BEFORE JIM CROW

Before Jim Crow

THE POLITICS OF

RACE IN POSTEMANCIPATION

VIRGINIA

Jane Dailey

The University of North Carolina Press

Chapel Hill & London

© 2000

The University of North Carolina Press

All rights reserved

Set in New Baskerville type

by Tseng Information Systems, Inc.

Manufactured in the United States of America

The paper in this book meets the guidelines for permanence
and durability of the Committee on Production Guidelines for
Book Longevity of the Council on Library Resources.

Library of Congress Cataloging-in-Publication Data

Dailey, Jane Elizabeth, 1963–

Before Jim Crow: the politics of race in postemancipation
Virginia / Jane Dailey.

p.   cm.—(Gender and American culture)

Includes bibliographical references and index.

ISBN 0-8078-2587-5 (cloth: alk. paper)—

ISBN 0-8078-4901-4 (pbk.: alk. paper)

1. Virginia—Race relations—Political aspects—History—19th
century.   2. Virginia—Politics and government—1865–1950.
3. Reconstruction—Virginia.   4. Race awareness—Political
aspects—Virginia—History—19th century.   5. Sex role—
Political aspects—Virginia—History—19th century.   6. Social
classes—Virginia—History—19th century.   7. Afro-Americans—
Virginia—Politics and government—19th century.   8. Afro-
Americans—Civil rights—Virginia—History—19th century.
9. Slaves—Emancipation—Virginia.   I. Title.
II. Gender & American culture.

F231 .D24   2000

324.7′089′960730755—dc21   00-057723

04   03   02   01   00   5   4   3   2   1

CONTENTS

ILLUSTRATIONS & MAPS

Illustrations

Maps

ACKNOWLEDGMENTS

I owe so many people my thanks for their support during the writing of this book that I scarcely know where to begin. The clearest debts are to institutions. Princeton University, the Virginia Historical Society, the Andrew W. Mellon Foundation, and Princeton's Council on Regional Studies all supported the dissertation that became this book. Rice University hired me when that dissertation was little more than promise; its growth and revision are thanks to Rice's generous institutional support via the Dean of Humanities and the Center for the Study of Cultures.

I have also been aided immeasurably by the librarians and research staff at the Virginia Historical Society, the Alderman Library at the University of Virginia, the Perkins Library at Duke University, and the State Library of Virginia, where John Kneebone and Brent Tarter taught me the ropes and continue to answer my questions. Kate Torrey of the University of North Carolina Press expressed interest in this project early on and waited patiently for it, while Pamela Upton shepherded it through the publication process. Two copyeditors, Jean Williams Brusher at Rice and Stevie Champion for the UNC Press, broke up my sentences, hoisted my dangling modifiers, and otherwise shored up my prose. Scott Marler, a graduate student at Rice, came to my rescue as a last-minute research assistant.

The book that will be cataloged under my name has its roots in the work of many other people, most of whom I have never met. Replacing footnotes with endnotes obscures the creative interchanges among scholars. I hope that the degree of my intellectual debts is clear from the notes that follow the text of this book.

Other obligations are more transparent. While I was an undergraduate at Yale, John Morton Blum ignited my interest in American history; Gaddis Smith directed the senior essay that gave me the confidence to go to graduate school. At Princeton, this project was stimulated and encouraged by the faculty and my fellow graduate students. There I enjoyed the massive learning and abiding humaneness of James M. McPherson and Christine Stansell. Daniel Rodgers planted my feet firmly on the path to a dissertation while Sean Wilentz taught me how to see the big picture and helped with my title ("Dates are death!"). Although a medievalist, Bill Jordan has always been a source of sane advice. Most importantly, Nell Irvin Painter embraced both my project and me with her characteristic warmth and vigor. Her example as scholar, teacher, and mensch continues to be a mark to shoot at and miss.

This book has benefited as well from the learning and contemplation of many other people. Edward Ayers read the dissertation and then helped me envision it as a book. Later, Suzanne Lebsock and a second reader for the University of North Carolina Press pushed me to be clear and sharp and unequivocal. Peter Bardaglio, Fitz Brundage, Vernon Burton, Glenda Gilmore, Steven Stowe, and Peter Wallenstein all read the entire manuscript toward the end. (Wallenstein even paid for the three-hour phone call to discuss his comments and gloat over various heinous grammatical errors and blunders in Virginia geography.) Glenda is an unending source of fun and wisdom, who does her best to tame my instinct to get myself in trouble. I couldn't ask for a better friend.

Other people shared their thoughts on bits and pieces of the manuscript: Eric Anderson, James Anderson, Anthony Badger, Patricia Bixel, John Boles, Krista Comer, Laura Edwards, Drew Faust, Gail Bederman, Richard Hamm, Thomas Haskell, Robin D. G. Kelley, Steven Kantrowitz, J. Morgan Kousser, Alex Lichtenstein, Reid Mitchell, James Tice Moore, Evelyn Thomas Nolen, Michael O'Brien, Carol Quillen, Howard Rabinowitz, Bryant Simon, J. Douglas Smith, Arnold Taylor, Elizabeth Hayes Turner, Brian Ward, Michael Willrich, and Richard Wolin. Their critiques often required radical rethinking on my part. I am thankful to have such disputatious friends and colleagues.

I owe a special debt of gratitude to Paula Sanders, computer wizard and Nota Bene goddess. While it cannot be said that I could not have written the book without her, it is a fact that I could never have printed it without her. Thank God I didn't have to try.

The people I owe most of all belong to my family. I have been as fortunate in my in-laws as in my teachers. Isabel and Ricardo Nirenberg read most of this book; their dislike of cant and moralizing, combined with their remarkable erudition, made for a far better result. My own parents, Judy and Bill Dailey, have sustained me over the years with their good humor and generosity. Included in my definition of family are Gloria Ayala and her sons Joel and Omar. It is safe to say that I could not have written either my dissertation or this book if Gloria had not been there to take care of my household and my son, not to mention the dogs!

There remain two people to thank. My son Alexander helped this work along by indirection; who would have dreamed a six-year-old could invest the phrase, "Oh, you're *working*," with such devastating sarcasm? Finally, anyone who knows David Nirenberg's work will see his footprints all over this book. He has shared his knowledge, his turns of phrase, his bent of mind, all freely. Yet through it all he has always insisted that I write my book in my own way. More than anyone else, this man—who knows his Lewis Carroll—has taught me to speak in French when I can't think of the English for a thing, to turn my toes out when I walk, and to remember who I am.

BEFORE JIM CROW

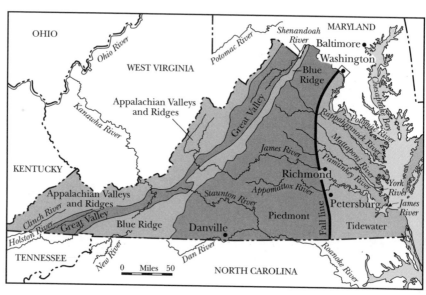

Map. 1. Virginia's Principal Geographic Regions

INTRODUCTION

In *Jazz*, Toni Morrison's novel set in the Harlem of the 1920s, the narrator fills in the past of the main characters, Violet and Joe Trace. They had come to the city from Virginia in the years just before the Great War, in search of diversion and anonymity, and to get away from want and white violence. When Violet was a child, the narrator tells us, her father had been forced to abandon his home and visit his family in secret because "he had been mixed in and up with the Readjuster Party, and when a verbal urging from the landowners had not worked, a physical one did the trick and he was persuaded to transfer hisself someplace, anyplace, else." That was not the end of it, though: the year Violet turned twelve, her father's crop failed and the landlord exercised a lien on the family's possessions in retaliation, the family supposed, for the father's "joining a party that favored niggers voting."[1]

The Readjuster Party—the party that "favored niggers voting"—was the most successful interracial political alliance in the postemancipation South. An independent coalition of black and white Republicans and white Democrats, the Readjusters governed Virginia from 1879 to 1883. During this period a Readjuster governor occupied the statehouse, two Readjusters represented the Old Dominion in the U.S. Senate, and Readjusters served six of Virginia's ten congressional districts. Led by the serenely improbable former Confederate general, slaveholder, and railroad magnate William Mahone, the coalition controlled the state legislature and the courts, and held and distributed the state's many coveted federal patronage positions. A black-majority party, the Readjusters legitimated and promoted African American citizenship and political power by supporting black suffrage, officeholding, and jury service. To a degree previously unseen in Virginia and unmatched elsewhere in the nineteenth-century South, the Readjusters became an institutional force for the protection and advancement of black rights and interests. Although the coalition controlled state politics for only four years, its legislative and judicial legacy endured long past 1883 and its political organization became the blueprint for modern politics in Virginia. For all these reasons, the Readjusters inspired both hope and foreboding outside the borders of the commonwealth. A main purpose of this book is to understand why the hope was so strong and the foreboding so deep.

Toni Morrison does not invoke the Readjusters in *Jazz* to celebrate their many achievements. For her, the narrative value of the coalition lies chiefly in its ability to stand for the white violence and intolerance that encouraged the northern exodus of southern blacks in the twentieth century. *Jazz*'s story of a black man and his family punished for the assertion of political autonomy is a familiar narrative of post–Civil War southern history. The tale of the Virginia roots of Joe and Violet Trace echoes the stories of thousands of other black Americans who moved from the rural South to the urban North after 1900.[2] Yet Morrison's evocation of the Readjusters subverts her sketch of the postwar South. Her allusion to the coalition reminds us that black southerners were not always denied a significant role in the New South. African Americans fled a region whose white ruling class took deliberate steps to circumscribe all possibility of black political, economic, and social power. Within the logic of white supremacy, the necessity of taking those steps was drilled home for many southern whites by the actions of people like the Readjusters. The votes of African Americans were not "meaningless in the post-Reconstruction South," as some scholars continue to assert.[3] Rather, the very success of black men in politics contributed to their eventual exclusion from public authority at the turn of the twentieth century. Legal barriers to African American power and influence—the creation of the Jim Crow South—grew out of white southerners' specific and concrete encounters with black social, economic, and political power.[4]

The Readjusters were not the only interracial political coalition in the postemancipation South. Although I have chosen to focus on black suffrage in Virginia and the possibilities that African American enfranchisement offered that state, the problem is a more general one. Between 1865 and the turn of the twentieth century every state south of the Mason-Dixon line experimented with political alliances that spanned the color line. Some were more successful, and some were more lasting, than others. The Republican Party provided the original example of interracial coalition during the late 1860s and 1870s. Even after the end of congressional Reconstruction in 1877—the year President Rutherford B. Hayes removed the last federal troops from those parts of the former Confederacy still occupied militarily—Republican electoral candidates at the county and congressional levels drew a considerable amount of support. In the Upper South in particular, Republican or "fusion" candidates, who represented coalitions of Republicans, Democrats, and later Populists, challenged Democratic attempts to define politics along race lines. Between 1876 and 1896, eighteen Republicans or Readjusters were elected to Congress from Virginia. Tennessee sent fourteen Republicans to the House of Representatives during those same years. North Carolina Republicans mounted a continual challenge to the Democrats and were able to carry seven out of nine congressional districts at least once in this period. Half of these districts elected Republicans repeatedly. In addition, four southern congressional districts sent one or more African Americans to Congress, including one each from North Carolina and Virginia.[5]

In the 1880s independent coalition parties eclipsed the Republicans as the vehicle for interracial political cooperation in the South. In both the Upper and Lower South, schisms among white Democrats made space for new alliances between black and white men. Southern Democrats splintered along a variety of fault lines, but one of the deepest chasms emerged out of disputes over public spending and activist government. In the context of explicit battles over state fiscal policy and priorities, black and white southerners dissatisfied with the local manifestations of their respective national parties identified a thread of common interest that emphasized class status and civil rights and downplayed race. In addition to unhappiness over questions of government spending and taxation, southern Independents opposed election fraud and intimidation and demanded a "free ballot and a fair count"; they denounced elite control of government, or what they called "ring rule"; they called for debtor laws that did not openly favor creditors; and they attacked Democratic white solidarity slogans for obscuring the class interests that bound nonelite white and black southerners. In general, Independents, Greenbackers, and later the Populists desired state and local government to work in the interest of the great mass of ordinary citizens by providing free public education, protecting men's political rights, and curbing the power of economic elites to exploit the labor of farmers and workers.[6] One Alabama Republican explained his vote for the Greenback-Labor Party this way: "There are questions of more vital importance in southern politics than banking and currency. . . . They are issues such as fair elections, an honest count, free thought, free speech, free government itself."[7] An independent-minded Georgian amplified these sentiments and addressed himself to the charge that Independents were "levelers": "All the leveling we have ever attempted," he explained, "is to *level upwards*. We wish to elevate the downtrodden to an equal participation in the blessings of Government, in as much as they are bound to bear more than their proportion of its burdens."[8]

In two southern states—Virginia and Tennessee—third-party interracial alliances gained control of the state government during the 1880s. In North Carolina, disaffected Republicans and dissident Democrats emboldened by the Readjusters' success coalesced in 1882. They lost, but they came close enough to winning to impress a young Furnifold M. Simmons—later known for his role in the white supremacist campaign of 1898—with the wisdom of appealing to the black vote in 1884.[9] Eight years later struggling white farmers began to desert the Democratic Party, and by 1894 North Carolina was governed by a Populist-Republican coalition. In Alabama the Greenbackers successfully combined the votes of white and black coal miners and farmers, while in Mississippi and Georgia black Republicans allied with moderate Democrats against both the GOP and a local Independent movement.[10] In gubernatorial elections during the 1880s across the South a quarter or more of white voters crossed the color line to vote for a black-majority party.[11] Far from being solid, as it has sometimes been asserted, southern politics in the post–Civil War era was exceptionally fluid. To scratch the surface of the "solid South" in the late nineteenth century was to discover multiple competing interest groups divided by region, race, ideology, and class.

African Americans were an important, though not monolithic, voice in this contest. The success of non-Democratic political parties in the South depended on the ballots of black men, who voted in most places throughout the late nineteenth century. Of course, as the fate of Violet's family in *Jazz* suggests, black men often exercised their right to vote at considerable cost. Black suffrage never went unchallenged in the postwar South, especially by members of the landowning and mercantile elites, who resorted to physical violence and intimidation when such impediments as the poll tax and ballot box fraud failed to eliminate the black vote. It was this class that was behind the drive to divest black men of the franchise once and for all through revision of state constitutions between 1890 and 1908.[12] Angry about the social and economic disaster of war and emancipation, elite southern whites nursed a more general anxiety over the political catastrophe of seeing black men raised to the status of voter and lawmaker.

The most central problem of Reconstruction was how to create interracial democracy in the South. How could newly enfranchised black men be incorporated into a preexisting political system? As the most successful interracial democratic political movement in the postwar South, the Readjusters are a splendid example of the problems faced by those looking for common ground between black and white southern men and the formulas they developed to enable politics across the color line. In making the methodological and narrative decisions involved in the writing of any book, I have chosen to focus here on only some of these problems. *Before Jim Crow* is not offered as a comprehensive history of the Readjuster movement or of Virginia politics between emancipation and disfranchisement. The riches of the William Mahone Papers have much to offer any scholar interested in those projects, although they have not been mine.

This volume is concerned chiefly with how Virginians formed ideas about race and how these ideas functioned politically within a specific context. At the heart of the book is the tension between, on the one hand, attempts to establish white supremacy, to remove African Americans from participation in the body politic, and, on the other, the struggle to build cross-race political coalitions. Historical scholarship has focused extensively on the first part of this narrative, stressing the incontestable fact that black suffrage and political influence were not irrevocably established throughout the South until after the passage of the Voting Rights Act of 1965, following a century of political, economic, and social discrimination. But this is the view from afar, in which recollections of nineteenth-century southern interracial movements are displaced by the history of the South after 1900. By then, almost all African Americans and a significant minority of white men had been stripped of political power through poll taxes, literacy tests, and Democratic electoral fraud and violence. By then, a rising tide of segregation laws had defined racial identity through genealogy and location, by putting and keeping African Americans in their "place."

By then, the South had become best known for the degenerate behavior of its white lynch mobs, which shot, hanged, and burned alive African Americans from Virginia to Texas. This is the South of living memory; this is the South memorialized in popular culture and most standard American histories; and this is the South whose overturning by the civil rights movement is rightly celebrated.

Faced with the obscenity and scope of the Jim Crow South, it is easy to see white supremacy as irresistible and to pass over attempts at interracial political cooperation between 1877 and 1900. But these attempts mattered just as much, and were often as heroic, as those of our more recent and eulogized past. The difference between them is that with the benefit of hindsight we can see that the nineteenth-century efforts to create a shared interracial political world failed. Knowing where we ended up, it has been difficult to imagine that we were ever elsewhere or that the route from there to here was not direct. By focusing intently on the hard-fought political battles of Readjuster Virginia, this book shows how significant these early encounters were. In particular, it demonstrates that late-nineteenth-century formulations of white supremacist racial ideology did not represent an easy continuation of past oppressions. It was not at all clear after the war that antebellum racial hierarchies could be reproduced in the context of the Reconstruction amendments to the federal Constitution, which outlawed slavery, embraced African Americans as citizens, and enfranchised black men. Although postwar southern society was eventually reranked according to racial hierarchy, the path from emancipation to Jim Crow was rockier than is sometimes realized, with many detours and switchbacks along the way. New forms of white dominance coalesced through the lived, and often conflictual, everyday experiences of black and white southerners after emancipation. The white supremacist South was not preordained, and its victory was never certain.

Others before me have challenged the interpretation that the Jim Crow South was inevitable. In 1955 historian C. Vann Woodward and novelist James Baldwin each confronted the aura of predestination surrounding southern race relations. In *The Strange Career of Jim Crow*, Woodward defanged southern racial apologists who defended legal segregation and discrimination by race as the foundation of the "southern way of life" by showing that the social and political relations of segregation that characterized the mid-twentieth-century South did not reach back to emancipation but had instead replaced a more flexible and integrated racial system that developed between 1865 and 1900. By reaching back into the decades before Jim Crow, Woodward showed that white supremacy was not timeless or natural but rather the result of individual actions undertaken as part of a calculated campaign to render African Americans political and economic dependents and social unequals.[13] The apparent seamlessness between the antebellum and the twentieth-century South's system of racial hierarchy was illusory, argued Woodward; what looked like continuity had been painfully forged out of a deep historical disjuncture in the thirty years between emancipation and disfranchisement. James Baldwin also spotlighted the contingent and discordant nature of southern race relations. "The history of the American Negro problem is not merely shameful, it is also something of an achievement," he remarked. "For even when the worst has been said, it must also be added that the perpetual challenge posed by this problem was always, somehow, perpetually met." Far from being static, Baldwin emphasized, the South's "Negro problem" was dynamic, a "perpetual challenge" that had to be repeatedly "met."[14]

What has become known as the "Woodward thesis" has held up best with reference to politics. Woodward's argument about the fluidity of southern race relations and the region's forgotten interracial political alternatives focused mainly on law and electoral politics; it was reinforced by studies published in the 1970s and 1980s that documented a significant hardening of white southern racial attitudes between 1888 and 1900.[15] In areas of life not generally considered overtly political, however, later work challenged Woodward's claims about the malleability and variety of race relations in the postwar South by showing that, from the moment of emancipation, segregation rather than integration characterized private sexual relations, most churches, militia companies, patriotic celebrations, voluntary organizations, schools, state and private welfare institutions, and a host of other activities.[16] This interpretational division between postwar southern politics and society has resulted in a curious narrative of southern history in which black southerners are seen to "retreat" into their own private world at precisely the same time that they form the most effective interracial political alliances before the civil rights movement.[17]

One purpose of *Before Jim Crow* is to demonstrate the analytic impossibility of isolating "politics" from these other "social" realms. This emphasis on the futility of distinguishing political and social concerns represents more than simply a desire to blend the insights of social and political history. A central theme of this book is the instability of social categories. By this I mean first the difficulty of pinpointing the boundaries between such categories as political identity, gender identity, and racial identity. But more important, in pointing out the instability of social, political, and cultural categories in Readjuster Virginia I mean to mark the points at which one category (say, partisan identity) cannot be constituted except through another (for example, racial identity). Rather than simply juxtaposing categories such as race, class, and gender, I try in this book to uncover and explain the dynamic interrelations among categories and to underscore the reliance of any one on a variety of others for definition and formulation within a particular setting.[18]

Because southerners worked out the margins of identity and the meaning of those margins over the last two decades of the nineteenth century, they saw the period as dynamic, filled with moments of hope and despair, rather than as an extended prelude to Jim Crow. This sense of movement, of possibility, has not dominated historical assessments of the period. Scholarly narratives of southern political history have in the past flattened out regional variations and drowned out local cadences in ways that have impoverished our appreciation of the complexities of racism and power in the postemancipation South. Harold D. Woodman's historiographical assessment of the postwar South is typical of a broader homogenizing approach, which tends to skip chronologically from 1865 or 1877 to 1900. "Once the adjustment to emancipation had been made and once the disruption and uncertainty of war and Reconstruction had ended, social and economic relations in the South remained stable for some three-quarters of a century," writes Woodman, who adds that "nowhere did political Reconstruction extend beyond 1877." Carl Degler, whose book *The Other South: Southern Dissenters in the Nineteenth Century* argued for the possibilities of an alternative southern political history, nonetheless undercut the importance of nineteenth-century attempts to realize this history when he categorized them as "failures." George M. Fredrickson, who is a sympathetic critic of nineteenth-century southern attempts to circumnavigate the race problem, still concluded that "viable movements transcending racial lines never came close to fruition during Reconstruction or after." Most recently, Leon F. Litwack, one of the most insightful interpreters of southern and African American history, has insisted that by the end of the 1870s "the promise of a biracial democratic society" had been betrayed in the South.[19]

The Readjusters contradict this view. It is not surprising, then, that they have often been dismissed (when they are not neglected entirely) as an aberration, compartmentalized as a historical accident of little or no consequence for the rest of the South or the nation. Rather than challenge the broad conventions of southern history, historians of Virginia frequently erase the Readjuster era. Crandall A. Shifflett's *Patronage and Poverty in the Tobacco South*, for instance, skips directly from 1876 to 1884, proposing a seamless trend toward less popular democracy in postwar Virginia. Charles Preston Poland Jr.'s *From Frontier to Suburbia*, which purports to be an inclusive history of Loudoun County from 1725 to 1972, omits the years 1877 to 1887 outright.[20] These are admittedly extreme examples. But even historians who have written about the Readjusters downplay the importance of the movement and their own work when confronted with the incongruence between Virginia's political history and the political narrative of the region as a whole. James Tice Moore, who restored the Readjusters to prominence in postwar Virginia historiography, later dismissed them and other late-nineteenth-century efforts to limit the political power of white elites.[21]

The most salient fact about the Readjusters—for historians as well as for Toni Morrison—has become their failure, because only through that failure can the coalition be trimmed to fit the standard narrative of post–Civil War southern history. Thus configured, the Readjusters' failure may be attributed to "the race issue"—to the implications of the Readjusters being "a party that favored niggers voting." The first scholar of the Readjusters, Charles Chilton Pearson, explained the downfall of the coalition as the predictable result of "race antagonism." Sixty years later James Tice Moore described the Readjusters as a movement that "collapsed after a few years, torn apart by racial antagonisms." A recent reconsideration of the failure of nonelite whites in one Virginia city to make common cause with their African American class allies concludes that white Virginians "could not divorce themselves from the ancient [race] prejudices and were thus reluctant to share power with blacks."[22] These explanations of the failure of interracial democracy in Virginia rely on the explanatory power of white racism, which is conceived of as timeless and unchanging—indeed, "ancient"—and simplify what was a complex nexus of partisan rivalry, political and economic domination, white and black male concerns over manhood rights and sexual access to women, racial identity, and everyday contests for dignity and respect.[23]

Asking how "the race issue" functioned in particular times and places by uncovering the moments when questions of racial identity and its relationship to other social categories took on political meaning makes it possible to challenge the teleological approach to late-nineteenth-century southern history. And seeing white racial ideology as grounded in social relations reveals the power of black and white southerners to both structure and resist new systems of racial domination. This focus on agency and context, this stress on the particular lived experiences through which social categories and political languages gained meaning and form in postemancipation Virginia, leads to a consideration of southern political culture in terms of a process in which white dominance was continuously re-created rather than a product that was simply perpetuated.[24]

Because this book is about the definition and interrelations of categories of identity and the politically combustible combinations of these categories, chronology has not proved the most useful organizing principle. Bounded loosely by Virginia's Radical Republican 1868 constitution and its disenfranchising successor of 1902, the chapters are organized thematically and overlap.

The book begins with electoral politics: both the politics that preceded the Readjusters and the practical politics necessary to the formation of the third-party coalition. Chapter 1 outlines the prehistory of the Readjuster movement from emancipation through the creation of the coalition in 1879. Unraveling the connections between suffrage, public education, debt, and taxation, this chapter explains how nonelite white and black Virginians came to perceive a common identity of interest powerful enough to override established partisan identities. While other black southerners in search of social and political autonomy packed their bags and headed west to Kansas, black Virginians put their faith in the ballot and exploited political division among whites. The formation of the Readjuster coalition reveals greater inclination among black southerners to ally with non-Republican whites than has previously been appreciated. At the same time, it is clear that the political behavior of nonelite southern whites cannot be explained solely—or at times even principally—in terms of race or racism.[25]

As Chapter 2 explains, after he was elected to the U.S. Senate in

1881, Readjuster leader William Mahone gained the federal patronage for Virginia through a combination of unlikely circumstances and nerve. Control of the federal patronage turned out to be crucial to the success of the Readjusters. Patronage power gave the coalition a strong material foundation and encouraged the formation of a cohesive interracial political community with a common identity and goals. But because patronage is fundamentally about public authority and hierarchy, the practical necessity of sharing patronage with black Readjusters posed certain social and political questions for the coalition's white members. The relations of domination and subordination explicit in patronage power enabled the Democrats to present Readjuster patronage policies as destabilizing to social hierarchies based on race. Black officeholding and jury service, for example, could be presented by opponents of the Readjusters as eroding white privilege. But black power in Virginia, as Chapter 2 details, did not result immediately in white backlash. Democratic zero-sum arguments that every black gain under the Readjusters represented an equivalent loss to white Virginians failed to draw white voters from the coalition.

Every effort to promote interracial cooperation in the postemancipation South was attacked by its opponents as an assault on white racial dominance. Warning sternly of the danger of "social equality," southern Democrats picked off interracial political coalitions and labor unions one by one. Chapter 3 considers the ideological underpinning of the coalition and the rhetorical and political strategies the Readjusters used to rebuff white supremacist assaults and contain racial anxiety and ill will. In an effort to protect the coalition from the corrosive effects of white men's fears about the future of white dominance in a world of enfranchised black men, the Readjusters turned to liberalism. Liberal ideals about masculine political equality and the sanctity of the home helped white Readjusters defend black suffrage but also gave them a rhetorical arsenal to repel Democratic arguments that interracial political cooperation led invariably to interracial homes. Drawing on the notion of a separation between public and private space at the heart of nineteenth-century American liberal theory and practice, white Readjusters argued that the line between the spheres paralleled the color line, and they insisted that liberalism could redraw political boundaries without disturbing the social status quo.

Drawing the color line parallel to the division between public and private space made room for political alliance among black and white men. But this strategy had dangers of its own. In essence, the question of where to draw the color line in Readjuster Virginia became rephrased as "at what point do black men encroach on white women?" Attempting to trump a racial hierarchy in the public sphere by retaining a gendered one in private, the Readjusters became vulnerable to political attacks by conservative critics who used gender to combat the racially progressive aspects of liberalism. A dramatic example of this may be seen in the collapse of the coalition in 1883 over issues of miscegenation manifested not through any epidemic of interracial sex or marriage but through black Readjusters' service in public office. Asserting a fundamental connection between black political and sexual power, Democrats argued that issues of public authority and private influence were related. There is nothing intrinsically obvious about the logic of such a claim, although that logic eventually became the cornerstone of racial politics in the New South. By investigating how that logic was formulated and resisted in Readjuster Virginia, we may reveal some of the processes that made the equation of black political power and sexual power seem both obvious and natural.

Strong enough to dissolve the old political order, the Readjusters could not master the social and ideological forces released by that dissolution.[26] The ramifications of interracial coalition extruded, in unanticipated ways, into daily life. Chapter 4 brings together the problems of how to define the boundaries of public space (and equality) and the interrelation of honor, gender, and race by focusing on the conception and performance of individual identity in public. In 1883 a dispute over street etiquette in the Piedmont manufacturing town of Danville escalated into a massacre when a white mob shot into a crowd of unarmed black men, women, and children. Following the shooting, white Democrats took control of the city in defiance of its elected Readjuster government and spread rumors of black insurrection throughout the state. Coming three days before an important state election, the violence in Danville and Democratic stories about it contributed significantly to the downfall of the Readjuster coalition.

The broad aim of Chapter 4 is to bare the links between civility and civil rights and between deference and violence in the postwar urban South. This chapter examines how black men and women in the New South enunciated their claim to civic equality through their behavior in urban public spaces and how some whites, determined to maintain their social, political, and economic control, responded to such behavior. In the absence of either a rigid system of racial hierarchy or mutually agreed upon conventions of public conduct between the races, questions of honor, hierarchy, and deference arose in every public encounter. Broad questions of racial domination and subordination were frequently distilled in public interactions on the streets of the urban South, and negotiation over the rules of common courtesy became a principal venue for the ongoing contest between blacks determined to assert their identity as civic actors and whites intent on denying blacks that power.

As observers of the South since Karl Marx have noted, emancipation and the actions of slaves and free people of color during the Civil War untied the formal connections in America between color and condition.[27] Without slavery to connect blackness and dependency, the meaning and worth of whiteness became unclear. As black men gained authority and visibility in Readjuster Virginia, white voters began to exhibit a heightened sensitivity to political languages of race. What W. E. B. Du Bois identified at the height of Jim Crow as the "public and psychological wage" of whiteness—deference on the streets, access to public spaces, control of the legal system, and superior public services, particularly schools—could be seen as threatened by interracial democracy and Readjuster patronage policies.[28] When black men supervised white postal workers or teachers or meted justice from the magistrate's bench or the jury box, white Virginians worried about the distribution of authority in public life and any fraying of traditional links between authority, race, and manhood.

The Democrats nurtured these anxieties by encouraging the idea that political alliance with black men could erode white men's racial identity. Chapter 5 shows how the practical political successes of the Readjusters undermined existing definitions of such categories of identity as party, race, and manhood. Because it supported African American civil and political participation, and distributed the material and honorific benefits of patronage to black Readjusters, the coalition could be presented as challenging both white superiority and white identity. Faced with the success of interracial rule under the Readjusters, Virginia Democrats stressed the interactive qualities of racial identity in an effort to realign the political and racial divide, and they encouraged the notion that whiteness was something that could be lost (but also regained).

In 1883 the Readjuster Party lost power in an election marred by violence, electoral intimidation, and fraud. Interracial democracy and black public power did not end with the defeat of the coalition, however. Between 1883 and the turn of the twentieth century various groups of black and white Virginians continued to make common political cause. These groups appeared in different guises: first as Republicans, then as Knights of Labor, still later as Populists. The task for the Democrats in Virginia as elsewhere in the late-nineteenth-century South was to constrain this coalition and with it the possibility for progressive politics in the South. As the Epilogue details, the Democrats pursued two simultaneous approaches to this end: they insisted that the categories of "white man" and "Democrat" were coterminous and exclusive, and they limited the popular vote through election laws and a new state constitution.

Together, the election laws passed in the 1880s and 1890s and the 1902 constitution ended most black voting in Virginia and cut the white electorate in half.[29] The expanded political universe that free and equal manhood suffrage had created in Virginia between 1868 and 1902 became after that the familiar white supremacist, one-party world of twentieth-century southern Democrats. But none of this was clear before 1902. Before then—before Jim Crow—nothing was sure and, it often seemed, anything was possible.

1

ORIGINS OF THE READJUSTER MOVEMENT

White southerners in the antebellum era liked to argue that racial slavery, far from being incompatible with democracy, was in fact the basis for equality among white men. "In this country alone does perfect equality of civil and social privilege exist among the white population, and it exists solely because we have black slaves," lectured the *Richmond Enquirer* in 1856. "Freedom is not possible without slavery."[1] The constitutional history of the southern states reflected this view, although the "perfect equality" of whites trumpeted by the *Enquirer* was never attained. In the 1810s and 1820s slave states in the South produced the most democratic state constitutions in the country, granting free white manhood suffrage before most of the states that would make up the Union did.[2] In a very real sense, this white political freedom was defined against black slavery. It should not be surprising, then, that the end of slavery shook white southern ideologies about hierarchy and equality to their very foundations. It was on the remnants of these foundations that the Readjusters later sought to build their own precarious edifice.

White Virginians had more reasons for anxiety than most other southern whites, for the civic status of nonpropertied white men there had shallow roots. These men gained the suffrage only in 1851, when the slavery crisis bore down on the nation. Even then the General Assembly insisted on retaining viva voce voting, which meant that patrons, landlords, and employers could monitor the electoral choices of their clients, renters, and workers.[3] At the local level, Virginia politics was dominated by an archaic system of elite-controlled, self-perpetuating county courts.[4] Statewide, the eastern planter elites of antebellum Virginia controlled the legislature through an electoral system that counted slaves for representational purposes. (The national electoral system, designed in good measure by Virginians, achieved much the same result through the three-fifths clause, whereby slaves were counted as three-fifths of a free person for the election of representatives to the house and the electoral college.) Throughout the South, many whites thought of their electoral privileges as dependent on black subordination, and emancipation put those privileges in doubt. Glancing back to antebellum Virginia reminds us that postwar political battles were fought in a world in which suffrage was highly unstable and recently exclusive. For many white Virginians, as for the freedpeople, the right to vote was a novelty not to be taken for granted.

But the freedpeople had the greatest cause to worry about representation. African Americans demanded civil and political rights even before they officially entered politics in Virginia during Reconstruction. Thousands of freed men and women assembled in Richmond only two months after Appomattox to demand citizenship rights and to protest their treatment at the hands of native whites and Union troops alike.[5] In a series of meetings in Norfolk from April to June 1865, black Virginians called for the suffrage as the key to their future as workers, citizens, and families.[6] That April, again in Norfolk, more than five thousand black men demonstrated their intention to assume the rights of citizenship when they tried to vote in a municipal election. A similar scene would be repeated in Alexandria in March 1866.[7] Earlier in 1865 freedpeople had assembled at a convention in Alexandria and insisted, "As citizens of the Republic we claim the rights of citizens; we claim that we are by right entitled to respect."[8] Already in this demand we see many of the keywords that would prove so important in the political sensibilities of the next thirty years, a vocabulary in which civic rights and civility, equality and respect, politics and honor, were so intertwined as to be empirically inseparable.

The black citizens of Alexandria insisted on rights that few whites in Virginia were willing to grant. At the head of the "loyal government" of Virginia in 1865 was Governor Francis H. Pierpont, who had been elected at a convention in Wheeling in 1861 in opposition to the Virginia secessionists. When West Virginia was admitted to the Union on the last day of 1862, the Pierpont government moved to Alexandria to administer the Union-controlled areas of Virginia.[9] After the Confederate surrender, the Pierpont administration oversaw the election of a new state legislature, which assembled in Richmond in December 1865. This legislature, like all that had preceded it in Virginia, was elected exclusively by white men. As William L. Royall, a prominent Richmond lawyer in the postbellum era, wrote without irony, "It was truly representative of the old State."[10]

When the representatives of the "old state" convened in Richmond in December 1865, they ignored Governor Pierpont's many suggestions, including the establishment of free schools, provision for widows and orphans, consolidation of the railroads, and, later, ratification of the Fourteenth Amendment. Pierpont's opponents claimed to resist him for his boorish western ways. He was, after all, a manufacturer, not a planter, and he pastured his cow on the capitol lawn besides.[11] We may be forgiven, however, for suspecting that Pierpont's detractors were probably more concerned about his relative progressivism. Totally unreconstructed, the General Assembly denied the existence of West Virginia, enacted a draconian vagrancy law that was denounced by the Union military commander of Virginia as "slavery in all but its name," rejected the Fourteenth Amendment, and suggested that the president replace Governor Pierpont with Robert E. Lee.[12] The legislature also vowed to pay the state's antebellum debt in full, including wartime interest. When West Virginia declined to "restore the ancient commonwealth" and, incidentally, assume responsibility for its share of the debt, Virginia's leaders declared that the state would assume West Virginia's share until it could be determined and apportioned.[13]

That debt, which would come to dominate postwar Virginia politics, originated in antebellum efforts to construct roads and canals. In this, Virginia was hardly alone. New York had led the way in 1817 with the Erie Canal. But Virginia's economic and political ambitions, when married to its topography, produced a multitude of competing claims for state funding. Pressed to link its vast western hinterland to the more settled counties of the east, the commonwealth tried at the same time to carve out a north-south juncture. Because capital was scarce in the new nation, Virginia and the other states turned to Europe to finance their improvement projects. In return for cash, the states issued interest-bearing bonds.

After 1845 the growth of railroads, whose enormous capital needs were incapable of being satisfied by private stock subscriptions, made Virginia the nation's largest borrower. To facilitate the construction of railroads, the state became the majority stockholder in the companies that built and operated them.[14] In 1861, on the eve of secession, Virginia's debt stood at $33.3 million, which translated into an annual interest payment to bondholders of about $2 million. With that money the state had constructed the James River and Kanawha Canal, which linked Richmond and the Shenandoah Valley, and 2,483 miles of rail that crisscrossed the commonwealth.[15] Four years later Virginia's transportation system, like the state itself, was undone by war. Nearly every rail line was wrecked.[16] Northern war correspondent Whitelaw Reid traveled at a snail's pace from Lynchburg to Bristol on straightened track whose gaps were plugged with stones.[17] English journalist John Kennaway spent most of his time on trains in Virginia peering out the window to see if the car had derailed.[18] About all that remained intact of Virginia's extensive antebellum infrastructure was the debt that the state had incurred to finance its construction.

It was unclear, to say the least, how Virginia expected to settle this debt after the war. The state had lost a third of its territory in 1861, when the Union convention in Wheeling passed an ordinance for the formation of the new state of West Virginia. The dismemberment of the state represented a severe financial blow to Virginia, as a third of its population—and nearly half of its taxpaying free men and women—lived in the mineral-rich regions of the west. In 1865 emancipation erased the chief form of taxable property in Virginia, and war-related damage cut the value of farmland in half.[19] Although northern visitors dismissed reports of mass starvation, even those least inclined to sympathize with the defeated Confederates noted the prevalence of scurvy and other nutritional deficiencies and remarked on Virginia's overall devastation. Infectious diseases such as typhus and tuberculosis carried away thousands in the immediate postwar years. So many African Americans were infected by cholera in the summer of 1866 that some suspected whites of poisoning them.[20] In this context of devastation, the "old state" legislature issued its declarations about honoring the debt and ignoring the political consequences of emancipation.

It was this kind of thing that convinced Congress that President Andrew Johnson's lenient policy of southern readmission to the Union jeopardized the social and political fruits of Union military victory. The Reconstruction Act of 1867 divided the eleven Confederate states (except Tennessee, which had ratified the Fourteenth Amendment) into five military zones. The act left in place state governments dominated by former Confederates, but it required that the states allow black men to vote for representatives to conventions called to create new state constitutions that would provide for universal manhood suffrage. In addition, the states had to accept the Fourteenth Amendment, which declared African Americans to be citizens and reduced the congressional representation of states that refused to enfranchise black men. The combined intransigence of the president and the white southern ruling elite had accomplished what Radical Republicans could never have done alone: the recognition of black suffrage as the cornerstone of Reconstruction.[21]

The 1867 Reconstruction Act nullified both the Virginia General Assembly and its fiscal intentions and reorganized the state as Military District Number One. While the other southern states elected new Republican legislatures and set about the process of congressional readmission, Virginia resisted and remained under military control until 1870. Most white Virginians preferred the indignity of military rule to the black-white coalition governments that ruled their neighbors. Referring to the declaration of martial law by Arkansas governor Powell Clayton and his use of black militias to suppress white terrorists, the *Richmond Whig* declared that U.S. troops were vastly preferable to "such characters as are now marauding Arkansas."[22]

While Governor Pierpont tried to forge a moderate consensus of Republican loyalists led by former Whigs, white and black Radical Republicans founded the Union Republican Party of Virginia. In 1867 this wing of the Republican Party dominated the state convention in Richmond and wrote a platform that celebrated the passage of the federal Civil Rights Bill of 1866, championed the equal protection of all men before the courts, advocated universal suffrage and the right of all Union men to hold office "without distinction of race or color," and called for a free school system.[23] Led by abolitionist and federal judge John C. Underwood and the Reverend James W. Hunnicutt, who had both served in Pierpont's Alexandria government, the Radicals spoke for the overwhelming majority of black Virginians and a significant minority of white voters as well. But they went too far for some white Republicans. Alienated by the Radicals' demand for black suffrage, the more conservative Republicans would ally in 1869 with the Conservative (Democratic) Party, which was founded in November 1867 in opposition to the Union Republicans.[24]

But for the moment, at least, radicalism had the upper hand. Radical Republicans predominated among the delegates elected in the fall of 1867 to the constitutional convention called to bring Virginia's laws into accordance with the federal Constitution prior to the state's readmission to the Union. Three-quarters of the convention members were Radical Republicans. Among them were twenty-four African Americans and thirty-three white men born outside Virginia.[25] The black delegates were hampered to a certain extent by a lack of formal education—as bricklayer George Teamoh recalled, "Agricultural degrees and brickyard diplomas, I found, passed for very little" in constitutional debate.[26] Nevertheless, the black delegates participated spiritedly in discussion and used their votes when words failed them. Often they appealed to the galleries, which were filled with men and women from Richmond's large black community.[27] Despite the obstructions of the minority Conservatives, and against the best efforts of the decidedly non-Radical military commander of Virginia, General John M. Schofield, the convention produced a constitution that upheld the 1867 Union Republican platform.[28] Denounced as the "Negro Constitution," its most hotly contested provisions were one that provided for black male suffrage and another that disfranchised all who had held civil or military office under the Confederacy. The disabling clauses that disfranchised former Confederates meant that virtually all native white Virginians would be barred from political office for the foreseeable future.[29]

With its provisions for black suffrage and Confederate disfranchisement, the new constitution stood a poor chance of ratification by the state's majority-white population. Without a new constitution, Virginia could not be readmitted to the Union. When General Schofield, who took a dim view of black suffrage, delayed the election on the constitution by refusing to release the state funds for it, Republicans and Conservatives sent delegations to Washington to argue for and against the proposed basic law. Reflecting the radical-moderate schism of 1867, which continued to rend the GOP in Virginia, the Republicans sent two committees, one radical and one conservative, that worked at cross purposes.[30] In the meantime, the conservative Republicans and the "Committee of Nine," a self-appointed group of ex-Whigs and moderate Republicans headed by Alexander H. H. Stuart, planned to make common political cause in the state election of 1869.[31]

The Committee of Nine may be credited with coming up with the winning slogan if not necessarily bending Congress to its will regarding the issue of the Virginia constitution.[32] The committee proposed a compromise settlement of "universal suffrage and universal amnesty" as a solution to the constitutional crisis in Virginia. This meant that two clauses—one requiring that all electoral candidates be able to swear that they had never held office in the Confederacy or in any way supported it and another that disfranchised former Confederates who had reneged on oaths of allegiance to the United States—would be voted on separately from the constitution as a whole. The final tally from the July 1869 constitutional referendum reflected the importance of this uncoupling in winning approval for black suffrage: the Underwood Constitution was ratified by a majority of voters, who simultaneously rejected both the test oath and the provision disfranchising former Confederates. In other words, only after four years of struggling to guarantee white suffrage without regard to loyalty could black suffrage be approved for the first time in Virginia.

In addition to establishing equal manhood suffrage, the Underwood Constitution called for the creation of a free public school system. Unlike its neighbor North Carolina and the states of the Lower South, which began to create state-supported common schools early in the nineteenth century, antebellum Virginia had only pauper schools, funded by a combination of local taxes, lotteries, and an anemic Literary Fund.[33] The majority of children in Virginia who received an education before 1870 were the sons (and, to a far lesser extent, the daughters) of the well-to-do, who could afford the tuition and board at academies organized by the planter and merchant elite. Ranging from about $125 per year to $250 and more, the cost of learning Latin, French, and geometry was beyond the reach of all but the most prosperous residents of the commonwealth. The middling classes were more likely to send their children sporadically to a local private school, where underpaid teachers provided a rudimentary education at best.[34]

Virginians had long differed about free public schools. In the antebellum era that split followed closely the regional division of opinion on equal white manhood suffrage and slavery. White support for public education was greatest in the west. It was also strong in the Shenandoah Valley, whose many small towns were a natural magnet for both schools and potential students.[35] The counties that routinely opposed the schools were clustered in northern and Southside Virginia, where wealth tended to be concentrated in a few white hands and the economy rested on black agricultural labor. In the 1830s and 1840s westerners joined their desire for public education to a demand for suffrage reform and a reconfiguration of regional allocation of state monies.[36] Since many supporters of free schools lacked enough property to vote, public education did not become a pressing political issue until after the adoption of the 1851 constitution, which admitted all adult white men to the suffrage.[37]

In 1854 popular desire for free schools and western complaints about the distribution of state aid for public improvements split the Democratic Party. Henry A. Wise, remembered chiefly as the man who hanged John Brown, was elected governor that year on a breakaway Democratic platform that proposed a free public school system and a more equitable distribution of state funds. Despite (or perhaps because of) being labeled a "reckless visionary" in thrall to the "agrarian notion of compelling the rich to pay for the education of the poor," Wise defeated his Whig opponent.[38] But he was prevented from putting his program into effect by Democratic rival Robert M. T. Hunter's states' rights men in the General Assembly, and local issues were soon subsumed into the broader national dispute over slavery.

The 1864 constitution, which was adopted by Francis Pierpont's Unionist convention in Alexandria, authorized the establishment of a free public school system.[39] But the legislature that convened in December 1865 made no provision for common schools, although it did allocate funds for the University of Virginia and "that miserable Military Institute," as Pierpont referred to VMI.[40] Lack of state provision did not dampen enthusiasm for free learning, however, either among those whites who had traditionally championed it or among the newer participants in the debate, Virginia's African Americans. Because it was forbidden to hold school for slaves and free people of color in Virginia after 1831, nearly all black Virginians were illiterate.[41] After the war, African American men and women of all ages flocked to school; Booker T. Washington, who was educated at Virginia's Hampton Institute, described the rush to learn as "a whole race trying to go to school." Searching for language to convey the passion for learning displayed by Virginia's freedpeople, one Freedmen's Bureau school official described them as "*crazy* to learn." Even the youngest understood the transformative social power of education. According to one freed slave in Warwick County, black children attending school there "thought it was so much like the way master's children used to be treated, that they believed they were getting white."[42]

The intensity of black southerners' desire for education was reflected in the hundreds of schools African Americans established throughout the postbellum South. The "native schools," as they were dubbed by John W. Alvord, the general superintendent of schools for the Freedmen's Bureau, were financed and operated by local black communities and churches.[43] Most were one-room affairs, "poor rooms with scant supplies of benches, desks, and books."[44] In some cases, however, grander buildings were pressed into service. When former governor Henry Wise visited his farm near Norfolk, an area occupied by the Union army since 1862, he relished the irony of discovering "John Brown's daughter teaching a negro school in my Mansion House!"[45] These schools provided the foundation for those established by the Freedmen's Bureau and northern missionary associations, which, in turn, nurtured popular demands for state-supported free public schools for all children.[46]

Black southerners had compelling reasons to press for universal public education. As the outward sign of inner reason, writing was valued by African Americans anxious to prove their cognitive abilities and rebut European and white American portrayals of blacks as mentally deficient. Less abstractly, in the new world of contract labor it paid to be able to read and cipher, not only to gain access to better-paying employment but also to avoid being cheated by white employers. Schoolrooms by day also served as citizenship schools by night. Danville blacks crowded into a small school founded by northern Quakers to read and discuss the Civil Rights Bill of 1866; a white observer found the discussion "rich and significant beyond description."[47] Finally, the education of black children represented an assertion of parental authority and mobility by black families, many of whom made decisions about where to live based on the accessibility of schools.[48]

Delegates to postwar southern state constitutional conventions were well aware of this broad enthusiasm for free public education among both blacks and nonelite whites. These conventions were dominated by Republicans committed to public schools, but sketching the contours of state-funded public education in places with no tradition of free common schools was not a trivial matter. Further, Conservatives strongly opposed free schools for a variety of reasons, including the traditional worries of an agricultural employer class about the effects of education on labor. One Conservative newspaper in Virginia would later complain that "the underlying idea of all our district school teaching seems to be . . . to educate all the scholars to be teachers in their turn" rather than reinforcing the notion that "all honest work is respectable."[49] Already concerned about the effects of "leveling" institutions such as equal manhood suffrage, elite white Virginians fretted that the schools would disrupt class and perhaps race lines by encouraging radical ideas of equality among lower-class whites and blacks.[50] These opponents of free schools concentrated on dividing white and black Republicans on the issue of segregation. Their success is evident in the extent to which the education debates during the 1867–68 constitutional convention revolved around this question. White parents would refuse to send their children to integrated schools, said the Conservatives, and the schools would therefore provoke taxpayer antipathy. Segregated schools were expensive and inefficient, integrationists countered, and constituted a denial of the sameness of citizenship.[51]

Virginia's African American delegates fought hard to ensure that the new public school system would be integrated. They lost this battle, but they did defeat Conservative attempts to establish separate schools funded according to the tax revenues generated by each race.[52] Instead, black delegate Samuel F. Kelso proposed a system of common schools "which shall give to all classes a free and equal participation in all its benefits," which Thomas Bayne, a dentist and former slave, amended to read "without distinction of color." In a telling attempt to remind white Virginians that they, too, had a past that required transcendence, James W. D. Bland, who was born free, proposed that every person have the right to attend any public institution of learning "regardless of race, color, or previous condition, or loyalty, or disloyalty, freedom or slavery."[53] But white Republican delegates refused to join their black colleagues in support of mixed schools. Despite a pointed reminder that without black electoral support the Republican Party in Virginia "would hardly be a skeleton," white Republican delegates pushed through an ambiguously worded call for public schools with no reference to race.[54]

The vagueness of the Underwood Constitution's provision for "a uniform system of free public schools" provoked a political crisis over the readmission of Virginia to the Union in 1870. Governor Gilbert C. Walker had vowed while a candidate that the constitution's school provisions "would never be enforced in a manner detrimental to the people," a statement that was understood to signal his opposition to integrated schools.[55] Black citizens, on the other hand, were desperate to prevent the inauguration of an educational system sure to be unequal if separate, and they persuaded Congress to incorporate a guarantee of equal school rights in Virginia's readmission legislation.[56]

As Virginia's first superintendent of public education made clear immediately, equal school rights did not mean integrated schools. William Henry Ruffner was appointed to his post in April 1870 with the support of the Conservatives, who considered him "a good, easy sort of half-way enemy to the common school system." Here they misjudged Ruffner, who threw himself into organizing the schools with precisely the degree of evangelical zeal that might have been expected of a mid-nineteenth-century Presbyterian minister educated at Princeton. At the end of his first year in office, Virginia's infant school system was instructing 131,000 students.[57] But Ruffner was equally zealous in his support of segregation.[58] Although pledged to "equal school rights" for all, the education bill he presented to the General Assembly provided for separate schools for white and black students. Black senator William P. Moseley, who had also been a delegate to the constitutional convention, sought to delete the separate schools clause because it favored "the continuance of caste and prejudice" and was "inimical to the theory of republican government." He was defeated by a large margin.[59] African American members of the House of Delegates also attacked the separate schools clause, but they were not supported by their white Republican allies. The school bill passed both houses of the legislature in July 1870 with the separate schools provision intact.[60]

The specter of racial mixing banished for the moment, most white Virginians quickly overcame any apprehension about the virtues of public education. Of the commonwealth's 105 county and city school districts, 73 passed local school tax measures in the spring of 1871.[61] Popular sentiment regarding the public schools became increasingly favorable as the decade wore on, even in those counties that had traditionally opposed them. In Spotsylvania County, for example, white nonproperty holders banded together with the minority black vote in 1872 to create a majority in favor of the schools.[62]

Free schools, of course, had to be paid for. Although Virginia benefited considerably from the largesse of northern educational missionaries such as George Peabody and continued to generate income from

"Practical Illustration of the Virginia Constitution." White Virginians worried that social hierarchy would be disrupted after the Underwood Constitution recognized African Americans' civil and political rights. (The Library of Virginia)

the Literary Fund, the principal state funding for education as fore-seen by the 1868 constitution were state and local taxes. Of these, the most important was a capitation tax of one dollar assessed on males of voting age.[63] In 1876 the Conservatives linked the issues of schools and suffrage by turning the capitation tax into a poll tax and making its payment a prerequisite to voting.[64] There was some grumbling about this new tax, particularly as Virginia experienced the effects of the depression that followed the national financial panic of 1873. But despite the planter elite's muttering about communism (the Paris Commune having just enriched beyond measure the metaphors of conservative America), local opinion favored the schools, and the most common complaint regarding schools and taxes during the 1870s was that the latter were insufficient to support the former. Superinten-dent of Schools Ruffner had claimed before the onset of the depres-sion that many citizens were willing to double or even treble their rate of taxation if that would increase the number of schools.[65] For those of us living in a period when the term "school bond" is almost synony-mous with political defeat, the willingness of Virginians to voluntarily increase their taxes to build more schools stands as striking testimony to their faith in public education.

This enthusiasm for free public education collided with the state's fiscal crisis in the second half of the 1870s. That crisis, too, had a his-tory. In 1869, when Virginians approved the amended Underwood Constitution, they also elected a new governor and legislature. That year the Virginia Republican Party split for good after the Radicals refused to agree to purge the constitution of its disfranchising provi-sions. Backed by Petersburg railroad entrepreneur and former Con-federate general William Mahone, moderate Republicans allied with progressive-minded Conservatives. Calling themselves "True Repub-licans," this coalition offered an alternative ticket headed by Gilbert C. Walker. A lawyer from New York, Walker had settled during the war in Union-occupied Norfolk, where he founded the Exchange National Bank and became a director of the Norfolk and Petersburg Railroad. He was, in short, a carpetbagger, a fact that he concealed behind a magnificent black mustache. (As one contemporary explained, Walker could not be "a *Yanky;* he don't look like one.")[66] Balancing the New Yorker on the ballot were two native residents of western Virginia: John F. Lewis, a prosperous farmer and former Unionist, and James C. Taylor, a former Whig and Confederate veteran whose political disabilities had been rescinded by Congress. Fearing the prospect of a Radical victory in the event of a split of the non-Republican vote, the Conservatives were induced to withdraw their candidate, Colonel Robert E. Withers. Walker won, and was joined in Richmond by a General Assembly dominated by Conservatives.[67]

Despite the "True Republican" slogan, Walker had been a Douglas Democrat before the war, and as governor he sided with the Conservatives in the General Assembly and in local power struggles across Virginia. His legislative legacy and his fiscal policy cut across partisan lines, however, and influenced Virginia politics for more than twenty years. In 1869 the legislature reiterated its intent to honor the antebellum state debt, which by then stood at $45 million. Two years later, in 1871, the General Assembly passed a measure funding two-thirds of the debt and unpaid interest in new 6 percent bonds, and offered "certificates of indebtedness" for West Virginia's share, which was still outstanding. Of pivotal importance for Virginia's later political history, the coupons on the new bonds were receivable for state taxes in lieu of cash.[68] The governor counted on increased tax revenues generated by an anticipated, if unduly optimistic, economic upswing to keep the state afloat.[69]

The controversial funding bill proved a fiscal disaster from the start. Criticism at first focused on the tax-receivable coupons rather than on the debt itself. When wealthy bondholders paid their taxes in coupons, there was not enough revenue to fund state services. Moreover, a far larger percentage of Virginians paid their taxes in coupons than ever owned bonds. This was because bondholders, rightly nervous about the ability as well as the inclination of the state to pay interest over the long haul, sold the coupons for less than their face value. The inundation of the state treasury by coupons rather than dollars created a fiscal crisis that would soon force the question of government priorities. Before the Funding Act, Virginia had run a modest budgetary surplus. After 1871, as the state accepted more and more coupons for taxes, that surplus turned into a ballooning deficit.[70] Popular anger at the situation was widespread, and the legislature elected in the fall of 1871 rode in on a wave of opposition to the Funding Act. Immediately it set to work to limit, if not eliminate, the tax-receivability of the coupons. But the General Assembly was thwarted by the Virginia Supreme Court, which ruled in 1872 that the promise to accept coupons in payment of taxes was a contract between the state and the bondholders that the legislature could not repudiate without violating the federal Constitution.[71]

Of necessity, the legislature turned its attention to taxation. Here, too, there was little room to maneuver. Before the Civil War, Virginians paid taxes on slaves and land, as well as for the right to vote. Like the other states of the former Confederacy, Virginia sharply increased land taxes during Reconstruction to make up for revenue lost owing to emancipation. By 1870 the property tax accounted for a staggering 77 percent of all state revenue, compared with 48 percent in 1860. As this statistic indicates, the postwar tax system rested squarely on the shoulders of landowners. With farmers already complaining that they were taxed beyond their capacity, raising the land tax was impracticable. Businesses got off relatively lightly during the period, contributing only about 27 percent of state revenue from 1870 to 1880.[72] Railroad companies in particular, which had been the chief beneficiaries of the debt, paid little taxes. Some railroads were exempted through charter agreements granted under the Walker administration, but most simply exploited unblushingly a law that permitted the companies to assess their own property for tax purposes.[73] New forms of regressive taxation on dogs and liquor—for example, the 1877 "Moffett Punch Law"—fueled popular outrage with Conservative management of the state and were widely evaded.[74] By 1878 Virginia was in the midst of a full-blown fiscal crisis. That year 47 percent of the state revenue was collected in the form of nonmonetary coupons from bonds. Annual income fell about $800,000 short of the budget. To meet all obligations, the state auditor estimated, would require a 75 percent tax increase, an impossibility given the depression.

Other southern states faced severe economic difficulties in the post-Appomattox era. But Virginia was unique in the solutions that it selected to address these problems. Presented with the same stark choice between maintaining social services and funding public debt, other states repudiated portions of their debt.[75] Virginia's Conservatives, on the other hand, began to slash state services. Many commonwealth institutions suffered from the deep cuts implemented in the late 1870s, particularly the state penitentiary and facilities for the mentally ill.[76] But it was the Conservatives' fiscal assault on the public schools that split wide Virginia politics and made possible a critique of Conservative rule that linked the debt, the schools, and suffrage. As early as

1872 Superintendent of Schools Ruffner had warned that revenue was being diverted from the school fund to service the debt.[77] In 1877 Ruffner calculated that the schools were owed more than $500,000; by 1879 that figure stood at $1.5 million.[78] Teachers went unpaid, and schools across Virginia began to close their doors. Almost half of the state's schools shut down during the 1878–79 academic year, and some one hundred thousand children—about half of the school population—were barred from school. Of those schools that remained open, many were forced to charge tuition.[79]

To justify these priorities, Conservatives invoked "traditions" of southern honor. John Warwick Daniel, a gubernatorial hopeful in 1877, thought it "better for the State to burn the schools" than repudiate any of the debt.[80] (Friends of Daniel later explained helpfully that his remark was "a figure of rhetoric, meaning that though friendly to the schools he preferred the destruction of public education to the disgrace of the state.")[81] Such representatives of the Virginia elite as Professor Bennett L. Puryear of Richmond College considered public education a northern innovation imposed on the state and worried that any extension of government functions through public schools would "relax individual energy and debauch public morality."[82] Even Jabez L. M. Curry, later famous as a reformer in southern educational circles, preferred scuttling the schools to readjusting the debt, which he denounced as "sheer demagoguism or communism."[83]

Conservative public officials and private citizens who placed the debt before the state's other obligations became known as "funders." James Lawson Kemper, governor from 1874 to 1878 and a firm funder, was an articulate exponent of this view. Applying to the state the same standards he exacted of himself as an individual, he insisted that the honor of the state as reflected in its creditworthiness was of greater value than the economy of debt scaling. Humiliated that "the best bonds of Virginia rate lower in the Stock Exchange of London" than those of such "darker" nations as "Egypt, Turkey, or Peru," Kemper lamented that "our credit ranks in the grade of such countries as Mexico and San Domingo. No grosser fallacy can be conceived," the governor concluded, "than the one which claims that a Commonwealth can flourish while its credit is in a state of prostration or dishonor."[84] Kemper's successor, Governor Frederick M. W. Holliday, recommended "economy, retrenchment, and self sacrifice" as a solution to the debt crisis.[85]

The funders were encouraged by the justices of the state supreme court, whose rejection of the legislature's attempts to void the tax-receivable coupons was also couched in the language of honor. In Judge Wood Bouldin's opinion, Virginia had "just emerged from a terrible trial—an ordeal of fire—without a stain on her escutcheon. Impoverished, crushed, and dismembered but not dishonored, she is now taking a new departure, and we would hope to see it in the right direction. In the language of a vigorous writer: 'Now is the seed time of faith and honor. The least fracture *now* will be like a name engraved with the point of a pin on the tender rind of a young beech, the wound will enlarge with the tree, and posterity will read it in full grown characters.'"[86]

Concern about the honor of Virginia could be—and in many cases probably was—both a class-based ideological position and a rhetorical cover. The funders drew on a specific rhetoric that called forth specific echoes. But not all, or even many, funders benefited directly from their prescribed debt policies. Although it is impossible to do a forensic accounting of the self-interest of the funders, we know that by 1874 only a fourth of all bonds were held by Virginians. True, the fact that the governor was prominent among them did little to further the funders' cause in the eyes of their critics,[87] but the typical funder, according to James Tice Moore, was "a middle-aged lawyer with a good family background, a University of Virginia education, and a distinguished war record as a Confederate officer." The majority of funders were professional white men in cities and towns; the faction (and later, the party) was dominated by doctors, lawyers, newspaper editors, businessmen, and merchants: men who professed to hold the sanctity of contract as a tenet of faith.[88] Filling the ranks behind them were northern Virginia's wealthy farmers, whose class interests and identity tended to align with the mercantile elite; white voters in the black-majority Piedmont, who were nervous about political schisms that could amplify African American political influence; and small businessmen in the cities concerned that ideas about "repudiation" would spread among their clientele.

Spread they did. Conflict over the debt had begun brewing in the interior of Virginia as soon as the funding bill passed in 1871. It intensified after 1876, when the Conservatives made payment of the school tax a prerequisite to voting. At this point the political discontent of western farmers angry over tax levels began to coalesce with the distress of less-propertied whites over the poll tax, which they perceived as a Conservative assault on popular governance. In the mid-1870s white farmers in the Valley and west took a page from black Virginians' political book and organized local chapters of the Grange, or the Patrons of Husbandry, to champion the cause of farmers against the interests of urban businessmen and professionals. H. W. Cosby of Halifax sounded the call to arms in the *Southern Planter and Farmer*. "We have long *begged* for our rights—let us now in *solid column demand* them!" Cosby exhorted. " 'In Union there is strength!' This is the colored man's secret. Let them agree on any measure, and they are *one* for that measure. Let us take a lesson." By the beginning of 1876 there were 685 Grange chapters in Virginia with a combined membership approaching 20,000. The Grange enjoyed modest success in its interventions in state politics in the 1870s, and by the end of the decade there was important overlap between the leaders of the Virginia Grange and supporters of what was coming to be called the "readjustment," or partial repudiation, of the state debt.[89]

Early white supporters of readjustment came from those western and Valley counties with the widest distribution of land ownership and the most rapid rate of population growth. These same counties tended to be enthusiastic about the public schools and to have the largest voter turnout in popular elections.[90] They were also, and not inconsequentially, heavily white-majority areas that had little immediate fear of black political influence. Centered west of the Blue Ridge Mountains in the Shenandoah Valley, these white critics of the debt policy had fought the social and political domination of eastern planters during the antebellum period, and they continued to resent the planters' political influence.

In addition to western white farmers, white and black urban workingmen and agricultural laborers, who had all been granted the suffrage late and grudgingly, objected to the Conservative plan to link the vote to the school tax. The ballots of immigrant Irish, German, and Jewish working-class voters, when cast alongside those of urban blacks, would also contribute to coalition victories in cities like Norfolk, Petersburg, Danville, Harrisonburg, Winchester, and Williamsburg.[91] These three groups—urban black and immigrant white workingmen, black agricultural workers and farmers in the heavily black eastern counties, and western white landowners—became the core constituency of the Readjuster Party when it formed in 1879.

Readjustment as a politically divisive issue originated in the Valley and found its first support among white yeoman farmers. But this does not mean that readjustment was an agrarian revolt against urban interests.[92] Rather than an obvious rural-urban struggle, the political alignments of postemancipation Virginia reveal the depth of the political and economic flux of the era. Ultimately, most of the coalition's leaders had at least one foot in the city, and many—like William Mahone—came from the periphery of the urban mercantile and professional classes.[93] As for class itself, although the funders attempted to portray those in favor of scaling down the debt as *sans-culottes* and enemies of all property, a majority of the insurgent white voters held property. As James T. Moore has noted, the areas of Virginia with the most concentrated white Readjuster votes were those counties where farm tenancy had made the smallest inroads—in other words, the Readjusters did best in areas where small to middling farmers predominated.[94] Furthermore, a number of elite Virginians, including former governor Henry A. Wise, state supreme court judge Waller R. Staples, and Colonel Lewis E. Harvie, a wealthy Valley agriculturist and prominent member of the state Grange, had all counseled partial repudiation from the beginning of the debt crisis. The claim that the Readjusters represented a movement of the have-nots rested mainly on the poverty of the coalition's black supporters, who tended not to own land.[95]

Maps 2 and 3 illustrate the spatial and racial geography of the Readjuster movement. Dividing Virginia into thirds, we can see that Readjuster support was concentrated in two areas: the largely black eastern counties and the overwhelmingly white region west of the Blue Ridge. These strongholds of readjusterism were divided by the central counties, which tended to vote Democratic. It is perhaps well to pause here and recognize that the coalition's white and black voters did not, in the main, live together. Although the Readjusters represented an interracial coalition at the state level, in most counties either white or black Readjusters predominated. It is possible that the success of interracial politics in Virginia can be attributed at least in part to the essentially segregated geographic distribution of the coalition. A significant exception to this pattern were the cities, where white and black Readjusters lived, worked, and acted politically day in and day out in close proximity.[96]

Whether in the city or the countryside, African American voters were among the most disaffected in Virginia. By the mid-1870s even

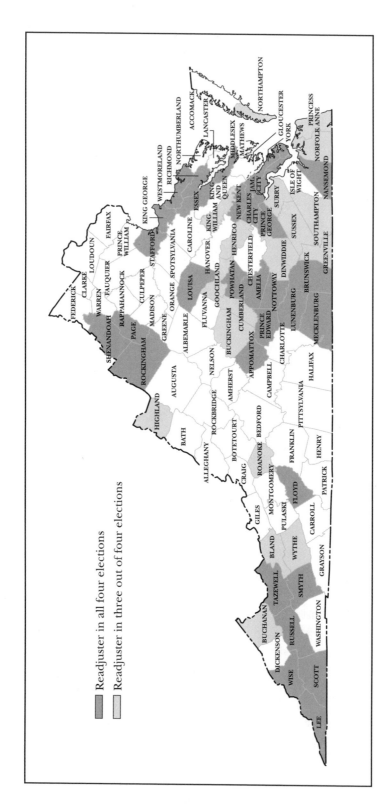

Map 2. *Readjuster Majorities in Virginia Counties, 1879–83*

■ Readjuster in all four elections

■ Readjuster in three out of four elections

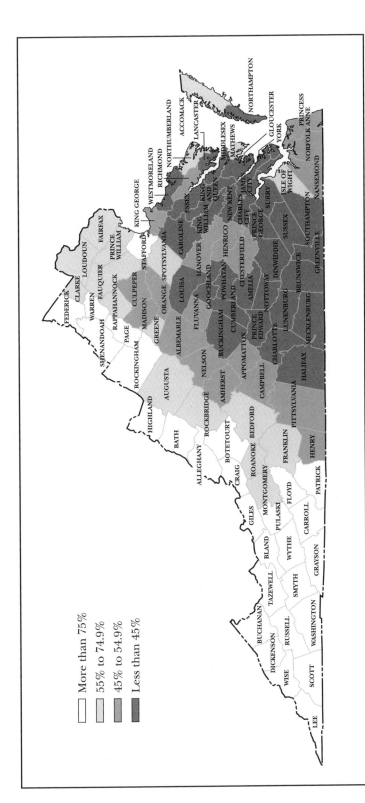

Map 3. *White Population of Virginia Counties, 1880*

Legend:

- More than 75%
- 55% to 74.9%
- 45% to 54.9%
- Less than 45%

the Republicans paid little attention to the political opinions of black Virginians. Although African Americans continued to support the Republican Party, the GOP occupied a minority position in Virginia politics and had little influence. This situation was in part the result of steps taken in the late 1860s. Like the Republican Party elsewhere in the South, the Virginia GOP had divided into radical and moderate factions that more or less paralleled the color line—black and a few northern white radicals to the left, moderate native whites to the right.[97] For a variety of reasons—including both ideological conviction and personal ambition on the part of leading individuals—the Radicals consistently refused to compromise with moderate Republicans and make common cause against the Conservatives. In the end, the white swing vote in Virginia—the "floating center of former Whigs, conditional Unionists, and political moderates"—was incorporated into the Conservative ranks following the "True Republican" alliance of 1869.[98]

Although the Republican organization occasionally rewarded individual African American politicians, the collective interests of black Virginians remained unrepresented in the 1870s. Dominated by a white leadership cadre, the Republicans typically nominated all-white tickets for the House of Delegates and saw little need to reward black voters either with a racially progressive legislative agenda or with federal patronage positions.[99] Prominent black Republicans such as Lewis Lindsay—who would soon lead black voters into the Readjuster camp—protested at the time, but to little purpose. The election of 1869 had sent thirty African Americans to the General Assembly, but by 1871 the black cohort in the House of Delegates had dropped to fourteen and the number of black senators had been halved, from six to three.[100] With their numbers so diminished, black legislators were unable to influence the course of debt policy or even to prevent the enactment of statutes that they considered abridged their rights, such as an 1870 law providing for convict labor.[101] Such legislation did not originate with Republicans, but the party of Lincoln drew clear boundaries around what it considered sufficient African American political power. By 1878 the Virginia GOP had become little more than a brokerage firm for federal patronage. To the dismay of the radical, largely African American wing of the party, Virginia Republicans did not even nominate a candidate for governor in 1877.

After 1873 Conservatives outnumbered Republicans three to one in the General Assembly, and they were emboldened enough to systematically wrest what rights they could from Virginia's African Americans. Amending the constitution, Conservatives abolished a third of local political offices. This undid a major contribution of the constitution, which limited centralized control over local politics. Turning their attention to the state level, Conservatives redrew election district boundaries in ways that diminished the possibility of black officeholding, and they reduced the membership of the House of Delegates by a third. In addition to linking the school tax to the suffrage, the General Assembly further circumscribed exercise of the franchise by nonpropertied blacks and whites by adding petit larceny to the list of actions that disqualified one from voting. Finally, the Conservatives disbarred from voting anyone punished by whipping, most commonly a penalty for petty theft. Sounding a class warning to poor whites, one of the state's few remaining black legislators, George Teamoh, remarked that this punishment was intended for the poor. "The rich man never . . . steals on a small scale," said Teamoh. "No danger of his being stretched upon that whipping post."[102]

Virginians skeptical about debt payment, angry about the restriction of the suffrage, and afraid of dwindling state support of the public schools came together in 1877 in the gubernatorial campaign of William Mahone. One of the most maligned political leaders of Gilded Age America, Mahone was also one of the most able. Compared to Cataline (by the Democrats), to Moses (by black Republican leader John Mercer Langston), and to Napoleon (by Mahone himself), the future Readjuster leader was born to slave-holding innkeepers in Southampton County in 1826.[103] Mahone studied engineering at the Virginia Military Institute, which he attended on scholarship. Although he ended life a wealthy man, Mahone's origins separated him from Virginia bluebloods and left him attuned to the political concerns of the laboring classes.[104]

Nothing in Mahone's earlier career prophesied that his name would become synonymous with race treason.[105] A native Virginian and a slaveholder, Mahone had supported secession and served in the Confederate army throughout the war. Although his political opponents, especially the vituperative General Jubal A. Early, tried to sully his war record, Mahone had risen to the rank of major general. Furthermore, he had achieved his greatest military success in his home state, at the Battle of the Crater outside Petersburg. At Petersburg, troops of the Ninth Corps of the Army of the Potomac used gunpowder to

William Mahone. This portrait was taken during Reconstruction, during Mahone's heyday as a railroad entrepreneur. (The Library of Virginia)

blow a hole underneath a Confederate fort. Led by an undistinguished Union commander with a drinking problem, however, white troops went down *into* the crater rather than fanning out to the right and left. They were followed by black troops, who were mowed down by Mahone's rebels, who also murdered a number of black soldiers trying to surrender. Mahone went on to become one of Robert E. Lee's most trusted advisers and was with Lee when the decision to surrender was made in April 1865. The troops Mahone led were part of the only two intact divisions of the Army of Northern Virginia to stack their weapons at Appomattox.[106]

Historians have tried to find hints of Mahone's political future in his military career. According to Douglas Southall Freeman, Mahone's leadership and military skills increased in proportion to his responsibilities: an unexceptional brigadier, he became one of the Army of Northern Virginia's most able divisional commanders.[107] Mahone was also something of an iconoclast. As tiny and bright-eyed as a leprechaun, he spurned military uniformity. One contemporary described his appearance in 1864 as that of "a Major General indeed, but wonderfully accoutered! A plaited brown linen jacket, buttoned to trousers of same material, like a boy's; topped off by a large Panama hat of the finest and most beautiful texture." [108] Can signs of future greatness be read in such a getup?

Mahone's prewar career may be more telling. Before enlisting in the Confederate cause, Mahone had used the education he obtained at vmi to initiate a flourishing career in Virginia's infant railroad industry. By all accounts a brilliant railroad engineer, the young Mahone was an enthusiastic and self-interested promoter of state aid to transportation.[109] His involvement with railroads led him immediately after the war into Reconstruction politics. It is difficult to overstate the influence of railroads on Virginia politics in these years. From the 1870s through the 1890s, nearly every state chairman of every political party in Virginia was a railroad president or chairman.[110] Railroad rates and the influence of railroad men on government were animating issues for the Grange in the 1870s and for the Farmers Alliance in the 1890s, as well as for the Readjusters in the 1880s. Those few leading politicians who were not personally vested in railroads were inevitably backed financially by railroad interests or were railroad lawyers; more than one election involved not only the outward clash of different political parties but also a behind-the-scenes conflict between competing railroad lines. At the center of these battles stood William Mahone, who championed local control (ideally, his own) over railroads, and various representatives of northern companies, all of whom were connected in the end to either the Baltimore and Ohio Railroad Company or to Tom Scott's Pennsylvania Railroad.[111] In 1869, when he backed Gilbert C. Walker for governor, Mahone was president of three different railroads extending west from Norfolk; his ambition was to consolidate these lines into one company, grandly named the Atlantic, Mississippi, and Ohio, which would dominate traffic between Virginia and the Midwest. He achieved this goal in 1870, when the General Assembly, with the advice and consent of Governor Walker, approved Mahone's consolidation proposal.[112]

Bankrupted during the depression of the 1870s, in 1877 the railroad man decided to campaign for the Conservative gubernatorial nomination as an antifunder. This represented a sharp change in policy. Mahone did not speak out against the Funding Act in 1871, and he supported Governor Kemper's debt policy in 1874.[113] Uncharitable observers have suggested that Mahone was motivated by a desire for revenge against northern and British men of finance.[114] More sympathetic portraits stress principle over opportunism. Mahone is easily seen as an archetypal New South man: an entrepreneur interested in technology, a supporter of European immigration to the South, a proponent of a protective tariff to encourage mining and manufacturing, a city man. Certainly Mahone fits this profile, but so did many funders who worried that a diminished state credit would stifle economic growth. Perhaps Mahone's political course was inspired by his own experience with education and his New South economic goals, which rested in part on the education of Virginia's labor force. Before beginning his career in engineering, Mahone taught school for several years, first at VMI (where he instructed cadets in tactics, Latin, and mathematics) and later at the Rappahannock Academy. But all this is biography. Whatever the exact proportions of personal ambition and ideological conviction, in 1877 William Mahone awoke to the economic and social peril—not to mention the political possibility—inherent in the funders' assault on the public schools.[115]

Mahone made three arguments regarding the debt and the schools in 1877. First, he asserted that by failing to meet scheduled interest payments on time, Virginia was already in the process of "practical, though unwilling, repudiation."[116] Accordingly, he and other like-minded Conservatives recommended "readjustment" (partial repudiation) of the debt. Second, he and other Readjusters (as the antifunders were soon called) took on funder rhetoric about honor and sacrifice. Mahone ridiculed funders who invoked honor while breaking their promises to the people. "This twaddle about the honor of the State . . . is sheer nonsense," he fumed, when considered alongside the "robery [sic] of the school fund."[117] Fellow antifunder John E. Massey went further, adopting the language of honor for the Readjusters by impugning the masculinity of the funders and, by implication, the voters who supported them. Lecturing that "there is virtue and heroism in patiently bearing evils which we cannot help, but it is unmanly to submit to injustice when the remedy of it is in our own hands," Massey accused Virginians of endangering the future of coming generations by submitting to funder debt priorities.[118] Balancing the interests of the people against those of the bondholders, Mahone recommended readjustment of the debt to "within the certain and reasonable capacity of the people to regularly meet" as the only way for the commonwealth to maintain its honor. This position must have seemed attractive to voters when compared with surprisingly frank funder campaign slogans such as "Poverty rather than dishonor" and "Taxation before Repudiation."[119]

Mahone's final argument was that funder debt policies were undemocratic, unconstitutional, and antithetical to the expressed will of the people, who had declared "unmistakably and irrevocably . . . in favor of the free-school system." Terming the attempts to redirect school funds "subversive of popular rights," he announced grandiosely that he would rather "let the very wheels of government stand still" than tolerate "so gross a violation of the will of the people, as the perversion or conversion of the public-school fund to any other purpose than that for which it was created."[120] Such language may well have reflected Mahone's own feelings with regard to the schools, but it also hinted at what would later materialize as a dramatic shift of political strategy: courting the black Republican vote to bolster the schism in white Conservative ranks. "You can operate on the negroes by telling them that it is the effects [sic] of the Funding Bill that is depriving them of a school now," advised D. C. Miller of Marion.[121]

By the time William Mahone entered electoral politics in 1877, the debt question had been a highly charged issue in Virginia for nearly a decade. But Mahone's actions made the debt the central focus of an election for the first time. Although he failed to win the Conservative gubernatorial nomination that year, his candidacy forced the party to consider openly the possibility of partial repudiation. In ambiguous terms that Readjusters ridiculed and parodied throughout the fall campaign, the Conservative platform rejected what it called "forcible readjustment" by state action but did not discount all possibility of voluntary readjustment through negotiations between bondholders and the state.

In the election of 1877 twenty-two independents, nearly all Readjusters of some sort, won seats in the Virginia House of Delegates. In their own minds, many of these men paired the debt and the schools. Among these were the representatives of organized white workers in Richmond who had declared that "education being the keystone of the arch that supports the whole superstructure of society," the school funds should be "sacred from all encroachments."[122] In 1878 Conservative dissenters in the house drew up the first piece of legislation aimed at readjusting the debt. The Barbour Bill, named for Conservative Readjuster James Barbour, argued that the three necessities of the state, in order of importance, were preserving the state government, supporting the public schools, and servicing the debt. Aimed at readjusting the priorities of government, the bill said nothing about readjustment of the debt. The hope was that if the claims of creditors were placed last on the agenda, the bondholders could be persuaded to forge a more equitable settlement with the state through the courts. Although he had said many times that he intended "to abide by the will of the people as to the debt" and had described the debt as "belonging properly to the legislature," Governor Frederick M. W. Holliday vetoed the bill.[123]

As Mahone had made the sanctity of the schoolhouse his point of attack on funder debt policies, so the funders turned on the schools in their rage over the Barbour Bill. Adopting Mahone's zero-sum approach to the debt and the schools, Governor Holliday argued that the debt had preexisting claims on the state that the schools did not. The debt, he intoned, "was due when free schools were scarcely, if at all, thought of." Alluding to the racial and political composition of the convention that produced the 1868 constitution and the school system, Holliday noted that in 1866 the debt had been acknowledged by "a legislature composed of men of the old *regime*—among the ablest, best and truest who ever grew upon Virginia soil," and he insisted that the new constitution "does not put [the schools] on any higher ground than the debt." In earlier messages to the legislature Holliday had advised those Virginians who wanted free schools to "pay for them out of their own means."[124] Now he elaborated:

Education is a great blessing when of the proper sort, and properly gained. But a state has no more right to educate its youths than an individual his children, at the expense of its creditors. . . . Our fathers did not need free schools to make them what they were. . . . Free schools are not a necessity. The world, for hundreds of years, grew in wealth, culture, and refinement, without them. They are a luxury, adding, when skillfully conducted, it may be, to the beauty and power of the state, but to be paid for, like any other luxury, by the people who wish their benefits.[125]

The people who wished the benefits of the free schools met in convention on February 25 and 26, 1879, at Mozart Hall in Richmond, to establish the Readjuster Party. About 175 delegates represented local conventions that were opposed to full funding of the debt. Reflecting the disintegration of party lines over the debt issue, moderate Conservatives mingled with Republicans, Greenbackers, and other flavors of independents. In the first official sign of his recognition that Republican votes would be needed to force the funders from power, Mahone had issued the invitation to attend the convention to all, "without distinction of color."[126]

The Mozart Hall convention was the most significant interracial political forum in Virginia since the constitutional convention. Rising to address the convention, William T. Jefferson of New Kent explained that he and the other African American men present longed for an opportunity to ally with progressive whites. Making his point with a biblical mixed metaphor, he said that blacks "had been waiting long for the waters to be troubled so that they might step in and be healed of the political leprosy which had fatally afflicted them."[127] Turning to the question of the debt, Jefferson told the assembly, "we [black Virginians] don't want to pay a cent of it. We think we paid our share of it, if it ever was justly chargeable upon us, by long years of servitude." Other sources uphold Jefferson's assertion. "The majority of colored voters here are in favor of not paying the debt," reported a Virginia correspondent to the *Southern Workman*, which was published at Hampton Institute. These voters felt that "when this debt was made, they were held as property as security for it, and they had no hand in making it. Therefore, they hold that they should not be taxed to pay it, nor the money taken from their free schools and their children left destitute of education."[128]

Moving from the debt to other issues in common between white and black delegates at Mozart Hall, William Jefferson commented shrewdly both on the hierarchy of social relations in Virginia and on the identity of interest binding white and black Readjusters. Couching an assertion of commonality of interest within the language of deference, he explained: "We are humble citizens—the humblest in the Commonwealth—and we treat white people invariably with a great deal more courtesy than we receive, because we are anxious not to offend you, and to win your good will. We are for peace, and we accept the overture made to us as heartily as it is tendered, for we feel that your interests and our interests are identical."

In 1879 the interest most capable of binding black and white voters together was shared outrage over the condition of the public schools. The arrogance of the Conservatives had convinced both groups that the government was actively working against the well-being of non-elite Virginians regardless of their position along the color line. In the weeks preceding the Mozart Hall convention, Readjusters across Virginia had met to consider forming an independent third party. They passed resolutions, sent to Richmond and printed in the *Whig,* that denounced the funders for destroying the public schools and made the case that "the preservation of the functions of the Government" outweighed the state's obligations to its creditors. The public school system stood first among the functions of government for these voters. As the Re-Adjusters of Washington County resolved, "we favor the maintenance of the free school system of Virginia, for the benefit of all her citizens, without regard to race, color or condition, under separate management as to white and colored, so that the white and colored people may reap the fruits of the system and become alike honest, industrious and useful citizens." Bland County Readjusters agreed: "We demand the maintenance of the public free schools, alike for white and colored—under separate organizations, so that education can be given to all citizens alike." Addressing the funder argument that to renege on the debt was dishonorable, Stafford County resolved "that we look on the misapplication, or robbery, of the school fund as the blackest stain that has ever been inflicted on our proud old State, and ought to be denounced by every honest man."[129]

Responding to funder arguments cast in the moral terms of manly honor, Readjusters presented the state as failing to live up to its word. One county superintendent of schools relayed the opinion of the people of his district this way: "The State, they say, has stipulated to educate the children of the Commonwealth in consideration of the payment of certain revenues by the people. The revenues have been paid, and the money used for other purposes. This is certainly bad faith, and just cause of complaint. The people have paid the State to educate their children, and now are required to pay the teacher. This is virtually raising or increasing taxes, which the people say should not be done."[130]

Like the Readjuster rank and file, Mahone argued the case for readjustment in terms of fairness, rights, and honor. Rebutting the funder position that public schools were a "luxury," he insisted on the one hand that the sons and daughters of Confederate veterans "have a rightful claim upon popular guardianship" and on the other that the freedpeople needed education to enable them to fulfill the duties of citizenship. As in the debate over the Underwood Constitution ten years before, the rights of African Americans were linked to those of former Confederates.[131]

In 1879 public anger over the misallocation of the poll tax, as well as the curtailment of the suffrage it represented, created a sense of commonality, of mutuality, among Virginians of the lesser ranks great enough to bridge the racial divide. As one new coalitionist put it at Mozart Hall, the Readjusters "had been sneered at for seeking the aid of the colored citizens. He desired nothing better than to add all the colored voters to the ranks of those who were fighting the battles of popular rights and interests." He had been told in Richmond that "we should not waste education on the 'd——d niggers.'" But, he said, "let the colored people stand fast by the Re-Adjusters and the Re-Adjusters will see to it that education shall be provided for the children of all colors."[132]

The legislative election of 1879 became a referendum on funder policies regarding the debt and the schools.[133] Reversing the Conservative litany of the citizen's duty and obligation to the state, the Readjusters asked what the state could reasonably be expected to do for

the citizen. To reach as many voters as possible, the Readjusters organized their party on a mass scale and sent dozens of lecturers into the
most remote regions of the state to explain the Readjuster positions
on the debt, the schools, and taxes.[134] "Our cause, which is the cause
of the people, gains by every fair discussion," John Massey scrawled
hastily in May.[135] Of course, not every audience had the patience to listen to three hours' worth of detail about the debt. One unsuccessful
funder candidate recalled years later that speeches had to be larded
with anecdotes and that invariably someone in the crowd would call
out, "Oh, damn the Coupons! Tell us that Bear tale" (a sentiment the
reader may by now share).[136] In many areas, four candidates—a funder
Conservative, a Readjuster, and pro- and anti-funding Republicans—
tangled over one legislative seat, and all sides competed for the black
vote to an extent not seen since 1869. In some counties the breakdown
of party lines apparently confused black voters, who reportedly failed
to vote out of fear of mistakenly casting a ballot for funding.[137]

Despite the rhetoric of the Mozart Hall convention and the appeal
of the debt—as articulated through the related issues of the schools
and the poll tax—to unify white and black voters, the Readjusters
balked at further identification with African Americans. Although
some Readjuster leaders admonished that "now is the time to carry
the war into Africa," most members of the new party feared that the
adoption of black issues and overt appeals for black votes would risk
the movement's gains among white workingmen and farmers.[138] African Americans, for their part, reserved judgment. Confronted with an
eleventh-hour appeal for Republican votes by the Readjusters, black
Virginians remained suspicious and for the most part voted Republican.[139] Those African Americans who did vote Readjuster did so because they saw it as a vote for the schools.[140]

Yet it was ultimately the black vote that cast the deciding ballot in
the conflict over the debt in Virginia. With the white vote split between the funder Conservatives and the Readjusters, the Republicans
won enough seats to hold the balance of power in both houses of the
General Assembly. Thirteen of the Republicans were African Americans, whose votes, if combined with the Readjusters', would give the
third party control of the legislature.[141] Leading Readjusters and black
Republicans immediately began to negotiate the terms of unification.
"To-day, a prominent Republican approached me, to know if they
should aid us in the organization of the House, what we would do for

them?" D. J. Godwin of Portsmouth wrote to Mahone in the second week of November 1879. "I could only say that we would deal justly and fairly with them. . . . We must do something for these men to get their co-operation, now, and in the future. We must give them something in the way of offices and also in a legislative point of view . . . to win the masses of that party. For instance: provide for the public schools. We must let them know that we are their friends."[142] Writing from the majority-black Southside, Richard S. Wise agreed: "If as the [black] preachers say we won through the negro vote we owe them much, and those of their color a debt which can only be paid by sticking to those principles for which their color voted."[143]

After the election, white Readjuster leaders courted their black Republican colleagues in an effort to outline the contours of coalition.[144] After surveying Littleton Owens, one of the black Republicans elected to the House of Delegates, C. B. Langley reported that the issues that mattered most to Owens were "the Fence Law, Public Schools, and the repeal of the qualification for voting."[145] Referring to legislative limits of black civic and political rights during the 1870s, Lunsford L. Lewis, the Republican U.S. district attorney for eastern Virginia, put matters more generally: "[T]he Republicans will cooperate with that faction of the Conservative Party which is willing to *do justice* to all classes in the State, and which will unite with them in repealing much of the odious and oppressive legislation . . . perpetrated by the Conservative Party. The Republicans, generally, I think, will take that view of it; and will help that faction which will help them."[146]

Coalition negotiations dragged on into December, when Mahone met personally with black Republican legislators to assure them of the Readjusters' willingness to address issues of concern to black Virginians, such as increased support for black schools, abolition of the whipping post, a voice in patronage distribution, and the severing of the poll tax from the suffrage. As the state passed into a new decade, the thirteen black legislators allied with the Readjusters to give the coalition a voting majority in the General Assembly.

2

EXPANDING THE CIRCLE OF HONOR

The Politics of Patronage

William Mahone never intended to challenge white supremacy in Virginia. He did not mean to be, as he was later depicted by John Mercer Langston, a white Moses leading black Virginians out of the political wilderness they found themselves in after 1873.[1] But the 1880 national election revealed to Mahone a fundamental truth about politics in postwar Virginia: the path to enduring victory for the Readjusters ran through the black community.

This reliance on the black vote was a fact of life for any party that hoped to challenge the Democrats in the postwar South. When federal Reconstruction ended in the South in 1877, a welter of oppositional parties sprang up to challenge the Democrats. Throughout the 1880s, Independent and Republican gubernatorial candidates received roughly a third to a half of all southern votes. The success of each of these parties depended on the ballots of African Americans, a fact the Democrats themselves came to appreciate. In 1876 Senator Benjamin H. Hill of Georgia noted the importance of the black vote when whites were splintered and declared himself "glad to be voted [for] by a colored Democrat."[2]

The urge to independent politics was not confined to the South. In 1878 the North and Midwest sent fifteen members of the Independent Party (Greenbackers) to Congress, and Greenback-Labor candidates took control of a number of northern cities. In the postwar South as well as the North, independent political parties reflected popular dissatisfaction with the conditions of labor, currency restriction, and elite-dominated government. At the same time that white and black voters cooperated through party politics, white and black workingmen forged new ties through local labor unions and such national organizations as the Greenback-Labor Party and the Knights of Labor. The boundaries between labor organizations and political parties were porous in the postwar period, and alliance in one arena often facilitated coalition in the other.[3]

In 1880 the National Greenback-Labor Party made a serious dent in the prospect of a solid Democratic South. Wild card candidates challenged the Democrats for control of Arkansas, Kentucky, Mississippi, and North Carolina. In Alabama Greenbacker congressman William M. Lowe was fraudulently denied reelection, and in Texas the following year Greenbacker candidate for governor Wash Jones barely lost to his Democratic rival. In Tennessee in 1880 the Democrats split into warring factions over the issue of the state debt and the Republicans returned to power.[4]

Southern politics was volatile in the 1870s and 1880s because large blocs of voters considered political, communal, and economic interests along with such factors as partisanship and race solidarity. The impulse to cross party lines ran strongest in state and local elections and held for black Republicans as well as for Democrats and white Republicans. African American voters weighed their needs, and the potential benefits of alliance with non-Republican southern whites, against a deep attachment to the party of emancipation. Despite the desire and attempts of white representatives of both major parties to control the black vote, black voters acted autonomously.[5]

Organized black voters could also act in concert. A dense network of community associations and religious organizations enabled the political activism of black men and women in the postwar South. In towns as well as in the countryside—which had a greater but more dispersed African American population—blacks formed fraternal and self-help societies, militias, political organizations such as the Union League, and churches.[6] Churches, militias, and the Union League complemented each other and served as a three-pronged tool of mass political mobilization.[7] Political meetings were often held in churches and schools (frequently the same building) and were guarded by armed militias. On Sundays, ministers did not shy away from making political recommendations from the pulpit. Although black ministers never commanded the unquestioned political obedience of their congregants, as southern whites often assumed, they were in most cases among the best educated of their community, which buttressed the moral authority that accompanied their calling. Indeed, the line between religion and politics was often blurry in the early postwar African American community. Studying the political culture of rural black laborers, Steven Hahn has found that the Union League's initiation ritual—in which new members "took a sacred pledge while forming a circle with clasped and uplifted hands"—resembled the ring shout and sounded other chords from traditional spiritual worship.[8]

The collective, cohesive nature of black politics meant that for a growing number of African American politicians in the South, maintaining an independent power base and wielding it to the best advantage of the black community often outweighed any sense of obligation to organized political parties.[9] This was as true in Virginia as elsewhere. Throughout the 1870s nearly all black voters in Virginia supported the Republicans, as most had in 1879 despite the creation of the new third party. Because of Mahone's December bargain with the thirteen Republican legislators in Richmond, however, the Readjuster Party now seemed most likely to further the interests of black Virginians.

The benefits of alliance with black Republicans were immediately apparent to the Readjusters: control of the General Assembly meant passage of debt legislation and Mahone's election by the assembly to the U.S. Senate.[10] Black support also promised greater electoral majorities and the possibility of electing a Readjuster governor in 1881.

The cost of coalition was less tangible. In part, this was because the African American coalitionists' agenda had yet to be incorporated into the Readjuster program. As long as readjustment itself could be thwarted by a Conservative governor's veto, the main focus of the party, and the glue holding it together, remained the debt. Doubts about the demands of the black wing could wait.

Black Virginians had greater cause for concern about the pros and cons of coalition. Even among the group of young black Republicans anxious to ally with the Readjusters there was anxiety over their new partners' past. Robert A. Paul, who was captain of a Richmond black militia unit and a respected—and critical-minded—Republican, made the case both for and against fusion. On the one hand, Paul argued that "there is no difference between the Readjusters and the Republicans so far as equal rights before the law are concerned."[11] But the context for coalition worried him. As he put it, "Those who had been the bitterest and most dangerous foes to the Colored People were calling for their support. The one [Mahone] who had hurled hundreds of colored soldiers into the death-fraught crater of Petersburg had announced himself the leader and director of the new party. They who had fought on the field of blood and labored in the arena of politics to deprive the Colored man of his constitutional rights now proclaimed that Colored men should enjoy the full rights and prerogatives of citizens." It was only prudent, under these circumstances, for black Virginians to hold back and wait to see if "any 'good thing could come out of Nazareth.' "[12]

The Readjusters had scarcely settled into their leadership role in the Virginia legislature before both national parties began to plot the coalition's destruction in the 1880 presidential election. Recognizing the difficulty of explaining to voters the relationship of debt readjustment to the election of congressional representatives and the race for the White House, both the Democrats and the Republicans planned to stress national issues and cultivate partisan loyalties and distrust among coalitionists. This strategy was sound. As one local coalitionist put it, "The trouble with this canvass is the people don't understand it. Funders tell them Readjustment don't have anything to do with Presidential Elections—they can't see behind or beyond that."[13] Readjuster state senator and presidential elector Harrison H. Riddleberger insisted that white Readjusters would vote "a straight [D]emocratic ticket without regard to State issues," and he strove to remind Mahone that "Readjustment is viewed as involving only dollars and cents—federal politics as involving all [D]emocratic and [R]epublican principles."[14]

In addition to concealing the debt issue and all that it represented, the national election threatened to sunder the coalition along lines of support for a president. Smelling the danger, Mahone attempted to head off disaster by proposing that Democratic and Republican Readjusters unite behind an independent ticket of unpledged presidential electors.[15] Neither the Democrats nor the Republicans in the coalition liked the idea of jeopardizing their presidential candidates in favor of local politics, however. Meeting at Staunton in April, the Virginia Republican Party divided over the question of fusion with the Readjusters and narrowly voted to field a regular Republican ticket.[16] The Democrats did likewise in May.

Unification with the Republicans was anathema for most white Readjusters, which left the party with two options: fuse with the Conservative Democrats, dividing the nominees for state and congressional offices between Conservatives and Readjusters, or field an independent ticket. The Greenbackers, who had nominated their own national slate, also made a play for coalition votes. Although there were influential Readjusters who supported fusion, most coalition leaders favored a third-party ticket because it maintained the coalition's organizational independence. In the end the Readjusters ran their own ticket but supported the Democratic nominees for the executive, Winfield Scott Hancock and William H. English.[17]

Realistically, the Readjusters were hardly in a position to decide otherwise: white coalitionists, who dominated the new party's leadership, were no more willing to undermine the Democratic effort to capture the federal executive than black coalitionists were to jeopardize continued Republican control of the White House.[18] But the decision to back Hancock and English virtually guaranteed a poor showing for the coalition in November by alienating black voters.[19] This in turn caught the attention of national Republican strategists, who reckoned that the Readjusters' slight to black voters coupled with the schism in the white Democratic ranks might tip the state for Republican nominee James A. Garfield.[20]

The existence of two tickets in Virginia supporting Hancock and English frightened the national Democrats as much as it heartened the Republicans. Concerned about Republican strength in Virginia, the Democratic National Committee ordered the Democratic factions there to fuse and form a single ticket.[21] This command was resisted by Readjusters worried about their congressional candidates,[22] but it found approval among those who feared that the Republicans might take the state. Should the Readjusters fail to fuse with the Democrats, one correspondent from a black-majority county warned, white Readjusters would scratch their ticket and vote with the Conservatives anyway.[23] When the coalition and the Conservatives failed to reach an agreement, the Democratic National Committee recognized the funder Conservatives as the regular Democratic Party.[24] Readjuster leaders predicted a "general stampede" in the direction of the regular Democratic ticket.[25]

Despite a last-ditch attempt to fool Republican voters into supporting the Readjusters by omitting the names of the coalition candidates (Hancock and English) from the top of the ticket, the Readjusters came in a distant third in November. Most Democratic Readjusters voted the regular party ticket, and black voters were not duped by the irregular ballots. The thirty-odd thousand votes cast for the coalition came largely from the majority-white counties in the mountain west, which sent two Readjuster congressmen to Washington.[26]

Two fairly obvious lessons could be drawn from the Readjusters' 1880 electoral defeat. The first concerned partisan identity and allegiance. To the extent that anyone in Virginia was a "Readjuster" in 1880, he was either a "Republican Readjuster" or a "Democratic Readjuster." This identity was pronounced in national politics but need not derail local political alliances. After November 1880, the Readjusters worked to foster local affinities of interest through a political agenda designed to overcome partisan loyalties and animosities. Forming the coalition in 1879 around the debt and schools platform had proved it could be done. Now the coalition had to set an agenda wider than the debt. If the Readjusters could succeed in doing this, wrote one martially minded correspondent to Mahone, they would win the gubernatorial election of 1881 and thereby "capture Richmond in far less time than the Yankees did."[27]

The second lesson of the 1880 election was demographic: defeating the Democrats in Virginia required almost unanimous Republican—which meant African American—electoral support combined with a sizable minority of white Democratic voters. Confronting their electoral disaster, Readjuster leaders conceded for the first time the importance of the black vote to the coalition. It was suddenly clear to white Readjusters that the future of the coalition turned, in the words of one local leader, on the actions of "our Republican friends."[28]

That the Readjusters had any Republican friends at all was thanks to the GOP's neglect of its African American constituency. Black Virginians' distrust of the state Republican organization reached back to the internal schism precipitated by the ratification of the Underwood Constitution. After 1870 the Republican Party had come under the control of native white Virginians more devoted to railroad construction than to black citizenship. The GOP candidate for governor in 1873, for instance, was Robert W. Hughes, a funder and former Confederate officer who had opposed the test oath provision of the 1868 constitution. Urban black leaders working through the Colored National Labor Union tried but failed to gain control of the party machinery in 1869 and 1870. Black radicals were unable as well to influence either the Republican Party platform or its electoral slate. Planks supporting equal access to public facilities and transportation and the right of black men to serve on juries met defeat, and the party nominated an all-white ticket for the General Assembly. Shortsightedly, the party of Lincoln failed to protect black political influence; Richmond blacks were furious when the GOP accepted Democratic gerrymandering of the city that concentrated black votes into a single district. Essentially a vehicle for the distribution of federal patronage, the Republican Party in Virginia reached its nadir in 1877, when it failed to even nominate a candidate to oppose the Conservative gubernatorial nominee.[29]

Unable to influence the Republican Party from within, black Virginians created new organizations that combined political and labor concerns in an attempt to shape public policy from without. In August 1875 delegates from more than forty counties assembled in Richmond for a black labor convention. There keynote speakers criticized the GOP's patronage distribution and organization and suggested scaling down the state debt to protect the public school system. Joseph T. Wilson of Norfolk declaimed his unwillingness to be the "political serf" of "unworthy white leaders," and Joseph P. Evans, a state legislator from Petersburg, declared that Virginia blacks should work in their own interest outside the bounds of the Republican Party.[30] The depression engendered by the panic of 1873 would limit black gains in the realm of labor between 1875 and 1880. But the combustive political situation in Virginia generated by the state debt presented black Republicans with unanticipated political power.

In 1880 black Republicans knew that the balance of political power in the Old Dominion lay, for once, in their hands. Shortly after the presidential election, African American supporters of coalition issued a call for a "Colored State Convention" to be held in Petersburg the following March. Intended as a declaration of independence from the Republican Party, the authors of the Petersburg call asserted the right of black Virginians "to be free . . . to control their own affairs in their own way" and announced their intention "to concert with the most liberal party in Virginia."[31] As John Oliver, a prominent labor and political leader in Richmond, had argued in the fall of 1879, the grievances of the black community outranked partisan loyalty, and "whatever party wants our votes must consider them."[32]

The grievances of black Virginians were no mystery to white Readjusters. But white recognition of black complaints, and blueprints for their remedy, were novel. In a letter to Mahone in the spring of 1881, George W. Booker, a white man in Henry County, outlined a strategy for the Readjusters based on a clearheaded assessment of the need for the black vote and what it would take to get it. First, Booker advised, the Readjusters should amend the Virginia constitution and abolish the article linking prepayment of the capitation tax to the suffrage, "as this enables the rich to control the votes of a large portion of the poor, black and white alike." Next, they should abolish the whipping post as a penalty for petit larceny. Although in theory stripes could be administered to anyone convicted of theft, in practice this intentional legacy of slavery remained a degrading punishment reserved for black men and women. Finally, the Readjusters should convince President Garfield to give them control of federal patronage. This would weaken the Republican organization in Virginia and, combined with a progressive legislative program, win over black voters to the coalition through the allure of civil service jobs.[33]

Students of realpolitik may wonder how Booker expected Mahone to persuade the president—who, we should recall, did not head the Readjusters' 1880 electoral ticket—to abandon the Republicans in Virginia and support the coalition. By May 1881 there was no need for explanation. Although elected U.S. senator by the Virginia legislature in December 1879, William Mahone was not sworn in until the special session called for March 1881. As it happened, the upper house of the Forty-seventh Congress was divided evenly between the two national parties, 37 to 37, with two new senators, Mahone and David Davis of Illinois, to be seated. Davis had been elected as an Independent but had declared his intention to vote with the Democrats. Mahone's vote would therefore determine whether the Democrats or the Republicans would control the organization of the Senate (through the election of officers and committee chairmen), since Republican vice president Chester A. Arthur could cast the deciding vote in case of a tie.

Throughout the winter of 1880–81, Mahone pondered formal alliance with the Republicans. In light of the large number of Readjusters who attributed the outcome of the 1880 election to white Virginians' hatred of the GOP,[34] Mahone's willingness to consider fusion with the Republicans suggests recognition of the demographic reality of third-party movements in Virginia: only with the backing of African Americans, who represented 40 percent of the electorate, could a white splinter movement beat the Democrats. Mahone's thoughts on fusion also reflected the alienation of Democratic Readjusters from their national party. In the minds of many Democratic Readjusters, Mahone and his followers had been excommunicated by the Democratic National Committee and were now free to act independently. "I wish you could be here to read the tone of all the letters I am getting," Mahone wrote to Harrison Holt Riddleberger, the prominent Readjuster leader from the Shenandoah Valley, in December 1880. "They would surprise you. They are all from [Readjuster] Stalwarts with two or three exceptions—and they absolve allegiance to the Demo. party and ask for a new departure. Some are ready without method to go—others by gentle and progressive steps—all would be glad to have the Rep. party come to us—and some would go there." [35] John E. Boze of Lynchburg was one of these incipient bolters. In early March 1881 Boze explained to Mahone that many Democrats who had voted the regular Democratic ticket in 1880 were now on the Readjusters' side and even supported coalition with the Republicans. "I myself am more Republican than I ever dreamed I would be when I used to be a Cat-O nine tales [*sic*] for the Old Democrats," Boze enthused. [36] The sentiments of John B. Lady of Rockbridge (a lifelong Democrat who had voted for every Democratic presidential candidate "not excepting Horace Greeley") are more representative of those expressed in letters to Mahone. Without referring to the Republicans by name, Lady advised Mahone to align himself in the Senate with whatever party "would do the most to rid Virginia of Bourbonism." [37]

Letters such as these propelled Mahone ever closer to the GOP. Finally he agreed to cooperate with the Republicans in exchange for assignments to four influential Senate committees and division of the federal patronage in Virginia between regular Republicans and Readjusters. [38] This decision caused considerable consternation on both sides of the Senate aisle—among Democrats, who claimed, justifiably, that Mahone had been elected by a *Democratic* Readjuster majority in the General Assembly, and among antirepudiationist Republicans, who were aghast to find the Readjuster claiming membership in their club. Through it all, Mahone insisted that he had been sent to the Senate without party affiliation to work in the best interests of Virginia. [39]

Because of the relationship between patronage jobs and electoral politics in Gilded Age America, the Readjusters' capture of the federal patronage strengthened the third party immeasurably. Before passage of the Pendleton Act in 1883, which established a Civil Service Commission and instituted merit examinations for many former patronage positions, most government jobs were distributed through local partisan organizations as rewards to loyal party members. In return, federal and state appointees paid assessments on their wages to support electoral campaigns.[40] Thousands of jobs that paid cash wages on time were tied to partisan control of the government. Patronage power bound many men's political identity to their livelihood, and this politics of obligation bolstered the party that controlled the patronage and discouraged local political experimentation among federal job-holders. The report of a black Readjuster from Portsmouth reflected this reality. A. H. Lindsay predicted a Republican sweep in 1880 in his black-majority district. He was sorry to lose, Lindsay wrote Mahone, but the Readjusters could not expect to win "with the whole influence and patronage of the Navy yard against us."[41]

Between the federal civil service and the local party machines stood a state's two U.S. senators. Elected until 1913 by state legislatures, U.S. senators controlled the flow of patronage between the executive and the states.[42] The new senator from Virginia wanted this power for the Readjusters, and he had reason to claim it. Republican patronage meant jobs for Readjuster supporters, assessments to finance future campaigns, and power to punish the foes of readjustment. Such power almost certainly meant the expansion of the coalition and promised to occasion multiple conversion experiences among former funder Conservatives and Republicans.[43] This, at least, was the opinion of one white Republican Readjuster from the mountain west who suggested that well-considered patronage distribution could aid the party and overcome Democratic distaste for the Republicans. "If you can get the Federal patronage and dispense it among readjusters irrespective of past party affiliations, it would make us invulnerable & invincible," he exulted.[44]

Virginia had considerable patronage opportunities; in the words of one disgruntled Conservative, "the blue book of the Civil Service reads like a book of official generation in which one bureau begets another."[45] In 1881 there were about two thousand jobs for Mahone to disperse among loyal Readjusters and their families. There were clerkships in Washington, laboring positions at the Norfolk and Portsmouth Navy Yards, jobs with the Treasury service. There were posts for federal judges, marshals, district attorneys, and their many clerks. And since Virginia was a coastal state, there were customs houses, lighthouses, and a lifesaving service to be staffed.

Best of all, there were hundreds of postal positions—masters and clerks—just waiting to be filled with Readjusters. Because of their control over the flow of information, post offices were at the center of local political life and therefore the most cherished and fought over of all Gilded Age patronage jobs. No post office was too small or insignificant to be coveted, and the Readjuster hierarchy showed no scruples against moving, in the words of a Democratic critic, "against the incumbent of some little pitiful postoffice in Virginia."[46] In addition to letters, partisan newspapers and broadsides flowed into—but not necessarily out of—the nation's thousands of post offices.[47] In 1880 there were approximately 43,000 post offices in America, and the master of each one of them was a local party notable or his friend. While cities such as Petersburg, Richmond, and Lynchburg had the sort of formal public building recognizable today as a post office, most late-nineteenth-century post offices in Virginia were crossroads affairs housed in local stores or even private homes. Having a post office in one's home might be inconvenient, but distributing the mail from one's store was good for business. Although he cast his argument in partisan terms, no doubt the postmaster of Liberty, who wanted his office transferred to his store half a mile down the road, dreamed as well of stealing his competitor's custom. "[Y]ou know I *dislike* to go in a democrat's store to open the Mail," he complained to his senator.[48]

By allying with the Republicans in the Senate and with their president in the White House, Mahone gained this patronage power for the Readjusters. At the same time he, in effect, transformed his white followers from dissident Democrats into Republicans. Many white Readjusters were happy to strike a blow at the ambitions of the national Democrats. "Northern democracy smot us, & hereafter we intend to smite them," wrote one. But this sort of internal rebellion was a far cry from embracing the Republicans.[49] Most white voters in Virginia loathed the party of Lincoln; in their eyes, the only thing worse than a black Republican was a white one. The word reserved for a native white southern Republican—scalawag—expressed this revulsion, conjuring up as it did an image that was equal parts pirate and cur.[50]

In other places, formal alliances between Independent movements and the Republicans led to large-scale desertion by white followers.[51] The Virginia coalition's alliance with the national Republicans would create grave problems of identity—political, racial, and gendered—for white Readjusters further down the road. In the short run, however, well-considered distribution of patronage eased the acceptance of affiliation with the Republicans and reinforced partisan loyalty to the coalition. Designed to breach old barriers of class, race, and party and to structure a new common sense of identity as a "Readjuster," coalition patronage distribution was considerably more inclusive than traditional party patronage politics. Although only "Readjusters" were eligible for positions, the definition of a coalitionist was far more elastic than old categories of "Democrat" and "Republican." Essentially, anyone who was known to have voted Readjuster (and by 1882 at the latest, the Readjuster precinct machines were tuned finely enough to possess this information) was considered, for the purposes of patronage distribution, a party member.

Mahone's patronage policy reflected his desire to ensure that every community in Virginia benefited materially from voting Readjuster. At the same time, such benefit provided an eloquent, if understated, argument in favor of black suffrage, which, after all, had underwritten the coalition's continued rule and eased its relationship with the Republican administration in Washington. Under Mahone's direction, Readjusters counted federal appointments by county and apportioned them equally among congressional districts. This division resulted in vastly increased representation from the mostly white mountain counties,[52] which demonstrated anew to voters there the coalition's ability to act in their interest. To ensure fair distribution by region, the senator instructed his county chairmen to send him the names and addresses of local people interested in employment in Washington: people who had good penmanship, were accurate with figures, or who would make suitable watchmen or messengers. Similar messages went out to fill jobs in federal installations in Virginia such as the state's two navy yards. In these missives, Mahone stated specifically that he hoped for the names of women and men, black as well as white.[53] Local residents greeted this protocol enthusiastically if incredulously, and Mahone and the Readjusters reaped considerable goodwill, especially among mountain whites who were used to being ignored by political leaders. A Carroll County Readjuster wrote to his senator to express his appreciation. "Up here in these Backwoods we never thought of a United States Senator sending to the people to recommend some of our Boys or Girls for positions in Washington," he said. "Heretofore it has been the Policy to give all positions to some Jackleg lawyer. . . . You have proven to us that you are the Representative of the People and for the People."[54]

More precisely, Mahone represented the Readjuster Party. Patronage applications were scrutinized for attachment to the coalition. Few office seekers fell through the cracks of its extensive local networks. "I find there is employed in the railway mail service on the Richmond and Charlotte route, R. S. Johnson who is registered as from Scottsville, recommended by Gen. Tyner," went one such query from Mahone to a local Readjuster leader. "Can you tell me anything of this person?" The reply was favorable, stating that although Johnson was a minor, his father Charles was one of the most influential Readjusters in the county. Not everyone got off so easily. The judgment on Jacob E. Putron in the Pension Bureau was harsh: this man was "perfectly unreliable, politically; would do anything to keep office, and sell his best friend."[55] Mahone kept a sharp eye on patronage recipients in Virginia, as indicated by his notes on lists of federal appointments. Opposite the name of one federal worker who was about to find himself unemployed, Mahone jotted: "one fourth Republican. Every fourth year, votes for the Republican candidate for President and at the same time for the Bourbon Democ. candidate for Congress."[56]

Women who received patronage positions under the Readjusters encountered the same inspection as men. Although formally disfranchised, women could, and did, influence the political behavior of the men around them. Since women could not vote, their political leanings were generally gauged by the Readjusters based on the behavior of male relatives. Sometimes, however, a woman's own political opinions outdistanced the control of her husband. Mrs. S. W. Willard, a Treasury Department employee, was married to an active Republican. Nevertheless, the Appomattox County chairman was "inclined to think she is a Bourbon of the most objectionable kind." Miss A. E. Matthews, also of the Treasury Department, had no living male relatives but received a clean bill of political health from the Loudoun County chairman in March 1882 based on her status as the daughter of a Quaker.[57]

As such scrutiny implies, the political economy of patronage was tight. The difficulty and desirability of attaining a patronage position helped create ties of allegiance among coalition members. These ties were relayed in the testimony of local Readjusters regarding an applicant's fitness for a patronage office.[58] In addition to making "voluntary" assessments to fill Readjuster coffers, patronage appointees were expected to fill leadership roles in the party and to stand by the Readjuster caucus and the national Republican administration.[59] In an interview explaining Readjuster patronage policies, Mahone commented on the damage that a single weak link could do. "Think of a janitor in a custom house, for example, coming out with a speech to the negroes abusing me and saying that the administration was not with us," the senator conjectured. "If he had not been in Government service it would have been all right. They would say he had been hired by the Funders to do it. But being in Government service they [w]ouldn't understand it."[60]

Competition for office also encouraged a culture of accusation and surveillance among party members that, in its own way, cemented loyalty among coalitionists. The briefest glance at Mahone's correspondence reveals scores of state workers writing to affirm their loyalty to the coalition and an equal number of letters accusing patronage appointees of political infidelity.[61] There was a certain logic to this—as one Culpeper County Readjuster put it straightforwardly, "If he is not for us, and does not show his 'Faith by his Works,' he is against us—and our party can't afford to feed and nurture its enemies, or men wholly indifferent to our cause." In this spirit, F. L. Slade of Norfolk brutally assessed the worth of railway mail employee J. Williams Jr.: "This man I do not consider of sufficient value to the party to retain the office."[62] When Edwin Harvie's father, prominent octogenarian and Norfolk Customs House employee Lewis E. Harvie, was summoned to meet with the collector of internal revenue, his son worried that someone had at last noticed "the fact that you had never been given any official duties."[63] The prize for inventive argumentation probably belongs to the Republicans of the Fourth Congressional District, who, in their petition to remove W. L. Furnald as collector of internal revenue at Danville, averred that "while he has very recently professed to be in sympathy with us he has never the less so acted, that we are constrained to believe that if sincere, his mind is impaired, and therefore [he] is unfit mentally to discharge the important and responsible duties of his position."[64]

Patronage power and partisan organization mutually reinforced one another in the effort to prolong Readjuster electoral success. Federal patronage appointees paid a voluntary 5 percent assessment on their salaries, which supported local precinct workers, absorbed the expenses of the coalition's corps of traveling lecturers, and financed the printing of campaign materials. Prodded by constant flyers from Mahone, local Readjuster leaders compiled intricate lists of precinct voters, painstakingly identifying the political affiliation of every man of voting age. Black Readjuster leaders came under sedulous cultivation as well, and detailed lists were kept of the names and political leanings of African American ministers.[65] In every precinct Readjuster voters fell into groups of ten organized by squad captains, who were paid $2.50 per campaign to march their charges to the polls on election day. Two lieutenants per precinct, one white and one black, who received $10.00 each, oversaw the numerous squad captains. The positions of squad captain and lieutenant were used to reward the party faithful and to remind Readjuster voters that partisan loyalty could be materially as well as politically beneficial. At the same time, local captains and lieutenants could protect Readjuster voters at the polls while monitoring their electoral behavior, since the secret ballot did not come to Virginia until the mid-1890s.[66]

Assessments on federal officeholders also bought votes—either through the payment of the poll taxes of indigent Readjusters or through out-and-out bribery. All three political parties in Virginia had access to state information detailing who had paid his poll tax and who was in arrears.[67] Before the separation of the poll tax from voting in 1883,[68] every political party in Virginia paid the taxes of some insolvent voters, but the Readjusters perfected a statewide system for this purpose first. Early in a canvass, the state Readjuster organization supplied local party workers with the names of delinquent taxpayers in their areas. The local Readjuster leaders, in turn, sent out precinct workers to convince the delinquents to pay up in time for the election. On the verge of the election, precinct leaders sent the list of those Readjuster voters who remained delinquent to the state committee, which sent back funds to pay the delinquents' taxes. There was an art to this; no one wanted to pay the poll tax of a supporter of a competing party or subsidize the taxes of someone who could afford to pay for himself. This was especially true for Readjusters, who represented the poorest voters in the state and therefore had to allocate a greater portion of their campaign budget for the payment of taxes. After explaining the procedure outlined above, one Valley party leader urged his precinct workers to economize, remarking dryly that "it would be well to keep from those who are able to pay the fact of our intention to finally pay their taxes."[69]

In addition to known Readjusters, county coalition leaders compiled lists of men whom they regarded as "doubtful" or "reasonably open to conviction." In response to a flyer from Mahone in 1883, one Rappahannock County leader sent along a list of vacillating white Democrats; he also requested that the weekly edition of the *Richmond Whig* be sent free of charge to twelve literate African American men in his district.[70] Sometimes political information was not enough to induce a switch in party affiliation, however. During the 1883 state canvass Isaac Herring of Petersburg submitted a list of men who had previously voted against the Readjusters but would, he thought, "if properly treated," come into the Readjuster fold. Herring was explicit about what sort of "treatment" was required, listing five men who if "talked to right" could probably be convinced to vote Readjuster and another nine who "for a trifle in the shape of money and in some cases whiskey . . . can be changed to suit the times."[71]

Most of the money that paid the poll taxes of the poor and persuaded doubtful voters in Virginia to support the coalition went through federal patronage offices or came from prominent Republicans in the North who supported Mahone and the efforts of southern independent parties to challenge Democratic dominance in the South. These funds were put to good use, as Mahone created a political organization that was unrivaled in the region. The strength of the Readjuster machine, in fact, differentiated it from other southern independent movements and gave the coalition favored-child status with Republican luminaries in the North.[72] In return for supporting the Readjusters in state and local elections, the national Republicans expected Mahone to back up GOP policy decisions in the Senate and the Readjusters to deliver Virginia's electoral votes to the Republican nominee in the presidential election of 1884.[73]

At the same time that they distributed patronage more broadly, the Readjusters tried to shift more federal money south. Working from the Senate, Mahone managed to add 347 new post offices to Virginia during his six years in office.[74] Gerrymandering congressional districts promised another two Readjuster seats. Replacing the boards of visitors of the University of Virginia, the Virginia Military Institute, and the various asylums for the deaf, blind, and insane promised additional plums for educated Readjuster supporters. Significantly, both in terms of patronage and the local functioning of the party, the Readjusters replaced county judges across Virginia. Circuit and county court judges served terms of six years and were, like the judges of the Supreme Court of Appeals, elected by joint vote of the General Assembly. In 1882 five Readjusters were elected to twelve-year terms on the Court of Appeals. In addition, the coalition was able to replace ninety-five county judges, thirteen corporation court judges, and five circuit court judges.[75] Although no African Americans served as judges in nineteenth-century Virginia, a significant number of black men won positions as local magistrates or justices of the peace in such cities as Richmond and Petersburg and in the heavily black counties of the peninsula and Southside Virginia.[76]

In addition to ruling on the cases that came before them, county and corporation courts were in charge of compiling lists of potential jurors. With one or two exceptions, Democratic county judges had excluded African Americans from the jury box. Furthermore, according to one Readjuster, the mission of "these little county judges . . . was to suppress the republican party in their respective counties." This ended with the advent of the Readjuster judges, who built up the coalition in their areas and recognized black men as jurors.[77]

Attempts by the Readjusters in the General Assembly to expand the coalition's patronage power by increasing the number of state patronage jobs in Virginia fell apart after 1882. That year four Readjusters in the state senate defected, joining the united opposition of the Democratic and Republican Funders. Defeated Readjuster proposals to vacate all the state notaries public and superintendents of schools would have opened up nearly a thousand jobs, and the coalition's scheme to create a commissioner of land sales would have generated a hundred more.

Although it never passed, the proposed commissioner of land sales bill generated the most intense controversy of any Readjuster legislation apart from the debt settlement. As conceived, the governor would appoint for each county and city in Virginia a general commissioner of land sales, who would arrange all transfers of real estate. The commissioner would sell all real estate decreed to be sold by the county court, collect the proceeds and deposit them in a bank, and receive for his services 2 percent in fees. He would be required to advertise each sale in a newspaper to be selected by him, and "this newspaper was to be the only legalized medium for the publication of all notices and orders emanating from the courts." Thus in addition to creating over one hundred new lucrative patronage positions, the Commissioner of Sales Bill would have supported numerous local partisan newspapers. The possibilities for influence and outright corruption were endless, particularly, as the Democratic press pointed out, "for shaping the politics of the debtor class."[78]

Within the Democrats' political vocabulary, "the debtor class" was code for African Americans. Even without the Commissioner of Sales Bill, however, Readjuster patronage power created opportunities for black Virginians and menaced (as it was designed to) their attachment to the Republican Party. The GOP had controlled federal patronage in Virginia since emancipation, but blacks, who represented far and away the majority of the state's Republican voters, were vastly underrepresented in patronage jobs. Rather than share the federal spoils with its African American rank and file, Republicans in some parts of the state joined forces with the Conservatives, swapping federal positions for Democratic state jobs, with the elite of each party guarding the interests of the other.[79] This policy weakened the Republican Party in Virginia and did little to promote institutional loyalty among Afro-Virginians.

Black coalitionists and their white Republican Readjuster allies wasted no time in enunciating the relationship between black electoral loyalty to the Readjusters and patronage distribution. With a savvy eye to the give and take of politics, Republican Readjusters reminded the third party's white leadership that its new patronage power was due in no small measure to the black vote. In the course of congratulating Mahone on his vote in the Senate, Shed Dungee, a black member of the General Assembly, remarked that he "boasts with pride that his action in the legislature helped turn the tide in the U S Senate."[80] In addition, as long as Virginia's remaining Straight-Out (unallied) Republicans retained power over some federal jobs,[81] black political leaders could threaten the Readjusters with loss of the black vote unless propitiated by patronage. James O. Corprew, an African American Readjuster from the Tidewater, argued strenuously for the replacement of black Republican patronage appointees in the navy yards with black Readjusters to further the coalition cause among black voters there. Corprew was having difficulties recruiting Readjuster voters, he said, because many of the area's leading black men held "good and honorable positions from the government." "As they were appointed by their friends from the straight-out Republican party," he continued, "some of them vigorously oppose the colored people forming an alliance with the Readjusters, because they say that as to yet, not one colored man in this section has been appointed to any position of honor by the Readjusters."[82] The threat of the loss of the black vote was neither idle nor empty. As one independent political journal warned, black Readjusters who felt ill-treated would bolt the coalition. Furthermore, noted the *Saturday Mail Carrier*, "the colored man is capable of bolting with a good deal of unanimity if he takes the notion."[83]

Mountain Republican Readjuster John F. Lewis echoed these sentiments in a letter to Mahone in the summer of 1881. "The fact is, that the negroes have been told [by the regular Republicans] that they do most of the voting on our side, and have no reward for their labor." The Republicans, on the other hand, succeeded in getting Virginia blacks secure jobs by appealing to Washington.[84] George L. Preston, a black Readjuster in Alexandria, put things more bluntly when he warned Mahone in late July that "the Collard People in alexandria is going Back on you mighty fast and i am sory to se[e] it[.] Robert Gains in alexandria had bin a strong readjuster [but] says [Republican leader] Sampson P. B[ailey] can get men something to due and you can due it and wont due it."[85] Future Readjuster governor William E. Cameron had said as much the previous spring. "We cannot expect to receive the means of victory from those people and monopolize the fruits," he lectured H. H. Riddleberger.[86]

The patronage power of Virginia's rump Republicans was shattered in the late summer of 1881 when President Garfield was assassinated by, of all people, a disappointed federal office seeker. Impressed by the success of the coalition in Virginia and worried about the diminution of GOP strength in industrial states like New York and Ohio, the new Republican president, Chester A. Arthur, inaugurated a policy of unrestricted aid to southern independent movements as the key to continued Republican domination of the executive. One of his first acts was to cut off Virginia's regular Republicans and distribute all federal patronage in the commonwealth through the Readjusters.[87]

Complete Readjuster control of federal patronage eroded black support for anticoalitionist Republicans. Mahone cooperated with black party leaders to find African American laborers to fill positions in the Construction Department, at the Norfolk Navy Yard, and in Washington. Jobs employing teamsters, firemen, engineers, riggers, iron platers, coopers, and day laborers paid relatively high wages of $1.50 per day.[88] Such positions held symbolic as well as pecuniary value: before the Civil War white mechanics at the navy yard had campaigned to eliminate black workers, and in the postwar years competition between the races for control of southern waterfronts continued to strain efforts at biracial cooperation.[89]

At the height of Readjuster power black men constituted 27 percent of Virginia's employees in the Treasury Department, 11 percent in the Pensions Bureau, 54 percent in the Secretary's Office, and 38 percent in the Post Office. Twenty-eight percent of the Virginians employed in the Interior Department were African Americans, including two black women, and blacks constituted 38 percent of Virginians employed by the navy. A fourth of these navy personnel were black charwomen and scrubbers. Although the majority of these positions were for manual laborers, skilled African American Readjusters found posts in Washington as clerks and copyists.[90]

Without doubt, black Republicans in Virginia wanted a larger share of the material prosperity that accompanied federal and state patronage. The *Nation*, which abhorred debt repudiation but supported black rights, spotted this part of the logic fueling the alliance of black Republicans with the Readjusters. It was easy, the *Nation* editorialized, to see the attraction of independent politics for Virginia's black voter: "He has seen white debt-paying carpet-baggers carry off all the available plunder, in the shape of Federal offices, while the white debt-paying 'brigadiers' have all the State offices. To the 'colored Readjuster' this looks like a conspiracy between Democratic and Republican debt-payers to 'perpetuate the color line,' and he accordingly favors repudiation as a means of splitting up the dominant parties and giving his race a chance."[91] But there was more to it than that. When the commonwealth's African American Republicans condemned the "feudalistic" attitude of the Republican Party in Virginia, as a conference of black Richmonders did as early as 1873,[92] they criticized not only the maldistribution of material resources but also a party hierarchy that denied black men the recognition, responsibility, and authority that accompanied patronage positions.

As much as black Readjusters wanted jobs, they desired recognition of their electoral support and influence within the party and their role in the public life of the state. Well before the 1880 election debacle one of Mahone's more farsighted local advisers observed that the patronage issue facing the coalition involved issues of honor as well as of treasure. "I can see no way [of gaining and keeping the black vote] except by sacrificing every mere sentimentality at the start," Robert A. Richardson wrote to Mahone. "[We must] show that our colored readjusters are to get beyond all doubt their *full* share of the party patronage. I am no advocate for giving too much, but we must give *enough*." Unusually sensitive to the political economy of honor inherent in patronage relations, Richardson added that the Readjusters must take care not to insult their black allies by offering only those offices "according to the old idea particularly fitted to the colored man—say for instance the doorkeepers."[93]

Patronage is fundamentally about public authority and hierarchy. Because of the relations of dominance and subordination explicit in patronage power—indeed, in the very etymology of the word—Readjuster patronage policies could be destabilizing, or presented as destabilizing, to social hierarchies based on race. As black Virginians were elected or appointed to public office, they became more visibly authoritative. Sixteen African American legislators served in the 1881–82 session of the General Assembly. Black Readjusters such as William N. Stevens, Ross Hamilton, Alfred W. Harris, and Richard G. L. Paige pushed for measures that would benefit their largely African American constituencies. Stevens, for instance, brokered the establishment of an asylum for the African American mentally ill (who under the Conservatives had been housed in local jails) and succeeded in placing the new institution under black supervision. Harris was the author of a bill that appropriated $100,000 for the Virginia Normal and Collegiate Institute, a new black college in Petersburg. Like Stevens, Harris won the battle for black supervision of this African American public institution. At the municipal level, particularly but not exclusively in black-majority towns, black Virginians gained in public stature and influence as they filled local political offices. By 1882 it was possible for one Readjuster supporter in Petersburg to boast of the numerous "positions of both profit and trust" held by black men in Virginia—black men who, in the words of another Petersburg party leader, handled "a pen, and not a hoe."[94] Whether occupying a seat on the board of education or sharing a political platform with a white man, black Virginians, especially men, became increasingly visible under Readjuster rule.

In addition to the federal and state patronage positions available in towns and cities, municipal institutions such as hospitals, asylums, and, especially, the local public school system offered qualified Readjusters steady wages and an entry into state power. White and black Readjusters often competed openly for these positions, and in the black-majority areas of the state or in cities where black Readjusters predominated among the coalition's voters, the distribution of patronage became enmeshed in broader disputes about racial privilege and rights in Virginia.

A case in point is the 1882 struggle in Petersburg to employ black teachers and principals in black public schools. Situated in the heart of the black-majority Southside, a key Readjuster enclave, Petersburg was Virginia's largest majority-black city. It was there that Mahone chose to have the Readjusters make an overt appeal for black support of the coalition in 1879.[95] The hometown of both Mahone and Governor William E. Cameron (elected in 1881), the city had been ruled continuously by the coalition since 1880, when local Readjusters gained a majority of seats in the Petersburg City Council. More than any other place in Virginia, Petersburg represented both Readjuster and African American political power. As testimony to the influence and loyalty of its black Republican-Readjuster community, Petersburg benefited disproportionately from state largesse. It gained the two new state institutions for African Americans, both of which were run by accomplished black men. Dr. John C. Ferguson, a physician, became assistant director of assemblyman Stevens's Central Lunatic Asylum, and James Storum presided over the Virginia Normal and Collegiate Institute, where students were taught a classical, not an industrial, curriculum. During the summer the Normal and Collegiate Institute sponsored an eight-week course to prepare black teachers to pass the state teacher examination.[96]

The Readjusters reached the height of their power in Petersburg in May 1882, when the coalition at last elected a Readjuster mayor to head the Readjuster-controlled city council. In confirmation of African American influence in local politics, the new council, which itself included several black men, selected four local black Readjusters for civic office. The most prominent of these was Dr. H. L. Harris, who was named one of Petersburg's four city physicians to the poor.[97]

Like their counterparts at the state level, Petersburg's Readjusters pursued a reform agenda. The city council lowered real estate and personal property taxes, raised licensing fees on businesses, and initiated a municipal capital gains tax on stocks and bonds. The city banned the chain gang, and the whipping post disappeared from Petersburg before the General Assembly ended the practice throughout the state. The Readjuster municipal government also paved streets, added sidewalks, modernized the city's water system, financed the creation of a new park and a race track, and subsidized prescription drugs for the poor.[98]

In addition, Petersburg had one of the strongest public school systems in Virginia. Its term was long (nine months, compared with the state average of four), and its teachers were well paid. There were five graded schools in 1882, two of which, Peabody School and the Jones Street School, were reserved for black students. But the city's single public high school admitted only whites.[99] And in marked contrast to such other Virginia cities as Richmond, Danville, and Lynchburg, as of July 1882 there was not a single African American teacher employed in Petersburg's public schools.

Throughout the postwar era, black Virginians remained concerned about the social and psychic cost of "a proscriptive system of public schools," in the words of Richmond party leader R. G. L. Paige.[100] African American legislators in Virginia persistently demanded integrated schools. Future Readjusters Thomas Bayne, William P. Mosely, and Lewis Lindsey had led the fight during the 1868 constitutional convention and in the early sessions of the postwar General Assembly.[101] But after William Ruffner and the General Assembly denied the possibility of integrated public schools in 1870, black Virginians shifted their focus from gaining access to neighborhood white schools to securing African American control of black schools. They doubled their efforts after the Civil Rights Act of 1875 failed to forbid segregated schools. In that year Richmond blacks petitioned their board of education for "a more equitable proportion" of black teachers and principals in the black schools.[102] Pledges to support public education drew black voters to the Readjusters in 1879, and the coalition's promotion of black authority within black public institutions perpetuated black electoral loyalty. When a Democratic speaker in Hanover County implied during the 1881 campaign that African Americans wanted mixed schools, he was refuted by a black man in the audience who shouted back, "No! But we want colored teachers for colored schools." The Readjuster candidate, John Goode, apparently lost no time in replying, "You shall have them."[103]

A variety of concerns motivated calls for African American teachers and principals in the South's black schools. The demand was certainly one of "justice and common sense," as the *Virginia Star* argued in 1882,[104] but other issues were involved. As time went on, more and more qualified African American teachers, who had been trained in the black normal schools and colleges springing up across the South, were available to teach in black schools. The traditional excuse southern school boards used for not hiring black teachers—that there weren't any—became less relevant with every passing year. By 1880 most of the ninety-six black men and women who had graduated from Richmond Normal and High had applied for teaching jobs in the city's black schools and had been rejected. That year Richmond had only eleven African American teachers, all at the elementary level, as a mass meeting of "colored taxpayers" noted and deplored.[105]

While white excuses that black teachers lacked "tone" sounded increasingly feeble, black complaints about the inadequacies of white teachers remained potent. White teachers assigned to black schools were frequently underqualified and uninspired. In Richmond, many white teachers who passed the teaching examination refused to teach black pupils. To staff the city's black schools with white teachers, the Richmond School Board had to dig deep into the pool of applicants who had failed the exam.[106] This practice led the *Star* to the conclusion that "our colored public free schools are charity concerns for the pensioning of white women who can not make a living at any other business." [107]

Compounding the problem of intellectual limitations was the social chasm between white teachers and black pupils and their families. As black Readjuster William Harris explained to the Petersburg School Board, a white Virginian "reared in the traces of slavery . . . cannot put himself down to associate with the families from which the scholars came, and cannot look at the matter as he should." [108] Black communities expected far more from their teachers than classroom instruction. Unlike the white teachers who taught in black schools, black teachers in other places lived among their pupils, frequently boarding with a family and worshipping with a local black congregation. As moral and civic exemplars, African American teachers were on duty twenty-four hours a day and were expected to correct their students in and out of the classroom. To encourage attendance, black teachers visited the homes of their students, something a white teacher would never do. Over a cup of tea or a glass of cool water black teachers convinced parents reluctant to part with the money their children earned in the fields to find a way to send these children to school. In addition, black teachers strove to make their students employable in the constricted southern labor market and spent extra hours teaching basic household skills. For instance, when Hampton Institute graduate Amelia Perry Pride was hired by a Lynchburg school in 1882 she taught cooking and sewing classes in the evening in addition to her daytime academic instruction.[109]

One further concern fed blacks' desire to see their schools staffed by African Americans. In the postbellum South jobs for educated black men and women were few and far between, and teaching stood as the main avenue for their advancement into the middle class. Given prevailing white attitudes about racial hierarchy and widespread white contempt for the intellectual attainments of African Americans, it was inconceivable for black teachers to instruct white students in the New South. Black schools were the only possible employers of black teachers; every classroom presided over by a white teacher meant one position denied to a potentially qualified black.[110]

For all of these reasons, Petersburg's black community desired African American teachers in its children's schools. In 1880 a group of prominent black citizens requested that qualified black teachers be hired, but they were rebuffed.[111] In the summer of 1882 the black community decided to try again. On July 10 they gathered at a mass meeting and delegated a group to speak to the Petersburg School Board. Two days later the citizens' emissaries demanded that the board employ "colored teachers for colored schools." Spokesman William H. Harris knew that he was asking the school board to do the unthinkable: turn out white teachers from their jobs and give those jobs to blacks. Mahone had already indicated that this proposal was beyond the pale when black Readjusters had asked for his help.[112] Shrewdly, Harris deployed his heaviest rhetorical artillery first and attacked the city schools along the color line. Pointedly rejecting the possibility—or even the desirability—of integrated schools, Harris requested that the color line be drawn more explicitly within public schools in Petersburg. "[W]e know that it is not the policy of this State Government to have mixed schools. We do not ask for them," Harris explained to the school board. But, he continued, "We want the schools, if they are to be kept separate, to be *entirely* so." Anxious that he not be misunderstood, Harris reiterated his position favoring strict racial segregation in schools: "We are not asking for mixed schools, but asking that they be *unmixed*." Explaining that white teachers were unfit to teach black students by virtue of their immersion in the dominant culture of white superiority, Harris warned that unless the board granted the petition, Petersburg blacks would not hesitate to use their political power to attain their goal.[113]

The Petersburg School Board was unmoved by Harris's arguments. In a sop to the black community, however, the board elected two African American teachers, William D. Hamlin and Kate D. Hill, the following week. But Hamlin and Hill remained unassigned to a school. Apparently reconciled in principle to black teachers, the school board refused to dismiss white teachers to create room for black ones.[114]

The issue of patronage—control over jobs and the channeling of jobs to one's own community—mattered to both white and black leaders in Petersburg. This was clear from the board's actions, as well as from William Harris's assertion that "Petersburg cannot rest as the only city where the schools are kept for the whites," by which he meant teachers, not pupils.[115] Then, as now, the public school system provided an extraordinarily fruitful source of state employment, and people fought for preference within it just as they jockeyed for other patronage positions.[116]

But other issues were interwoven in this conflict. While some members of the school board may have favored white control over black schools as a matter of principle, Petersburg's black community felt just as strongly that white teachers were incompetent, as black Readjuster leader Spencer Green put it, to "fairly develop the negro's intellect." [117] White Virginians who had matured before the war or during the sectional conflict itself were tainted, in the eyes of black Virginians, by their experience with and allegiance to slavery. Moreover, both the political power of black men in Petersburg and their right as fathers to direct the education of their children were being thwarted by the school board in a particularly public and galling way. This last concern was highlighted by the *Lancet*, Petersburg's leading black newspaper, when it reported that the Manchester School Board, which the paper characterized as controlled by Democrats, had replaced the white teachers in the city's black schools with African Americans. "And why is it that we are not treated thus?" asked George Bragg Jr., the *Lancet*'s Readjuster editor. Using language usually applied by southern whites toward blacks, Bragg fumed that the Petersburg School Board's "bold audacity and unbounded insolence towards the colored people of this city is unparalleled in a free country." [118]

Rebuffed by the school board, black leaders in Petersburg met again on July 18 at the Union Street Methodist Church to consider their course. This meeting was riven by a factional dispute over leadership between black Readjusters and Straight-Out Republicans. But on July 25 the Readjusters succeeded in organizing another mass meeting of more than five hundred black residents, in which citizens were invited "to give expression to their views about the education of their children." Spurred on by W. H. H. Parker's incendiary charge that "the colored janitors held colored children at Peabody School in order that they might be whipped by white men," the participants vowed to boycott black schools as long as white teachers remained in them.[119]

Petersburg's black Readjusters also decided that it was time to speak to the governor. As he was a former newspaper editor, William Cameron's past sentiments regarding black political participation were readily at hand and had been displayed by the Democrats and Straight-Out Republicans any number of times in an attempt to discredit him with black voters. In an 1868 editorial, for example, the future Readjuster governor had insisted that "the evils which result from universal suffrage" would soon lead to "universal suffering." Equating black men with white women and children, Cameron had denied the freedmen's claims to social and political authority. In light of African American inferiority, he had maintained in 1868, white men should give black men "precisely those political rights which they give to their own wives and daughters, and to their sons during their minority."[120]

In 1876 Cameron was elected mayor of Petersburg, capping a Conservative sweep of municipal government that had begun in 1874. While mayor, however, he established a rapport with Petersburg's black community. According to Walter T. Calhoun and James Tice Moore, Mayor Cameron displayed a newly acquired social conscience where African Americans were concerned, treating leniently youthful black offenders brought before his Mayor's Court. Calhoun and Moore also document the emergence of Cameron as a calculating political strategist who as governor fought to transplant the state mental hospital for African Americans (and its jobs) from Richmond to Petersburg and who assiduously courted black votes in the city and surrounding countryside.[121]

William Cameron had changed since 1868, in ways that exemplify the willingness of some southern whites to envision an expanded, if not equal, public role for African Americans after the Civil War. Already in 1882 Cameron urged a closer alliance with the national Republican Party. Later he would join other Readjusters in opposing Mahone's leadership of the Virginia GOP.[122] Now he did not shrink at the prospect of recognizing, even advancing, black political influence. In Petersburg to address the participants of the State Institute for Colored Teachers, which prepared African American teachers for the state's qualifying examinations, the governor met with Dinwiddie County superintendent of schools E. B. Branch on August 9. On that occasion Cameron instructed Superintendent Branch to declare the Petersburg School Board invalid and to replace it with one that would be willing to employ black teachers in black schools.[123]

To justify this action, the governor turned to a law passed the previous May that required state officeholders to take an oath recognizing the civil and political equality of all men before the law.[124] None of the members of the Petersburg School Board had taken this oath. Their defenders claimed that the oath law was not intended to be retroactive and should therefore not apply to members elected before May 1, 1882, but by August 16 Petersburg had twelve new school board members. On that day, in an address to the members of the State Institute for Colored Teachers, Governor Cameron extolled the benefits of black education.[125] Overjoyed, the *Lancet* crowed, "Can it be possible that the body of men who sat in the High Schools building a few weeks ago and with such arrogance flaunted in the face of the colored people a power conferred upon them . . . must now step down and out?"[126]

After holding new examinations for teachers, the new school board dismissed one-fourth of Petersburg's white teachers and replaced them with African Americans. Readjuster leader and Lincoln University graduate Alfred S. Pryor became the new principal of Peabody School, and William S. Hamlin, another prominent Readjuster and a graduate of the Hampton Institute, was chosen to head the Jones Street School. The two men presided over new faculties composed entirely of African Americans.[127]

The issues surrounding schools and patronage in Petersburg emblematized contests elsewhere in the state. Black Readjusters in other cities followed Petersburg's lead and made African American control of local black schools an issue. By December 1882 black teachers had been substituted for whites in the black schools of Lynchburg, Norfolk, Hampton, Danville, and Charlottesville, as well as in those of a number of smaller towns.[128] Between 1879 and 1883 the number of African American teachers and principals and the number of black schools in Virginia tripled.[129] Although white Readjusters stead-fastly opposed any efforts by black coalitionists to integrate the public schools, the General Assembly did mandate equal pay for white and black teachers.[130] This principle of salary parity regardless of race was repealed by the Democrats after the coalition loss in 1883. But the coalition precedent was reasserted sixty years later in a 1940 case from Norfolk that was a landmark legal victory on the way to the *Brown* decision.[131]

The success of Petersburg's African American Readjusters in their quest for black teachers in black schools, as well as the patronage gains of black Readjusters across Virginia, illustrate the ability of southern blacks before Jim Crow to wield political power in meaningful ways. Education in particular reinforced political power, especially once suffrage was linked to literacy.[132] Black public power was also a tangible sign of interracial democracy in action. In places like Petersburg, the elevation of black men to "positions of honor and emoluence," as one black Readjuster put it, undermined any construction of Virginia as "a white man's country." Implicit in this denial was black men's assertion of their status as men and heads of households and their related right to play a governing role in civic life. Celebrating the new black teachers and principals in Petersburg and the political power that had provided them, *Lancet* editor George Bragg boasted, "This is the result of the manly stand taken by the colored people in the matter."[133]

Black Virginians were proud of the public authority that African American men wielded in places like Petersburg. But an equal or greater number of white Virginians were increasingly uneasy about this renegotiation of public power. The *Staunton Spectator*—always hostile to the Readjuster enterprise—stoked this anxiety when it interpreted events in Petersburg in 1882 as paradigmatic of Readjuster rule throughout the commonwealth. "What has happened in one Virginia city," warned the inland paper, "will happen in all the others in which the Mahoneites gain control."[134] So far, the political and material resources of coalition power and patronage had overridden whites' suspicion of black power. But it remained to be seen if the Readjusters could continue to balance the claims of the party's black wing against white fears of African American authority. How long, and in what ways, could black and white Virginians share power? George Bragg's formulation of the issues involved as rotating around black manliness gave a hint of the trouble to come.

3

DRAWING THE LINE BETWEEN PUBLIC & PRIVATE

Sex, Schools, & Liberalism

As the battle over the Petersburg public schools shows, black Virginians made tangible gains under Readjuster rule. Yet black power in Petersburg, and in Virginia generally, had its limits. Despite considerable agitation on their part, African American Readjusters in the black-majority Fourth Congressional District, which included Petersburg, did not succeed in their quest to have a black man nominated in the 1882 congressional election.[1] Throughout the Readjuster years, white Virginians continued to dominate high office, they owned the lion's share of property, and their sons alone attended the elite University of Virginia and the College of William and Mary. As John S. Wise put it later in an autobiographical novel, there was never a time in Virginia after the Civil War "in which negroes or alien and degraded whites were in a position to oppress" native white Virginians.[2]

The former Readjuster congressman and heir to one of Virginia's leading political dynasties wrote those words from his home in New York after he was hounded out of Virginia by white supremacist Democrats. From Wise's perspective, the Democrats had no rivals of note for oppressiveness. The white teachers dismissed from their posts in Petersburg's black schools might have argued the point with Wise, however. Many white Virginians—particularly nonelite white Virginians—regarded the authority invested in African Americans by the Readjusters as a direct challenge to their own autonomy. John Wise was unlikely to ever feel oppressed by a black man. But when federal revenue officials appointed a black Readjuster storekeeper to an Augusta County distillery, the owner objected mightily to the idea of a black man carrying his keys, doling out his grain, and "otherwise dictating and controlling" him.[3]

Broad-based distribution of patronage helped ease the minds of white Virginians worried about the possibility of black men "dictating and controlling" them. But material interest—with its logical corollary of rational behavior—cannot alone explain political actions. What were the ideological underpinnings of the coalition, and how did they help the interracial alliance cohere? What beliefs did black and white Readjusters share across the color line? How did the coalition balance the claims of African American Readjusters against the fears of black power exhibited by many whites? In what ways did ideology contribute to the downfall of the coalition? Because historians have traditionally taken the victory of Democratic race baiting for granted and have seen white racial animosity and anxiety as inevitable, they have not considered seriously the political ideologies that interracial parties employed to contain racial ill will. Although it is important to "search for the social roots" of political movements, political activity and rhetoric themselves remain important windows through which to view the aspirations and beliefs of white and black southerners.[4]

In an effort to extend the coalition, the Readjusters redefined themselves as liberals in 1881.[5] The first question that must be asked of the new "Liberal party," as prominent Readjusters began to refer to the coalition, is what the Readjusters might have meant by liberalism. The answer to such a question is not obvious.[6] A main aim of Reconstruction policy was to instill in southern whites and the freedpeople "the *values* of a bourgeois society: regularity, punctuality, sobriety, frugality, and economic rationality."[7] But as social and political historians have shown recently, the missionary liberals from the North did not succeed entirely in uprooting traditional southern notions of social, political, and economic hierarchies during Reconstruction. Liberal ideals of free labor may have been "sanctified by the North's triumph." But the social and labor relations of the postwar South remained marked by a disparity between faith and practice, as both the freedpeople and their white neighbors and employers were baffled by and balked at liberal precepts of contract, marriage, and domestic and civil governance.[8]

The conflicted nature of southern liberalism that emerges from recent studies coincides with scholarly views of American liberalism as a whole. Liberalism—in the nineteenth century as today—meant different things to different people at different times and places.[9] There is no need to assume, as the noted Swedish sociologist Gunnar Myrdal did in 1944, that there is a stable taxonomy of liberalism against which the southern variant can be measured and found wanting. Remarking on the obvious inequalities that even those who considered themselves liberals supported in the Jim Crow South, Myrdal declared that "Southern liberalism is not liberalism as it is found elsewhere in America or the world. It is a unique species."[10]

Though admitting that Readjuster liberalism may not be any more recognizable to us than it would have been to Myrdal, we must still ask what it meant to coalitionists. The renaming of the coalition did not signal an embrace of laissez-faire economic theory, although the party did promote a generally liberal economic program. Rather, it denoted a commitment to an essentially rights-oriented political language and program. Sounding more like Tom Paine than John Locke, the Readjusters trumpeted the rights of man.

At the core of the Readjusters' conception of liberalism lay a commitment to equal rights. Confronting a society whose members continued to draw on a variety of political languages and concepts, the Readjusters used liberalism to bind together coalitionists with divergent goals and to provide a common idiom within which to pursue those goals. In Virginia, Readjuster liberalism allowed blacks and whites with radically different a priori assumptions about fundamental rights and social organization to cooperate politically and to participate in a common discourse of equality.[11]

By focusing on a political movement and not simply on the white southern cultural elite, we can see that white southerners did not necessarily reject liberalism out of hand because they considered public equality for blacks inseparable from social equality.[12] As we will see, it was possible for white southerners to accept liberal political precepts such as one man, one vote without necessarily diluting their commitment to white superiority. In Virginia, interracial political cooperation leading to a more equitable distribution of social and political power was accomplished despite a dominant social and ideological discourse of white supremacy. To put it another way, though white Readjusters' hearts and minds may have remained prejudiced, that did not stand in

VIRGINIA.—THE READJUSTER STATE CONVENTION AT RICHMOND.—MR. MASSEY MOVING TO MAKE UNANIMOUS THE NOMINATION OF COL. W. E. CAMERON FOR GOVERNOR, JUNE 2d.—FROM A SKETCH BY WILLIAM GOODALL.—SEE PAGE 287.

"The Readjuster State Convention," from Frank Leslie's Illustrated Newspaper, 1881. This cartoon drawing of the 1881 Readjuster convention, which nominated William E. Cameron for governor, captures both the exuberance and the interracial nature of the coalition. (The Library of Virginia) the way of significant redistribution of social, political, and economic power toward black Virginians.

According to William Mahone, the first right, and the precondition for liberalism in Virginia, was "a free and priceless ballot."[13] Implicit in this right was a commitment to universal equal manhood suffrage. In 1876 the Conservatives had made payment of the capitation tax a prerequisite for voting. Three years later, African American assemblymen in the House of Delegates insisted on the separation of the tax from the suffrage as a condition of their alliance with the Readjusters.[14] In 1881 leading Readjusters drew on the already established commitment to suffrage among poorer whites and blacks, who were most likely to vote Readjuster, to further articulate an ideology capable of sustaining the coalition.

In the spring of 1881 Mahone declared that the fall canvass would be fought on the issue of a free and equal suffrage. The anti-Readjuster *New York Times* noted the change in Virginia politics in the summer of 1881. "The debt question has receded to the background," wrote the paper's Virginia correspondent, "and questions affecting the rights of citizens, the purity of elections and a generally progressive policy have come to the front."[15] In addition to satisfying the demands of black Readjusters, a commitment to free suffrage and an honest count softened the resistance of national GOP leaders protesting the alliance with debt repudiators.[16]

The 1881 Readjuster Party platform joined the coalition's commitment to liberal notions of civic equality for men to issues of free public education and tax relief. In an address to coalition members in January, Mahone pronounced the party dedicated to "the complete liberation of the people, the preservation and improvement of the public schools, the final readjustment of the public debt and restoration of the public credit, the overthrow of race prejudices, the removal of unnecessary causes for sectional contention, the liberalization and equalization of the laws."[17] In February the *Whig* declared the purpose of the new Liberal Party to be "the harmonious union of both colors, to forward mutual interests and to protect mutual rights, without sacrificing either race to the other."[18] By June the coalition's gubernatorial candidate, William E. Cameron of Petersburg, proclaimed, "I am going forward to preach Liberalism."[19]

As the Readjusters ventured further into the realm of liberal politics, the national media portrayed them as more than merely repudiationist. The *New York Evening Post* slipped from quoting Readjuster self-assertions to editorializing in their favor, showing how the coalition's agenda had expanded beyond the issue of debt settlement to denounce the traditional nemeses of liberalism: "They say they are fighting caste. They assert that they represent the dignity of labor. Their hero is a man of the people. . . . They champion the rights of man against the privileges of an aristocracy of office-holding families."[20] Even the antirepudiationist *New York Times* conceded that the Readjusters stood for "the securing of human rights to the poor whites and the poor blacks" and cheered the coalition's "formation of politics on other than the color line." "It becomes more and more evident every day," the *Times* continued, "that the Readjuster party in Virginia is engaged in a cause that is broader than that State and deeper than the debt question. . . . The main contest is against the old intolerant and proscriptive conservatism which will not accept the doctrine of equal rights, but connives at all manner of iniquity and injustice in order to perpetuate its own ascendancy."[21]

In addition to equal suffrage for all men, free schools, and fair taxes, the Readjusters moved to solidify the support of workingmen and small farmers in ways that reflected both local concerns and the national context of rising workingmen's power.[22] The 1881 platform advocated a protective tariff to encourage industry in the New South, a mechanics' lien law to favor workers over creditors, and Granger proposals for railroad regulation and fertilizer inspection. These planks were shrewdly designed to maintain the sympathy of rural voters while encouraging urban white workers to desert the Democrats, and they mirrored the resolutions passed by a convention of black Republican-Readjusters in Petersburg in March 1881.[23] Beyond the inducements to workers and farmers, the Readjusters broadened their vision to consider such reforms as corporate taxation, federal aid to mining and manufacturing, free vaccinations during epidemics, a food distribution program in case of crop failures, and increased state funding of hospitals, asylums, and penitentiaries. The entire Readjuster program was both populist and statist, sounding alarms at the national Republican level as well as among Virginia Conservatives.[24]

Liberal language and ideals helped the coalition repel Democratic race rhetoric during the 1881 campaign. Against the Readjusters' race-neutral platform of liberal equality and expanded state services, Democrats paraded the specter of Negro domination, warning white voters to remain unified against the threat of a black electorate that would exploit any breach in white ranks.[25] But Democratic hopes that white voters would privilege race chauvinism over economic and educational self-interest withered under blistering Readjuster pronouncements on class bias. Readjuster speakers blasted Democratic proclamations of race solidarity as hypocritical and reminded voters that "the lines of demarcation are as distinct between whites as between whites and colored."[26] Many white men found this line of argument so compelling that by October 1881 Democrats were changing their tune. John W. Daniel, a Democratic candidate for Congress from the party that in April had fulminated against governance by "illiterate, non-taxpaying voters," now sold himself as "the friend of the laboring man."[27] Increasingly desperate, the Democrats designated class-consciousness a "false doctrine" and admonished white voters to fight against "all the low arts of the demagogue, against the race prejudice of the negro and the class prejudice of the white man, which [had] been incited, fomented and stimulated" by the Readjusters.[28]

In spite of Democratic appeals to racial chauvinism and denials of class differences among whites, the gubernatorial vote of 1881 turned out to be the Readjusters' greatest electoral victory. The coalition elected its ticket by a majority of twelve thousand votes, retained control of both houses of the General Assembly, and added the governor to its ranks. The election of William E. Cameron as governor eliminated the final obstacle to the passage of debt reduction legislation and thus represented the achievement of the Readjusters' original call to arms.

The Readjusters interpreted their victory as the rejection by white men of race as a political issue. After the election, the *Culpeper Times* denounced the Democrats for their position "that there could be no honest ground for agreement between black and white citizens" and interpreted Cameron's election as evidence that reflective white Virginians had dismissed the racial divide in politics. "[S]uch a verdict as that given to Cameron by the great Democratic strongholds of Southwestern Virginia and the Shenandoah Valley proves that the white people of Virginia have thrown off the shackles of the narrow party tyranny," the editor of the *Times* lectured, "and have endorsed the principles of Liberalism and Nationalism which our speakers and our platform have proclaimed to them."[29] For the coalition as a whole, whose fate was ever more enmeshed with that of Virginia's African American minority, liberalism had come to mean the repudiation of the race issue in politics. Interested outside observers drew the same conclusion and announced optimistically that "the triumph of the Readjuster and Republican coalition in Virginia shows that with time the prejudice of the Southern whites against Negro suffrage, is fast giving way and disappearing in practical politics."[30] Playing off national concern about the Readjusters' plan to scale down the state debt, the partisan *Norfolk Review* insisted that "if there is repudiation in Virginia by the Liberal Party, it is the repudiation of sectional hate and race prejudices."[31]

The new governor reflected these sentiments in his inaugural speech, which was a virtual paean to liberalism: "Virginia, always in the van of great national events, furnishes a grave upon her soil for the vexed question of [the] color line in politics. Today Virginia stands before the world offering all the blessings of free citizenship, of absolute freedom in politics and religion, to those who may seek her borders. . . . The laws of Virginia guarantee equal protection and privilege to every citizen; and the people of the commonwealth have ordered that all departments of the government shall execute the spirit and letter of those laws."[32] The "Liberal revolution" appeared triumphant.

Liberal political theorists of their time or ours would not necessarily recognize any carefully articulated Readjuster philosophy of liberalism. Rather than concern themselves with outlining a consistent liberal ideology, Readjuster leaders turned to a liberal vocabulary because it offered them a way of expressing positions that made the coalition politically viable. One of the first white Readjusters to define the party's mission in "liberal" terms was future state school superintendent Richard R. Farr. According to Farr, the Readjusters were "contending for human rights—liberalism—and a break up in the Solid South." Notwithstanding his espoused commitment to human rights, he did not embrace a definition of liberalism as encompassing complete equality before the law. For Farr, liberalism meant "maintaining all those rights, which are guaranteed to all, by laws adopted by the people."[33] This was equality hedged around the edges. Whereas black Readjusters, as we will see, saw in liberalism absolute parity of manhood rights, most white Readjusters believed that they had found a political philosophy and rhetoric capable of separating some rights from others.

What Richard Farr and other white Readjusters saw liberalism capable of separating was social life, particularly sex, from civil rights and political equality. Especially useful to the Readjusters was the way nineteenth-century liberal thought divided the world into a public sphere of justice and equality and an associational private sphere that allowed discrimination. These two spheres were explicitly gendered in American thought and considered complementary: the public world of commerce and politics belonged to men, while the home and its occupants were left to women.[34]

The public and private spheres, of course, were ideological rather than physical spaces. As such, they were never clearly defined. Determining the boundaries of the public and private spheres was hard enough in the urban North, whose social organization conformed to the capitalist and bourgeois model that was the basis for the liberal notion of separate spheres. The boundaries between the spheres were even fuzzier in the slave South, where life revolved around extended rural households and the civic equality of a minority of propertied white men depended not on their own individual independence but on their mastery over their wives, children, and (in some cases but not all) slaves at home. Antebellum white southern "freemen" derived their public rights not from their status as autonomous individuals, but from their position as household heads, as masters of their own, however small, domains. This entanglement of public and private distinctions in antebellum southern political culture helped give the defense of slavery the broadest possible social foundation.[35]

The Civil War and emancipation disrupted the social relations of antebellum southern households and the system of public and private power rooted in those relations.[36] But the war and Reconstruction did not completely destroy political vocabularies or mindsets. Southerners had a variety of conceptual languages and models of social organization available to choose from in refashioning their lives after emancipation. As the new histories of Reconstruction have revealed, the problem of defining public and private rights and responsibilities for the freedpeople was embedded within a broader question of the meaning of freedom for black men and women and the definition of African American gender roles. In their attempts to have their households legally recognized through marriage and the control of their dependents validated, black men and women showed their understanding of the relationship between the private and public orbits of power, and they asserted their standing in each.[37]

In this context, the trick for the Readjusters was to construct a public/private divide firm enough to contain white household heads' fears about their ability to control their own dependents—especially the sexual behavior of their wives and daughters—while creating room for black men in politics. The separate spheres doctrine promised the possibility of a racially integrated political realm, in which black men could be included as public actors, and a segregated private sphere, within which white women and children could be shielded from black men. Making use of this strand of liberalism, the Readjusters created an opening for interracial political alliance among men by stressing the possibility of public and private spheres that were sharply delineated along lines of race as well as gender.

The separate spheres doctrine gave white Readjusters a way to differentiate between civil or political rights and what they called social rights. The rights that most white Readjusters considered bound to liberalism were, in the words of one Abingdon Readjuster, "all constitutional provisions in relation to political or civil rights."[38] This translated in practical terms into a guarantee of black suffrage, officeholding, and jury service. But the boundaries between social and political rights and spaces were difficult to mark with precision. Although it seemed clear to everyone that the home was the essence of the private, there remained many intermediary spaces whose status needed to be determined if the Readjusters' racialized public/private split were to work. State buildings such as courthouses could easily be seen to fall within the domain of the public. A man's home remained his castle; as Readjuster congressman John S. Wise made a point of explaining to white audiences, he always met with African American constituents on his back porch or in his kitchen.[39] But where did a post office located in a store or the front room of a private home—fairly common situations—belong? And did African Americans have the right to sit in the orchestra of the Richmond Theater when the black gallery was closed, as black assemblyman Richard G. L. Paige insisted?[40]

Separation of public and private rights was crucial for the Readjusters because of one highly contested "right" in particular, that of masculine sex right as a whole and the related question of black men's sexual access to white women. Feminist political philosophers such as Carole Pateman have argued that both civil society and masculine political identity are predicated on male sex right, defined as the right to enjoy equal sexual access to women.[41] It is not necessary to agree with Pateman to see how the problem of reconciling universal equal manhood suffrage with racial restrictions on sex and marriage complicated interracial democracy in the South in general and Readjuster political strategy in particular. The issue of black men's sexual authority underlay congressional debates over emancipation, and the elusive definition of African American "equality" plagued supporters of black suffrage.[42] From the moment of emancipation, white men and women conflated the political and sexual power of black men, insisting that black suffrage would lead to sexual liaisons between white women and African American men. Republican congressional leaders rebutted the association between sexual and political equality among men, wondering how marriage with a white woman would result "because a colored man is allowed to drop a little bit of paper in a box."[43] Nevertheless, throughout the postwar era southern white supremacists continued to press the connection between black suffrage and sex.[44]

The rhetorical link between black suffrage and interracial sex has been denounced as "the *reductio ad absurdum* of the congressional debates," but the logic was far from absurd.[45] We might dub this issue the Othello problem: once the black man has been admitted to the republic, is there any way to limit his rights in private? Definitions of political rights that tied them explicitly to manhood, as the Fourteenth and Fifteenth Amendments did, suggested that there was not.[46] Contemporaries were well aware of the conflation of masculine sexual and political identity. As one champion of black suffrage, North Carolina carpetbagger Albion Tourgée, explained, the Reconstruction amendments defined the body politic as "the manhood of the nation" and "recognized and formulated the universality of manhood in governmental power."[47] The sexual dimension of universal manhood suffrage complicated the work of white men who wanted to find a way to incorporate African American men into the polity without at the same time allowing them access to white women and girls.

The Readjusters relied on Virginia's laws forbidding interracial sex and marriage to mark the outer boundaries of black civil equality and to serve as the barrier to the white private sphere. Drawing the color line at the threshold of the home served the coalition by allowing it to champion black rights while limiting its vulnerability to charges of race treason. As the collective voice of the coalition, the *Richmond Whig,* explained in 1883, "Our party . . . encourages each race to develop its own sociology separately and apart from unlawful contamination with each other, but under a government which recognizes and protects the civil rights of all."[48] Joseph Porter, an 1883 candidate for the legislature, was more specific: "I am opposed to Mixed Schools, Mixed Marriages, Miscegenation, or ANY AND ALL PROMISCUOUS MIXING OF TWO DISTINCT RACES OF PEOPLE; believing these things to be injurious to the morals and repulsive to the better instincts of both." But, Porter continued, "still claiming for each equal and exact justice before the Law," he left black and white Virginians "to work out their appointed destinies under a common government."[49]

The main legal barrier to the promiscuous mixing of citizens and destinies in Virginia was the commonwealth's law forbidding interracial marriage. Beginning in 1691, the colony and then the commonwealth prohibited marriage across the color line. After the Civil War the antebellum antimiscegenation statute was incorporated into the Revised Code of 1873.[50] Between 1873 and 1924, when Virginia passed its "Act for the Preservation of Racial Integrity,"[51] changes in the law of sex and marriage revolved around racial definitions, penalties for infraction, and enforcement mechanisms.

White Readjusters admitted that the Reconstruction amendments to the Constitution guaranteed black men equal civic rights. Interracial marriage, however, was considered outside the bounds of civic rights. White Readjusters defined the private sphere as contiguous with the laws of sex and marriage, just as postwar southern jurists did. This theoretical move, as Michael Grossberg has noted, "forestalled the classification of marriage as a political rather than a social right."[52] Viewing marriage as a hybrid of status and contract, white southerners erected a barrier against the new contractual capacities of African Americans in the postemancipation South and limited the influence of liberal rhetoric centered on the equal right to contract.[53] Essentially, white Readjuster liberals denied one type of contract to preserve others. There was, and would continue to be, they argued, an area of postwar southern life safe from the solvent of contractual liberalism.

Although they deployed the same liberal idiom as their white coalition partners, black Readjusters differed radically in their approach to the antimiscegenation law. They also drew different lines between the public and private spheres. Black Readjusters regarded the law forbidding marriage across the color line as an illegitimate assault on equality and the prerogatives of citizenship. In 1879, as the African American community considered abandoning the Republican Party to ally with Mahone's dissident Democrats, speakers at the Colored Citizens Convention denounced the antimiscegenation law as an oppressive abridgement of "our privileges as citizens of the State" and pledged "every effort" to have "the obnoxious and unconstitutional law wiped out." Threatening to emigrate from Virginia to other American states or territories "where there is no distinction on account of color," the delegates expressed their sympathy for and solidarity with Edmund Kinney and his wife Mary, who were currently performing hard labor in the state penitentiary for marrying in defiance of the ban on interracial unions.[54]

The fifty-nine African American Republicans who met that May in Richmond represented the black vote that ultimately transformed the Readjusters from a Democratic faction to an interracial third party. Many black leaders, including the president of the 1879 convention, attorney William C. Roane, carried their commitment to repealing the state's proscriptions on interracial sex and marriage into the Readjuster coalition. Between 1879 and the coalition's downfall in 1883, the black wing repeatedly identified restrictions on marriage as inequitable and indefensible in a liberal political system. In 1880 an unidentified African American speaker argued that black Virginians must trade their political support for a promise to repeal the laws regarding the whipping post, disfranchisement for petit larceny, and miscegenation, "all of which were enacted with one purpose—to bear against the new citizen."[55] In 1881 the *Virginia Star* was still complaining that "the oppressive laws" that had been enacted "expressly to oppress our people" were still on the books.[56]

When white Readjusters insisted that the boundary between the spheres necessarily paralleled the color line, black Readjusters disagreed. They considered marriage a political right, with the marriage contract itself serving as the boundary between spheres that were fully integrated.[57] This color-blind definition of the spheres grew out of a vision of liberalism that saw the ideal of "equal rights before the law" as founded in masculinity. It is not surprising that black Readjusters focused on masculinity—so did white Readjusters. In a world where women remained disfranchised, political power was vested in "the manhood of the nation," as Albion Tourgée had put it, and the connections between masculine sex right and political right were not hard to see: this is how Democrats had argued against African American enfranchisement during Congressional Reconstruction. Drawing on conceptions of liberalism by such African American political leaders as Frederick Douglass and John Mercer Langston, black Republican Readjusters defended equality as grounded in citizenship and manhood. As Langston had insisted in 1874, black men demanded, and the Fourteenth and Fifteenth Amendments guaranteed, "complete equality before the law, in the protection and enjoyment of all those rights and privileges which pertain to manhood, enfranchised and dignified."[58] This sentiment was echoed in 1882 by Readjuster George F. Bragg Jr., who edited the *Petersburg Lancet*. After the war, Bragg wrote, "The slave . . . was made a freeman and a citizen[;] while, before, he was a mere chattel, or thing, he was left a man and a sovereign."[59]

The masculinity that was so important to the assertion of the male as a political actor was not taken for granted. Masculine identity, like other forms of identity, was grounded in personal relations and could be strengthened as well as put at risk through social and political interactions. Reflecting on the enhanced position of African American men in Virginia under the Readjusters, one young black Richmonder claimed for African Americans the connection between public power and masculinity visible in the political system at large when he exulted, "Under the Readjusters, now for the first time black men feel like men."[60] Writing from the other side of the Jim Crow divide in 1906, W. E. B. Du Bois still spoke in terms that Langston and Bragg, as well as the young man in Richmond, would have understood. In his statement of principles for the Niagara Movement, the predecessor to the National Association for the Advancement of Colored People, Du Bois declared that "with the right to vote goes everything: Freedom, manhood, the honor of your wives, the chastity of your daughters, the right to work, and the chance to rise. . . . We are men; we will be treated as men."[61]

When southern blacks defined their political rights and individual autonomy as rooted in their masculinity, they asserted their commonality with white men through their essential difference from women and established themselves as citizen-patriarchs. As Laura F. Edwards has argued, African American men after the Civil War "harnessed a traditional definition of the household" and their place in it to serve the radical end of black enfranchisement and civic power.[62] An assembly of Alabama freedmen articulated these principles as early as 1865. "We claim exactly *the same rights, privileges and immunities as are enjoyed by white men*," they declared, because "the law no longer knows white or black, but simply men."[63] That African American political leaders could use the Fourteenth and Fifteenth Amendments to justify their participation in the polity in terms of their manliness testifies to the diversity of political ideology and vocabulary in the post–Civil War South. The Reconstruction amendments, which stood as the guarantors of African American equality within the liberal polity, were themselves links with the past through their grounding of political right in sexual identity and men's implied domestic majesty.

The foundation of men's domestic sovereignty was marriage, an institution that bore the weight of a world of symbolic meanings in the nineteenth century. Understood as the basis of society as well as its reproductive unit, marriage also served as a crucial boundary marker of the intersection between the private world of the household and the public world of the state, with the husband and father serving as intermediary. It was through this interrelated role of husband and father that matrimony established a clear relationship between sexual self-determination and civic power.[64]

Along with negotiating contracts, voting, and exploring their legal rights through the court system, black southerners after emancipation used marriage to signify their new identity as civic coequals.[65] Although many freedpeople and poor whites frequently practiced and defined marriage differently from the way white southern spokesmen did, everyone recognized that the right to marry was a significant marker of freedom.[66] Marriage may also be seen as constituting a recognition of equality: not between the partners but between the families of the betrothed. Indeed, marriage is such a recognition of equality that the definition of equality itself has become bound up over the years with that of marriage so that, as anthropologist Edmund Leach has remarked, cultures determine the standing of a group by asking, "Do we intermarry with them?"[67] As far as black Readjusters were concerned, laws that limited the right to marry limited a free exchange of property (sexual and material, in the form of a wife's labor) as well as social alliances among families, thus fencing in equality itself.

African American Readjusters considered race-based restrictions on marriage a flagrant denial of the liberty, the autonomy, the individual authority, that liberal citizenship was meant to confer. As they had in the antebellum era, postwar black Virginians (and an equal number of white Virginians) resisted restrictions on marriage.[68] We may infer postbellum marriages between black and white Virginians from the passage by the General Assembly in 1878 of an evasion provision to the criminal section of the antimiscegenation law. This new provision denied legitimacy to miscegenous marriages performed according to law outside the borders of the commonwealth and was directed at couples who went to Washington, D.C., to marry and then returned home to Virginia.[69] The 1878 law was tested in court that year and affirmed. It was reconfirmed in an 1885 case that also ruled that the children of miscegenous marriages were illegitimate.[70] Despite the increasing pressure of the law, however, many mixed-race couples in Virginia simply carried on without legal sanction;[71] the subjects of at least one successful state prosecution continued to live together with their children in Augusta County.[72] When confronted with the law, yet others challenged the official construction of their racial identity.[73] And from emancipation until 1967, when the U.S. Supreme Court ruled in a case from Virginia that bans on interracial marriage violated the Fourteenth Amendment,[74] black Virginians fought to change the law.

African Americans' protests against the antimiscegenation law became sterner as the Readjuster coalition succeeded. Calling for the repeal of the ban on interracial marriage, the state's leading black newspaper insisted: "The American colored man will never be satisfied until he has all the rights of any other American citizen. We want a good honest government that does not make a difference on account of the color of the skin."[75] To this end, black Readjusters in the General Assembly worked to overturn the prohibitions on interracial marriage. Practically, they were concerned with protecting black women who were already in common-law marriages with white men and the mixed-race children of those unions. More abstractly, these black legislators acted out of dedication to their vision of public equality *before the law* as enunciated in the Readjuster Party platforms. These attempts failed when white coalitionists refused to cooperate. Black assemblyman Shed Dungee's 1880 resolution to revoke the law fell by a 77–10 margin, and Petersburg leader Armistead Green's 1881 bill to repeal the law languished in committee.[76]

Black Virginians' objections to the antimiscegenation law were not centered on a desire to marry whites. Rather, black men were worried about equality. African American Readjusters saw clearly that within the logic of liberalism as articulated by the coalition, the antimiscegenation law was an explicit attempt to render black men less than fully political. This is not to say that black Virginians saw male equality as grounded in sexual domination of women. But within the Readjuster formulation of equal manhood rights, the selective privation of rights through the antimiscegenation law—the creation of a clear asymmetry of rights—angered and insulted them. By insisting on the absolute equality of all men before the law as the essence of liberalism, African American Readjusters made explicit the relationship between public and private life that white Readjusters had gone to such efforts to conceal.

White Democrats recognized and resented the connections between black masculinity and political power that were apparent under Readjuster rule. The self-confident assertion of African American political influence was increasingly equated by the Democratic press with a breakdown in the racial balance of power generally. When Daniel Norton, an influential black Readjuster from Williamsburg, presided in the state senate in the absence of the majority leader, the *Wytheville Enterprise* denounced the masculine universalism that it identified with liberalism to note sourly, "It is the first time in the history of Virginia that a colored 'brother' has taken such high ground and it remained for the 'Liberal' party, so-called, to usher Sambo into such prominence."[77]

"Sambo's" prominence in the coalition was always a delicate issue for the Readjusters, particularly in light of black and white Virginians' understanding that racial and gender identity were in part constructed through social performance, where both racial identity and masculinity could be gained or lost. To the extent that masculinity was politically emancipatory, it called into question the capability of liberalism and the separate spheres ideology to effectively protect whiteness from dissolving, and it heightened anxiety about competition between men over both white and black women. From the Democratic point of view, black gains in manhood could result only in white losses. Allying politically with African Americans and distributing patronage to them— encouraging black men to climb "the ladder of authority," as Mahone put it[78]—opened the possibility of interpreting the Readjuster coalition as destabilizing social hierarchies based on race. When black men supervised white postal workers or teachers, drafted legislation for the commonwealth, or simply asserted their right to space on the public byways, white Virginians worried about the distribution of authority in public life and any fraying of traditional links between authority, race, and manhood. Just as black Readjusters had done, white Democrats stressed the zero-sum nature of masculine assertion by shifting the discussion as much as possible from one of civil rights to one of masculinity, sex, and honor.

When whites spoke about masculinity and public authority in zero-sum terms, they spoke in the language of honor. It is probably not too much to say that the language of the performance of masculinity *was* the language of honor, for blacks as well as whites. In the antebellum South honor had been linked explicitly to both race and gender identity. Honor was reserved for white men, who granted none to women (except in the negative), children, slaves, and free men of color. In addition to identifying the gender boundaries of southern honor, historians of the Old South have shown the essential interrelatedness of white honor and African American slavery. If not founded in slavery, southern honor was nonetheless buttressed by it; white freedom was defined with its degrading opposite near to hand.[79]

Like racial and political identity, honor was never something a southern man could take for granted. Honor had to be asserted and reasserted daily through social interactions. The assertion of honor relied on its recognition by people in the same way that other markers of identity did. Scholars of southern honor all note the system's distinguishing behavioral marks: the ethos of reciprocity among equals, the preoccupation with reputation and outward appearance, the control of subordinates, the disposition toward conflating the personal and the social. Described variously as a language, an ethos, and a mentality, we may understand honor as an interpretational system that makes sense of social actions in a hierarchical world.[80]

The depth of scholarship on honor in the antebellum South cannot be found for the postbellum period. Indeed, the fact that nearly every book on southern honor ends with the Civil War unintentionally leaves the impression that the war and emancipation destroyed the culture of honor as well as its material foundation.[81] The field of postbellum southern honor has been abandoned to journalists and social psychologists, who often interpret honor reductively as a tendency toward violence or other forms of aggression. A University of Michigan psychologist has even devised a test to measure residual levels of southern honor, which is considered, for the purposes of science, to be synonymous with testosterone. When jostled while walking and then insulted verbally, white southern men tend to react with anger, demonstrating "a Southern sensitivity to insult and disposition to violence."[82] (Of course, the problem may lie with the northern control sample: as Walker Percy once remarked, "It's impossible to insult anybody from Michigan.")[83]

Despite this lack of scholarly attention, honor as a cultural touchstone and interpretive language remained politically important in Virginia long after emancipation. The Readjusters had always had to define themselves with one eye on the expectations of honor—in 1879, recall, the new party was compelled to articulate its positions vis-à-vis funder Conservatives' insistence that debt repudiation would publicly disgrace all white Virginians. All through the Readjuster era, Virginians continued to interpret ideas about both hierarchy and equality through the lens of honor.

This had important implications for the politics of sex and race. As many anthropologists and historians have emphasized, honor may be partly understood as a language in which hierarchy is sexualized, in which masculinity and authority are conflated and venerated, and in which the feminine is seen both as a way of speaking about dishonor and the point at which honor is most at risk. Both before and after the Civil War, white women were a principal flash point of white honor. In the white supremacist South, where white men sexually exploited black women with impunity and contributed to the region's mixed-race population, white women carried the sole responsibility for the perpetuation of the white race. Only by their refusal to engage in sexual relations with nonwhite men could the white race endure. As the physical embodiment and rhetorical repository of whiteness, white southern women assumed ever greater political importance in the postwar South. The first laws that segregated space rather than legal relationships were defined with white women in mind, to create a cordon sanitaire around them as they ventured into public spaces of work and transit and consumption in the New South.[84]

As suggested by the later Jim Crow laws segregating the public spaces where white women congregated, white anxiety about the sexual power inherent in black masculinity could be transferred to a variety of seemingly nonsexual areas. The Readjusters had considered the antimiscegenation law a necessary but sufficient barrier to accusations of black social equality in a liberal political system. But the interracial nature of the Readjuster political machine, particularly coalition patronage policies, upset white supremacist social dynamics. Readjuster patronage reshuffled social hierarchies, giving black men —and sometimes black women—authority over white women and men. Because of the explicit relations of deference and hierarchy visible in patronage, patronage politics were especially liable to be analyzed using the vocabulary of honor. To the extent that hierarchy was sexualized within the lexicon of honor, the authority of black men *anywhere* was capable of being sexualized. Crucially for the everyday life of the coalition, black authority was *not* sexualized in most instances, because the Readjusters had taken such care to plant it in the public sphere. "Negro domination" rhetoric was deployed by the Democrats constantly, but until 1883 it had little effect because black authority under the Readjusters never seemed to really threaten the fiction that the separate spheres ideology was deployed to maintain: that there was an impermeable barrier between public and private space.

One of the most basic conceptions of masculine honor was the ability to protect and govern one's women and children in the private sphere. This capacity had been of concern to black Readjusters in Petersburg in 1882, and it was exactly this sense of honor that Democrats called on when they warned of race mixture and mixed marriages, which both blacks and whites considered the most dramatic form of social equality. After its initial failure in 1881, this Democratic strategy gained a hearing among white Readjuster voters when black men won entry to a place that already seemed to breach the public/private divide: the public schools.

In the spring of 1883 Governor Cameron replaced Richmond's Democratic, all-white school board with one dominated by Readjusters. Repeating the procedure he had used so successfully in Petersburg, Cameron disqualified the sitting school board members for failing to take their oath of office on time. He replaced them with nine coalitionists, including two African Americans, Richard Forrester and Robert A. Paul. Educated and propertied, Forrester and Paul had influenced black politics in Richmond since Reconstruction. Each had held public office before his appointment to the school board.[85] Richmond's African American Readjusters were delighted at Forrester and

Paul's elevation; a mass meeting of Richmond blacks at the First African Church celebrated the governor's action and once again articulated their understanding of liberalism as "the great principles of equal political and civil rights for all classes, irrespective of race and color."[86]

Local Democratic leaders were outraged, but the state's leading Democratic newspaper drew some interesting distinctions. Although murmuring a protest against the increased African American influence over public institutions under the Readjusters, the *Richmond Dispatch* departed significantly from New South Democratic dogma by allowing that there was a sphere of legitimate black authority in public life. "There is no insuperable objection" to electing black men to the General Assembly, to city councils, or as magistrates and the like, the *Dispatch* conceded. But it drew the line at black influence over white schools, expressing incredulity that "any white man should raise his voice in defense of such a wrong."[87] That the most prominent Democratic newspaper in Virginia should admit, however reluctantly, the right of black men to serve in local and state government is in itself a reminder of the political fluidity that enabled the sort of shifting allegiances represented by the Readjusters. But the logic of the *Dispatch* is unclear. If black men were acceptable as magistrates, then why not as members of local school boards?

The answer to this question has to do with the location of white women and children in Virginia and the role of schools in reproducing the social unit. In the nineteenth-century South, as in the twentieth, schools most clearly exposed the fiction that there was an absolute barrier between private and public life. Try as they might, parents could not entirely control the education of their children in the public schools. Schools became the place where the socially transformative possibilities of liberalism were most clearly articulated: in this public space, it was hoped—or dreaded—that old hierarchies based on race (and later, gender) would be erased, and new generations of children would take what they learned at school home with them to create a different social reality.[88] Just as African American men in Petersburg had resented the implied insult to their authority as fathers when white teachers were employed in black schools, so did white men in Richmond worry about the expansion of African American authority over their own children. The anger of Petersburg blacks in 1882 about the authority of white men and women over their children was echoed by

Richmond whites worried about black power over *their* children. During the fall campaign Richmond Democrats published a cartoon depicting an African American male teacher about to spank a white girl. In the background of the drawing was a blackboard, on which was written the word "Coalition" next to a crude sketch of a mule's head, a traditional symbol of miscegenation. This drawing was widely circulated, although not without the opposition of an important cog in the Democratic publicity machine: black newsboys in Richmond refused to sell the *Lynchburg Democratic Campaign* because it contained a copy of the cartoon, and they beat up a white newsboy who tried to distribute the paper.[89]

In its portrayal of spanking, the Democratic cartoon suggested both the domination and subordination inherent in any hierarchical relationship and the specific sexual risks involved in hierarchical relations between men and women. These relationships held particular stakes for white southerners. In most societies in which the sexual purity of women is protected as the gate of entry to the caste, women lead highly restricted lives.[90] According to white Readjusters' representation of the separate spheres doctrine, white women should have remained apart, sheltered from the rough-and-tumble public world in their private domestic oases. But they did not. The same unpredictable forces of emancipation, urbanization, and industrialization that mediated the entry of African American men into public space expanded the worlds of black and white women. As women entered public space as workers, patrons, volunteers, and consumers, the definition of the private became less and less clear, and the places where women congregated became charged with sexual potential.

The most explosive of these locations in Virginia turned out to be the public schools. Public schools in the nineteenth-century South were a primary locus of patronage in the form of state employment.[91] After the Civil War, those employees tended to be women. Most children in Readjuster Virginia were taught by white women who were hired, promoted, and supervised by local boards of education.[92] In appointing Richard Forrester and Robert A. Paul to the Richmond School Board, Governor Cameron placed them in a position of direct authority over white women teachers. Because of the subordinate role played by white women in schools, the Democrats' more general progression from black men's civil authority to black men's sexual authority was easier to make. The danger schools posed for the Readjusters could now be constructed as different in degree, but not in kind, from that posed by the issue of intermarriage. By placing black men in positions of authority over white women teachers, the integration of the Richmond School Board threatened to expose the potential relationship between political right and sex right that the Readjuster emphasis on the separation between public and private space was meant to suppress.

In May 1883 the *Richmond Dispatch* reluctantly agreed in principle to black management of black schools if the Readjusters considered that necessary to the maintenance of the coalition, begging only that the white schools not be "degraded and ruined by having negroes placed over them."[93] At the same time, the paper contributed to the Democratic campaign by focusing on fears of black male power over white women teachers, straining at the boundaries of its own tortured logic to argue that two black men on a nine-member school board constituted a "majority": "Of the nine new trustees, two are negroes; that is to say, as five members constitute a majority of the board, and can elect teachers, and three members constitute a majority of that majority, it may probably happen that the fifty or sixty young lady-teachers, as well as the principals and other school officials, may have to depend upon the good will of these two negroes for their places." As if such reliance on black patronage power were not galling enough to whites, the *Dispatch* played up the sexual implications of black male school officials examining and hiring white women teachers and concluded the editorial with a statement resonating both of marriage and of rape, intoning, "The outrage has been consummated."[94]

Richmond Democrats fought Cameron's replacement of the school board in the courts and lost. Then they took the fight to the people, making the authority of black men over white schools an issue in the spring election. From South Quay, Thomas H. Cross reported that "our efforts to do something for the negroes drew many white men from us. . . . I fear many of our best white men have left us permanently as they object to the appointment of negroes to School Board in Richmond."[95] John J. Deyer of Handsoms concurred and complained that he was handicapped by having an African American on the local Readjuster ticket.[96] Not that the Richmond School Board issue was always decisive. R. L. Henley of New Kent explicitly rejected this logic in explaining the Readjusters' loss in his county. "It has been claimed here that the defeat of the Readjuster ticket in this county was caused by

Gov. Cameron putting colored men on the Richmond School Board. We have had a colored Trustee for a long time in James City & it has never hurt us there." Instead, Henley attributed the coalition's defeat in New Kent to the behavior of the local Readjuster candidate for the state legislature, who had "been drinking and carrying on in such a way that the people would no longer submit to it."[97] In Hanover County, the Readjuster candidate for magistrate even managed to overcome Democratic efforts to paint him as a supporter of integrated schools.[98]

Despite the mixed success of the school issue in the spring election, the Democrats made the conjunction of black male political and sexual power the main theme in the election of 1883. All through the fall Democratic newspapers asserted that mixed school boards led to mixed schools, which led inevitably to miscegenation. The Democrats were aided by the decision of the U.S. Supreme Court to overturn the Civil Rights Act of 1875. There was nothing to prevent a Readjuster legislature from passing a civil rights bill in Virginia, and the Democrats nursed this fear when they urged white voters to reject a "Miscegenation—Civil Rights—Mahone Legislature."[99] The *Lynchburg News* abjured white voters to remember that readjusterism meant "Negroes to control the schools to which your little children go" and insisted that a vote for the Readjusters was a vote for "mixed schools now and mixed marriages in the future."[100] The Democratic cartoon of the black teacher spanking a white girl made the same argument in visual form to reach illiterate voters. All of this left C. J. Heermans of Blacksburg worried about the Readjusters' prospects. "[Democratic] Men are employed by the day to ride and visit the people and the only song is nigger, nigger," he reported, adding that the race rhetoric was scaring off Readjuster voters.[101] Former Confederate general T. J. Kenny, reporting on the southwest to white Republican leader James Brady, agreed. "The Funders are resorting to any means in their power to weaken the Re-Adjuster strength by a cry of Negro supremacy, Union or Mixed Schools and personal attacks on General Mahone. And it seems to me from observations made on the ground that they are meeting with some success."[102]

The integration of the Richmond School Board appears to have convinced a considerable number of white voters in Virginia that black male political and sexual power marched hand in hand.[103] In November 1883 the coalition lost control of the state in a close election that turned on the race question. Commenting on the campaign, J. M.

Gills, Readjuster chairman for Amelia County, wrote Mahone that "it surpassed anything ever before known for unfairness, misrepresentation and meanness. Bulldozing and intimidation was the order. Mixed Schools, Mixed Marriages, Social Equality and Negro rule and Negro supremacy was the cry of [Democratic] precinct leaders, used in the presence of women in every private family." Gills continued, "In my Precinct [Democratic] chairmen rode to the doors, called out the women and after going through the catalougue [*sic*] of ills that would follow if the Coalitionists succeed, would wind up by asking the women how they would like (calling a most objectionable Negro by name) to visit and examine their daughters."[104] White Readjusters who could support African American voters and jurors balked at the presence of black men in charge of white schoolmarms.[105] The Warren County coalitionists, for example, passed a resolution supporting the civil and political rights of African Americans but opposing "social equality" and the appointment of Forrester and Paul to the Richmond School Board.[106] Such an act points to both the relative success of the liberal rhetoric of separate spheres in masking the relationship between political right and sex right and to the Democratic success in merging the two in the school issue in 1883.

There is some irony in the fact that the public schools proved more dangerous than intermarriage to Readjuster liberalism, for the latter has seemed the more fundamental issue to a number of nonsouthern, twentieth-century liberals. In her famous essay "Reflections on Little Rock," Hannah Arendt questioned the wisdom of launching the assault on segregation through America's schools. Rather than expecting children to solve the nation's race problems on the playground, Arendt argued that the fight against legalized racial discrimination should focus on voting rights and on "what the whole world knows to be the most outrageous piece of legislation in the whole western hemisphere": the antimiscegenation laws that, in 1959, made marriages between American citizens a criminal offense in twenty-nine states. Combined with the South's denial of African Americans' right of suffrage, these marriage laws, wrote Arendt, constituted "a much more flagrant breach of letter and spirit of the Constitution than segregation of schools." If the purpose of the civil rights movement was to abolish legal enforcement of social and political discrimination based on race, how could the Civil Rights Act of 1957 leave untouched "the most outrageous law of Southern states—the law which makes mixed marriages a criminal offense?" And why were American liberals so quick to dismiss the issue of black sexual rights, insisting, as Sidney Hook did in a reply to Arendt, that African Americans were "profoundly uninterested" in the antimiscegenation laws?[107]

Despite Arendt's impression that antimiscegenation laws were not under attack, most mid-twentieth-century Americans understood that in integrating the public schools the nation was implicitly addressing the question of intermarriage.[108] More clearly than Arendt, they saw that the schools had become the site on which white anxiety about the relationship between political rights and sex rights had been displaced. This displacement was not the foreordained result of any inherent logic of liberal politics, but neither was it some perversion of liberal ideology. Instead, it resulted from the strategic deployment of liberal assumptions in a particular time and place. To insist, as Arendt did, that sex rights and political rights could meet only in the field of marriage was to ignore the many ways in which sexual boundaries had been displaced by those seeking to enlarge the political arena for African Americans as well as by those seeking to restrict it. She might have learned from the story of the Readjusters and their enemies what Alabama Governor George Wallace seems to have understood intuitively as he made his "stand in the schoolhouse door" in 1963: that (to quote Mary Douglas) "the homely experience of going through a door is able to express so many kinds of entrance."[109]

4

DEFERENCE & VIOLENCE IN DANVILLE

As he finished his autobiographical *Lanterns on the Levee: Recollections of a Planter's Son*, William Alexander Percy—planter, writer, and (as he supposed) racial liberal and "friend of the Negro"—fretted over the increasingly acrimonious state of race relations in the South. Published in 1941, just before the southern legal and cultural edifice of racial segregation and official white supremacy began to dissolve under the ideological strain of World War II, *Lanterns on the Levee* included a "Note on Racial Relations" in which Percy worried about the erosion of black manners. Referring to white violence, he "noted that the Negro is losing his most valuable weapon of defense—his good manners." He continued: "When a Negro now speaks of a 'man' he means a Negro; when he speaks of a 'lady' he means a Negress; when he speaks of a 'woman' he means a white woman. Such manners are not only bad, they are not safe, and the frame of mind that breeds them is not safe. Covert insolence is not safe for anybody, anywhere, at any time."[1]

Identifying and interpreting "covert insolence" among the subjugated has become something of a cottage industry in the academy since Percy condemned its deployment by black southerners. Inspired by the work of social historians such as Eric J. Hobsbawm and E. P. Thompson, the search for what James C. Scott called the "hidden transcript" of resistance has become a central pursuit of scholars interested in questions of domination and resistance. The uncovering of what Scott dubbed "infrapolitics" and what Czech philosopher Václav Benda called "the parallel polis" has focused scholarly attention on the political subtext of acts of resistance that stop short of open rebellion. The definition of *politics* has been broadened to include the breach of manners so vexing to Will Percy.[2]

Historians of the American South have profited in particular from the insights gained mining the hidden transcript. Several scholars whose work preceded Scott's formulations—Herbert Aptheker, Eugene D. Genovese, Lawrence W. Levine, Albert J. Raboteau, and Gilbert Osofsky—applied the concept of underground resistance to relations between masters and slaves in the antebellum South.[3] More recently, historians have explicitly used Scott's approach to analyze black-white relations under Jim Crow. Robin D. G. Kelley, for example, employed Scott's notion of infrapolitics to draw attention to African Americans' broad repertoire of acts of everyday resistance in the segregated twentieth-century South in order to show "how seemingly innocuous, individualistic acts of survival and opposition shaped southern urban politics, workplace struggles, and the social order generally."[4] While documenting and fully appreciating the importance of urban black working-class opposition at home, in the community, and in the workplace, Kelley urges scholars to focus on black resistance to white domination in public space and "to rethink the meaning of public space as a terrain of class, race, and gender conflict." It was, Kelley argues, urban public space—a city's parks, its streets, and particularly its public transportation system—that provided most of the opportunities for acts of resistance and simultaneously embodied "the most repressive, violent aspects of race and gender oppression" in the Jim Crow South.[5]

What had been the hidden "weapons of the weak" in urban public spaces of the antebellum South—the "accidental" jostling of whites on the sidewalk or on a city trolley, the profanities and depredations muttered under one's breath—would later become acts of covert resistance during the more rigid days of the Jim Crow era. But during the crucial transition between slavery and Jim Crow, these same acts emerged as the open and public actions of an enfranchised and politically empowered people. In the years after emancipation and before the codification of the white supremacist South, African Americans devised a series of strategies to resist white definitions of black rights, opportunities, and sociability. Not unexpectedly, conflicts arose between black and white southerners over what was proper, acceptable, or demeaning behavior in public arenas. The forms of black behavior now recognized as covert resistance in the antebellum and Jim Crow eras—such as a refusal to yield to whites on the sidewalk or the reservation of appellations of gentility for themselves—were precisely those through which black men and women asserted in public their claims to citizenship and equal civil and political rights with whites. Such assertion by blacks risked violence by whites, either individually or in groups, and urban spaces during the New South era frequently became battlegrounds over public behavior. Eventually, segregation regulated both public space and civil behavior by dividing each according to race, along phantasmagoric "separate but equal" lines. As Howard N. Rabinowitz demonstrated twenty years ago, the postwar South's urban spaces were the first settings for the rationalized system of racial segregation that by World War I characterized the region as a whole.[6] But even segregation could not solve fully—to the satisfaction of whites—the issue of black behavior in public space. As the work of twentieth-century historians shows, African Americans continued to assert their claim to civility, and to dignity, in public.[7]

The story of what historians know as the Danville Riot illuminates the ways that disagreements over civil behavior between white and black urban southerners intersected with other social and political developments. In November 1883 a dispute over street etiquette in the burgeoning industrial town of Danville escalated into a massacre when a white mob shot into a crowd of unarmed black men, women, and children. White Democrats then took control of the city and spread rumors of black insurrection throughout the state. Coming only three days before an important state election, the violence in Danville and Democratic stories about it contributed to the downfall of the Readjusters. As occurred more notoriously in Wilmington, North Carolina, in 1898, white men in Danville usurped the power of the state through violence and overthrew a democratically elected interracial government.

This chapter will explore the whys and hows of the violence in Danville, but its broader aim is to reveal the links between civility and civil rights and between manners and massacres. As we will see, the actions of white and black Virginians on the streets of Danville made a mockery of the posited divisions between "public" and "private" so central to Readjuster enunciations of liberalism. The sequence of events that led to gunfire in Danville began with a confrontation over sidewalk space between a white man and a black man. Central to the analysis here is the idea that, particularly for people (such as women and racial and religious minorities) whose identities have traditionally been defined spatially, as "place," the act of appropriating public space—whether on a New South city sidewalk or a Jim Crow streetcar—is a political and subversive act. The appropriation of public space was an important way for African Americans in this period to assert their humanity, demonstrate their political rights, and stake their claim to equal citizenship. When black men and women stood their ground on the streets of Danville, insisting on the impartial rule of law, white men responded violently and reclaimed the streets, and ultimately the political arena, for themselves.

The struggle for black equality in the New South was fought on many fronts. Exercising the right to vote and to make contracts were two of the most obvious means by which African Americans proclaimed their new civil status. Appropriating public space was another. Although the racial politics of Congress and the state legislatures are better documented, the streets of the urban South had a politics of their own. It was here, in the everyday pushing and shoving of white and black southerners, that broader questions of political, economic, and sexual competition were enacted and represented daily.

By the time of the automobile, black "place" was so firmly defined by the racial code of Jim Crow that southern cities found nothing odd in barring black motorists from public streets.[8] By the 1930s the inner side of the sidewalk was designated in custom if not in law as "the 'white man's right of way.'"[9] But this was not yet the case in the 1880s or even on the eve of the twentieth century in areas of the South where black political influence survived or was resurrected. In such places, in the absence of either a rigid system of racial hierarchy or mutually agreed upon conventions for public conduct between the races, questions of honor, hierarchy, and deference arose in every encounter in public. Broad questions of racial domination and subordination were frequently distilled in public interactions on the streets of the urban South, and negotiation over the rules of common courtesy became a principal venue for the ongoing contest between blacks determined to assert their identity as civic actors and whites intent on denying blacks that power.

In a column entitled "Manners," published in January 1884, Orra Langhorne, a white woman who regularly contributed to the Hampton Institute's monthly news publication, the *Southern Workman*, decried the public behavior of the new generation of black southerners—those born in freedom. "It is a common thing in the towns of Virginia," she charged, "for several Negro boys to lock their arms together and parade the streets, rudely jostling passers by, for whom they refuse to make way, and terrifying ladies and children." Langhorne herself had recently been knocked off the sidewalk by a group of young men that included the son of one of her tenants, "good old Uncle Ben." She reported the incident to the father, and the son was sent to apologize. He was not, he explained, drunk (as Langhorne supposed) but "was only projeckin'." Langhorne did not favor such projecting. Rather, she urged Virginia blacks to recall "the amiable and gentle manners which once distinguished the southern slaves" and recommended the advice that "old aunt Hester" gave to a young African American man excited about passage of the Civil Rights Bill: "Don't you mine so much 'bout Civil Rights—Civil Rights is very good in dere place, but you try civil manners an' behavior an' you'll git along wid white folks."[10]

It was a commonplace among postwar white southerners that black civil rights had eroded black civility, especially on the public streets. Countless white diarists and political commentators left behind stories of black rudeness in public. Planter Henry W. Ravenel's impression of postwar Charleston is typical of contemporary accounts: "It is impossible to describe the condition of the city—It is so unlike anything we could imagine—Negroes shoving white persons off the walk—Negro women drest in the most outré style, all with veils and parasols for which they have an especial fancy—riding on horseback with negro soldiers and in carriages."[11] Georgia Bryan Conrad, a young white woman, first realized the magnitude of the postwar transformation of southern social life when "a huge Negro soldier" compelled her "to take to the gutter, to escape coming in contact with him," and her father did nothing. Complaining of similar behavior in postwar Memphis, Elizabeth Avery Meriwether remarked that "any stranger, seeing those negroes, would have supposed the Blacks not the Whites, were masters in the South."[12]

These images are familiar because twentieth-century authors and filmmakers used them to represent the social and political inversions of Reconstruction. Margaret Mitchell made "niggers pushin' white folks off the sidewalks" a defining feature of Republican-ruled Atlanta. In his 1915 film *Birth of a Nation*, D. W. Griffith used disputes between whites and blacks over sidewalk space as a synecdoche for the decline of black deference toward whites and the corresponding loss of white power and prestige. As Griffith has the mulatto carpetbagger Silas Lynch explain to one white protagonist, "The side walk belongs to us as much as it does to you, Colonel Cameron." And in his 1941 magnum opus *The Mind of the South,* W. J. Cash deplored in blacks "the dangerous manners learned in carpetbag days—to pour into the towns on Saturday afternoon and swagger along the street in guffawing gangs which somehow managed to take up the whole breadth of the sidewalk."[13]

If the existence of prohibitory legislation is a legitimate indicator of the occurrence of the forbidden, even antebellum southern cities found it difficult to regulate black behavior on the streets. Slaves exulted in the relative liberty of the city; as Frederick Douglass put it, "a city slave is almost a freeman." Richmond's 1857 "Ordinance concerning Negroes" addressed itself specifically to the behavior of free blacks and slaves in public. Regarding street etiquette, the ordinance specified that "Negroes shall not at any time stand on a sidewalk to the inconvenience of [white] persons passing by. A negro meeting or overtaking, or being overtaken by a white person . . . shall pass on the outside; and if it be necessary to enable such white person to pass, shall immediately get off the sidewalk." As for rude or threatening behavior, Richmond's law provided thirty-nine lashes for any black who used "provoking language" or made "insolent or menacing gestures to a white person, or [spoke] aloud any blasphemous or indecent word . . . in any streets or other public place."[14]

Richmond was not unusual in its attempt to establish public decorum. By the mid-nineteenth century, cities as far afield as New York and San Francisco had turned to legislation to coerce proper urban behavior. According to Mary P. Ryan, the majority of arrests in nineteenth-century American cities were prompted by violations of street etiquette—such as being drunk or boisterous in public.[15] But there is a difference between the generalized rules of public engagement— for instance, the prohibition of spitting—that are symmetrical (applicable to all) and rules that are explicitly hierarchized (applicable only to members of a prescribed group and useful in establishing and maintaining asymmetries of power).[16] Richmond's requirement that blacks yield sidewalk right-of-way to whites is, of course, an example of the latter, as were sumptuary laws restricting slave dress. In 1822 Charleston residents petitioned the legislature to prohibit African Americans from wearing "silks, satins, crapes, lace[,] muslins, and such costly stuffs, as are looked upon and considered the luxury of dress." The purpose of such an appeal was to impress on blacks of every legal status the slave society's determination to maintain "every distinction . . . between the whites and the negroes, calculated to make the latter feel the superiority of the former."[17] Such asymmetrical rules typify societies that are dominated by an ethos of honor. Fundamentally opposed to "a universal and formal morality which affirms the equality in dignity of all men and consequently the equality of their rights and duties," the honor-based society establishes "two opposing sets of rules of conduct"—one that governs relations between equals and another for relations between dominant and subordinate individuals.[18]

For postbellum black southerners, casting a ballot and signing—or refusing to sign—a contract signified the attainment of a degree of agency and independence.[19] But there were other, more quotidian, ways in which they reminded southern whites of African American selfhood. Chief among these was their behavior in public, in particular their physical actions and presence and their speech and forms of address. It was no coincidence that whites frequently coupled complaints about the conduct of black men and women on the streets and sidewalks of the urban South with objections to their forms of address. Both speaking and walking may be seen as acts of appropriation that assert and confirm selfhood.[20] Refusing to yield the sidewalk to a white man or woman and referring to oneself as a "gentleman" and to a white man as a "man" were acts of self-definition for African Americans, acts that were intimately bound up with the freedmen's emerging identity as citizens.[21] As important as the discursive public sphere may be, public space *as space* is essential to the definition of citizenship because, along with suffrage and contract, it is a primary location for the establishment of the autonomous individual.[22] While attempts by whites to circumscribe the basis of black equality by limiting the right to vote and contract were clearly part of an overall goal of restratifying southern society, it was in white efforts to undercut black claims to public space that notions of honor most clearly inserted themselves into the process of redefining black "place."

When black southerners appropriated titles such as "lady" and "gentleman" and expected white men and women to step aside on public streets, they did more than assert themselves—they demanded whites' *affirmation* of African American civil equality. This was a demand that few white southerners were prepared to grant. In the context of the profound and simultaneous social, political, and economic transitions that made the New South new—urbanization, industrialization, emancipation—it is not surprising that people became uncertain about the rules of social conduct. As German political scientist Norbert Elias reflected from experience in 1939, during transition periods "the social situation itself makes 'conduct' an acute problem." In such circumstances, as postbellum historian Philip Alexander Bruce put it, the "fear of being misunderstood" was marked.[23]

Orra Langhorne's 1884 column on manners was itself composed in the context of a crisis of conduct. Three months before the editorial appeared, and days before a crucial election for the Readjusters, a dispute over street etiquette involving a black man and a white man in Danville had turned into a massacre of black citizens by a white mob. Langhorne clearly considered manners related to massacres. Although concerned in general with the behavior of young black men on city streets, she disapproved of the white crowd's action in Danville; she accepted the black version of the violence and called the white action cowardly. Just as she criticized white men as imperious, she recognized the combustive combination of white pride and black assertion. "It is this coarse and rude conduct of the colored youth, with the fierce and arrogant behavior of the young white men, that in times of political excitement culminate in tragedies" such as the one in Danville, she argued.[24]

Langhorne's awareness of her own "times of political excitement," and her association of personal conduct and politics, anticipated Elias's "periods of transition" in which everyday conduct becomes a social problem. Since 1879 Readjuster reforms had validated African American male equality in the political arena and encouraged black activism in other walks of life. The power of the biracial coalition to legitimize, even promote, a renegotiation of power relations between the races was most apparent in the cities, where blacks and whites met frequently in public situations.

Although the New South remained overwhelmingly rural (even in 1900, only one in six southerners lived in cities), the postwar trend was in the direction of urbanization. In the half century between the end of the Civil War and World War I, the southern rate of urbanization outpaced that of the rest of the nation. In 1860 the South was home to only 51 of America's nearly 400 urban places (defined rather loosely by the federal census as having 2,500 or more inhabitants). By 1910, the number of southern towns or cities had jumped to 396, or almost 18 percent of urban America.[25]

The freedpeople led the way to the cities of the South; indeed, the migration of rural black southerners to these areas after 1865 was so significant that southern urban historians have termed it "the first phase of the Great Migration." Plagued by economic depression and outbreaks of infectious diseases such as cholera and yellow fever, most cities in the South—but not in Virginia—failed to grow during the 1870s.[26] By 1880, however, the region experienced a major spurt of urban growth; between 1880 and 1890 the urban population increased by 49 percent. This statistic is all the more remarkable when read alongside the substantial rate of southern out-migration. While many rural southerners moved to town between 1865 and 1900, thousands more left the region altogether.[27] Of all the southern states, Virginia saw the greatest percentage of its population leave between 1870 and 1910. This happened in two main waves, the first between 1880 and 1900 and the second between 1920 and 1930.[28]

The southern anchor of an emerging northeastern metropolitan corridor, Virginia was always the most urban of the southern states. This status was unchanged by emancipation. In 1880 Virginia led the South with eleven cities boasting over 4,000 inhabitants.[29] After emancipation the process of city building accelerated in the Old Dominion. As a percentage of total population, urban inhabitants grew from 13.1 percent to 16.8 percent between 1880 and 1890. This represents a whopping 40 percent increase in the state's urban population.[30] When the high out-migration rate is factored in, this gain in cities becomes all the more significant. The state as a whole may have been stagnating demographically, but the cities were growing.

The greatest urban growth occurred in the heavily black coastal and tobacco-growing regions of the state. Rural black Virginians moved to town for a variety of reasons: to avoid the oppressive labor conditions of the countryside, to bring children within the orbit of schools, to live in an environment in which it was easier to vote,[31] to earn the higher wages paid by urban manufacturing concerns. In Virginia as elsewhere, there was an obvious reciprocal relationship between urbanization and industrialization: as manufacturing took off after 1880, wage work in the cities drew in ever more agricultural workers. Whereas older cities such as Richmond expanded only marginally or even declined during the 1890s, newer towns in the tobacco country grew by leaps and bounds. Norfolk's population increased by 25 percent during the decade, while the number of people in Danville grew by a third.

Big Lick's 669 residents in 1880 multiplied to rival Roanoke's 21,495 twenty years later.[32]

Thus while the South as a whole remained predominantly rural, the trend was toward towns and cities. This current was stronger in the Upper South than in the Lower South (except for Texas) and in Virginia more than anywhere else. In this context, what happened in places like Danville, Petersburg, and Richmond under coalition rule could easily be seen as predictive of the future of the state.

It was in the many public spaces of Virginia's growing towns and cities, with their concentrated populations, that disputes between white and black citizens over questions of public equality, deference, and civility most commonly arose. Complicating this social renegotiation was the definition of public space itself. Public buildings such as the capitol or the police station could easily be seen to fall within the domain of the state. Public streets, including sidewalks, were communal space. But where did restaurants and theaters belong? And what rules governed a privately held factory? When William P. Graves, a white tobacco merchant and factory owner in Danville, struck a black employee in 1883 for bumping into him with a basket of tobacco, the worker complained to the authorities, and Graves was arrested and later fined.[33] From the black point of view, the fate of William Graves was an admirable example of the rule of law and the impartial workings of justice. From Graves's angle, however, his ability to enforce in his own factory a private sense of race-based honor—his social autonomy as a white man—had been usurped by the Readjuster state.

In Readjuster Virginia the amplified political power of black men altered the behavioral status quo. The new status of African Americans was reflected in white anxiety over what whites considered to be assertive black behavior. It was also apparent in the novel consequences of long-accepted white behavior toward blacks, as William Graves discovered to his cost. In these ways, disputes over protocol were also political contests, as black women and—particularly—men asserted their rights as citizens and political actors. In this context, public behavior between members of different races became more consequential. Events in Danville provide a dramatic example of just how consequential such encounters could be.

Like so many other towns in the rapidly urbanizing postwar South, Danville boomed in the 1870s and 1880s, more than doubling its prewar population. Located just north of the Virginia–North Carolina

border, in Pittsylvania County, Danville had a U.S. government building (the seat of the U.S. Court for the Western Division of Virginia) and
an armory. As in many other southern towns, there were two militias—
the white Danville Grays and the black Douglass Guards. Tobacco factories continued to be the principal employer of industrial labor, but
some entrepreneurs hoped to harness the power of the Dan River and
replace the tobacco factories and their black workers with textile mills
and a white workforce.[34] The hilly downtown was dominated by the
Opera House and the Arlington Hotel, but nestled in their shadows
were ramshackle bars and a few "Houses of Ill Favor." The streets of
Danville were increasingly crowded, especially on court and market
days.[35]

This was the setting for the local Readjuster victory in 1882. In the
spring of that year the Readjuster-controlled General Assembly divided Danville into three wards, two of which had a black majority.[36]
This division resulted in the election that summer of a Readjuster majority to the Danville Common Council, which thereafter consisted of
four white Democrats, four white Readjusters, and four black Readjusters. The most immediate and visible effect of Readjuster rule in Danville was the election of the African American councilmen, Julius W.
Payne, Henry W. Swann, D. F. Balls, and R. A. Arrington, and the selection by the council of a black policeman, Walter S. Withers.[37]

Prior to the Readjuster victory, the Danville Common Council was
mainly occupied with tasks that were common to a growing late-nineteenth-century city: establishing sewer and telephone systems; paving
city streets and sidewalks; running the public schools, poorhouse,
cemeteries, and jail; and keeping the peace amid the uproar. After
the Readjusters won a majority on the council, it continued to be concerned with these matters, but there was a shift of emphasis toward
serving the black population. The long-promised house for the sex-
ton of the black cemetery was finally built. Streets were paved and
sidewalks constructed in black neighborhoods. Schools for both black
and white students were expanded and improved, and discrepancies
in funding between them, though not eliminated, were narrowed.[38]

As in any city, there was violence, and arrests for felonies kept pace
with population growth. More commonly, Danville men found themselves behind bars for one or more of three misdemeanors: carrying a
concealed weapon, selling intoxicating liquors without a license, and
engaging in unlawful gaming.[39] Considering the arguments that would

be made later regarding Readjuster rule in Danville, it is important to note that the crime level—measured by arrest rates—fell consistently under the Readjusters.[40] If crime is a reliable index of social stability, then Readjuster Danville was a model city. But, ominously, even as the overall number of arrests declined between the summer of 1882 and the fall of 1883, the number of men arrested for violation of the concealed weapons law rose, skyrocketing in October 1883 as the political campaign intensified with the approach of the state election.[41]

Around the first of October 1883, the local Democratic leadership published a pamphlet entitled *Coalition Rule in Danville,* known popularly as the Danville Circular. Addressed to the residents of southwestern Virginia and the Shenandoah Valley, the circular lay before that white, predominantly Readjuster population "a few facts from which you can form some idea of the injustice and humiliation to which our white people have been subjected and are daily undergoing by the domination and misrule of the Radical or negro party, now in absolute power in our town." The circular claimed to enumerate the many grievances of Danville's white population and ended with a fraternal plea that "fellow-citizens" to the west deliver the whites of Danville "from this awful state *of humiliation and wretchedness . . .* by voting for the Conservative-Democratic candidates for the Legislature, for *unless they are elected we are doomed.*"[42]

The Danville Circular was a partisan attempt to persuade Readjuster voters in white majority counties to vote for Democratic candidates. As such, it cannot be considered uncritically as testimony about life in Danville under the Readjusters. Rather, the value of the circular lies in its representation of everyday life in Readjuster Danville and its connection of politics to civility and the articulation of urban social relationships. The heart of the circular concerned the control of public spaces in Danville and three interrelated issues regarding African Americans: their appointment to public offices, their prominence in the public market, and their behavior on the public streets and in the homes and offices of white employers.

The first item in the circular's "litany of shame" was the appointment of African American police officers. Black postmasters and legislators were grudgingly tolerated by whites in the South, but black men representing the law—armed and with the authority to arrest and detain white men and women—were bitterly resented.[43] Danville's Readjuster government had appointed black policemen, and these appointments were emphasized and their number exaggerated. The circular charged that four out of nine policemen were black. In fact, of nine regular policemen serving in October 1883, only two were black.[44] In addition, there was an African American weighmaster of the public scales, Benton T. Fields.[45] The town health officer, Dr. Paulus Irving, was a white Democrat, but the sanitary policeman empowered to enforce city sanitary regulations was black Readjuster leader Squire Taliaferro.[46] As for the circular's charge that African American policemen were sent to arrest white men, it seems that black officers preferred not to and generally did not serve warrants on whites.[47]

Democrats were also aggrieved at the election of an African American as a magistrate of the police court. The police court was composed of the mayor, the president of the common council, and three magistrates, all popularly elected. Of these five people, only one, a man named Jones, was black. According to John D. Blackwell, himself a judge in Danville, the black justice was "the best of the lot," and the chief complaint against him (other than Democratic tirades about his color) came from members of the black community who insisted that his judgments against them were more severe than those he issued against whites. Perhaps because of this, postulated another magistrate, white people in Danville preferred to have their cases heard before Justice Jones.[48]

Whatever the number of black officials, both blacks and whites took the political involvement of African American men to mean that Danville blacks had influence under the Readjusters. In addition to the redistribution of patronage represented by the employment of African American men, their presence in public and official settings served as a constant reminder of the participation of black men in the political process and may have, as whites charged, encouraged other forms of African American assertion and outspokenness.

Close on the heels of the allegations regarding the black police officers was the assertion that black hucksters were controlling the public market and pushing out white sellers. "Out of the 24 stalls and stands at the market place, 20 are *rented out by the council to the negroes*," maintained the Danville Circular. In addition, the document's authors fretted over what they portrayed as the degradation of manners in public commercial space. The market, they charged, which was previously "occupied in all its stalls by polite white gentlemen, with their clean white aprons, and the most enticing meats and vegetables upon their boards, is now the scene of filth, stench, crowds of loitering and idle negroes, drunkenness, obscene language, and petit thieves." Testimony taken after the violence refutes the idealized description of the market before the Readjuster period but verifies the presence of significant numbers of African American sellers. There were twenty-nine stalls in the market, which the city leased each year in a competitive auction. Fifteen of these were rented to black merchants who sold oysters, fish, and fowl, while the remaining fourteen stalls were divided between white butchers and hawkers. Standing in front of the stalls were tables belonging to African American vegetable sellers. This made for an extremely cramped space, where people were liable to be jostled and crowded regardless of race.[49]

There is an obvious economic theme in the circular's complaints about African American public officials and conditions in the city market: good jobs, with regular salaries and social prestige, were going to African Americans, and black sellers were competing successfully in the marketplace. Indeed, the Danville Circular was not the first formal criticism of Readjuster administration of the market. The previous January, a group of whites who rented stalls and stands had used "disrespectful language" in a complaint to the common council involving rents and bidding practices and made unsubstantiated charges that the council's committee on the market had artificially run up the price of stalls during the annual auction.[50] One final concern lay below the surface of the circular's protests against black police officers, hucksters, and loiterers but emerged clearly in its central attack on black behavior on the city streets. This was a lack of what whites considered good manners and due deference from blacks in public situations.

In words akin to those chosen later by Orra Langhorne, the Danville Circular complained of "squads" of black vagabonds "who impede the travel of [white] ladies and gentlemen, very frequently forcing them from the sidewalk into the street." This behavior, it asserted, was not limited to black men: "*Negro women* have been known to *force ladies* from the pavement, and remind them that they will '*learn to step aside the next time.*'" The circular also charged that black women in Danville were intent on ascribing for themselves gentle status in words as well as actions: "It is a very common practice for the negroes who are employed about our houses to allude to white ladies and gentlemen as *men* and *women,* and to negroes as *ladies* and *gentlemen.* This is a practice almost without exception with the negro women."[51]

The use or denial of appellations such as "sir" and "Mrs." and the granting or assertion of right-of-way are ancient markers of status and submission. Blacks in the New South complained bitterly about the refusal by whites to accord African American men and women honorific titles, and these memories are buttressed by whites' recollections of having been taught to omit such titles when addressing black people.[52] As for the public right-of-way, competition over street space seems to be an eternal fact of urban life. Nevertheless, encounters on the street that telegraphed power relations among social groups could have far-reaching consequences. In 1863 Confederate soldiers outside of Jackson, Mississippi, spread the rumor that the Jackson City Council had come within three votes of passing an ordinance "forbidding *soldiers the use of the pavement* and *sidewalks* and forcing them to walk in the middle of the streets."[53] It is unclear whether the citizens of Jackson ever contemplated such an action or why they would have. What is important for the present purpose is that Confederate soldiers anxious about their position and role in southern life should cast their concerns in terms of the right to walk the public streets on an equal basis with the rest of the white community.

In Danville, disagreement between the races over sidewalk protocol often turned city strolls into wrestling matches. William P. Graves, a tobacco merchant and a Democrat who was elected mayor in 1884, described walking on Danville streets in territorial terms, as a personal battle for space:

> Frequently, in walking the streets I have encountered negroes, more particularly negro women; I have generally turned to the right, and I have very frequently come in contact with them. I first gave the way, but I found if I continued to do it they would press me off the sidewalk altogether, and I generally [walk] straight along on the right hand, and if I come in contact with any one, why, they generally give the way; I [don't] strike her with my fist or anything of that kind; I generally strike them with my shoulder, and pass on; I have had frequent occurrences of that sort.[54]

Historians of the American South in recent years have argued that African American appropriation of Victorian gender roles and white refusal to validate black gender differentiation were part of a broader struggle over the legitimization of black manhood and citizenship and over economic and sexual control of black women.[55] Self-confident or aggressive behavior by African American women—whether on the streets or in the kitchen—bothered whites not only because of what it said about black women but also because it simultaneously reflected black men's new identities as patriarchs and citizens, capable of protecting and exploiting black women through individual action or the law. This explains in great measure the tendency of both whites and blacks in Danville to interpret sidewalk shoving matches as political statements. When "leading white men" in Danville later recalled witnessing altercations between the races on sidewalks, they associated the disputes with Readjuster rule. William N. Ruffin, a real estate agent, insisted that black-white relations had not always been so contentious: such incidents had occurred only since Danville's black population had been "under Readjuster dictation or training."[56] Blacks also linked public altercations in Danville with politics but put the blame on white shoulders. Walter Gay, a black resident, reported being shoved off the sidewalk by white Democrats.[57]

It is impossible to say whether public interactions between Danville's white and black citizens were more acrimonious under the Readjusters than in the 1870s or the immediate postwar years, or whether the origins of the tension of 1879–83 lay in that earlier period. The local newspaper is the likeliest source of stories about black-white relations, but a fire at the turn of the century destroyed the office of the *Danville Register,* taking with it back copies for the nineteenth-century. Furthermore, unless an arrest was made, street altercations of the sort documented for the Readjuster era are unlikely to surface in existing police records. Only the records of the U.S. Senate's investigation of the causes of the Danville Riot permit a partial reconstruction of life on the streets under the Readjusters and an educated guess as to what degree Readjuster rule, through its legitimation of black political power, resulted in a recalibration of social relationships in Danville.

What can be said with assurance is that Readjuster rule put black-white relationships in a new light and opened up new interpretative strategies for altercations across the color line. In both very real and figurative senses, black and white people in Readjuster Danville jostled for position every time they faced each other in public, and both whites and blacks in Danville associated what they considered aggressive behavior with opposing political allegiances. This conflation of the social and political effects of biracial rule was manifest in the *Lynchburg Democratic Campaign*'s complaint that "[w]hite women are rudely shoved off the pavements by dirty buck Negroes and encouraged to do it by the truculent Negro policemen appointed by the Mahone ring."[58] These redefined social relationships were themselves political insofar as they seemed to have been caused by a political revolution and were perceived to be, as the Danville Circular suggests, susceptible to reversal through politics.

On November 3, 1883, white men repossessed Danville—politically and physically—through violence. In a dramatic affirmation of the power of the white minority population to negate the rights of the African American majority, white citizens reinscribed the boundaries of black "place" in a bloody confrontation on Main Street.

The multiple, contradictory, and fundamentally incompatible versions of the riot produced by its participants and interpreters underscore the inability of white and black residents to agree about what happened in Danville. The contemporary disagreement about the riot centered on disputes over manners, honor, and status and who controlled public space. These issues led to the riot, and no consensus between whites and blacks could be reached after the fact—as an early historian of Danville acknowledged. "The Danville Riot . . . was nothing more nor less than a street fight between whites and blacks," wrote Beverley Munford in 1905, "the immediate occasion for which was an inconsiderate jostling of a white man by a colored man, or vice versa, on the sidewalk."[59]

We can say more than that about the violence in Danville, though Munford's brevity is instructive. The event that resulted in an armed revolt by Danville's white anti-Readjuster minority began as an altercation over street etiquette.[60] Around lunchtime on Saturday, November 3, Charles D. Noel, a young white grocery clerk, was walking up Main Street when he stumbled over the foot of one of two young black men traveling in the opposite direction.[61] According to Noel, he turned to the black man whose foot he had stumbled over, Hense Lawson, a waiter, "and asked him what did he do that for. His reply was, in a very insolent manner: 'I was getting out of the way of a lady, and a white lady at that.'"[62] Noel told Lawson that was all right and continued on his way. Only a few steps farther, he heard Lawson's black companion, Davis Lewellyn, a tobacco worker, tell Lawson that it did not matter if Noel thought it was "all right"—Lawson had apologized and was in no need of pardon.[63] At this point, Noel turned and struck

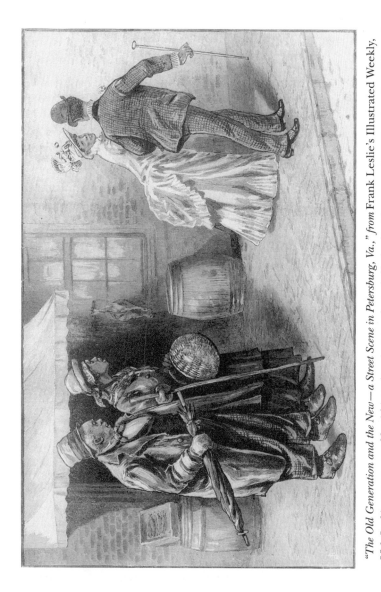

"The Old Generation and the New—a Street Scene in Petersburg, Va.," from Frank Leslie's Illustrated Weekly, 1886. In this cartoon, an older African American couple, probably freedpeople, comments on the separation of lines of race and class under the Readjustors. Referring to a well-dressed black man and woman strolling past, the man asks, "Whar am de white folks now, Dinah? Jes' look dar: arn't dey a-bilin' along!" (The Library of Virginia)

Lewellyn, who fought back, hitting Noel and twice knocking him off the sidewalk into the gutter. Seeing that he was beaten, Noel left, and Lawson and Lewellyn did the same.

What did Noel and Lewellyn fight over? It was Lawson, not Lewellyn, who stepped on Noel's foot, violating Noel's personal space,[64] but this was put right by Lawson's explanation—though, with its implicit denial of a natural equation between "lady" and "*white* lady," the apology may have irritated Noel more than it appeased him. Noel appears to have been angered by what he might have termed Lewellyn's "insolence," that is, his remark that it made no difference whether Noel was satisfied with Lawson's explanation because Lawson had apologized and the matter was closed. Lewellyn's lack of concern for Noel's opinion drove the white man into a rage.[65]

Tempers were running high that Saturday. The night before, William E. Sims, chairman of the Readjuster Party in Pittsylvania County, had spoken in Danville and denounced the Danville Circular. The crowd was variously described as placid or whooping (depending on the politics of the observer), and Sims was "as severe as could be" in his criticism of the creators of the circular. In fact, he outraged whites in Danville by invoking the language of honor to denounce the signers of the circular, calling them "liars, scoundrels and cowards!"[66]

On Saturday, November 3, the day after Sims's speech, the Third Ward Democratic Club met at the Opera House at the request of George C. Cabell, Danville's Democratic congressman. The meeting was called to reaffirm the truth of the Danville Circular in the face of Sims's denunciation.[67] That Saturday afternoon nearly every white Democrat in Danville was cloistered in the Opera House, as Cabell was determined to get the signature of each and every one of them.[68]

While the Democrats were meeting, Davis Lewellyn was knocking Charles Noel into the gutter. After the fight, Noel stopped at the Opera House to check on the assembly and discussed the trouble on Main Street with his friends George Lea and W. R. Taylor. Noel decided to confront Lewellyn, taking his friends along for support. Walking down Main Street, the three white men approached Lewellyn, Lawson, and a third black man, James Love, from behind. Noel grabbed someone by the collar and ended up, not with Lewellyn, but with Lawson instead.[69]

As Noel struck Lawson, Taylor and Lea moved (as they put it later) to insure "fair play."[70] Lea brandished his pistol to keep Love and

Lewellyn from interfering. As "Noel had the advantage of two or three inches of length in the arm," Lawson got the worst of the fight. At this point, as was routine with a street fight, a crowd began to gather. Because it was Saturday afternoon, the traditional market time for African Americans in Danville, there were many people—mostly blacks—on the street.[71] Lawson was bleeding profusely;[72] somebody shouted "murder," and R. J. Adams, an African American policeman, came running. Adams moved to separate Noel and Lawson, identifying himself as a police officer, but Lea resisted. Jeff Corbin, a white man, affirmed Adams's office, and the policeman separated Lawson and Noel and sent them to wash off the blood.[73]

The fight over, a small group of two or three white men and a half-dozen black men loitered; things seemed to be quieting down. This was all routine in a medium-sized southern city. But suddenly George Adams, a black man (no relation to Adams, the policeman), tackled Lea and rolled him into the gutter in an attempt to wrestle away his pistol. Adams failed to disarm Lea, got up, and ran away. As Adams ran, Lea shot at him from the gutter.[74] Hearing the shot, more people gathered. Officer Adams blew his whistle for reinforcements. This brought a second black policeman, Walter Withers, and a white policeman, Charles Freeman. Black men, women, and children drifted over,[75] and white men began to come down from the Opera House. A white man, Joel Oliver, captain of the local Democratic militia, approached Officer Adams and ordered him to disperse the crowd. E. M. Hatcher seconded Oliver's order, saying, "Damn it, make these niggers get off the street." Officer Freeman (the white policeman) responded that the black crowd was doing nothing and "if you all don't bother them they won't bother you."[76]

While the white men on the sidewalk were demanding that the street be cleared, the blacks in the street called for the arrest of Lea—the man who had fired at George Adams—for violating the concealed weapons law.[77] All three policemen and a few white men were circulating among the black crowd, which had grown to perhaps a hundred people, asking the blacks to leave. The twenty or so white men on the sidewalk were angry about (and perhaps a bit afraid of) the size of the black crowd, and they exhibited their pistols as they repeated their demand that the people go home. But the blacks in the street were defiant: they felt that an arrest was called for and "were not willing to move off, on the order of the white men."[78] The crowd "intended to have their rights," meaning the right to have Lea arrested for shooting at George Adams and to remain on the street until that happened. When Officer Freeman pleaded with the blacks to go home, they replied that they would not be run over and told him to make the white men leave.[79]

There seemed to be a standoff. A young Democrat, Walter Holland, perhaps thinking to join the men urging the blacks to disperse, stepped off the sidewalk and walked through part of the crowd toward a policeman. When Holland was a few steps away from the sidewalk, the white men raised their pistols and opened fire on the crowd. Some reported that they had heard a command to "fire!"; others said that the shooting began spontaneously, with no warning. Members of the white group later testified that at first they fired in the air; nevertheless, Holland fell on that first volley, shot through the back of the head. Between seventy-five and two hundred rounds were fired in the space of two or three minutes. When the smoke cleared, three black men, among them Terry Smith and Edward Davis, lay dead beside Holland on the street. A fourth black man died later.[80]

The crowd began to run at the first shot, and by the time the firing ended the street was nearly empty. A few white men pursued the retreating blacks and attacked a number of people. Their targets appear to have been prominent black citizens. Charles Adams, brother of police officer Robert Adams, left the safety of Nicholas and Hessberg's store to calm his horses. William P. Graves approached Adams and leveled his pistol at him. According to his later testimony, Adams attempted to mollify Graves through a show of deference. "I said, pulling off my hat to him, 'For God's sake, Capt. Graves, don't shoot; I am not doing anything.'" Graves shot anyway, breaking Adams's arm, which he had raised to protect his head. Jack Redd, a black Readjuster leader, was beaten and kicked, and the white crowd was preparing to shoot him when Congressman Cabell intervened and stopped them.[81] Meanwhile, the men who remained at the Opera House, hearing shots, poured out of the building onto the street despite the efforts of the Democratic organizers to remain in session until all the men had signed the new affidavit validating the Danville Circular.[82]

With the streets empty of African Americans, the white men of Danville organized themselves into patrols to augment the local militia. Despite Readjuster mayor J. H. Johnston's plea that "all good citizens . . . resume their usual avocations; [and] cease appearing upon the streets armed with shot-guns or other weapons," all that afternoon and night groups of armed white men patrolled the streets, sending a clear message of possession.[83] Sophie Powell, a Danville resident, testified that squads of white men armed with shotguns policed her neighborhood on the weekend of November 3 and 4. She said that at night she and her family could hear sounds of gunfire "all around" and that "we were surely scared & did not know when we would be killed."[84]

In the election held the Tuesday following the massacre, the Democrats carried the state, gaining majorities in the white mountain counties that had previously voted Readjuster.[85] But the importance of the Danville Riot lies less in its effect on the 1883 election than in the stories told about it. The Democratic victory in Virginia was narrow, and the violence in Danville provided William Mahone with a convenient basis for congressional investigation into fraud and intimidation at the polls. In an attempt to have the election results overturned, the Readjusters portrayed the massacre in Danville as the centerpiece of a Democratic campaign strategy to overthrow the coalition through violence. In response, the Democrats crafted a narrative that characterized their actions as self-defense, making their case in terms of honor and courtesy. They denied that they had shot into an unarmed crowd of black men, women, and children. Recasting the violence as a struggle among equals, the Democrats insisted that the black crowd in the street had been armed and had fired shots and that the white men on the sidewalk had responded in their own defense. One participant lectured his Readjuster uncle that the men who fired "were not bullies and rowdees but were in the main your equals in every particular which goes to form honorable manhood & integrity."[86]

Shifting the blame for the violence from Danville's white to its black population was central to Congressman Cabell's response to the allegation that the Democrats had planned the violence as part of their campaign strategy. "The charge that the disturbance at Danville was premeditated," Cabell fumed, "is false and absurd. The truth is that Mahone's orators had inflamed the minds of the colored people to a dangerous pitch." In Danville that Saturday afternoon the streets had been crowded with working-class blacks "influenced by liquor and bad political teaching" and looking for a fight. Conceding that "each race was in an excited state of mind," Cabell viewed the "row" as spontaneous, unexceptional, and the result of the coalition's lamentable effect on manners. Whoever's manners were most lacking, Cabell was probably right about the spontaneity of the explosion of violence.[87]

Cabell's statement anticipated the report of the Committee of Forty, the predominantly Democratic local committee impaneled to investigate the causes of the violence. After examining thirty-seven witnesses, the committee concluded that the black crowd had been armed and that the white men had acted in self-defense. The melee was presented as the natural result of coalition rule, which had encouraged, by appointing African Americans to public office, Danville's black population to become "rude, insolent and intolerant to the white citizens of the town."[88]

The report of the grand jury, formed to determine individual responsibility for the five deaths, paralleled the findings of the Committee of Forty, including the charge that Danville's black community "rushed upon the scene from all quarters, advancing upon the whites with drawn pistols."[89] The jury unanimously concluded that the whites used their firearms in self-defense "and by their courage and pluck in standing up against such odds saved the lives of hundreds of people in this city." No indictments were issued, and no one was ever tried for the violence on November 3. The solitary African American member of the grand jury, Preston Watkins, later testified that no evidence was ever put before the jury that black men had carried firearms but that he had assented to the report because he "never expected" to ascertain the true facts, saying, "It was a heart-rending mystery to me, and I wanted to get off it as soon as possible. . . . [W]e had seen men dead and of course somebody was responsible for it, but we didn't think we would get any nearer to it."[90]

Investigations of violence in the New South have focused on lynching, which was largely a rural phenomenon.[91] But postbellum southern cities also sustained high levels of personal violence.[92] Particularly in times of black political influence, violence erupted into riots and other forms of mass action. Many of these disturbances were organized attempts by whites to prevent or discourage African American participation in politics—which lent a degree of credibility to the Readjusters' claim of Democratic premeditation in Danville. Others, though, were spontaneous and were commonly precipitated by disputes between black and white city dwellers over the control of public spaces, as, for instance, in the 1866 and 1867 riots over segregated streetcars in Richmond and the 1866 Norfolk Riot set off by a parade of black militiamen celebrating the Civil Rights Bill. A third example occurred in March 1875, following passage of the Civil Rights Act of 1875, when a near-riot erupted in Richmond after two black men, in accordance with the new law, sat in the white section of the Richmond Theater.[93]

Of course, not all altercations across the color line ended in riots. An interracial fistfight in Charleston in 1876, which began under circumstances similar to those of the Danville massacre, was limited to the immediate participants. Still, the potential for communal violence was never far from the surface of life on the streets of the postwar urban South. For example, in Atlanta in 1881 two hundred blacks fought white police officers after they had clubbed a black man accused of pushing a white woman off the sidewalk.[94]

Mob violence such as the massacre in Danville or the Atlanta police riot undercut the efforts of urban leaders to project an image of an orderly New South. After the November 3 violence, the Danville Common Council, in an attempt to legislate civility, proposed a fine for any pedestrian not yielding to the right on city sidewalks. In its effort to define a uniform and equitable standard of behavior on sidewalks, this color-blind rule might have formed the basis in Danville for a common urban identity. Such a measure, based on the collective ownership of the city by its citizens, was diametrically opposed to the hierarchical predispositions of white residents, and the Committee on Public Ordinances rejected the proposal as unenforceable. In a postscript to its decision, the committee expressed the belief "that in future the general rules of common politeness will be observed and that we will not need such an ordinance."[95]

The Danville Common Council's rejection of a color-blind standard for street etiquette goes to the heart of the dispute over public space between whites and blacks in the postwar urban South. For African Americans, white civility toward blacks in a public arena stood first and foremost as the marker of black equality. For southern whites, such behavior meant precisely the same thing, and such gestures were often seen as tantamount to admitting defeat and dishonor. This was exactly the meaning that filmmaker D. W. Griffith meant to convey in the street encounter between Silas Lynch and (future Klansman) Colonel Ben Cameron in *Birth of a Nation*. Again and again, both in primary historical documents and in contemporary popular representations of the era, altercations over sidewalk space serve as a metaphor for broader questions of racial domination and subordination. Thus did African American author Charles W. Chesnutt satirize white concerns in his 1901 novel *The Marrow of Tradition*. Much as the Danville Circular did, Chesnutt combined white social, political, and economic anxieties. As he has a member of the white elite remark, "Things are in an awful condition! A negro justice of the peace has opened an office on Market Street, and only yesterday summoned a white man to appear before him. Negro lawyers get most of the business in the criminal court. Last evening a group of young white ladies, going quietly along the street arm-in-arm, were forced off the sidewalk by a crowd of negro girls. . . . Something must be done, and that quickly!"[96]

Southern whites' insistence on enforcing race-based standards of social deference reflected their disinclination to recognize the civic equality of African Americans, just as blacks' insistence on white civility reflected African American civic claims and revealed the impossibility of marking the boundary between public and private with any surety. Sometimes the refusal of whites to recognize the public equality of blacks resulted in resistance to African American authority. One such example occurred during the Danville Riot. As George Lea later explained when asked why he had leveled his gun at Officer R. J. Adams after Adams had attempted to separate Hense Lawson and Charles Noel, "He [Adams] came up with the rest of the niggers." On being persuaded that Adams was a policeman, Lea had lost no time in attempting to take charge, "ordering," as he testified, Officer Adams to separate Lawson and Noel. When asked what right he had to command an officer of the law, Lea answered, "Well, we generally speak that way to that class of people down there [in Virginia]. We are in the habit of ordering them. . . . I would not speak to them in the same way I would speak to a white man."[97] More often, the white urge toward domination revealed itself in small, routine, and seemingly insignificant ways, such as a calculated bump with a shoulder or an imperious demand for an "explanation" when jostled on the street.

The point here is not that black and white southerners could not understand each other because they spoke different social languages, but just the opposite. The issue was not conflicting standards of civility: black and white men and women agreed on the meaning of civil behavior. Black southerners wanted the rules of civil behavior to apply equally to white and black alike, however, while white southerners continued to promote two opposing standards of conduct—one for relations among whites and another for relations across the color line. In the clash between honor and equality, the discourse of civility itself became a primary mode of confrontation for black and white southerners. It was the very convergence of black and white opinion on markers of status and face in the postwar urban South that turned public behavior into a zero-sum game where one person's gain was another's clear loss.

The social and political consequences of this disagreement over civil behavior become clear when the theorization and representation of public behavior in the urban spaces of the postwar South are contrasted with those observed by Friedrich Engels in mid-nineteenth-century England. Peering at the crowded streets of London, Engels reflected that as "people of all classes and ranks of society jostle past one another . . . their only agreement is a tacit one: that everyone should keep to the right of the pavement, so as not to impede the stream of people moving in the opposite direction."[98] No such agreement was forged along urban southern sidewalks because racial divisions precluded it. In the postbellum South, fractured along the race line, there could be no collective ownership of the streets, no space for the sorts of collective action feared by urban elites and lionized by champions of the people. In the absence of a common urban identity—as reflected in the inability of city dwellers to recognize one another as part of a collective and conform to uniform tacit standards of acceptable public behavior—the urban white leaders of the region looked for an alternative way to end urban violence and forge a race-based civility.

They found it in Jim Crow. Legal segregation of the races, through demarcation of the public space allotted to each race, was meant to provide a clear answer to the question of who owned the streets in the New South and, in the process, end extralegal violence in southern cities.[99] Certainly, segregation limited the opportunities for conflict between black and white urban southerners. Segregation greatly reduced the possibility of an urban lynching such as the one that occurred in 1900 in Augusta, Georgia. In that city, a well-known white man was killed by a black man following a dispute over seating on a streetcar. The killing prompted both the lynching of the black man and the city council's passage of a Jim Crow law that separated blacks and whites on streetcars.[100]

Around the turn of the century, what had been an open and public conflict—white-black altercation on the streets hammered out in an agonistic political climate—was forced underground by segregation and became the "hidden transcript" of opposition to Jim Crow. Yet, despite the Jim Crow laws, the sidewalks remained a juncture between overt and covert resistance, and encounters between the races on the public streets revealed the incomplete dominance of white supremacy. Although the color line could be drawn with precision on trains and in theaters, one's position on the public streets and sidewalks was always ambiguous.[101] Spatial ambiguity promoted conflict between the races in two ways. As one of the few public spaces that defied racial segregation by law, the streets had an etiquette that required enforcement by individuals, not by civil authorities. Second, the ambiguity of street space intensified interaction between the races—was a violation of white racial etiquette by a black man or woman intentional or not?—and nourished in dominant white minds fear of the revenge fantasies of the weak. The intensity of white anxieties over breaches in the color line is revealed in the way street encounters between whites and "uppity" blacks became, for white southerners, symbolic of all that was wrong with the New South.

It is appropriate to refer to Thomas Dixon's 1902 novel *The Leopard's Spots* in this context—for, as the seventeenth-century French writer Claude Fauchet reminded his readers, "Any writer, including the most wretched, can be occasionally useful, at least as a witness of his own age."[102] Dixon's portrayal of black "insolence" and white violence in the fictional town of Independence, North Carolina, has rightly been read as a thinly disguised version of the 1898 Wilmington Riot. The standard historical narrative of the massacre turns on an editorial in which black journalist Alexander Manly, in the process of rebutting Rebecca Latimer Felton's defense of lynching on the grounds of black rape of white women, suggested that sex between black men and white women was often consensual.[103] When set in context—black North Carolinians had achieved unprecedented political power via their participation in a third-party government similar in composition and goals to that of Danville under the Readjusters—white revolution seems explicable, if not justifiable.[104] But in his re-creation of the riot, Thomas Dixon did not center his story on the Manly editorial.[105]

In *The Leopard's Spots*, which is set during the Spanish-American War in the context of biracial rule in North Carolina, a black soldier walking down the street in Independence refuses to yield the sidewalk to a young white woman and her escort. Instead, the black man bumps into the woman, "jostling her roughly," and her white companion knocks the black soldier down and beats him to death. The death of the African American soldier enrages local blacks, who form a mob with the intention of killing the hero of Dixon's novel, a white supremacist politician named Gaston. The black mob fails to kill Gaston, but its action convinces the town's white citizens that the political and social deference of blacks must be restored through violence.[106] In Thomas Dixon's version of the Wilmington Riot, it is not whites' outrage over the Manly editorial but disagreement over social conventions between the races, and the broader implications of that disagreement, that leads to violence.

The altercation on the sidewalk between the black soldier and the white couple portrayed in *The Leopard's Spots* did not in fact occur, but its "poetic plausibility," to borrow a phrase from Carlo Ginzburg, is punctuated by the complaints of white Wilmington residents prior to the November 1898 violence.[107] In addition to reports of increased black criminality, biracial rule in Wilmington was deemed responsible for the deterioration of African American manners where whites were concerned. According to the *New Bern Journal,* black men liked to obstruct the sidewalk, forcing white women to abandon the walk and pass in the street. Whites portrayed the behavior of black women as even more outrageous. In an instance cited by the *Wilmington Star,* a black woman forced a white woman off the sidewalk and then, to underscore her intent, hit "the white woman over the shoulder with an umbrella." A black man standing nearby shouted his approval. On another occasion "a colored woman passing along the street insolently shoved her elbow into the face of a white man who was standing in his yard leaning over the fence."[108]

By the time *The Leopard's Spots* was published, open confrontation between black and white southerners on city streets was largely a thing of the past. Implacable white hostility toward African American self-assertion—political, economic, and social—had driven black resistance underground. By the early twentieth century, the sort of behavior that was an overt act of defiance in Danville could be exhibited openly only under the cover of childhood or lunacy. Even then, the sensations of such moments, however fleeting, exposed the submerged possibilities of daily existence, as the young Katharine DuPre Lumpkin discovered in South Carolina around 1905:

We knew the streets were the white man's wherever he chose to walk; that a Negro who moved out into the gutter to let us pass was in our eyes a "good darkey." I could have been hardly more than eight when a little Negro girl of our age, passing a friend and me, showed a disposition to take her half of the sidewalk. We did not give ground—we were whites! Her arm brushed against my companion's. She turned on the Negro child furiously. "Move over there, you dirty black nigger!" I know why this recollection stayed with me while others did not. It outraged us so because this particular colored child did not shrink or run, but flared back at us with a stinging retort, remaining dead in her tracks, defying us, and we had no choice left us but to move on.[109]

5

MAKING BLACK WHITE & WHITE BLACK

The Politics of Racial Identity

Classifications—social, racial, sexual—are constantly disputed in everyday social interactions and in the civic and political sphere. Danville's citizens argued about such classifications on sidewalks. Other Virginians clashed in more esoteric settings. Legislation and court cases involving the definition and establishment of racial identity are two of the best vantage points from which to see classification in movement. Take the prominent example of Virginia's various attempts to define "nonwhite" for the purpose of antimiscegenation legislation. In 1705 a "mulatto" was said to possess at least one-eighth African ancestry. When the 1705 act was amended in 1785, the percentage of African ancestry necessary to be defined as nonwhite was raised to one-fourth. This meant that those who had been classified as mulatto under the 1705 act by virtue of a single African American great-grandparent might, in 1785, claim status as "white." The twentieth-century descendants of many of these nineteenth-century families crossed back again in 1910, however, when the General Assembly redefined black persons as having one-sixteenth or more "negro blood." The fractional loopholes of this law were drawn even tighter in 1924, when Virginia adopted the "one drop" rule, which required that persons designated "white" have "no trace whatsoever of any blood other than Caucasian."[1]

Racial recategorization by legal fiat was not a strictly southern occupation. For an example from the national level, we may look to the federal government's oscillating attempts to categorize racially the nation's assorted European immigrant groups. The Naturalization Law of 1790 reserved naturalized citizenship for "whites."[2] But who was white? In 1909 the United States declared that Armenians were "Asiatics" and thus ineligible for citizenship.[3] A year later the federal courts held that Indians from the Asian subcontinent were Caucasians and entitled to all the rights of "free white persons." The Armenian decision was overturned almost immediately, and Armenians were granted white racial status for cultural and historical reasons—because, in the words of the decision, "the outlook of their civilization has been toward Europe." Immigrants from India apparently looked the wrong way. They were stripped of their citizenship in 1923 because they were not (or no longer) "white" according to the "understanding of the common man."[4]

The malleability of racial identity visible in legislation and legal decisions has been useful to biologists and social scientists who point out that there is little genetic justification for speaking of "race."[5] Historians, anthropologists, and cultural critics of various academic backgrounds have articulated increasingly precise and persuasive definitions of race that are centered around the linkages between social interactions and the construction of individual identity. A growing number of historians now consider race a social relationship, made "within the ordinary and everyday," articulated in the "small gestures of everyday life."[6] W. E. B. Du Bois demonstrated this way of defining race back in 1923, the year that Indians were declared nonwhite. "The black man," Du Bois said, when pressed for a definition, "is a person who must ride 'Jim Crow' in Georgia."[7]

Even as scholars debunk biological definitions of race, however, we continue to assume that the "common man" employs a strictly biological or phenotypical model of race. As Evelyn Brooks Higginbotham has declared, the late-twentieth-century common man "knows race when he sees it."[8] This chapter argues the opposite for the late nineteenth century. Far from being self-confident about the "natural" boundaries of race, Gilded Age Virginians, especially "white" Virginians, were extremely anxious about race because they—like Du Bois—saw it as at least partly constructed through social, cultural, and political meanings.

Contemporary legal decisions contributed to such anxieties. In 1892, for instance, the Virginia Supreme Court of Appeals determined a man's race posthumously. In the civil case of *Scott v. Raub,* Sarah Raub claimed the inheritance of her father James Scott against her uncle, Robert Scott. Raub was born in 1862 to Ann Settles, a slave of mixed heritage who cohabited with James Scott, to whom she had been hired out by her master. The union was not recognized as a legal marriage since Settles, as a slave, was incapable of entering into a contract. When James Scott died intestate in 1888, Sarah Raub argued in the Albemarle County Circuit Court and before the Virginia Court of Appeals that her father had been a free man of color and that as such his relationship with Ann Settles had been formalized by an 1866 act of the Virginia General Assembly. This act recognized unions between slaves and blacks begun before emancipation as marriages under the law and conferred legitimacy on the children born of such unions.[9] James Scott's brother Robert disputed Raub's depiction of her father as black, insisting that his brother, like himself, was white. As a white man, Robert Scott argued, James's relationship with Ann Settles violated Virginia's law prohibiting interracial marriage,[10] and the child born of this liaison was illegitimate. Sarah Raub, the bastard issue of this forbidden union, could not inherit.

Under Virginia law at the time, anyone possessing one-fourth "negro blood" was defined as "colored." In other words, having one black grandparent made one black as well. Although admitting that "the evidence tends to show that these people, both James and Ann, had less than one-fourth of negro blood," the Court of Appeals also conceded that "there is no clear proof offered, and probably none attainable, as to the degree of colored blood possessed by either one." Despite having declared in 1885 that no one should be presumed black "until he is proved to be such," the court nonetheless ruled in this case that James Scott was not white and that Sarah Raub was his legitimate heir.[11] The basis for this decision was not genealogical but social. As Justice Benjamin Watkins Lacy explained, both Ann Settles and James Scott were "classed as colored persons, socially speaking." Both had apparently belonged to a church "established and attended by colored persons generally," and James Scott had first voted "when other colored people voted, and not before." Ann Settles, for her part, had "always passed as a colored person," an argument that implies that she was light-skinned enough to have lived exclusively among whites after emancipation had she chosen to do so.[12] We can only guess at Robert Scott's reaction to the court's decision, as he found himself proclaimed the brother of a black man.

In his judgment in *Scott v. Raub*, Benjamin Watkins Lacy defined race in Du Boisian terms. "I base my opinion [regarding Scott's race],"

Lacy wrote, "upon the privileges he enjoyed." Lacy's (admittedly circular) reasoning reveals an important social fact about the South at the end of the nineteenth century: in that place, at that time, racial identity was intimately wrapped up with "privileges," social and political. Where did Scott worship? Lacy asked. Did he vote? Such questions highlight something that Erving Goffman has noted: "While it may be true that the individual has a unique self all his own, evidence of this possession is thoroughly a product of joint ceremonial labor" between a person and his social group. In other words, identity—including racial identity—is situational and historical, created and sustained through social interactions.[13] This does not mean that the creation of social identity is a process of free play: as this chapter will show, symbolic actions gain meaning from context; identity, rather than being a question entirely of self-fashioning, is one of disputation and negotiation. It may be useful to think of this as a tension between self-fashioning and ascription, a tension that is never fully resolved in one direction or another.

As far as racial identity in the South is concerned, novelists have seen this more clearly than historians.[14] Confusion over identity and the loss of identity have been major themes in southern literature since the Civil War. The problem of racial knowledge has been approached by such authors as George Washington Cable, Charles Chesnutt, Frances Watkins Harper, Kate Chopin, Thomas Dixon Jr., Mark Twain, Ralph Ellison, and William Faulkner, who all concerned themselves with questions of racial identity and blood. Indeed, the protagonist of Faulkner's *Light in August* (1932), Joe Christmas, may be seen as the allegorical southerner: born a "white" man, lynched as a "black," Christmas is tormented throughout his short life by his unclear racial ancestry. Unable to fall back on appearance (Christmas is "parchment-colored"), the citizens of the fictional town of Jefferson rely finally on gossip and hearsay in an attempt to fix Joe's identity.[15]

When we look carefully at the politics of race in the nineteenth century, it becomes clear that real-life southerners also supplemented a biological model of race with behavioral definitions. In a region full of "parchment-colored" people governed by a legal system that defined race in fractions, the clearest indicator of identity was often, as the court in *Scott v. Raub* acknowledged, social actions and affiliations. This is not to say that contemporaries did not make biological arguments. Such arguments were an important part of the construction of white racial ideology and identity. But they were only one part, and one that did not inspire enough confidence about the integrity of racial categories to preclude great anxiety about other, more obviously cultural, aspects of racial identity.

Contemporaries had as much difficulty pinpointing the boundaries between such categories as political identity, gender identity, and racial identity as historians have had. In the previous two chapters we have seen why the drawing of certain boundaries was so important to the Readjuster coalition's success and how black Readjusters and non-Readjuster whites challenged both those boundaries and their social and political meanings. The Readjusters' initial success in separating an interracial political sphere from a segregated private world depended on drawing and maintaining clear boundaries between stable categories of partisanship, race, and gender. But these categories of identity were neither stable nor independent; by changing some cultural and political variables, interracial alliance in Virginia affected the definition of others. To the surprise of the Readjusters, changes in partisan affiliation altered the definition of whiteness—affecting even the biological conception of race. Nearly always against their will, coalitionists' new political allegiances demonstrated the reciprocal relationship between individual knowledge about oneself and one's identity and public construction and affirmation of both.[16] Once we realize just how dynamic the relationship between categories of identity was, it becomes possible to take the racial rhetoric of Readjuster Virginia more seriously, and to see it as an indicator of the ongoing process of complex ideological formation rather than merely as a chauvinistic attempt to cover up the "real" interests—in other words, the material or economic interests—at stake in any political contest.

Of course, every "white" Virginian had a material, cultural, and political interest in his or her whiteness. Even before legal segregation, whiteness had its privileges. But in the 1880s the wages of whiteness were not yet standardized and they were not purely material. Dignity, "honor," the right to consider oneself an autonomous subject and citizen—these qualities were not bound exclusively to whiteness after 1865.[17] The social and political worth of whiteness remained in flux in the late-nineteenth-century South. Such instability was a constant irritant to the Readjuster coalition and a source of opportunity to its opponents.

The "race issue," as white southerners put it (or, as African Americans liked to phrase it, "the white problem") was always present in postwar life, but it did not always carry the same political charge. In the beginning, the Readjusters were able to kindle an affinity of interest between white and black Virginians centered around shared social and economic priorities. But could white and black Virginians change their political behavior and alliances without altering other axes of identity? Certain groups in the post–Civil War South—among them the Readjusters—saw the liberal political community as fundamentally unrelated to other human associations. Other southerners—in this case, Democrats and some black Readjusters—stressed the essential interrelatedness of political allegiance and other forms of identity. Although the conclusions reached here may be generalized to other parts of the South, the inner workings of the Readjuster coalition in Virginia provide an especially good vantage point from which to view the intersection of African American political power and the white social and political imagination.

When William Mahone cast his lot with the Republicans in the Senate in 1881, he effectively transformed the partisan identity of his white followers from dissident Democrats into Republicans. This transformation was no small thing. Wartime Republican governor Francis H. Pierpont warned Mahone of the danger that this switch in political identity involved for white Virginians, most of whom hated the party of abolition: "You have in Va. a great work yet to perform. The name is the great scarecrow now in the way. I don't know that you fully appreciate the difficulty in getting men to adopt a new name and especially one that has been so odious. . . . But Readjusters now have to act with Republicans in Congress and it will continue to be pressed on all Demo[ocrats] in Va. who are acting with the New Party [that they are, in effect, Republicans]."[18]

Shrewd distribution of patronage eased white Readjusters' affiliation with the Republicans and reinforced partisan loyalty to the coalition. At the same time, many white Readjusters resisted any construction of the coalition as revolving around African American interests. Such resistance often manifested itself in local disputes over patronage distribution and black influence in party affairs. Despite official pronouncements directing the sharing of power along race lines, some whites rigged the selection process for local leadership committees to favor white Readjusters. "We have two kinds of readjusters in this county, roman nosed and dishfaced," the white chairman of the Tazewell County Executive Committee informed Mahone. "[F]or this reason I will not select [the committee] until Court. I want to be sure I select from the roman nosed tribe."[19] Even so, by 1881 a good number of whites who had been with the movement since 1879 were being passed over for patronage positions in favor of black men in the interest of cementing the Republican-Readjuster alliance. More than one angry letter to Mahone complained about the favoring of these "side-door seekers."[20]

White opinion on black influence in the coalition spanned from professions of complete equality among men that emanated from a few Republican Readjusters to fears of "Negro domination" that prompted Readjuster congressional candidate John S. Wise, in black-majority Petersburg, to reassure his audience that there was not "too much nigger in the Readjuster party." More representative of the Readjusters' white rank and file was the view of "Old Commonwealth." Writing from Rockingham County, which was represented in Congress by Readjuster John Paul, Old Commonwealth proclaimed in 1881 that his district was "not ready for colored supremacy, although we do not deny to the colored brother any of his legal and constitutional rights."[21]

The position of Old Commonwealth on the problem of black equality and power was not far removed from that of many Democrats or of those white Readjusters who jumped ship after Mahone's alliance with the Republicans. In 1882 John "Parson" Massey, a former Readjuster with patronage and political grievances against Mahone, challenged John Wise in the race for congressman-at-large.[22] Outlining the reasons why white Readjusters should vote for him, Massey preached the primacy of identity politics. Like Old Commonwealth, Massey claimed to support the rights of black men under the law. At the same time, however, he asserted an identity of interest between all white men and the Democratic Party, arguing that he favored "white men being the governing power in Virginia." The *Staunton Spectator,* a leading Valley paper, had been making Massey's point for a year. Combining race and gender language, the *Spectator* insisted that "the question is, whether Virginia is to be ruled, in effect, by negroes or by white men."[23]

It is certainly possible to read such rhetoric as a simple demographic statement: the coalition's membership, if not its elected representatives or leadership cohort, was African American by a clear majority.[24] It was easy to argue, as the Democrats did, that Readjuster rule meant rule by a black-majority party: in the local vernacular, Readjuster rule was "Negro rule." But there were other layers to such language. When the Democrats equated Readjuster rule with black rule, they assaulted white coalitionists' race and gender identity. White Readjusters understood that their opponents' underlying claim was that white Readjusters were, somehow, no longer white men.

The Readjusters had been vulnerable to race baiting since the first days of the coalition, but before 1882 Democratic attempts to bring race into play were easily deflected. In the 1881 gubernatorial canvass, for instance, Democratic hopes that white voters would privilege race chauvinism over economic self-interest came to nothing. When Democratic newspapers read in the white-majority Valley and western counties accused white Readjuster voters of deserting their race, the Readjuster press responded with complacency.[25] Noting the popularity of Readjuster policies on the debt, the public schools, and the poll tax, the *Smyth County Patriot and Herald* declared: "There is nothing left for Funderism [the Democrats] but to resort to its worn out cry of 'honor and integrity,' 'Democracy and a white man's party!' But they tried these same things last fall and the people rebuked them. The bait of Funder 'honor and integrity' was not taken, the false cry of 'Democracy' did not deceive, and the yell of 'nigger!' failed to alarm."[26]

The rising fortunes of black Virginians changed this. By 1882 black men had gained authority and visibility in Readjuster Virginia and had recalibrated the traditional relationship between political authority and the social meaning of gender, race, and class relations. Beginning in 1882 white voters in Virginia began to exhibit a heightened sensitivity to political languages of race. The reason for this was not some new susceptibility on the part of white voters to racist ideology, but the more common experiences of whites with the growing public influence and confidence of black Virginians in public office, in patronage jobs, in schools, and on the street. Because the coalition supported African American civil and political participation, and distributed the material and honorific benefits of patronage to black Readjusters, the Readjusters could be depicted as challenging white social, political, and economic superiority. What W. E. B. Du Bois later called the "public and psychological wage" of whiteness—deference on the streets, access to public spaces, control of the legal system, and superior public services, particularly schools—was, according to white Democrats, threatened by interracial rule, as black men gained positions of power and trust through Readjuster patronage and electoral strength.[27] When the coalition filled public offices with black men elected and appointed, it suggested that neither the value of whiteness nor that of blackness was intrinsic. Although nearly all white Virginians benefited by Readjuster rule (whether from lowered property taxes, an economic upswing generated in part by resolution of the debt, or the growth and prosperity of the public schools), the Democrats were increasingly able to capitalize on a nagging fear among whites that their "possessive investment in whiteness"—the social and political worth of white racial identity—was being devalued.[28]

Not surprisingly, the Democrats worked to turn potential white anxieties into real ones. What is more, they encouraged the idea that political alliance with black men could erode white men's gender and racial identities. While black Readjuster William Jefferson had hoped in 1879 that the coalition would cure black Virginians of their "political leprosy," the Democrats made much of the contagious nature of that disease. To borrow Horace Mann Bond's 1935 words regarding white fear of integrated schools, Virginia's Democrats manipulated the notion that "perhaps black is catching."[29] Bond's words were a bitter reference to white anxieties that integrated schools would encourage interracial sex and marriage, leading to mixed-race children: in this way, white families might "catch blackness." The danger to white "race purity" through miscegenation was proximate, not immediate, however, and the links between politics, sex, and race abstract.

But there were other ways to "catch blackness" in the New South, according to Virginia Democrats—ways in which to alter one's racial identity in the here and now. Borrowing the language of crossbreeding from the agricultural world, Democrats argued throughout the Readjuster era that by cooperating with black men the Readjusters were attempting to "hybridize" Virginia. Although a few examples exist from the seventeenth century, the word "hybrid" entered the common vocabulary only in the mid-nineteenth century with the work of Charles Darwin and Thomas Henry Huxley. Huxley differentiated between "mongrels" and "hybrids," but nonspecialists used the words interchangeably. In agriculture and animal husbandry hybridity was associated with superior offspring, blending the strengths of different strains to achieve resilience and eliminate weaknesses. Where humans were concerned, however, nineteenth-century Americans used concepts of hybridity to argue against miscegenation, insisting that hybridity among humans resulted in degeneracy.[30]

The language of hybridity was meant to evoke in the imagination of white voters the violent and corrupting grafting together of naturally distinct bodies.[31] For the Democrats, this included the alliance of white and black men in the Readjuster Party. The 1881 address of the Conservative State Executive Committee, for example, denounced Readjuster efforts to "hybridize" Virginia. The *Richmond Dispatch* built on this rhetorical foundation when it linked and equated racially mixed political and sexual alliance, as it described the "active amalgamation and miscegenation of the Mahoneites and the Republicans" in the spring of 1881.[32] The *Lynchburg Advance* joined the fun when it decried "the tendency . . . to political mongrelism" in Virginia, and a Democratic stump speaker, J. Randolph Tucker, insisted in September that the Readjuster Party was "a hybrid, the product of a vile miscegenation."[33] If the coalition had a face, it was mulatto.

Democratic references to Readjuster hybridity and miscegenation stigmatized coalitionists as enemies of white supremacy and also branded them as practitioners of "unnatural" political, and perhaps sexual, liaisons. This was not the first time that the word "amalgamation" was used as a double entendre in regard to the politics of race: rumors of amalgamation and lechery among abolitionists were published by the proslavery press in the antebellum era in an attempt to discredit the antislavery cause.[34] During the campaign of 1883 Democrats put another phrase with a past into play. In a frontal assault on Readjusters' masculinity (which constituted, in part, an attack on their fitness to exercise political rights), Democrats denounced Mahone and other Readjusters as "political hermaphrodites."[35] In case anyone had missed the point, John Warwick Daniel, the finest political orator in Virginia and Mahone's eventual replacement in the U.S. Senate, put the matter succinctly in 1883. Daniel was a Democrat, he explained, "because he was a white man." Readjusters, he implied, were neither white nor men.[36]

The language heard on the hustings in Virginia between 1881 and 1883 was not unusual for the postemancipation South. Anyone who advocated interracial alliance of any sort—whether a political party or a labor union—opened himself up to charges of being labeled a gender-neutral "white negro," as a North Carolina Democrat put it in

1866. In the 1880s North Carolina Democrats argued that whites who joined the Republican Party surrendered their racial status. When the Knights of Labor succeeded nonetheless in organizing across the color line and entered politics as a third party, the Democrats poured forth their usual arsenal of race-based abuse. Complained one white Knight of his Democratic opponents, "They pointed at us with scorn and kept crying 'Nigger! Nigger!' until the two words 'nigger' and Knight became almost synonymous terms."[37] A decade later South Carolina Democrat Ben Tillman defined race in terms of political behavior. Referring to those who had supported interracial fusion politics in his state, Tillman recalled that the coalition "had some people of white skin, but I . . . consider that a man with a white skin who consorts with negroes, hugs and kisses them to get votes, is not a genuine white man."[38]

What is significant about the deployment of this gendered rhetoric of race and politics in Readjuster Virginia is its differential success rate. Cries of "negro domination" did not prevent the coalition from organizing in 1879 or hinder its growth and success in 1881 and 1882. In the election of 1883, however, such language gained greater purchase with white voters. The Democrats' basic rhetorical building blocks remained the same between 1879 and 1883, but the social and political context for this language changed. The assertion by black Virginians of their status as civic equals and white concern about the erosion of race privilege evolved dialectically, with constant reference to each other.

In 1883 African American assertions of civic equality and customary notions of white racial privilege collided in a telling way. In mid-October William M. Flannagan, a candidate for the Virginia legislature, knocked a political opponent from a platform during a debate in Richmond. The next day Flannagan, by now at home in Powhatan County, received a telegram from the man he had struck challenging him to a duel. Although its delivery by telegram departed from tradition (representing a modernization of convention if not content), the challenge to mortal combat resulted from a familiar overstepping of partisanship to an assault on masculine honor when Flannagan punched his opponent in the nose.[39]

The man who had been attacked on the political dais, and who demanded satisfaction from Flannagan, was black. By issuing "the first challenge to mortal combat on the field of honor between a white man and a colored man in Virginia," this African American Readjuster made a series of elegant assertions about his equality, his manhood, his liberty, his literacy, his possession of a weapon, and his honor. Every one of these rights and qualities had been categorically denied him before emancipation. Indeed, his former subordination and legal and social inferiority were the very foundation of the code of honor he now appropriated.[40]

Although prohibited by law, dueling enjoyed a brief vogue in Readjuster Virginia. This fact is noteworthy in itself, for dueling was never as popular in antebellum Virginia as in the Deep South and Gulf Coast states; only two duels were fought in Virginia in the first fourteen years after Appomattox.[41] During the four years of Readjuster rule, however, six duels were fought, and several others—as in Flannagan's case— were avoided by a combination of publicity and police action. Each of the six duels involved prominent white coalitionists who were determined to keep their social claim to honor after public attacks on their integrity. In asserting their claim to honor, white Readjusters also reiterated the relationship between honor and race. Most white Readjusters continued to associate honor with whiteness and saw an attack on one as involving the other. Congressman John S. Wise, *Richmond Whig* editor William C. Elam, Supreme Court of Appeals judge Lunsford L. Lewis, and U.S. senator Harrison Holt Riddleberger all fought duels in the early 1880s.[42]

William Mahone managed to avoid becoming involved in a duel, although he came close twice. In 1879 a contest between Mahone and former governor James Lawson Kemper was narrowly averted after Kemper backtracked from an attack on Mahone's honesty. Of greater interest is Mahone's refusal to duel with longtime irritant General Jubal A. Early in 1881. After Early denounced Mahone during the legislative campaign as "a miserable coward and a base liar"—a more formulaic call for a duel is hardly imaginable—Mahone refused to consider the challenge, claiming that Early "could give me no satisfaction."[43] In dismissing his former colleague in arms as an unworthy challenger, Mahone evoked the cultural understanding of dueling as something done between equals to deny this status to Early.[44]

In 1882 and 1883 Virginia Democrats matched their physical and verbal assaults on white Readjusters with social ostracism. William

Royall, a leading debt payer, urged social death and economic ruin on Readjusters by "all decent white people," and a Brunswick County Readjuster reported that funder leaders had exhorted local Democrats to shun Readjusters.[45] Across Virginia, Democratic merchants called in chits, Democratic landlords threatened to raise rents or turn tenants off land, and Democratic churchmen boycotted Sunday school classes taught by Readjusters.[46] The possibility of severed lines of credit in a largely agricultural society was an enormous threat to the economic viability of families, and unless balanced by Readjuster patronage positions could easily result in lost votes for the coalition. In some cities, small businessmen who voted Readjuster were boycotted and urban workingmen lost their jobs. In December 1883 a physician who desired a patronage position explained that all his Democratic patients had left him since he joined the Readjusters. Earlier that year white workingmen in Lynchburg worried about finding jobs had asked Mahone to erect a public building in their city to reassure working people that "they will not be permitted to suffer should they be denied work because they work & vote according to their own convictions."[47]

Such a line of argument may have exaggerated Democratic repression in order to jump the patronage line. But the Democrats' social and economic shots often hit their target. By becoming a Readjuster a man could spoil his own or his daughter's marriage prospects, disrupt his wife's social life, and splinter his church. One Readjuster wrote Mahone that "Funders have been heard to say that they would not allow a Readjuster to enter their houses." The woebegone author of this letter added that he had felt compelled to resign as vestryman of his church, a position he had held for seventeen years, because all the other vestrymen were funders.[48] A Prince George County correspondent complained that families who had pledged to contribute to the building of a church backed out when they discovered that it was being built by Readjusters.[49] Stressing the disapprobation of his family and neighbors, one unemployed young Readjuster precinct worker wrote to Governor Cameron in 1882 that "I stood alone at my precinct when I was the only white person who had the courage to stand up & fight for the rights of the People. My brother & kinsfolk were against me. I have been threatened with political ostracism & cannot obtain a position on that account."[50] A Readjuster vote could even result in the loss of filial piety. In an excess of emotional blackmail M. B. Nesbitt, a Democratic precinct leader, was said to be "guilty of telling his parents that if they voted the readjuster ticket he would not visit them when sick[. T]here seams to be nothing to mean for this man to do to gaine a political advantage."[51]

In addition to turning their backs on their white Readjuster friends and neighbors, Virginia Democrats raised the possibility that the color line, as well as the social line, could be breached. In 1883 the Democratic press warned in increasingly shrill tones that whites who cooperated with the coalition would become black by association. In an attempt to realign the political and racial divide during the spring and fall elections of 1883, the Democrats presented "black" as socially constructed and encouraged white voters to consider how their actions could affect racial boundaries. Articles circulated in the *Alexandria Gazette* intimated that white men who voted the Readjuster ticket would henceforth be classed with blacks. This was certainly the point of the young Dinwiddie County Democrat who equated coalition with miscegenation when he told an older white Readjuster that "all white men who voted for the Readjuster candidate ought to be made to associate with & sleep with negroes."[52] The intent of the Democrats in 1883 was to read Readjusters out of the category of white man.

Anthony M. Keiley, Richmond's energetic Democratic leader and future mayor, distinctly articulated this white supremacist strategy. In a bid to woo back white Readjuster voters, Keiley asserted the primacy of the race issue over all others. While stressing the commonality of whiteness, Keiley exposed its social, political, and economic worth. "There are other things even more valuable to me personally than the right of creditors," he wrote. "I do not own a State bond, and never owned one. But if I owned [a] thousand I would regard my interest in the supremacy of the white people vastly more valuable than my interest in the public securities. And to secure that, if I had to let go my hold on either, I would drop the interest of the creditors without a sigh." In the interest of white supremacy, this prominent Virginia Democrat alerted New York and Washington, debt repudiation would henceforth be regarded as a dead issue.[53]

Throughout the summer and fall of 1883, Readjusters across the state reported that local Democrats were depicting the coming election as a choice between "white government or negro" and equating whiteness with the Democratic Party.[54] Democrats went door-to-door asking potential white voters, " 'Are you going to vote with the whites, or niggers, this time?' "[55] Exposing the connections between racial and gender identity in the postwar South, Readjusters in Spotsylvania County accused of voting against their race were faulted as well as for failing to live up to the standards of white manhood by voting against the interests of their wives and children. The threat of being rhetorically or socially reconfigured as black compelled some Readjusters to assert their whiteness against Democratic charges of race treason and transformation. "We are all white in Wise County, but Readjusters nevertheless," one local Readjuster assured Mahone. "[I]n every speech I made," a Blacksburg Readjuster explained later, "I adopted this policy—that we were as white as they, that if a real race issue came that we would be formed side by side with our white people."[56]

Two events—the integration of the Richmond School Board and the shooting in Danville—seemed to call for a definitive decision about racial alliances and identification on the part of white Readjusters. The replacement of the Petersburg School Board in 1882 had passed without controversy. But Governor Cameron's decision to supplant the Richmond board set off a firestorm of white supremacist rhetoric. This reflected in part the differences in political makeup of the two cities: black-majority Petersburg, the hometown of both Cameron and William Mahone, was controlled locally by the coalition. White-majority Richmond, on the other hand, remained decidedly Democratic, despite a strong Readjuster organization among white and black workingmen. In addition to reflecting demographic and political patterns, the response of Richmond's Democratic leadership also represented a more widespread concern among white Virginians about the reallocation of state resources from whites to blacks and the ways in which such reapportionment could corrode white dominance. As one white newspaper put it during the Richmond School Board controversy, if Readjuster patronage policies continued on course, soon black Virginians would demand representation on school boards equal to their numbers in school districts. Then, "once in control of the school funds he [the black superintendent] will not recognize the fact that a teacher of a higher grade is demanded for the white school than the colored school, or that more money should be expended in one direction than another."[57] Black education and black suffrage and office-holding endangered white supremacy, and southern whites and blacks knew it.

Democratic electoral candidates and the Democratic press in Virginia used the integration of the Richmond School Board to make concrete previously abstract rhetoric about "Negro domination" of whites under the Readjusters. This rhetoric was reported to have been effective in some county elections in the spring of 1883. From Culpeper County came the news that a Colonel Gibson would sweep the white vote in the fall because he "is opposed to mixed schools, Negro Trustees or Negro managers where white children are going." W. E. Talley of Hanover County lost his race for magistrate, he said, because the Democrats "got up a hard lie to defeat me. They said I was in favor of mixed schools." This was a common Democratic tactic that prompted numerous speeches and handbills of denial by white Readjusters. But the new, integrated Richmond School Board was only the most recent and sensational investiture of black Readjusters. Generalizing from the narrow issue of the school board decision to the broader question of African American social and political power under the Readjusters, Thomas H. Cross of South Quay put matters squarely in a letter to Mahone. Cross was running for sheriff, and the voters of his district objected to his plan to appoint a black man, Jordan Thompson, as a deputy. "They say," Cross reported, " 'the Readjuster party has too much niggers in it for them.' "[58]

The integrated school board in Richmond was a convenient lightning rod for white dissatisfaction with the redistribution of state resources under Readjuster rule. But this was an old critique of the coalition and one that it was experienced at repelling. More ominously for the future of the third party, the Democrats interpreted the new school board as a direct threat to white racial purity. The *Lynchburg News* thundered that a vote for the coalition in 1883 was a vote for mixed schools then and mixed marriages in the future. The *Staunton Spectator* left nothing to the imagination, warning in sexually charged language against "submission to the wishes of the negro," and argued that it was but a short distance from mixed school boards to the time when "every other form of an abhorrent social equality will stare us in the face."[59]

The most immediately recognizable form of such "abhorrent social equality" was mixed-race children, whom the Democrats considered a direct threat to white racial identity. Insisting that the Readjusters intended to integrate schools and repeal the law forbidding racial intermarriage in Virginia, one Democratic paper made the extravagant claim that soon "everything will look like Africa."[60] Extending the language of pollution and corporeality to politics, Democratic newspapers argued that the Readjuster coalition corrupted the white body politic and warned that the integrity of white Readjusters' racial identity was compromised by political alliance with black men. While the *Staunton Spectator* contented itself with raising issues of purity and contact when it worried about the effects of white Readjusters' "touching elbows right and left" with their black coalition partners, former Readjuster John Massey posed the question of outright racial transformation through political alliance. Massey understood why a black man might want to be a white man, but he could not comprehend the reverse; on election day he wondered "how many white men in Lynchburg will go back on their race and make negroes of themselves today." [61] Massey was not alone in posing this question. The *Abingdon Virginian* put the matter crudely but unmistakably when it editorialized, "If you would skin a Mahoneite, you would find a black hide under a white skin!" [62]

The theme of racial transformation through politics evident in John Massey's question and the *Abingdon Virginian*'s biopsy found its echo in the Democrats' 1883 campaign song, "This Way, Freeman!" In addition to alluding to old equations between race and freedom, the tune's lyrics argued explicitly the case for racial disinheritance (or, alternately, redemption) through political action:

Ho, this way, freemen! If ye will not heed,
Then never call yourselves Virginians more;
For men will mark you as some mongrel breed,
Unworthy of the name your fathers wore.[63]

If the prospect of severing oneself from generations of white Virginians past was not traumatic enough to white Readjusters, the Democratic press anthropomorphized white-black political coalition and speculated about the relationship between political alliance and racial identity for the sons of white Readjusters. In September the *Lynchburg Advance* reported the following story: "Little Ambrose, son of Major R. W. Page, had heard persons talking about coalition, white and black, etc. A few days ago he fell down the steps and broke his arm. Before the bandages were on his arm it had become discolored by the bruised blood. The little fellow, with tears streaming down his face, appealed to his father, 'Is it going to be a coalition arm?' " [64]

Little Ambrose's purported anxiety that his arm might be transformed into "a coalition arm"—that a political alliance of one generation could be revealed in the flesh of its sons—raised fears about the future of Virginia and mirrored the concerns of many white Readjuster voters. We should not misunderstand these concerns: white Virginians did not expect to wake up one morning looking any different. Rather, corporeality was used metaphorically: the boundaries of the body were used to represent other boundaries that were threatened or appeared precarious.[65] In the case of coalition rule, the boundary that seemed to many white men to be threatened was that of whiteness itself. When they asked how many "white" men would "make niggers of themselves" by allying politically with African Americans, the Democrats revealed that racial identity in Virginia was neither static nor superficial.

As white Virginians weighed Democratic arguments about the relationship between political behavior, race, and individual identity, the city of Danville exploded into violence. As we saw in Chapter 4, more than manners was at stake in the public confrontations between whites and blacks that led to the bloodshed. In contesting the rules of civility, black Virginians challenged a primary social interaction through which racial identity was claimed and performed. In insisting on uniform standards of public behavior, African Americans denied white privilege and struck at both the boundaries of whiteness and the assumptions and purposes of racial categorization. The meaning of whiteness, as both Justice Benjamin Watkins Lacy and W. E. B. Du Bois understood, lay mainly in the privileges accorded it. Strip whiteness of privilege and its meaning and boundaries became unclear. This is what the Democrats meant when they accused the Readjusters of corrupting whiteness through interracial government. Insisting that "white men in Danville were being forced to walk in blood to assert their rights," Virginia Democrats turned the 1883 election into a referendum on black rule and white racial identity.[66]

White voters were not caught entirely unawares by the violence in Danville, as the Democrats had already made tensions there a subject of the fall campaign through the medium of the Danville Circular. Before the shooting, coalitionists generally managed to rebut the circular.[67] Readjuster Party workers in the Valley and mountain counties displayed in their store windows testimonials from Danville residents who denied the claims of the circular and used their extensive rural network of local precinct workers and postal employees to pass informational flyers from hand to hand. As late as Halloween, the Readjusters were lighthearted in their attempts to downplay Democratic arguments about the elimination of racial boundaries and privileges under coalition rule. In a speech in Roanoke that appears to have backfired, Governor Cameron even teased the crowd, saying, "I understand there are white people here who are afraid that their daughters will have negro babies."[68]

But the coalition failed to factor in the organizational strength of the Democrats. Under the leadership of new party chairman John Strode Barbour, a railroad magnate like Mahone, the Democrats finally had a party machine that rivaled the Readjusters'. Cameron's "negro babies" speech was broadcast across the state. In stoutly Readjuster Tazewell County, Democrats circulated a printed script of the governor's reported remarks, and prominent Readjuster Richard F. Walker complained that Democrats in Richmond had distributed "lying handbills about 'Cameron and the white ladies of the State.'" Most Readjusters insisted that the speech had been misrepresented; others tried to shrug off the story by claiming that Cameron had been drunk on the podium.[69]

The new Democratic organization also came in handy for publicizing and misrepresenting the violence in Danville. Although it appears that the Democrats did not plan the Danville Riot, they nevertheless used it to their advantage in the election. Democratic presses worked overtime on Sunday, November 4, to print flyers declaring that Danville was currently in a state of race war as a result of coalition policies. These circulars were distributed throughout the state by train and horseback.[70] A circular entitled "War Declared between the Races" was distributed in Patrick County the night before the election, and Botetourt County was the recipient of a flyer screaming "WHAT COALITION RULE MEANS! The People of Danville Sustain the Accounts Heretofore Given of the Condition of Affairs There! A BLOODY ROW IN DANVILLE! Democrats! Save the State from a War of Races!"[71] By the time election day dawned the following Tuesday, the news that whites and blacks were fighting to the death in Danville had been nailed to half the trees in Virginia.

The news of the shooting in Danville, including the false claim that the violence had been precipitated by blacks, sent a shiver up the collective spine of white Virginia. Rumors of black violence exploited deep-seated anxieties of white Virginians and called on memories of slave insurrections and postemancipation insurrectionary scares.[72] Now as then, white Democrats stoked and manipulated this fear of

African American violence to alter the political balance of power in Virginia. In some counties, the combination of the Danville Circular and reports of the violence convinced white voters to desert the Readjuster Party. A coalition leader in Amelia County reported that the Democrats' portrayal of themselves as "the white man's party" coupled with "the fraudulent Danville circular and their false representations as to the 'Danville Massacre' had the effect of making many of our men, who were either weak or timid, vote with the Funders or remain away from the polls." From Abingdon came the news that "the Danville circular and massacre frightened a number of our timid friends, especially among the Tunkers [Dunkers] and Mennonite religious societies. These people being non-combatants would take no part in an election out of which they were made to believe a war was to come."[73]

The violence in Danville also checked the black vote in Pittsylvania County and adjacent areas. Black voters there feared that if they went to the polls, they would be fired on by Democrats. William Powell, a black Readjuster in Danville, stated succinctly black men's reasons for not voting, testifying later that "while we were attached to our party, we were afraid to risk our lives for the right of suffrage."[74] Democratic scare tactics did not always work as intended, however. Although the party's drawing of the color line secured it "many white cowards who had heretofore voted with the Readjuster party" in Essex County in the east, the same tactics enraged black voters and assisted the coalition "in polling a much larger colored vote than usual." And though white Readjusters in Abingdon "deserted, like rats from a sinking ship," J. H. Ballard reported, the town's black Republican Readjusters "stood to their guns like men—[I] never saw them more determined, or united." Robert W. Hughes, a federal judge and a longtime political ally of Mahone, concurred: "Almost throughout the state, they [black Readjusters] voted fully the usual strength, and with a quiet and manly courage and unanimity that I cannot but admire."[75]

Heavy turnout by black voters could not overcome the state's white majority, however, and the Readjusters lost control of Virginia. White voters newly enfranchised by the separation of the school tax from the suffrage, a Readjuster reform implemented for the first time in this election, flocked to the Democratic banner of white solidarity. The formerly Readjuster mountain counties that had been the target of the Danville Circular went Democratic. In the mountain southwest, the coalition vote declined from over 60 percent in 1882 to 48 percent in

1883.[76] One white Readjuster compared the hysteria whipped up by the Democrats in 1883 to that of the New York City draft riots twenty years earlier. According to this correspondent, "men shaking with fear threw away the Coalition Ticket. They came to vote, and rallied under the Bourbon cry against the 'Nigger party.'"[77] The Readjusters' loss at the state level was a blow not only to the interracial coalition but also to the national Republicans, who had counted on Virginia's electoral votes to offset expected Democratic gains in Ohio, New York, and Pennsylvania in the 1884 presidential election.[78]

Historians of the Readjuster movement have uniformly attributed the coalition's defeat in 1883 to "race antagonism" leavened to a greater or lesser degree by charges of Democratic fraud and intimidation and by local Readjusters' resentment of William Mahone's autocratic style of leadership. But in treating "the race issue" as static and unchanging, scholars have missed the fluidity of racial identity and the process of its formation.[79] On the day of the election, wrote a Richmond Readjuster, "[a] certain class of ignorant white men . . . feared they would be classed by funders with Negroes unless they voted the funder ticket" and felt that "nothing but a funder vote could distinguish them from 'Niggers.'"[80] When they voted Democratic, "a certain class of ignorant white men" in Virginia—the tenor of our source suggests that this class was closer to the bottom than to the top of the economic ladder—believed that they were reclaiming their whiteness. Through the action of distancing themselves from the interracial coalition, white men asserted their racial identity and laid claim to its attendant privileges.

Black Virginians appear to have understood both the competitive and the strategic qualities of racial definition. In December 1882 the *Richmond Star,* the city's foremost African American paper, editorialized on the arbitrariness of racial categories in a story about disputed racial identity in the North. The children of Mason Brown had been excluded from the white public schools of Cedarville, Ohio, in 1880 on the grounds that they were black. Two years later the children were "declared to be white by the courts" and admitted to the white school. "That is very much like the work of the foolish prejudice against color," commented the *Star.* "It will make black white or white black as the case may be, if thereby it can effect its end."[81]

Much remains to be done to document and decode the ways in which it was possible to "make black white or white black" in the postemancipation South. To begin, we must take seriously the fears of white men that they endangered their own identity as "white" by allying politically with African Americans.[82] Whiteness had to be *maintained* in the postwar South; white people in Virginia could, it seems, jeopardize their racial status through a variety of actions. In 1881, to give one final example, the *Marion Conservative Democrat* carried a story that exemplified the ways in which an action could alienate a person's racial identity. That spring a white girl who had worked as a servant for an African American family quit her job and returned to the local white public school. Claiming that the girl had "lost caste" through her dependent relationship with African Americans, the other children protested her attendance and then boycotted the school until the school board barred the girl as "colored."[83]

Rhetoric about the precariousness of racial identity, rhetoric that made plain the relationship between racial identity and economic and political actions, was always available to be put into play politically. Such stories as the one about the "white" girl ostracized by her peers did not galvanize political opposition to the Readjusters in 1881. In 1883, similar language did. Neither the definition of whiteness at law nor white racial mores had changed. The Readjusters had left alone the legislative definition of whiteness, as articulated in Virginia's anti-miscegenation law. But Readjuster political and patronage practices had invigorated white supremacist rhetoric, and made people more receptive to its claims, by undermining the customary privileges of whiteness. As many whites in Danville, Petersburg, and Richmond were only too happy to explain, coalition government in Virginia ate away at important props of white supremacy. By leaving untouched the state's articulation of the genealogical foundation of racial identity, the Readjusters failed to challenge the construct of "race" outright. But through their support of black voting rights, officeholding, jury duty, and political leadership the coalition challenged Democratic notions of the value of whiteness. This was, as people recognized at the time, a threat to white privilege: in a world where identity is constructed in the everyday interactions between people, it is possible, even easy, to be misapprehended and reclassified.

One architect of the Democrats' 1883 white supremacy campaign soon had occasion to know just how much his whiteness was worth and how his own social alliances affected the value of that asset. After serving as mayor of Richmond in the newly Democratic Virginia, Anthony Keiley, a Catholic, was appointed ambassador to Austria under President Grover Cleveland. To Keiley's consternation, Vienna protested this appointment on the grounds that Keiley's wife, the former Rebecca Davis, was Jewish. According to the Austrians, "the position of a foreign envoy wedded to a Jewess by civil marriage would be untenable and even impossible in Vienna." Keiley's name was withdrawn, but not before the almost-ambassador denounced his fate in terms that Du Bois could barely have improved. "It is proclaimed that in the official regard of Austria," Keiley expostulated, "Hebrew blood brands us with a leprosy, not only excluding all tainted with it from high honor at Austria's hands, but . . . so fatal indeed, that even a marriage connection with it by a citizen of whatever blood or belief, unfits him for the representation of a foreign and friendly power at this imperial and royal court." As Keiley and others had argued to such purpose in the 1883 Virginia campaign, there was more to whiteness than met the eye.[84]

EPILOGUE

The Voice of the People

What lessons can we draw from the defeat of the Readjusters in 1883? Certainly the potency of race as a political issue cannot be denied. As one Richmond party leader concluded in December of that year, "There is no doubt that every issue was absorbed in the one issue, [the] Race issue."[1] But as this quotation makes clear, race was never experienced independently of other social relationships. It was always in flux, always connected with the articulation of other social categories. As I have tried to show throughout this book, the implications of race become clear only when they are anchored in specific political, cultural, and economic circumstances. Whether in the post office, on the sidewalk, or in the schoolroom, white and black Virginians worked out the meaning of "race" in local encounters.

Grounding racial rhetoric in everyday experience ought to help us avoid treating race as the most transcendent of all social categories. In many ways, the master narrative of postemancipation southern history is true: the cry of "Nigger!" was (and is) always a potent cry in the South. But recognizing this tells us nothing about how race functioned politically in the postwar South. The power of racial rhetoric and the divisiveness of racial politics derived from the everyday experiences of individual white and black southerners, not from any essential political meaning of "race." Of course, to say this is also to say that the example of Readjuster Virginia cannot be paradigmatic; it cannot (nor can anywhere else) stand as "the most southern place on earth."[2] Every southern state had its experience of black-white political coalition after emancipation, and each community can in some sense be said to have inscribed its own particular history of racism. But the problems that a history of the Readjusters confronts are common problems throughout the South, and the methodology I have adopted to approach those problems is in that sense generalizable.

By embedding politics within the lived experience of people, by viewing Virginia politics from within its broader culture, I have tried to get at the sense of possibility, of movement, that people on the ground sensed in the late-nineteenth-century South. At the same time, however, I have been conscious of the limits of possibility in postemancipation Virginia, particularly when a new departure required individuals to challenge so much of what supported their own sense of who they were and who they expected to become. In this sense, then, this book is not only about the chronological and cultural space before Jim Crow: it is also about the origins and meaning of Jim Crow.

The possibilities for interracial democracy in Virginia seem to have constricted suddenly in 1883. In many ways, the political history of the state for the next twenty years confirms this view. Yet at the time, few Virginians spoke of the coalition loss in catastrophic or celebratory terms. Certainly no one viewed it as permanent. African American Readjusters regarded the electoral defeat as a momentary setback, not the end of an era. The popular vote was close, and ten black Readjuster Republicans won election to the General Assembly.[3] Prodded by William Mahone, the U.S. Senate launched an investigation of the contested election. Surveying the damage, R. A. Paul remained optimistic that Virginia blacks would be able to keep afloat "the bark of equal rights amidst the raging elements of an adverse world."[4]

Virginia's Democrats appear to have agreed with Paul. In the months that followed, the Democrats implemented the lessons that *they* had learned from the 1883 campaign and election. Above all, the actions they took in 1884 reveal their apprehension that ideology—specifically, white supremacy—would be insufficient to safeguard the Democratic victory. In an effort to strip the coalition of the compelling social and political issues that sustained it, the Democrats adopted the Readjuster platform. In tacit recognition that the coalition program had become the status quo, the former funders accepted the Riddleberger debt settlement law.[5] Nor did the Democrats attempt to repeal other progressive legislation passed during the four years of Readjuster rule. They did not tamper with school appropriations, they did not raise the taxes of farmers or workers, and they made no attempt to reestablish the whipping post. Their early experience with containing a mass opposition party served the Democrats well in later years. When confronted with the Populist Party in the early 1890s, Virginia Democrats knew just what to do: "First denounce it, then accept its platform, and then force the party out of existence."[6]

Among the most important lessons of 1883 was that continued Democratic dominance of local politics required constant partisan organization. New Democratic Party chairman John Strode Barbour, a railroad man who had clashed with Mahone in business and political circles, was disinclined to underestimate the continued strength of the Readjusters. Under Barbour's leadership the Democratic State Central and Executive Committee resolved in late November 1883 to "maintain and perfect" county, city, and precinct organizations. Barbour exhorted local Democratic leaders to keep party workers fired up. In a speech in Richmond a few weeks after the election James Barron Hope, the editor of the *Norfolk Landmark,* thundered that "organization is power" and lectured the crowd on the importance of maintaining local Democratic clubs.[7] The roots of Virginia's legendary twentieth-century Democratic machine lay in the organizational innovations of the Readjusters and the Democrats' adoption of those innovations for themselves after 1883.[8]

Organization alone could not constrain anti-Democratic politics in Virginia indefinitely, however. The votes of African American men, if joined with those of a minority of whites, stood as a constant threat to Democratic dominance. Moving quickly, the Democrats introduced legislation to control the election process at the local level. The 1884 Anderson-McCormick election law, which gave the Democrats two out of three election judges at every precinct across the state, was passed over William Cameron's veto. Billed by proponents as designed "to perpetuate the rule of the white man in Virginia"—presumably by intimidating dissident white and black voters at the polls or by counting them out afterward—the new law was an open invitation to electoral fraud. The first draft was struck down by the Supreme Court of Appeals, where Readjuster-appointed judges sat until 1895, but a second version stuck.[9] The Anderson-McCormick law did not go into effect soon enough to aid the Democrats in the presidential election of 1884. But fraud and intimidation in the Black Belt tipped the state toward Democratic nominee Grover Cleveland, despite Virginia's strong Readjuster machine and large Republican vote. In the same election Virginia Democrats carried eight of ten congressional districts. Republicans cried foul, but to little result, and Cleveland became the first Democratic president elected since before the Civil War. The new president did not waste any time in stripping the Readjusters of federal patronage power.[10]

The combined tactics of Democratic assumption of Readjuster issues, perfected partisan organization, control of the election machinery, and redirection of federal patronage resulted in the election of a Democratic governor in 1885. Fitzhugh Lee, the amiable nephew of Robert E. Lee, defeated John S. Wise in a contest in which both candidates campaigned as friends of labor and supporters of free public education.[11] Of the variables that contributed to the Democratic victory in 1885, partisan organization stands out. That same year the Democrats gained control of the General Assembly and were able to choose Mahone's successor in the U.S. Senate. John Barbour's friends fought hard for him, but the honor went to John W. Daniel. Piqued by this slight, Barbour nursed his wounds in Europe and left the Democrats to organize themselves for the 1886 congressional race. Despite the Anderson-McCormick law and Republican factionalism, six members of the GOP won election to Congress. Barbour returned to conduct the successful Democratic state campaign of 1887 and was rewarded in March 1888 with Virginia's other U.S. Senate seat, replacing Readjuster Harrison H. Riddleberger.[12]

Contrary to expectations, the Anderson-McCormick election law failed to control politics in Virginia adequately (from the Democratic point of view). The Republican Party, led by Mahone until his death in 1895, continued to mount credible electoral challenges throughout the 1880s. Even after Republicans split over Mahone's leadership — he seemed to become more authoritarian with each passing year — the GOP still posed a potent threat to Democratic political control. In 1888 John Mercer Langston declared that it was high time the Fourth District sent a black man to Congress and volunteered his services. Mahone refused to back Langston, insisting that his candidacy would scare off white voters, which would be particularly damaging to the party in a presidential election year. This decision alienated many black Republicans and precipitated a split between Mahone and some of the most prominent white Readjusters-turned-Republicans, including John Wise and William Cameron.[13] Even then — with one wing of a splintered Virginia GOP running a black man for Congress in a three-way race, and with the election machinery controlled by Democrats—Democratic incumbent Grover Cleveland barely squeaked by in the Old Dominion, carrying the state by a margin of only 1,530 votes out of a total of more than 300,000 cast.[14] The election in the Fourth District was marked by disappearing ballots and heavy vote buying on all sides. As one Republican Party worker complained, "While we were buying Langston votes, Langston and [Democratic candidate E. C.] Venable were buying ours." Langston was counted out but was granted his seat belatedly after a congressional investigation into electoral fraud in Virginia.[15]

John Mercer Langston's victory in the Fourth District in 1888 was more an echo of past political successes than an omen of things to come. Even as interracial political alliances shook the pillars of Democratic dominance in other southern states in the late 1880s and 1890s, in Virginia anti-Democratic politics were most successful in cities and were commonly associated with labor movements. In the late 1880s the Knights of Labor spread the gospel of interracial unionism across the urban South and then ran for office. The Knights attracted black and white workingmen across urban Virginia, and in 1887 the order's electoral slate won control of Lynchburg's city council on a platform that supported public education and shared patronage between whites and blacks.[16] A year earlier a Workingmen's Reform fusion of Republicans and Knights had carried off a surprise victory in Richmond municipal elections. Inexperienced and undermined by both local Democratic and Republican leaders, the Reform coalition was short-lived in largely Democratic Richmond.[17] But these local successes were not mirrored at the state, county, or congressional levels. The Virginia GOP disintegrated after the 1889 election, in which Mahone was defeated for governor by Democrat Phillip W. McKinney. There was no statewide political organization to replace it.[18]

As the 1880s gave way to the 1890s, populism came to the Old Dominion. By 1888 white Virginians in the Shenandoah Valley were organizing local suballiances of the Farmers Alliance; by the fall of 1890 African Americans had organized twenty-five lodges of the Colored Farmers Alliance.[19] But in marked contrast to other southern states such as Georgia, South Carolina, North Carolina, and Texas, where white and black Populists and Republicans constructed viable interracial coalitions, in Virginia Populists spurned the black vote. Faced with a Democratic organization that had cut its teeth on interracial coalition in the 1880s, white Populists had no desire to travel the road trod by the Readjusters. Not a single African American attended the 1892 Virginia Populist Party convention that nominated Edmund Randolph Cocke for governor. Of course, Cocke was no William Mahone. In 1890, musing over the political future of his state, Cocke had suggested the repeal of the Fifteenth Amendment on the grounds that "depriving the negro of suffrage . . . might have a good effect [on southern politics]." Two years later Cocke and the Populist Party went to considerable trouble to dissociate themselves from African Americans by not seeking black men's votes and by insisting loudly that they did not want them.[20]

Compared with other southern states, populism in Virginia lacked substance. Even so, the Democrats felt unsure of their dominion and resorted to their old standby weapons of fraud and intimidation to defeat their opponents. Virginia Populists complained bitterly about the "bacchanalia of corruption and terrorism" of the 1892 election.[21] Traditional Democratic skullduggery did not keep black men from voting in Norfolk, however, where the local newspaper complained that the polls were crowded "with sable exponents of the fourteenth and fifteenth amendments."[22] In cities with significant black populations, the Democrats were reduced to more ingenious devices to curb dissident political power. One trick was to print ballots containing false names similar to those of Republican candidates. In 1890 black voters in Richmond confronted ballots in which genuine Republican candidate John Mitchell Jr. was opposed not only by a Democrat but by "John Mitchell," a "ghost" candidate or "political apparition."[23]

But Virginia Democrats were becoming fatigued at having to work so hard to win elections. Furthermore, as long as the GOP dominated Congress, it could reject Virginia representatives who had been elected in campaigns tainted by fraud.[24] In 1894 state senator M. L. Walton proposed a solution to both electoral competition and fraud in Virginia. A secret ballot law, the Walton Act discriminated against illiterates. Under its provisions ballots printed by the state and distributed at the polls could no longer contain party names or symbols. Alone in the polling booth, a voter had two and a half minutes to draw a line three-quarters of the way through the name of every candidate for whom he did *not* wish to vote. As Democratic governor Phillip McKinney noted at the time, the Walton Act practically disenfranchised illiterate voters, particularly black voters. "Negroes often hesitated in getting a Democratic election judge to assist them in marking their ballots," McKinney explained; "others were timid or ashamed to acknowledge their ignorance; and many who attempted to vote could not correctly mark their ballots in the allotted time." The estimated percentage of black votes cast for opposition (non-Democratic) candidates in Virginia dropped from 42 percent in 1893 to 2 percent in 1900.[25]

Black Virginians, of course, opposed Democratic disfranchising measures. But the space for black political action constricted almost daily. The Republican Party deserves considerable blame for this situation. As in North Carolina, Virginia's GOP deserted black voters just at the moment they needed their party most.[26] With the black vote all but eliminated by the Walton Act, Virginia Republicans failed to see the benefit of being identified as the party of "Negro dominance." The Republican Party had always had a lily-white faction, but now it gained the upper hand. John Mitchell Jr., a black teacher who had lost his job as a school principal in Richmond after the Democratic victory in 1883, helped found the *Richmond Planet* in 1884 to "agitate the political equality of all men before the law."[27] When he objected to the Republicans' decision not to contest Democratic congressional candidates in 1894, he was thrown out of the party. By 1896 white Republicans in Virginia had succeeded in Jim Crowing all party meetings, on one occasion allegedly resorting to stringing a clothesline down the center of an auditorium. Infuriated black Republicans boycotted party events and threatened to withhold their votes.[28] The angry black men in Richmond who founded the Negro Protective Association in 1897 grieved at "how the Negro has been wounded in the house of his friends . . . how he has been snubbed and smitten by those whom he elevated politically" and declared that the only solution to such betrayal was "Negro organization."[29]

Organization did not help black men regain a position of influence within the Virginia GOP. But it did frighten Democrats. Referring to black Virginians' network of churches, one Democrat complained, "the negro race is organized from one end of this State to the other in a way that is impossible among the white race. . . . You can give notice of anything that is to happen tomorrow night in almost any county in this Commonwealth, and it will, before that time, be known from one end of the county to the other by the negroes."[30] Haunted by persistent black organization and the possibility of black-white political cooperation, the Democrats called for revision of the Underwood Constitution.

The idea of altering the 1868 constitution was opposed by a majority of Virginians, and constitutional convention referenda were defeated in 1888, 1893, and 1897. In 1900 a referendum on constitutional revision was passed by fewer than 18 percent of Virginia's eligible voters. Overall turnout in the off-season May election equaled less than a third of the electorate. According to the most thorough student of late-nineteenth-century suffrage patterns, 60 percent of those who had opposed the convention in 1897 appear not to have voted in 1900. The referendum was passed by Democrats from black-majority counties and by urban whites swayed by white supremacist rhetoric and the patronage of the now well-oiled Democratic political machine. It was opposed by the old Readjuster coalition of eastern and urban blacks and mountain and Valley whites.[31]

The 1900 referendum passed because rural white voters outside of black-majority counties did not go to the polls.[32] Why did so many white men fail to vote? Perhaps they were ignorant of the oddly timed election. Perhaps they had grown tired of the perennial Democratic attempts to call a convention and had resigned themselves to a new constitution. Perhaps they believed the Democratic slogan about making politics safe for white men by disfranchising African Americans. Maybe they truly thought that eliminating the black vote would realign old hierarchies of race and status and make room for political disagreement among white men. Not caring enough to vote against the referendum but not really supporting it either, white men west of the Blue Ridge did not see the danger to their own rights in their failure to stand up for those of black men. For many nonelite white men in Virginia, the election in which they did not bother to vote represented their final chance to cast a ballot at all.[33]

Proponents of amending the constitution had insisted all along that their purpose was to end election fraud. Casting the issue in moral terms, Democrats blamed black Virginians as the root cause of corruption and bewailed the psychic damage to young white men forced to resort to fraud to protect Virginia from "negro rule." This rhetorical turn was denounced at the time as paradoxical to the point of depravity. "The remedy suggested here is to punish the man who has been injured," complained Albert Gillespie, a white Republican convention delegate, who despaired at the disfranchisement of African Americans "to prevent the Democratic election officials from stealing their votes."[34] But election fraud was only the most obvious symptom of the deeper Democratic fear of black political power and interracial alliance. The animating issue of the convention was suffrage restriction.

Although dominated by Democrats, the constitutional convention divided deeply over the issue of black disfranchisement. Even at this point it is impossible to see race as either uncontested or triumphant politically. While all but a handful of western Republicans favored stripping black men of the vote, more than the Republicans worried about how this could be accomplished without denying suffrage to many white men as well. The Fifteenth Amendment prohibited denial of the right to vote along race lines but left the door open for other criteria for disfranchisement. In 1898 the U.S. Supreme Court upheld Mississippi's 1890 disfranchising constitution, which limited black political participation through a combination of complicated registration procedures, a poll tax, a literacy requirement, and what was dubbed an "understanding clause." The purpose of the understanding clause was to guard the interests of illiterate white voters, who, while unable to read the state constitution if asked, could presumably provide a "reasonable interpretation" of it.

The Virginia convention could not agree on the terms of disfranchisement. The lines of division followed the familiar east-west contour of the state, with western whites anxious that their constituents would be disfranchised along with African Americans by eastern Democrats. Men such as former funder and public school enemy John Warwick Daniel, who headed the suffrage subcommittee, had never been convinced that the suffrage was a right and not a privilege. As the negotiations in the suffrage subcommittee dragged on, Allan Caperton Braxton, a lawyer from Staunton, despaired of solution. "Our conferences are like pandemonium," he wrote. "I do not believe any two members entertain the same views on the question of suffrage."[35] Eventually the convention agreed that to vote in Virginia a man had to satisfy one of three broad criteria: he could be a Union or Confederate war veteran or the son of one, he could pay property taxes of at least one dollar a year, or he could read and explain any section of the constitution. If unable to read, he could rely on the provisions of a temporary understanding clause, which was to be in effect until January 1, 1904. All voters were required to pay a cumulative poll tax six months in advance of an election.[36]

The adoption of the understanding clause is the clearest indicator that democracy, not fraud, was the chief target of the constitutional convention. Such clauses contributed to fraud rather than eliminated it, because they could be administered in a discriminatory manner against blacks and white Republicans. When this point was raised in the convention, a triumphant Carter Glass, at the beginning of his influential career as a Democratic power broker, congressman, and later U.S. senator, declared, "Discrimination! Why, that is precisely what we propose; that, exactly, is what this Convention was elected for—to discriminate . . . with a view to the elimination of every negro voter who can be gotten rid of." [37] Further repudiating popular democracy, the Democrats proclaimed the new constitution rather than submitting it to a popular referendum, as the party had promised in its 1900 platform.[38] Neither the disfranchising clauses nor the proclamation of the new constitution by fiat provoked censure from Washington. National Republican leaders, in thrall to the theories of Anglo-Saxon superiority currently in vogue and intent on restricting suffrage in Hawaii and the Philippines, were studiously silent on the topic of southern disfranchisement. Although they had pressing political motivations, the authors of Virginia's suffrage restrictions were also part of this broader intellectual current. In preparation for the deliberations of the suffrage subcommittee, Allan Caperton Braxton ordered a copy of Charles Darwin's *Origin of Species* from a Richmond bookseller.[39]

The effect of the 1902 constitution on black voting in Virginia was immediate and catastrophic. Black disfranchisement was most apparent in the cities, with their concentrations of black voters and strong African American political organizations, but African Americans in the countryside fared just as poorly. In 1900 Richmond claimed more than 6,000 registered black voters; by 1902 that number had dwindled to 760. In Jackson Ward, long the hub of black power in Richmond, registered black voters plummeted from nearly 3,000 in 1900 to 33 just three years later. During the same period Norfolk's black vote was reduced by nearly three-quarters, as was Petersburg's. Black Belt counties such as Elizabeth City, Brunswick, and Goochland, which had all voted heavily Readjuster, saw their black electorates reduced by more than 75 percent. Overall, the suffrage restrictions of the 1902 constitution cut the Virginia electorate in half. William Pendleton, the white editor of the *Tazewell Republican,* a vociferous critic of the new constitution, complained that Democratic registrars had disfranchised 90 percent of black voters and 50 percent of white voters. Illiterate white Republicans faced with "the humiliation of having their educational qualifications passed upon by ignorant and bitterly partisan boards of registration" simply stopped trying to vote. The *Lynchburg News*, owned by Carter Glass, was unsympathetic to those white men who had "voluntarily disfranchised themselves. . . . It is their own fault, and they have no body to blame but themselves." Together, the 1902 constitution and the Walton Act dramatically lowered popular participation in government and represented a definitive reversal of the most significant Readjuster reforms. Between 1905 and 1948 state employees and officeholders cast approximately one-third of all votes in Virginia's state elections, an ironic conclusion to William Mahone's ideal of an identity of interest between the citizen and the state.[40]

Given this narrative of narrowing possibilities for a shared, interracial political world, it is tempting to neglect analysis of resistance and change and sit back and wait for the timely arrival of a deus ex machina in the form of the Freedom Riders. But this would be to ignore the people who did the resisting and who did not see resistance as futile. African Americans in Virginia never considered the possibility that if they waited long enough, the civil rights movement would arrive to save them. Even from the perspective of 1902, black Virginians defy the interpretational reduction to abjection. As they had done since emancipation, black Virginians continued to look for space in the world of electoral politics. Then as now, they turned to familiar instruments of political power such as mass meetings, lawsuits, and partisan organization.

The first step was to challenge the constitution. Black Republicans initiated court cases to combat the suffrage articles before the constitution was even adopted. Abandoned by the GOP, the Negro Industrial and Agricultural League, a nonpartisan organization, engaged former Readjuster John S. Wise as counsel for the disfranchisement cases and paired him with black attorney James H. Haynes.[41] In *Jones et al. v. Montague et al.*, Haynes and Wise asked the State Board of Canvassers to delay delivering certificates of election to Virginia members of the House of Representatives because the new state constitution denied African Americans their right to vote under the Fifteenth Amendment and violated the terms set for Virginia's readmission to the Union in 1870. After winding its way through the state court system, *Jones* ended up in the U.S. Supreme Court, where the justices dismissed it and a similar case without ruling on the constitutionality of Virginia's new basic law. Bursting with indignation, John Wise deplored the lack of sympathy for southern blacks in Washington: "Congress doesn't want to do anything, the Supreme Court doesn't want to do anything, and so it goes. The Supreme Court passes the question along to Congress, and Congress politely passes it along to the Supreme Court. It is a game of 'After you, my dear Alphonse,' and it is amusing to everybody, except the Negro."[42]

Disfranchisement did not mean that black Virginians wielded no public power or that they ceased to act politically. Urban African Americans in particular enjoyed considerable consumer power, which they used both to found black banks and businesses and to punish white establishments that offended them. As white legislators began to pass Jim Crow segregation laws in an effort to define African Americans' place with greater specificity, black Virginians fought back with the weapons at hand. In 1904, for example, black businesses and associations in Richmond supported John Mitchell's call to boycott the Virginia Passenger and Power Company after it decided to segregate the city's streetcars. The streetcar company went bankrupt after a nine-month boycott by black riders, and its assets were sold at auction in December. The new management, however, was just as committed to segregation as the old one. The cars remained segregated, and most black Richmonders (although not John Mitchell) eventually returned to them. But even Jim Crow failed to solve the everyday dilemmas of racial identity. During the boycott light-skinned African Americans confounded streetcar conductors by sitting in the rear and refusing to move into the section reserved for white passengers. Commenting on the continuing difficulties of racial categorization, John Mitchell suggested that all streetcar passengers "wear tags certified by officers of the streetcar company" designating their official racial identity.[43]

In a speech delivered to celebrate the Democratic victory over the Readjusters in 1883, General Jubal Early had alluded to the Danville Riot and warned black Virginians that from now on "the Negroes must know that they are to behave themselves and keep in their proper places."[44] Judging by the actions of Virginia's black voters between 1883 and 1902, it seems clear that black men considered their place to be in politics. But faced with a public world that grew more restrictive by the day, many blacks decided that their place was no longer in the Old Dominion. Mobility was always a main weapon of freedom for African Americans after emancipation. The first stop for most rural blacks was southern cities, places like Danville and Petersburg and Richmond, that swelled with newcomers in the thirty years after the Civil War ended. Following the Readjuster loss in 1883, however, black Virginians began to look farther afield for the space within which to conduct their lives with dignity and respect. After disfranchisement every southern state experienced significant African American out-migration. In Virginia, the wave of heavy black migration to the North came earlier and corresponded with the defeat of the Readjusters. Before 1900 Virginia had the highest rate of black out-migration of all the southern states.[45]

Of course, more black Virginians stayed than went. And the state even gained some interesting new residents like Professor Luther Porter Jackson. Born in 1892 to former slaves in Lexington, Kentucky, Jackson was educated at Fisk University and went on to receive a Ph.D. in history from the University of Chicago. In 1922 he joined the faculty of Virginia State College, the black college founded by the Readjusters. One of the pioneers of African American history, Jackson prepared compilations of black property and officeholding in Virginia that remain vital sources for historians of the state. Prescribing a combination of nonpartisan political organization and African American memory to combat white supremacy, he published *Negro Officeholders in Virginia, 1865–1895* (1935) in a conscious attempt to inspire black Virginians to regain the political influence they had wielded before Jim Crow.[46]

Jackson's quest was not as quixotic as it may appear at first glance. Despite the impediments placed in their way, those blacks who remained in the Old Dominion never stopped voting entirely. Between 1902 and 1928, black voters and their leaders continuously strove to convince a skeptical state Republican Party that it needed black votes as much as the Readjusters had thirty years earlier.[47] When this tactic failed, blacks looked to the other possibility, the Democrats. Since 1905, Democratic electoral nominees in the Old Dominion had been nominated in a closed, all-white primary. Because the state GOP was so weak after 1902, the winner of the Democratic primary invariably triumphed in the general election. In 1928 Virginia blacks won the first of a string of judicial victories against the white primary. By 1931 the Democratic Party was open to all. A year later the majority of Virginia blacks who voted cast their ballots for Franklin D. Roosevelt.[48]

After this victory over the white primary, the biggest obstacle to black voting in Virginia was the poll tax. In 1941 Luther Porter Jackson organized the Virginia Voters League, a nonpartisan interracial organization established to encourage black voters to pay their poll taxes and register to vote.[49] Working in tandem with the National Association for the Advancement of Colored People (NAACP), the Congress of Industrial Organizations (CIO), and the Southern Conference for Human Welfare (SCHW), Jackson worked throughout the 1940s to increase the number of registered black voters in his state. In 1946 Nansemond County elected the first black man to public office since 1896.[50] Between 1940 and 1950—four years before the Supreme Court's decision in *Brown v. Board of Education* would finally annihilate the legal notion of separate but equal—black voter registration in Virginia quadrupled.[51]

As this final sketch of twentieth-century politics suggests, there was always the possibility of interracial alliance in postemancipation Virginia. The newest work on twentieth-century Virginia politics has begun to explore the alternative narratives enabled by focusing on these moments.[52] Seen this way, the meaning of the Readjusters becomes less emblematic of the failed possibility of interracial cooperation in the postemancipation South and more of an inspiration for change. The most important thing about the Readjusters was not their failure but their existence and their legacy.

Neither novelists nor historians understood this in 1900. A Virginian and Pulitzer prizewinning author, Ellen Glasgow saw the Readjusters' defeat in 1883 as representative of the processes that transformed the idea of black-white coalition in the South from hopeful possibility to failure. In her 1900 novel *The Voice of the People,* set in Virginia at the turn of the twentieth century, poor but clever Nicholas Burr wins the governorship as the leader of a popular reform movement within the Democratic Party. In the book's penultimate scene, Governor Burr rushes to his hometown jail to prevent the lynching of a black man accused of raping a white woman. Determined to enforce the rule of law in the face of a white mob and protect the black inmate inside, Burr covers the entrance to the jail with his body. Suddenly he is overwhelmed with the consciousness of a common identity with the black man; as he acts to protect him, Burr realizes that they will share a common fate. Standing with his back to the jail door, he tries to speak to the crowd:

"We'll be damned, but we'll get the nigger!" called someone beside him. The words struck him like a blow. He saw red, and the sudden rage upheld him. He knew that he was to fight—a blind fight for he cared not what. The old savage instinct blazed within him—the instinct to do battle to death—to throttle with his single hand the odds that opposed. With a grip of iron he braced himself against the doorway, covering the entrance. "I'll be damned if you do!" he thundered. A quick shot rang out sharply.[53]

In 1900, as the constitutional convention assembled in Richmond, it seemed safe to consider interracial democracy a thing of the past rather than of the future. In that year one could write plausibly of a champion of the people killed by his own white allies in defense of a black man's rights. By then, too, it was possible to reflect on the repercussions for nonelite white Virginians of their failure to see their common interest with black men, and to contemplate the price whites paid for their decision to privilege racial identity over all others and to dissociate themselves from African Americans. *The Voice of the People* signified the end of any possibility that remained in the story of the Readjusters—a position implicit in a comment of the aristocratic Judge Bassett on hearing a welcome report. "It's good news you bring me," he exulted. "I haven't had such news since they told me the Democratic Party had wiped out Mahoneism."[54] Concurring with Bassett, historians have tended to fix the end of interracial democracy in Virginia with the end of the Readjusters. But it is important to remember that many southerners living through the advent of Jim Crow—like young Luther Porter Jackson, eight years old in 1900—would have disagreed and gone on to prove them wrong.

NOTES

INTRODUCTION

1. Morrison, *Jazz,* 100, 138. Cheers to Simon Newman, who spotted this reference to the Readjusters oh so many years ago.

2. On the migration of black southerners to the North, see Henri, *Black Migration;* Grossman, *Land of Hope;* Emmett J. Scott, *Negro Migration;* Trotter, *Great Migration;* and Lemann, *The Promised Land.* For nineteenth-century precedents of mass African American migration from the South, see Painter, *Exodusters.*

3. See, e.g., Nathan Glazer's review of Williams, *Voice, Trust, and Memory,* in *Times Literary Supplement,* June 18, 1999, 7.

4. In a historiographical overview of scholarly works analyzing the political participation by black southerners in the 1880s and 1890s, LaWanda Cox ("From Emancipation to Segregation," 248) came to the same conclusion. "[T]he second generation of black political leaders were sufficiently effective

to have helped trigger their own undoing, the white racist reaction that led to the displacement of partial by total disfranchisement and the hardening of de facto into legal segregation." This assessment of African American political leaders may be generalized to black southerners as a whole, who by their votes and their assertion in a variety of venues inspired white repression. See also Holt, *Black over White*, 4, 206, and Cartwright, *Triumph of Jim Crow*.

5. See *Congressional Directories* for the sessions between 1877 and 1897. On fusion, see Argersinger, "Fusion Politics and Antifusion Laws." See also DeSantis, *Republicans Face the Southern Question*, 133–81, 227–62, and "President Hayes's Southern Policy"; Hirshson, *Farewell to the Bloody Shirt*, 94–98, 105–22; and Goodwyn, "Populist Dreams and Negro Rights." On Arkansas, see Kenneth C. Barnes, *Who Killed John Clayton*, 3, 56–57, 61, 65. For an excellent introduction to biracial coalition in North Carolina, see Eric Anderson, *Race and Politics*.

6. For a succinct discussion of the animating issues of intraracial southern independent movements, see Hyman, *Anti-Redeemers*, 167–91.

7. Quoted in Woodward, *Origins*, 81. On southern independent movements before populism, see the entries in n. 5 above and Woodward, *Origins*, 75–105; Kousser, *Shaping of Southern Politics*, 11, 18, 25–28, 73; Degler, *The Other South*, 264–315; Hyman, *Anti-Redeemers;* Rogers, *One-Gallused Rebellion;* Hahn, *Roots of Southern Populism*, 225–38; Cartwright, *Triumph of Jim Crow*, 29–41; Burton, "Race and Reconstruction"; and DeSantis, "Independent Movements in the South."

8. Quoted in Hyman, *Anti-Redeemers*, 196.

9. Eric Anderson, *Race and Politics*, 96–113, 136–37. Anderson (p. 138) reports that Simmons considered his victory secured by the support he received from "the better class of colored men" (quoting *Raleigh State Chronicle*, February 2, 1884). In Charlotte in the 1880s, middle-class whites allied with an emerging black bourgeoisie against alcohol. This coalition was mirrored by working-class black and white antiprohibitionists who formed an interracial Liberal Anti-Prohibition Party. See Greenwood, *Bittersweet Legacy*, 77–113. For more on the emerging African American middle class, see Escott, *Many Excellent People,* and Gatewood, *Aristocrats of Color.*

10. Hyman, *Anti-Redeemers,* 187–88 (Alabama), 170 (Mississippi and Georgia); see also Gutman, "Black Coal Miners." On interracial unionism in Alabama in these years, see Letwin's excellent new book, *Challenge of Interracial Unionism.* See also Halsell, "Republican Factionalism" and "Chalmers and 'Mahoneism.'" Other Georgia blacks supported William Felton's Independent candidacy for Congress. See Hyman, *Anti-Redeemers,* 173, 187, and Painter, *Exodusters,* 40–43.

11. Kousser, *Shaping of Southern Politics,* 27, table 1.3, and 28, table 1.4. The numbers and dates are (with some stretching on my part regarding Louisiana and the definition of one-fourth) Arkansas, 1888—29 percent; Georgia, 1880—28 percent; Louisiana, 1884—24 percent; Tennessee, 1884—31 percent; and Virginia, 1881—26 percent.

12. See Kousser, *Shaping of Southern Politics* and "Post-Reconstruction Suffrage Restrictions." See also Key, *Southern Politics in State and Nation.*

13. As Woodward put it later, his thesis in *Strange Career* was "first, that racial segregation in the South in the rigid and universal form it had taken by 1954 [the year of the first *Brown v. Board of Education* decision] did not appear with the end of slavery, but toward the end of the century and later; and second, that before it appeared in this form there occurred an era of experimentation and variety in race relations of the South in which segregation was not the invariable rule." Woodward, "The Strange Career of a Historical Controversy," *American Counterpoint*, 237.

14. Baldwin, *Notes of a Native Son*, 175.

15. See Rabinowitz, *Race Relations*, 330–33; Cell, *Highest Stage of White Supremacy*, 82–102; Joel Williamson, *Crucible of Race*, 180–223; Wynes, *Race Relations;* Cartwright, *Triumph of Jim Crow;* and Wright, *Life behind a Veil.*

16. Rabinowitz made this point most forcefully in his book *Race Relations in the Urban South.* For the scholarship that stresses segregation over integration, see Rabinowitz, "More Than the Woodward Thesis" and "From Exclusion to Segregation." See also Wade, *Slavery in the Cities,* and Joel Williamson, *After Slavery.*

17. For a recent example of this interpretation, see Hale, *Making Whiteness*, 19. Judith Stein ("The Political Economy of Racism," 422) made more or less the same point as I in 1974, when she noted that "while the social and cultural historians have found that black community life was rich and vital, the political historians have treated the popular resources of black political leaders as passive, needing either massive exhortation or opportunistic compromise." More recently, work that focuses on the actions of black and white women has challenged this bifurcation by showing how women working on the margins of formal politics influenced public life in the South between about 1890 and 1920. See, e.g., Gilmore, *Gender and Jim Crow;* Hall, *Revolt against Chivalry;* and Elsa Barkley Brown, "Negotiating and Transforming the Public Sphere."

18. My formulation of this issue is owed to Butler, *Bodies That Matter*, 168. Alexis de Tocqueville made a similar observation about America in *Democracy in America* (1835). In the formulation of Pierre Manent (*Tocqueville and the Nature of Democracy*, 105), "the distinction between civil society and the political institution is not fundamental; both are only what they are, and are distinguished only to accomplish a common project. This project, in itself, is neither social nor political: it includes 'the greater part of human actions.' "

19. Woodman, "Economic Reconstruction," 273, 255; Degler, *The Other South*, 1–10, and *Place over Time*, 108; Fredrickson, *Arrogance of Race*, 157; Litwack, *Trouble in Mind*, xiv.

20. Shifflett, *Patronage and Poverty*, 82; Poland, *From Frontier to Suburbia.*

21. Woodward makes this point in *Thinking Back* (p. 71), commenting on Moore's essay "Redeemers Reconsidered."

22. Pearson, *Readjuster Movement*, 175; Moore, *Two Paths*, xii, and "Black Militancy," 167; Tripp, *Yankee Town, Southern City*, 254.

23. The cost of such an approach to white racism for American history in general has been made most forcefully by Barbara Fields in "Ideology and Race in American History" and "Slavery, Race, and Ideology."

24. In this I follow Sabean, *Power in the Blood,* 94–95.

25. In 1980 J. Mills Thornton ("Fiscal Policy") criticized a historiography that explained nonelite white voters' rejection of Reconstruction regimes largely in terms of racism. He showed how white anger at increased taxes and decreased state services, especially schools, contributed to the defeat of Republican governments in the Lower South. Never denying the power of white racism, Thornton aimed in this article to reintroduce class considerations into historical writing about white disaffection with Reconstruction. The rise of the Readjusters in 1879 (and the concurrent defeat of the Conservatives) suggests both that his conclusions are applicable to the Upper South and that they are reversible. That is to say, economic considerations could also lead to the defeat of the more racist party and to the victory of the more racially progressive.

26. I am indebted to Carl Schorske for this formulation. See his *Fin-de-Siècle Vienna,* 118.

27. Marx, *Capital,* 1:301. See also W. E. B. Du Bois, *Black Reconstruction,* 727 and passim, and Roediger, *Wages of Whiteness,* chap. 8.

28. W. E. B. Du Bois, *Black Reconstruction,* 700–701.

29. Moger, *Bourbonism to Byrd,* 192.

CHAPTER 1

1. Quoted in Oakes, *Ruling Race,* 141. Henry A. Wise, who was governor at the time and who had long argued for equal white male suffrage, agreed: "Break down slavery, and you would with the same blow destroy the great democratic principle of equality among men." Quoted in Fredrickson, *Black Image in the White Mind,* 62.

2. E.g., Maryland, South Carolina, Alabama, Texas. See Watson, *Liberty and Power,* 50–52, and Oakes, *Slavery and Freedom,* 127.

3. Viva voce voting was replaced by the secret ballot in the 1868 Underwood Constitution, which was drafted by Republicans. The only other southern state with significant property restrictions on the suffrage was North Carolina. On suffrage restriction in antebellum Virginia, see Chilton Williamson, *American Suffrage,* 223–41.

4. On sectional tensions in antebellum Virginia, see Ambler, *Sectionalism in Virginia.*

5. Elsa Barkley Brown, "Negotiating and Transforming the Public Sphere," 113. See also O'Brien, "From Bondage to Citizenship," chaps. 5–9. See as well the petition of Virginia blacks to their "fellow citizens" of the North, which calls for the suffrage, and *The Liberator,* September 5, 1965, excerpted in Sterling, *The Trouble They Seen,* 63–64.

6. *Address from the Colored Citizens of Norfolk, Va., to the People of the United States:*

Equal Suffrage in Norfolk, Virginia (June 1865), in Foner and Walker, *Proceedings,* 83–108. At this time black Virginians also organized Union League clubs in Hampton and Williamsburg. On African American political activity in early postbellum Virginia, see Lowe, *Republicans and Reconstruction,* 112–20.

7. Foner and Walker, *Proceedings,* 92; Maddex, *Virginia Conservatives,* 45; McConnell, *Negroes and Treatment,* 110.

8. *Proceedings of the Convention of the Colored People of Virginia,* 12.

9. Ambler, *Pierpont,* 81, 89, 162, 220–23, 227–28.

10. Royall, *Virginia Debt Controversy,* 14.

11. Ambler, *Pierpont,* 307.

12. Ibid., 281–83, 292; Maddex, *Virginia Conservatives,* 39.

13. *Acts,* 1865–66, 79–80; *Acts,* 1866–67, 499–500. The constitution of West Virginia, ratified in April 1862, obliged the state to assume an "equitable proportion" of the antebellum Virginia state debt as of January 1, 1861. When Congress admitted West Virginia to the Union on December 31, 1862, it sanctioned this agreement. Ratchford, *American State Debts,* 197; Randall, "The Virginia Debt Controversy."

14. The state owned the majority of nearly every antebellum railroad's stock. Moger, "Railroad Practices," 426.

15. Ratchford, *American State Debts,* 124; Pearson, *Readjuster Movement,* 3–4.

16. Stover, *Railroads of the South,* 41.

17. Reid, *After the War,* 330–40.

18. Kennaway, *The South after the War,* 193.

19. A legislative committee in 1877 estimated Virginia's economic losses from the war at $457 million, which included the value of slaves freed. Pearson, *Readjuster Movement,* 7 n. 25.

20. Taylor, *Negro in the Reconstruction,* 41, citing *Richmond Enquirer* of September 13, October 13, 1866, October 30, 1867, and April 11, 1868.

21. McPherson, *Ordeal by Fire,* 521; Eric Foner, *Reconstruction,* 276. As Peter Wallenstein pointed out to me in conversation, black suffrage in the South—in the elections of representatives to the state constitutional conventions—*preceded* the Fourteenth Amendment.

22. *Richmond Whig,* December 15, 1868, quoted in Maddex, *Virginia Conservatives,* 47. On Arkansas, see Eric Foner, *Reconstruction,* 440.

23. Allen, *Reconstruction,* 230–32 (text of the platform); Taylor, *Negro in the Reconstruction,* 24, and Ambler, *Pierpont,* 299–300 (1866 events); *Richmond Times,* April 18, 1867, quoted in Taylor, *Negro in the Reconstruction,* 212. In 1867 Hunnicutt explained that he expected whites and blacks to be accorded exactly equal rights.

24. For an illuminating overview of the Republican Party in Virginia, see Lowe, *Republicans and Reconstruction.* Underwood also implemented his progressive ideas in his capacity as a federal judge. In May 1867, e.g., he impaneled a grand jury for the U.S. circuit court at Richmond that included six African Americans. Among them were several men who would play prominent political roles in postwar Richmond: George Seaton, Cornelius Harris, Fields Cook,

and John Oliver. A few days later Underwood included twelve black men on the petit jury of the circuit court that was meeting to try Jefferson Davis, former president of the Confederacy. See Taylor, *Negro in the Reconstruction*, 214–15.

25. Maddex, *Virginia Conservatives*, 57.

26. "George Teamoh's Autobiography," manuscript, Carter Woodson Papers, Library of Congress, quoted in Sterling, *The Trouble They Seen*, 121.

27. As the *Richmond Dispatch* correspondent noted, "Not only had Sambo gone to the Convention, but Dinah was there also." Quoted in Elsa Barkley Brown, "Uncle Ned's Children," 330. On the participation of blacks in the gallery in the constitutional debates, see Brown, 332–34.

28. African American delegates such as Lewis Lindsay argued explicitly that the constitution should reflect the platform formulated in Richmond in April 1867. See Knight, "Reconstruction and Education," 32–33.

29. By the spring of 1869 more than half of the state offices in Virginia were unfilled "owing to the difficulty in finding men able to take the test-oath," as General George Stoneman, the new military commander, explained. Quoted in Lowe, *Republicans and Reconstruction*, 158–59.

30. Maddex, *Virginia Conservatives*, 59–73; Lowe, *Republicans and Reconstruction*, 159–63.

31. Lowe, *Republicans and Reconstruction*, 162, citing Stuart, *Narrative*, 51–52.

32. Jack P. Maddex (*Virginia Conservatives*, 71) has concluded that the moderate Republican delegation led by Franklin Stearns "probably changed more minds than did the nine," who did, however, apparently succeed in winning President-elect Grant over to their side. See also Lowe, *Republicans and Reconstruction*, 161. The constitutional convention sent its own group of delegates to argue in favor of the proposed law. See *Debates and Proceedings*, 557–58, for discussion of the delegation.

33. Before the Civil War state-supported public school systems were established in every Lower South state save Mississippi. Although the depression that followed the panic of 1837 reduced funding, Lower South states resumed support in the 1840s. Both Louisiana and Alabama had centralized, state-supported public school systems in 1860. On the antebellum school systems and the tendency of historians to neglect their existence in favor of the argument that public schools in the South were a Reconstruction innovation, see Thornton, "Fiscal Policy," 378–80.

34. On the early history of education in Virginia, see Maddox, *Free School Idea*, 12–15, 46–75; Heatwole, *History of Education in Virginia*, 4–61, 102–6; Knight, *Documentary History of Education*, 2:94, 140, 155–56, 550–63, 3:129–36, 180–83, 4:5–20, 85–89, 92–109; and Stevenson, *Life in Black and White*, 123–33, esp. 124 n. 92 and 131–32.

35. The Valley had the largest concentration of small towns in Virginia; in 1850 it had ten towns with a population of more than 1,000. Shade, *Democratizing the Old Dominion*, 39–40.

36. Ibid., 243, 248, 266. These reforms were associated mainly with the Whig Party, which drew its vote in Virginia from the western regions and the

cities. See Sellers, "Who Were the Southern Whigs?," 342–44. On southern Whigs during and after the Civil War, see Alexander, "Persistent Whiggery."

37. Virginia's 1830 constitution used a complex formula that enfranchised all adult white men who owned lands or lots worth $25, or who paid at least $20 rent for lands for five years or more, or who were state taxpaying, housekeeping heads of families. It is estimated that nearly half (45.6 percent) of Virginia's adult white males remained disenfranchised under this constitution. See Freehling, *Drift toward Dissolution*, 76 n. 79. See also Chilton Williamson, *American Suffrage*, 234.

38. *Richmond Whig* quoted in McFarland, "Extension of Democracy," 19–24. For more on Wise's stand on public education, see Eaton, "Henry A. Wise," 485.

39. Ambler, *Pierpont*, 222.

40. Quoted in Ambler, *Pierpont*, 296. Pierpont was not VMI's only enemy: anti-Confederates hated the institution both for its elitism and for its contribution to the militarization of political culture prior to the war. David G. Carr, a delegate to the 1868 constitutional convention from Prince George and Dinwiddie Counties, proposed closing the academy, confiscating its funds, and selling its property to fund common schools. See *Debates and Proceedings*, 210.

41. In the early 1800s a series of slave rebellions led by literate black men culminating in the Nat Turner revolt in Southampton County convinced white Virginians of the dangers of African American education to the slave system. Nevertheless, some Virginia slaves and free blacks did learn to read and write. A small number of free blacks were taught in integrated Quaker schools; others taught themselves or were the beneficiaries of white scofflaws. John Janney of Loudoun County recalled that Quakers "who had colored boys living with them sent them to school along with their own children. There were two mulatto and one negro boy who attended our school, and they were taught and treated just as the other children were by both teacher and pupils." Janney and Janney, *John Jay Janney's Virginia*, 50–56, quoted in Stevenson, *Life in Black and White*, 276. Margaret Douglass, a white woman in Norfolk, was prosecuted in 1853 for teaching a black school there. See Foner and Pacheco, *Three Who Dared*, 57–95. In an 1865 petition to President Andrew Johnson complaining about Reconstruction policies in Richmond, black Richmonders estimated that three thousand members of their community could read and at least two thousand could read and write. *New York Tribune*, June 17, 1865.

42. W. E. B. Du Bois, *Black Reconstruction*, 641 (Booker T. Washington); Litwack, *Been in the Storm So Long*, 473 (second quotation, emphasis in the original), 474 (last quotation). On the freedpeople's desire for education, see Taylor, *Negro in the Reconstruction*, 137–73; Du Bois, *Black Reconstruction*, 637–67; Franklin, *Reconstruction*, 38, 52, 107–9, 140–41, 191; McPherson, *Abolitionist Legacy*, 143–295, and "White Liberals and Black Power"; Gutman, "Schools for Freedom"; Jones, *Soldiers of Light*; Morris, *Reading, 'Riting, and Reconstruction*; and James D. Anderson, *Education of Blacks*. Many of these books portray southern whites as hostile or indifferent to education; see esp. Anderson, *Education*

of Blacks, chap. 1, epilogue, and his article "Ex-Slaves and the Rise of Universal Education." Huntzinger ("The Birth of Southern Public Education," esp. 56–106) presents evidence of native white southern support for public education. Peter Wallenstein (*From Slave South to New South,* 152) points out that, given the postwar economic situation of white southerners, many who had previously sent their children to private schools could no longer afford tuition and transferred both their children and their allegiances to the public schools.

43. Alvord (*Inspector's Report,* 9–10) estimated in 1866 that there were at least five hundred such schools scattered throughout the South.

44. William Hepworth Dixon, a London editor, describing Richmond schools in 1866, quoted in Gutman, "Schools for Freedom," 270–71.

45. King, *The Great South,* 598; Ambler, *Pierpont,* 323 (quotation). Wise was undismayed by the school, although he did eventually petition to repossess the building. Like some other notable white Virginia men of honor, he appreciated the manly courage of John Brown and declared that he was "a great man." On Wise's respect for Brown, see Barton H. Wise, *Life of Henry A. Wise,* 247, and Kenneth S. Greenberg, *Honor and Slavery,* 90–91.

46. James D. Anderson, *Education of Blacks,* 15–16. On sabbath schools, see Horst, *Education for Manhood,* 13, 15, 21, 54, 60–63, 67, 73–74, 87, 90, 125, 157, 160, 166.

47. Gutman, "Schools for Freedom," 276.

48. Eric Foner, *Reconstruction,* 447; Litwack, *Trouble in Mind,* 57.

49. *Marion Conservative Democrat,* December 8, 1882.

50. Noting the outspoken opposition of the planter elite to free schools, historians of post–Civil War Virginia have mistakenly ascribed this position to white farmers and laborers. In his insightful study of rural education in Virginia, e.g., William A. Link nonetheless generalizes elite antagonism to public schools to the population at large. See Link, *Hard Country,* 16, where he describes an atmosphere of "deeply rooted and pervasive hostility to public education" in Virginia.

51. Conservatives made the same argument when Congress debated the 1874 Civil Rights Bill. Virginia's representatives and other white southerners threatened that the bill's provision prohibiting schools segregated by race would destroy the public school system in the South. Despite strong Republican counterarguments, the bill passed minus the schools provision. John T. Harris of Virginia read a letter from state Superintendent of Schools William H. Ruffner declaring that "the passage of the civil-rights bill now before Congress would immediately wipe out, or practically destroy, the public-school system of Virginia." See *Congressional Record,* 43d Cong., 1st. sess., vol. 2, pt. 1, 343–458 (December 19, 1873, January 5–7, 1874), esp. 377 (Ruffner), 385, 454.

52. *Journal of the Virginia Constitutional Convention,* 121, 299, 301. Black leaders also resisted segregated transportation facilities. For protests against segregated steamboats, see *Debates and Proceedings,* 150. Black southerners often disagreed about the desirability of integrated schools, in large part because of

the resistance of whites to hire African American teachers for mixed schools. But in *Dead End,* J. Morgan Kousser examined eighty-two cases between 1834 and 1903 concerned with racial discrimination in public schools. In addition to complicating the history of Jim Crow, Kousser documents convincingly that African American litigants "wanted integration, and they won it in a majority of the cases whose outcome is known" (pp. 5, 7).

53. *Debates and Proceedings,* 96, 150, 209–10. The citizens of Elizabeth City and Warwick Counties presented a petition "that there be no separate schools; but simple Christian legislation such as becomes a people who believe that 'God hath made of one blood all nations of men.'" Biographical information on Bland and Bayne is from Jackson, *Negro Office-Holders,* 2–4, and Newby, "'The World Was All before Them,'" 185.

54. *Journal of the Virginia Constitutional Convention,* 336–37, 340; Virginia Constitution, art. 8; Vaughn, *Schools for All,* 72–73. Ambiguity did have its uses: Thomas Bayne noted toward the end of the convention that he had promised his constituents that he would try to make a constitution that would not have the words "black" or "white" in it anywhere. *Debates and Proceedings,* 251. The Virginia Code of 1873 (title 23, chap. 78, sec. 58) provided that "white and colored persons shall not be taught in the same school, but in separate schools, under the same general regulations as to management, usefulness and efficiency."

55. Walker was quoted in congressional debate; see *Congressional Globe,* 41st Cong., 2d sess., 402, 543 (January 12). See also Kelly, "Congressional Controversy," 537–63, 541.

56. Petition of "Loyal Republicans of Virginia" to Congress, *Congressional Globe,* 41st Cong., 2d sess., pt. 1, 390, 440–41, 493–95, 502, 643–44, 720. See also Kelly, "Congressional Controversy," 542. The Readmission Act is in *U.S. Statutes at Large* 16 (1870): 62–63. The actual wording of the Readmission Act was "that the constitution of Virginia shall never be so amended as to deprive any citizen or class of citizens of the United States of the school rights and privileges secured by the constitution of said State." The imposition of "fundamental conditions" on Virginia that went beyond the Reconstruction Act of 1867 precipitated a split among congressional Republicans. Nineteen GOP senators and thirty-seven representatives, including future president James A. Garfield and New York power broker Roscoe Conkling, opposed the conditions appended to Virginia's readmission legislation. See Eric Foner, *Reconstruction,* 453.

57. Walter J. Fraser Jr., "William Henry Ruffner," 275 (quotation), 259, 269.

58. In the historical literature Ruffner is often called the "Horace Mann of Virginia" and portrayed as a racial progressive whose "idealism, vision, and scholarship with regard to the black man far surpassed that of his most learned contemporaries." Walter J. Fraser Jr., "William Henry Ruffner," 271. Although black Virginians did praise Ruffner for his industriousness in organizing the schools, they did not confuse him with a racial progressive. Not

only did Ruffner ensure that Virginia's public schools would be segregated, but he also played a leading role in the white southern assault on the proposed congressional Civil Rights Act of 1874, which initially prohibited public schools segregated by race. In May 1874 he wrote a brief article for *Scribner's*, a leading northern magazine. The article, which presumed a hierarchy of the races, insulted African Americans' sexual morality, and predicted the destruction of southern public schools if Congress outlawed segregation, prompted a rebuttal from at least one black church organization in Virginia. Ruffner, "Co-Education of the White and Colored Races," *Scribner's Monthly;* Minutes, Shiloh Baptist Association, August 1875, Virginia Baptist Historical Society, Richmond.

59. Virginia Legislature, *Senate Journal,* 493–95, 499, 505, 507.

60. *Acts of Virginia, 1869–1870,* 413; Virginia Legislature, *House Journal,* 471, 541, 568, 602, 606–7, 610, 615; Vaughn, *Schools for All,* 73; Jackson, *Negro Office-Holders,* 28. Black legislators felt that white Republicans had gone back on the spirit of the 1867 Union Republican platform hammered out in the first months of freedom at Richmond's First African Church. Indeed, in debates on the schools during the constitutional convention, Peter Jones had argued that failure by white Republicans to support mixed schools would signify the repudiation of their party's platform. See *Journal of the Virginia Constitutional Convention,* 339.

61. Ruffner, *First Annual Report,* 13, 153. Circumstances varied in the twenty-five counties that failed to pass a local school tax. According to Ruffner, these failures did not represent opposition to the school system but rather economic destitution. No school tax elections were held in the cities, which accounts for the discrepancy in numbers.

62. Ruffner, *Second Annual Report* (Richmond, 1873), 33, quoting the district supervisor of Spotsylvania County.

63. Peabody Fund administrator Barnas Sears moved to Virginia during Reconstruction and served at one time as school superintendent for Augusta County. Between 1870 and 1882 the Peabody Fund gave a fifth of all its donations to Virginia's free schools. Maddex, *Virginia Conservatives,* 212. Public schools of the antebellum era were typically financed by poll taxes as well. See Thornton, "Fiscal Policy," 353, 377.

64. Virginia Legislature, *Senate Journal,* 1876–77, doc. 17: *Communication from the Auditor of Public Accounts in Response to a Senate Resolution Calling for a Statement concerning Capitation Tax for the Year 1875,* 4.

65. Ruffner, *Second Annual Report,* 23.

66. James W. Walker to Mahone, April 11, 1869, quoted in Maddex, *Virginia Conservatives,* 75.

67. On the 1869 GOP convention and the formation of the True Republican ticket, see Lowe, *Republicans and Reconstruction,* 165–79. Walker had always dreamed of high national office—as a senator, as the vice presidential candidate on the 1872 Liberal Republican ticket, etc. See Maddex, *Virginia Conservatives,* 91, and the character assessment in Shifflett, "Gilbert Carlton Walker,"

61. Nevertheless, Walker was popular in Virginia—one of only a handful of transplanted northerners who were—and he served two terms as a congressman from Virginia after leaving the governor's mansion.

68. General Assembly, *Acts and Joint Resolutions*, 1870–71, 378–81.

69. Governor's Message, March 8, 1870, Virginia Legislature, *Senate Journal*, 1869–70, 158.

70. When James L. Kemper replaced Gilbert Walker in the governor's mansion in 1873, Virginia was receiving almost half of its revenue in coupons. Virginia Legislature, *Senate Journal*, 1874, doc. 3: *Communications from the Auditor of Public Accounts . . . Calling for Information as to What Amount of Taxes of the Present Fiscal Year Has Been Paid in Coupons, and What Amount in Currency*, 1–2. More taxes were paid in coupons than the percentage of bondholders living in Virginia would indicate: many bondholders sold the coupons to state residents for the express purpose of using them to pay taxes. Between January 1873 and October 1878 an average of nearly $1 million in coupons was received for taxes annually. Ratchford, *American State Debts*, 201–3.

71. *Antoni v. Wright*, 22 Grattan 833 (1872). Article 1, section 10, of the federal Constitution forbids states from "impairing the obligations of contracts."

72. Maddex, *Virginia Conservatives*, 171. An important difference between the tax histories of Virginia and other southern states during Reconstruction is that Virginia raised taxes while under Conservative, rather than Republican, rule. The fact that the Virginia Conservatives suffered more or less the same fate as Republicans elsewhere in the South bolsters J. Mills Thornton's ("Fiscal Policy," esp. 391) analysis of the relationship between tax hikes and Reconstruction politics.

73. Maddex, *Virginia Conservatives*, 148. There were a few other taxes, but they raised minimal amounts: taxes on gross receipts of transportation and insurance companies, license taxes on certain professions, and a sales tax, as well as a license tax, on liquor. Pearson, *Readjuster Movement*, 45. In 1879 two-thirds of the state's revenue came from land taxes (p. 94). According to Pearson (p. 170 n. 26), realty contributed 59 percent of the tax revenue in 1871 (compared with 36 percent in 1883).

74. Pearson, *Readjuster Movement*, 57; Moore, *Two Paths*, 20–21.

75. Virginia and Mississippi were the only former Confederate states that did not scale down state debt during Reconstruction. The other states lowered the amount of their obligations through statutes, constitutional amendments, and court decisions. See Ratchford, *American State Debts*, 192, table 15; McGrane, *Foreign Bondholders*, 282–389; and Thornton, "Fiscal Policy," 384. An early student of southern debts concluded that southerners used repudiation as a "weapon of defense and retaliation" against the Reconstruction governments supported by the North. See Randolph, "Foreign Bondholders," 74.

76. Considerable concern was expressed that the mentally ill were being housed in jails because there was no money for the asylums. Clippings, n.p., 1877, Mahone Scrapbooks, vol. 7, box 208, MP.

77. Ruffner, *Second Annual Report*, 1872, xi, xiv, 20, 26–29.

78. Ruffner, *Seventh Annual Report,* 1877, 12–13.

79. Ruffner, *Ninth Annual Report,* 1879, v.

80. Daniel quoted in *Richmond Whig,* December 3, 1880, recalling his earlier campaign against the schools.

81. *Staunton Spectator,* August 16, 1881.

82. Puryear quoted in Dabney, *New Dominion,* 381.

83. Curry quoted in Woodward, *Origins,* 93.

84. Virginia Legislature, *House Journal,* 1874, 347–48. Although gravely injured at Gettysburg and in debt after the war, Kemper refused to take advantage of personal bankruptcy laws. He did, however, consider the Funding Act a political and financial blunder. Moger, *Bourbonism to Byrd,* 22. For another example of funders' use of the rhetoric of honor, see John W. Daniel to M. Glennan, July 21, 1877, Daniel Papers, AL. This letter was published as a broadside in Lynchburg.

85. *Communication of the Governor of Virginia in Response to the Resolution of the Senate,* March 7, 1878, 12, VHS.

86. *Antoni v. Wright,* quoted in McGrane, *Foreign Bondholders,* 369.

87. Second Auditor, *Report,* 1874, cited in Pearson, *Readjuster Movement,* 8 n. 27. Pearson (p. 12) observes that bonds "were rapidly passing out of the hands of native [Virginian] owners." Royall, in *Virginia Debt Controversy,* 6, says that "almost all" of the bondholders were foreign; in *Some Reminiscences,* 118–19, he notes that "most" of the bondholders lived in England. Governor Walker, who signed the first post-Reconstruction debt legislation, was certainly financially interested. Pearson, *Readjuster Movement,* 32.

88. Moore, *Two Paths,* 27–28.

89. Kerr-Ritchie, *Freedpeople,* 144 (Cosby). In 1872 the Grange secured the appointment of a state chemist to analyze fertilizers, and in 1877 it convinced the legislature to establish a railroad commissioner and a department of agriculture. Lack of enforcement limited the benefits of these gains, however, and contributed to the atmosphere of political insurgency among farmers after 1877. The Grange was also associated with the Greenbackers in Virginia, where free silver enjoyed wide support, even among funders. On grangerism in Virginia, see Kerr-Ritchie, *Freedpeople,* 143–50; Pearson, *Readjuster Movement,* 59, 147; and Sheldon, *Populism,* 62. On grangerism in the South, see Saloutos, "Grange in the South," and Buck, *Granger Movement.* On greenbackerism in Virginia, see Moger, *Bourbonism to Byrd,* 106, and Pearson, *Readjuster Movement,* 81. On greenbackerism in the South, see Abramowitz, "Arena for Greenback Reformers"; Green, "Greenbackerism in Georgia"; Barjenbruck, "Greenback Political Movement"; and Roberts, "William Manning Lowe."

90. Moore, *Two Paths,* 51, table 1 (Readjuster Vote in Urban Areas), 52. According to Moore (p. 51 n. 14), the areas with the most concentrated white Readjuster votes were those counties where farm tenancy had made the smallest advances.

91. The coalition also won in many towns: e.g., Suffolk, Salem, Burkeville,

Farmville, Nottoway Court House, and Lunenburg Court House. See Moore, *Two Paths,* 50 n. 11, and *Richmond State,* November 4, 1879. The election returns published in the *Richmond Dispatch* on November 19, 1879, reveal the extent of the Readjusters' urban victory. This is not to say, however, that the Readjusters won the votes of all urban white workers. The city with the largest concentration of white workers, Richmond, remained safely Democratic, although a good number of white men voted for the coalition there. On the Readjusters in Richmond, see Rachleff, *Black Labor,* chap. 6.

92. See, e.g., Woodward, *Origins,* 75–106, in which the Readjusters are situated as latter-day Jeffersonians. Early scholarship on the Readjusters emphasized the rural origins of the party—see, e.g., Pearson, *Readjuster Movement,* 104, 130, 154–55, and Morton, *Negro in Virginia Politics,* 119.

93. See app. C, "Biographical Information on Prominent Readjusters," and app. D, "Occupational Background of Prominent Readjusters," in Moore, *Two Paths,* 140–56. Many Readjuster leaders combined farming with medicine, law, teaching, newspaper editing, or business.

94. Moore, *Two Paths,* 51 n. 14.

95. African American Readjuster legislators, like black Republicans, tended to have both more property and more education than the black electorate at large. Of the African American Readjuster legislators, five were farmers, and at least two of these owned their land. Black Readjuster assemblymen also included a lawyer, a doctor, a merchant, a teacher, and two ministers. See biographical entries in Jackson, *Negro Office-Holders.*

96. My thanks go to Peter Wallenstein for leading me to this insight.

97. On the importance of factionalism in weakening the southern GOP, see Thomas Holt, *Black over White,* 123–24, 175–76, 220; Alexander, "Political Reconstruction in Tennessee"; Curry, "Crisis Politics in West Virginia"; and Balk and Hoogenboom, "Origins of Border State Liberal Republicanism."

98. Lowe, *Republicans and Reconstruction,* 87 (quotation), 96.

99. Wynes, *Race Relations,* 8–10; Taylor, "The Negro in the Reconstruction," 525–26.

100. Jackson, *Negro Office-Holders,* 72–79; Blake, *William Mahone,* 137.

101. In the fall of 1871, African American men and women accounted for 672 of 895 prisoners in the state penitentiary (609 men and 63 women). Of the men, 433 were contracted out. Keve, *History of Corrections in Virginia,* 90. The convict labor system was an immediate target of black Readjusters. Although it contracted out convict labor, Virginia never leased its entire prison operation to private contractors, as other states of the former Confederacy did. This was in part because of black political power; other reasons advanced for the lack of leasing in Virginia include the existence, even in the antebellum era, of a state penitentiary (rejuvenated and expanded by the Readjusters) and a state prison farm. On convict leasing in the South, see Ayers, *Vengeance and Justice,* 185–222; Mancini, *One Dies, Get Another;* and Lichtenstein, *Twice the Work of Free Labor.*

102. Teamoh quoted in *New National Era,* January 26, 1871. Virginia's 1866 Black Code included stripes as a penalty for petty larceny. See Wilson, *Black Codes,* 102.

103. Cataline was a Roman whose name became synonymous with conspiracy. For instances of Mahone compared to Cataline, see clipping, January 9, 1880, George W. Bagby Scrapbook, 1877–81, Bagby Family Papers, VHS. For Moses, see undated broadside, 1877 Broadside Collection, AL. For Napoleon, see *Richmond Whig,* July 27, 1877.

104. Funder extraordinaire William L. Royall, perhaps Mahone's most persistent political antagonist, sniped at his background at every opportunity, as when he described Mahone as having received "what education he had at the State's expense" at VMI. Royall, *Virginia Debt Controversy,* 47. The standard biography of Mahone is Blake's *William Mahone.*

105. Allen W. Moger (*Bourbonism to Byrd,* 69) recalled that in the 1930s and 1940s "the worst charge that could be brought against an [anti-Democratic] opposition candidate was that he had been associated in any way with Mahone and the Readjusters."

106. Freeman, *Lee's Lieutenants,* 730, 749–50. The description of the Battle of the Crater comes from McPherson, *Battle Cry of Freedom,* 759–60. Mahone's major engagements were in the Wilderness, where a wounded James Longstreet recommended Mahone's promotion to major general, and the Battle of the Crater, both in 1864. The other division at Appomattox still in fighting form was that of Major General Charles W. Field.

107. Freeman, *Lee's Lieutenants,* 552–54.

108. Quoted in ibid., 553. Mahone's small stature earned him the nickname "the little General." His thinness, caused by dyspepsia, was legendary. When informed that her husband had been injured during battle but had received only a flesh wound, Mahone's wife reportedly cried, "Flesh wound? It can't be a flesh wound; the General hasn't any flesh!" Blake, *William Mahone,* 45.

109. Blake, *William Mahone,* 35.

110. Woodward, *Origins,* 5. On politics and railroads in Reconstruction Virginia, see Moger, "Railroad Practices." For a broader survey of these issues, see Martin, "Troubled Subject of Railroad Regulation," and Summers, *Railroads, Reconstruction.*

111. Every gubernatorial election in the 1870s turned on the railroad issue. In Mahone's camp were Governors Walker, Kemper, and Holliday, but Walker's brother James represented the Pennsylvania Railroad's interests. Colonel Robert E. Withers, who fought Kemper for the Conservative nomination in 1873, was connected with the Baltimore and Ohio, as was Republican state chairman Williams C. Wickham.

112. Consolidation, like other acts of incorporation, required an act of the legislature—hence its politicization. Further complicating matters was the state's interest as stockholder in railroads being considered for consolida-

tion. Consolidation in Virginia was not unopposed from within, although the prominence of the agents of the Baltimore and Ohio among the enemies of consolidation bolstered Mahone's construction of consolidation as the preservation of "home rule" over transportation in the commonwealth. On the 1870–71 legislature and the railroads, see Blake, *William Mahone*, 111–23, and Moger, "Railroad Practices," 437–40. On state aid to railroads during Reconstruction, see Goodrich, "Public Aid to Railroads."

113. See speech of John W. Johnston in *Congressional Record*, 47th Cong., Special Senate Sess. (1881), 56.

114. In 1876, unable to satisfy its New York and London creditors during the depression, the Atlantic, Mississippi, and Ohio (AM&O) was delivered into receivership. Leading the forces of repudiation of the state debt, which was held principally by New Yorkers and Englishmen, may well have appealed to Mahone. William Royall (*Virginia Debt Controversy*, 24) explains that Mahone lost his railroad and "[f]inding himself without a job, he turned to politics as his field and took up the public debt as his theme." Maddex (*Virginia Conservatives*, 249) follows Pearson (*Readjuster Movement*, 71) and argues that Mahone hoped to use the office of governor to resume control of the AM&O.

115. For a sympathetic but not uncritical appraisal of Mahone, see the sketch in Degler, *The Other South*, 271–76. On Mahone's teaching career, see Blake, *William Mahone*, 14–19. Public education for both races was central to Mahone's vision for the expansion and modernization of Virginia's economy. What form that education should take—whether it should have an academic or a vocational focus, especially where African Americans were concerned—was not of especial interest to Mahone, although this topic dominated the general conversation on education during most of the period from 1870 to 1915. On business interests and education in the New South, see James D. Anderson, *Education of Blacks*, 79–109, and "Ex-Slaves and the Rise of Universal Education," 19. See also Carl V. Harris, "Stability and Change," 377, 387–89.

116. *Richmond Whig*, July 5, 1877. The 1871 Funding Act stipulated that Virginia would pay 6 percent interest to its bondholders. In fact, the state never achieved this level of interest, paying in some years 5 percent and in others 4 percent. In 1881 the Readjusters' debt legislation, the Riddleberger Bill, lowered the interest level to 3 percent.

117. Mahone to Harrison H. Riddleberger, August 31, 1877, RP.

118. Massey to *Staunton Spectator*, special supplement, June 27, 1877.

119. Quotations from Gilbert C. Walker's speech, printed in *Whig*, October 6, 1877.

120. Mahone to Major Alfred R. Courney (member of the Richmond School Board), June 29, 1877; Clipping of reprint, n.p., n.d., Mahone Scrapbooks, vol. 7, box 208, MP.

121. Miller to Mahone, November 2, 1877, box 12, MP.

122. *Richmond Dispatch*, October 5, 1877.

123. Blake, *William Mahone*, 170 (first quotation); *Communication from the*

Governor of Virginia in Response to the Resolution of the Senate, March 7, 1878 (second quotation), VHS. The Barbour Bill required that half of all incoming government revenue go to government operations, a fifth to the schools, and three-tenths to servicing the debt, and that the government and the schools should receive their shares in cash. These terms, of course, were unfulfillable without voluntary debt scaling on the part of the state's creditors. At the same time that he rejected the Barbour Bill, Holliday vetoed a proposal by John Massey to collect school taxes separately and in cash. Hancock, *Massey,* 135–41.

124. *Annual Message from the Governor to the General Assembly of Virginia,* 14.

125. Virginia Legislature, *House Journal,* 1877–78, 425–30.

126. This invitation to black Virginians had precedents. In 1878 the "Committee of 39," a Conservative group dedicated to full funding of the debt, had invited the cooperation of "every citizen of Virginia to preserve the credit of the State." Blake, *William Mahone,* 182. The Readjusters referred to this organization as the "Last Dollar Debt Paying Organization," and its members as "Last Dollar Men," which could be interpreted both as paying the entire debt or paying every last dollar in Virginia's coffers to creditors. On the Readjuster response to this position, see Wythe G. Bane to C. H. Payne, April 14, 1879, published as a flyer, in Mahone Scrapbooks, vol. 8, box 208, MP.

127. Jefferson quoted in *Richmond Whig,* April 6, 1881, in an article recalling the 1879 convention. Jefferson was referring to the story of the pool of Bethesda told in John 5:1–15. My thanks to John Boles for pinpointing this citation.

128. *Southern Workman,* December 1879. The *Workman's* editors favored payment of the debt, as did other prominent black Virginians. See Taylor, *Negro in the Reconstruction,* 268.

129. *Richmond Whig,* January 31, February 5, 7–8, 10, 12, 15, 17–18, 1879, in Mahone Scrapbooks, vol. 9, box 208, MP.

130. Ruffner, *Ninth Annual Report,* 1879, x.

131. Mahone quoted in Blake, *William Mahone,* 149.

132. *Richmond Whig,* April 6, 1881.

133. After the Barbour Bill was vetoed, brokers in New York made one last attempt to negotiate a legislative settlement between Virginia and its bondholders. Former U.S. secretary of the Treasury Hugh McCulloch presented a bill to the General Assembly during the 1878–79 session that lowered the state's interest payments and released Virginia from liability for West Virginia's portion of the debt. Readjusters objected to a number of the bill's provisions, particularly its continued support for tax-receivable coupons. Moderate Readjusters were induced to support the bill when it incorporated Readjuster D. W. Henkel's proposal to authorize city and county tax collectors to deliver three-fourths of their estimated school revenue in cash to a special local school fund. The negotiations surrounding the McCulloch Act exemplified the competition between the debt and the schools. On the McCulloch Bill, see Pearson, *Readjuster Movement,* 85–89.

134. The Mahone Papers are full of cards and letters from all over the state requesting election education materials—copies of Mahone's speeches on the debt, copies of Conservative debt legislation (the Barbour and McCulloch Bills) and Readjuster critiques of it, the Conservative Party platform, etc. See, e.g., G. R. C. Phillips to Mahone, March 31, 1879; R. A. Finnell to Mahone, June 12, 1879; R. T. Thorp to Mahone, August 21, 1879; and John E. Massey to Mahone, May 17, June 10, 1879. See also Richard A. Wise to Mahone, March 17, 1879, in which Wise outlines how to improve distribution of the *Whig* and argues the importance of newspapers in the canvass. All in boxes 15–16, MP.

135. Massey to Mahone, May 17, 1879, box 15, MP.

136. Munford, *Random Recollections*, 148. Munford may have been speaking about the election of 1882, but the point holds.

137. *Southern Workman*, January 1880.

138. Walter N. Newman to Lewis E. Harvie, June 3, 1879, Harvie Family Papers, VHS.

139. J. B. Rust to Mahone, November 7, 1879, box 16, MP. See also Rachleff, *Black Labor*, 90; Pearson, *Readjuster Movement*, 128; Blake, *William Mahone*, 180; and Moore, "Black Militancy," 171.

140. Johnston, "Participation of Negroes," 225; Wynes, *Race Relations*, 20.

141. The thirteen African American legislators were, in the House of Delegates, Edward D. Bland, G. W. Cole, Johnson Collins, Shed Dungee, William D. Evans, Ross Hamilton, Nevison Lewis, Robert Norton, Richard G. L. Paige, Archer Scott, and Henry D. Smith, and, in the Virginia Senate, Cephas L. Davis and Daniel Norton. *Richmond Dispatch*, November 14, 1879. Jackson (*Negro Office-Holders*) also counts thirteen black Republicans elected to the General Assembly, but he omits Cole and adds Littleton Evans.

142. Godwin to Mahone, November 12, 1879, box 16, MP.

143. Wise to Mahone, November 12, 1879, ibid.

144. See, e.g., 1879 letters to Mahone from R. W. Arnold, November 5; R. T. Thorp, November 6, 12; W. W. Newman, November 10; Richard S. Wise, November 11–12; B. F. Jarratt, November 12, 17; E. E. Hathoway, November 13; Rutledge P. Hughes, November 13; L. L. Lewis, November 14; A. H. Lindsay, November 17; H. C. Brightwell, November 19; Robert P. Hughes, November 24; Robert A. Richardson, November 23; and T. E. Burford, November 25 —all in boxes 16–17, MP.

145. Langley to Mahone, November 12, 1879, box 16, MP. In the late nineteenth century, southern state legislatures battled over whose responsibility it was to protect crops from stock animals: should the crops be fenced or the stock penned? On common grazing rights and the fence issue, see Hahn, *Roots of Southern Populism*, 58, 60–63, 240, 243–46, 252–53, 282, "Hunting, Fishing, and Foraging," and "Common Cents or Historical Sense?"; Kantor and Kousser, "Common Sense or Commonwealth"; and Kantor, *Politics and Property Rights*.

146. Lewis to Mahone, November 14, 1879, box 16, MP.

CHAPTER 2

1. Langston quoted in undated broadside, 1877 Broadside Collection, AL.

2. Kousser, *Shaping of Southern Politics*, 27, table 1.3; Woodward, *Origins*, 75–105, 80 (Hill). Ayers (*Promise of the New South*, 46–47) writes that "the years between 1880 and 1884 marked the high point of independent voting in the South."

3. On the Greenbackers in the South, see Hahn, *Roots of Southern Populism*, 226–38; Saloutos, *Farmer Movements*, 48–54; Hyman, *Anti-Redeemers*, 4, 18–19, 22–23, 82, 172–76, 183–93; Rachleff, *Black Labor*, 82–85, 92; Letwin, *Challenge of Interracial Unionism*, 55–87; Abramowitz, "Arena for Greenback Reformers"; Barjenbruck, "Greenback Political Movement"; Green, "Greenbackerism in Georgia"; Gutman, "Black Coal Miners"; and Roberts, "William Manning Lowe." With its commitment to democratic ideas and its tentative embrace of interracial solidarity, the Knights of Labor in particular both contributed to and benefited from interracial democracy in the South. On the Knights in the South, see McLaurin, *Knights of Labor*, and Kahn, "Knights of Labor." On the Knights in Richmond, see Fink, *Workingmen's Democracy*, 149–77; Rachleff, *Black Labor*, 124–78; and Painter, *Standing at Armageddon*, 27–30. Knights won control of Lynchburg's city council in 1887 on a platform that supported public education and shared patronage between blacks and whites. See Schewel, "Local Politics in Lynchburg." For a more general treatment of the Knights, see Voss, *Making of American Exceptionalism*, and Weir, *Beyond Labor's Veil*.

4. Hyman, *Anti-Redeemers*, 193; Woodward, *Origins*, 84–85.

5. Reviewing the literature on black political participation in the 1880s, LaWanda Cox ("From Emancipation to Segregation," 248) noted that "black voters, rather than lapsing into confusion and apathy after redemption, responded whenever an avenue remained open to some measure of power or meaningful self-assertion." In the late 1880s a significant minority of black leaders called for Afro-American alliance with the Democrats on the ground that the GOP had failed to represent black interests. For evidence of African American overtures to the Democrats in this period, see Rabinowitz, *Race Relations*, 300–303. On black dissatisfaction with the Republican Party, see Eric Foner, *Reconstruction*, 537–39; Ayers, *Promise of the New South*, 38–43; and DeSantis, "Negro Dissatisfaction with Republican Policy."

6. Historians of Reconstruction have revealed black southerners' intense organizational activity in the years following emancipation. In the countryside, black men formed militias that guarded black families and served as collective bargaining intermediaries between the freedpeople and their employers. See Hahn, *New Jerusalem*, chap. 4, "Reconstructing the Body Politic," MSS 18–21, and Saville, *Work of Reconstruction*, 146–51. On the important role played by freedwomen in black community politics, see Elsa Barkley Brown, "Negotiating and Transforming," and Sharon Ann Holt, "Making Freedom Pay." Urban blacks organized legions of voluntary associations in the late 1860s

and 1870s. In Richmond alone, there were more than thirty secret societies by 1866. Sometimes these organizations offered services that southern municipalities refused to provide for their African American residents, such as burial services. In other instances the associations served educational, spiritual, or civic purposes. On African American associations in Richmond, see Elsa Barkley Brown, "Uncle Ned's Children," 294–313.

7. Hahn, "Politics of Black Rural Laborers," 22, 28.

8. Ibid., 22. For a fascinating discussion of the formation of rural black political culture in the immediate postwar years, see Hahn, " 'Extravagant Expectations.' " On the Union League, see Fitzgerald, *Union League Movement.*

9. Rachleff, *Black Labor.*

10. Until 1913—with the ratification of the Sixteenth Amendment—U.S. senators were elected by state legislatures, rather than by popular vote.

11. *New York Times,* April 27, 1880, quoted in Rachleff, *Black Labor,* 99. Paul had a history of opposition to the GOP. He first entered politics in 1874, when he denounced "ring" rule in the Republican Party during mass meetings in Richmond. In 1878 Paul became a local organizer for the Greenbackers, and although he did not support the Readjusters in the 1879 election, he was converted in 1880 by their legislative program.

12. Williams, *Capt. R. A. Paul,* 16–17. The reference is to the Battle of the Crater (1864), in which troops under Mahone's command slaughtered black Union soldiers.

13. W. C. Balch to Mahone, October 2, 1880, box 22, MP.

14. Riddleberger to Mahone, March 25, 1880, box 18, MP.

15. *Richmond Whig,* January 31, 1880.

16. On the GOP convention, see *New York Times,* April 23–27, 1880. Cf. *Nation,* April 29, 1880. The Virginia Republican Party, like the national party, did not favor debt repudiation. By 1880, however, the state's GOP leaders had split over the issue of coalition with the Readjusters. Different Republican factions favored alliance with the Readjusters for different reasons. Black Republican Readjusters saw coalition as their best chance to gain influence within the Republican Party itself. Among this group were Robert A. Paul, Norfolk assemblyman Richard G. L. Paige, and former customs house official Collin T. Payne. Others viewed the Readjusters chiefly as the best chance to defeat the Democrats in Virginia. This latter group included former U.S. senator John F. Lewis, federal judge Robert W. Hughes, Internal Revenue collector James D. Brady, John Tyler Jr. (the antebellum president's son), and Richmond postmaster George K. Gilmer. As James Tice Moore points out, most of these men were native Virginians, and many had collaborated with Mahone and Gilbert C. Walker in the 1869 "True Republican" campaign. The Republican anti-Readjusters were led by Mahone's old enemy from his railroad days, Williams C. Wickham, and included U.S. congressmen John F. Dezendorf and Joseph Jorgensen as well as most of the state's federal officeholders who feared (rightly) for their jobs under Readjuster control. See Moore, *Two Paths,* 70–

71, and Woodward, *Origins,* 99–100. On black Republican Readjusters, see Rachleff, *Black Labor,* 41, 46–47, 66, 92–93, and Williams, *Capt. R. A. Paul,* 18–19.

17. James Kernan, a Greenbacker journalist, encouraged Mahone to organize Virginia for the Greenbackers, arguing that "There is little difference between a Re-Adjuster and a Greenbacker—one is local and the other National, and that is all." Kernan hoped that if the election were thrown into the House of Representatives (as occurred in the presidential election of 1876), Virginia's presidential electors would tip the balance in favor of the Greenbacker candidates. James Kernan to Mahone, July 1, 1880, box 20, MP. Cf. Henry Nichols, New York City, to Mahone, June 3, 1880, box 19, MP.

18. The national GOP's decision to center its campaign on support of black rights made it even more difficult for black Virginians to consider voting the Readjuster ticket. On Republican strategy in the 1880 election, see Hirshson, *Farewell to the Bloody Shirt,* 79–86.

19. Readjusters in black-majority counties were understandably more concerned about the loss of the black vote than Readjusters elsewhere. The complaint of William M. Hessing of Powhatan County that "very few if any [N]egroes will vote our Electoral Ticket," even with strenuous campaigning by black Readjusters, failed to arouse Readjusters in white-majority portions of the state. Hessing to Mahone, September 28, 1880; see also Charles H. Miller to Mahone, September 14, 1880—both letters in box 22, MP.

20. The Republicans had won in Virginia as recently as the 1872 presidential election and since the Civil War had garnered about 40 percent of the presidential vote.

21. Resolution of the National Democratic Committee, September 7, 1880, box 22, MP.

22. George P. Hughes to William Elam, September 8, 1880; E. W. Greer to Mahone, September 9, 1880; E. D. Hundley to Mahone, September 13, 1880; W. M. Elliott to Mahone, September 14, 1880—all in box 22, MP.

23. S. E. Edmonds to Mahone, September 14, 1880; see also J. W. McBroom and S. W. Aston to Mahone, September 9, 1880, and John D. Foster to Mahone, September 23, 1880, box 22, MP.

24. *Richmond State,* October 22–23, 1880. For Mahone's reaction to the national committee's decision, see the October 22, 1880, broadside, "Address to the Re-Adjusters of Virginia," Williams Papers, AL.

25. H. Alexander to Mahone, September 28, 1880, and George W. Batte to Mahone, October 14, 1880, box 23, MP. See also John D. Blackwell to Mahone, July 31, 1880, box 20, MP.

26. The Republicans came within 13,000 votes of winning the state, lending credence to Democratic anxiety over the effects of schism. The final tally was 96,449 for the Conservative Democrats, 84,020 for the Republicans, and 31,527 for the Readjusters. The Readjusters elected to Congress were John Paul from the Seventh District and Abram Fulkerson from the Ninth. For letters to Mahone detailing the loss of the black vote for the coalition, see

William H. Henning to Mahone, October 29, 1880; William Baskerville to Mahone, October 30, 1880; and A. H. Lindsay to Asa Rogers, November 1, 1880. On white defection from the coalition, see C. H. Causey to Mahone, November 6, 1880; Horatio Davis to Mahone, November 6, 1880; and John Aldridge to Mahone, November 9, 1880. All letters in box 23, MP.

27. Charles H. Causey to Mahone, November 6, 1880, ibid.

28. Charles H. Miller to Mahone, September 14, 1880, box 22, MP.

29. Rachleff, *Black Labor*, 63–74.

30. Ibid., 77–78.

31. Broadside, "The Lightning Vat!," December 30, 1880, Williams Papers, AL. The call was signed by seventeen prominent African American Republicans and workingmen, including Cornelius Harris, a freeborn lay preacher, shoemaker, and longtime GOP activist; Stephen D. Harris, a tobacco worker and labor activist; and James H. Williams, second vice master of the State Assembly of the Industrial Brotherhood, a black labor organization. Both Harris and Jones were delegates to the March 1879 Richmond convention that reevaluated the relationship between black Virginians and the GOP. Rachleff, *Black Labor*, 42, 62, 68, 79, 87. See also "An Address to the Republicans of Virginia and Our Sympathizers beyond the Borders of This Commonwealth," March 1881, Mahone Scrapbooks, box 211, MP. Written by black Republican Readjusters, this address called for an alliance with "that party which would be most liberal in securing to [black Virginians] the full and complete enjoyment of their political rights."

32. *Richmond Virginia Star*, September 27, 1879. John Oliver, a free black carpenter from Boston, was elected president of the Richmond chapter of the Colored National Labor Union in 1870. Another up-and-coming young black man active in that union was Lewis Lindsay, who would become an important Readjuster. On Oliver, see Rachleff, *Black Labor*, 36, 41, 56, 61–69, 90–99, 103, 187.

33. Booker to Mahone, May 29, 1881, box 30, MP.

34. E.g., John Aldridge to Mahone (November 9, 1880, box 23, MP), who wrote that white Readjusters were alarmed by the activity of the Republicans in Virginia and voted Democratic. See also E. E. Hathaway to Mahone, November 10, 1880, box 23, MP.

35. Mahone to Riddleberger, December 2, 1880, box 1, folder 7, RP.

36. Boze to Mahone, March 11, 1881, box 25, MP. Boze was encouraged in his apostasy by the vows of black Republicans in Lynchburg to support his bid for office in the 1881 fall election.

37. Lady to Mahone, November 14, 1880, box 23, MP. Readjusters such as Lady used "Bourbonism" as shorthand to refer to Conservative management of the state—management that, as explained in Chapter 1, inhibited the growth of manufacturing, failed to support educational facilities, etc. As for Horace Greeley, in 1872 schism within GOP ranks had produced the Liberal Republicans, who nominated the *New York Tribune* editor for president. Formerly a die-hard opponent of the Democrats and a defender of black civil

rights, by 1870 Greeley was denouncing the Freedmen's Bureau and exhorting black southerners to "Root, Hog, or Die!" His platform stressing "local self-government" in the South was amenable to southern Democrats looking for a way to beat the regular Republican candidate, General Ulysses S. Grant, and the Democratic National Convention endorsed the Liberal Republican candidate and platform as its own. On the Liberal Republicans and the 1872 election, see Eric Foner, *Reconstruction*, 499–511.

38. Although happy to replace Democrats with Readjusters in federal patronage positions, the president refused to abandon Virginia's Republican officeholders. "I will not remove Republicans to appoint Mahone men," he insisted. Garfield to John Hay, May 29, 1881, quoted in DeSantis, *Republicans Face the Southern Question*, 147. On the patronage issue, see DeSantis, 150. On Mahone's decision to ally with the GOP, see DeSantis, 144, and Blake, *William Mahone*, 206.

39. The Democratic leader of the Senate, Ben Hill of Georgia, charged Mahone with betraying the voters of Virginia. Printed speech of Benjamin H. Hill, "Fidelity to Trusts the Highest Duty," in the U.S. Senate, March 14, 1881, 6. In his March 28 response, Mahone relied on the old Whig elevation of "statesmanship" over "partisanship." Mahone was supported in his efforts to join the GOP by the powerful senator from New York, Roscoe Conkling, and his close friend, secretary of the Senate and editor of the *Washington, D.C., National Republican* George Gorham. Against the Readjuster stood the Garfield wing of the party, which included such senators as James G. Blaine and John Sherman. On the political calculations of Republicans regarding Mahone's course in the Senate, see Rothman, *Politics and Power*, 32–33.

40. Patronage assessments averaged 5 percent of salary to support professional party workers, finance the printing of campaign materials, and, in Virginia as elsewhere in the South, pay the poll taxes of the indigent. The Pendleton Act outlawed *compulsory* contributions and political services from federal officeholders but left the door open for "voluntary" assessments and partisan labor. Assessments declined toward the end of the nineteenth century and were replaced with corporate financing and private donations. On assessments, see Skowronek, *Building a New American State*, 48, 53, 61, 65–66, 74–78. On the Pendleton Act, see Hoogenboom, "The Pendleton Act," 301–18, and *Outlawing the Spoils*, 200–203, 210–19, 238–564, and Aron, *Ladies and Gentlemen of the Civil Service*, 78, 107–20.

41. Lindsay to Asa Rogers, November 1, 1880, box 23, MP. As J. H. Merchant, a black Readjuster from Lynchburg explained, "[Black Republicans] have had to fight not only Funders but our own party leaders known as gripsacks. . . . The colored people will not be able to cast their votes to their own advantage as long as those gripsacks have control of Federal patronage." Merchant to Mahone, November 25, 1880, quoted in Robert Euell Brown, "Rise and Fall of the Lynchburg Readjusters," 20.

42. Keller, *Affairs of State*, 310–14; Rothman, *Politics and Power*, 179–81. By the 1890s patronage distribution had become so burdensome to senators

that some were demonstrably relieved when the Civil Service Commission curtailed senatorial power in this area. As California senator Stephen White complained to Civil Service Commission chairman Theodore Roosevelt, "At present, members of Congress and Senators are annoyed from day to day by the persistent demands of persons for place, and it is a question whether we were elected to legislate, or procure employment." Quoted in Rothman, *Politics and Power,* 180.

43. "The desirability of being a Re-Adjuster will begin to awaken an interest in the bosoms of a good many who now like to be classed with the Funders," the *Alexandria Picayune* predicted in April 1881. In Mahone Scrapbooks, 1881, box 211, MP.

44. Frank S. Blair to Mahone, November 20, 1880, box 23, MP. This point of view was not unopposed, although it triumphed. In a letter to H. H. Riddleberger, Mahone reported on the difficulties he had persuading the two Readjusters elected to Congress in 1880, John Paul and Abram Fulkerson, to abandon the Democratic caucus in the House of Representatives. When confronted by Mahone's arguments regarding black support for the coalition and the benefits of controlling federal patronage in Virginia, Paul, replying that his people were Democratic Readjusters, "said his people cared nothing for Federal patronage." Mahone to Riddleberger, December 30, 1880, box 1, folder 7, RP.

45. John Warwick Daniel, 1880 campaign speech, Daniel Papers, AL.

46. Pearson, *Readjuster Movement,* 154; *Staunton Spectator,* May 17, 1881, quoting *Charlottesville Chronicle.* Regarding Mahone's energetic exploitation of his patronage power, one Readjuster opponent complained: "No new member of congress ever did more tramping from one department to another, or more interviewing of heads of those bureaus and chiefs of divisions than does Senator Mahone. . . . The most insignificant employee hailing from Virginia is not beneath his notice and becomes a lever in his hands to move the readjuster forces." *Boston Globe,* September 5, 1882, quoted in Brooks Miles Barnes, "Triumph of the New South," 202.

47. Printed material was delivered to post offices in open sacks, which made it easy for postmasters to tamper with the mails. Persecuted by Democratic postmasters, one Readjuster complained in 1883 that he had to hire men to deliver Readjuster mail. D. S. Hale to Mahone, December 19, 1883, box 82, MP.

48. James E. Hughes to Mahone, June 22, 1883, box 73, MP. Federal law forbade the creation of a new post office within a mile of an existing one. (Otherwise, every block would have had its own!) For records of Readjuster post office appointments, see boxes 181–87, MP.

49. Dr. Joseph B. Strayer to Mahone, November 15, 1880, quoted in Moore, *Two Paths,* 76. According to W. S. Fernald, the collector of internal revenue for the Fourth Congressional District (at Danville), Judge Anderson of the Court of Appeals granted a divorce to the wife of a certain Latham because, she alleged, her husband was a Republican and she did not know that when she married him. Fernald to General G. Raum, April 9, 1881 (copy), box 28, MP.

50. The term "scalawag" was also associated with "race traitors"; see, e.g., the *Lynchburg Advance* article, quoted by the *Staunton Spectator* (April 5, 1881), recalling that "The Southern people regarded . . . men born on the soil of the South who joined the Republican party and attempted to organize the black vote, and lead it as deserters of their race and principles."

51. White voters bolted coalition movements after their formal alliance with the GOP in Mississippi in 1881 and Georgia in 1882. See Hyman, *Anti-Redeemers,* 190. Hyman also notes (pp. 174–75) the propensity of southern Independents to refer to themselves as the "true Democrats" of the South and to steer clear of formal alliance with the Republicans.

52. Frank P. Ruffin, "Mahoneism Unveiled," November 28, 1881, box 198, MP; McKinney, *Southern Mountain Republicans,* 104.

53. Flyer, Mahone to County Chairmen, June 24, 1882, box 187, MP. See also Flyers, Mahone to County Chairmen, July 9, 1882, box 179, and September 7, 1882, box 56, MP; and Navy Yard Scratch Book of Names for Appointment of Laborers and Mechanics, box 180, MP.

54. Thomas J. Jennings to Mahone, n.d., September–October 1882, box 58, MP.

55. For Johnson, see patronage form for June 2, 1882, Railway Mail Service, box 187, MP. For Putron, see printed list of Pension Bureau employees, n.d. [1882–83], box 179, MP.

56. Lists of federal appointments from Virginia, box 187, MP.

57. W. C. Franklin to Mahone, March 1882, and G. W. Hoge to Mahone, March 30, 1882, box 187, MP. Politicians in Virginia who attributed partisan allegiances to women did so based on the women's experience in the political system. Despite the fact that they could not vote, white women in Virginia had participated in political rallies and elections since 1840 and were considered to have political opinions. For an illuminating discussion of this topic, see Varon, *We Mean to Be Counted* and "Tippecanoe and the Ladies, Too." See also Rebecca Edwards, *Angels in the Machinery.* After emancipation, African American women in Virginia, as Elsa Barkley Brown has shown in "Negotiating and Transforming the Public Sphere," also took partisan stands and mediated black men's political relationships in a variety of ways.

58. The language and argumentation of the petition of the citizens of Elizabeth City County to Mahone (n.d. [1882]), is typical: "We the undersigned Readjusters and Republican Coalitionists of Hampton and the County of Elizabeth City, most respectfully urge that Mr. Kennon Whiting be retained as Postmaster at Hampton. Mr. Whiting was a consistent Union man during the war and has never cast a democratic vote and since the organization of the Readjuster party has zealously supported the Coalition movement. We the petitioners most seriously believe the displacement of Mr. Whiting will be injurious to the interests of the Readjuster Republican party of this county." Box 187, MP. See also Petition from Readjusters of Nelson County, November 28, 1881, to Mahone regarding Judge George S. Stevens, box 198, MP; Broadside, November 28, 1881, William H. Beveridge for position of sergeant at arms of

House of Delegates, box 199, MP; and Broadside, n.d. [November–December 1881], W. G. R. Fraser petition for position of doorkeeper in House of Delegates, box 200, MP.

59. Black Readjuster leader Lewis Lindsay revealed the criteria for patronage appointments in his report on Treasury Department employee John W. Cromwell. According to Lindsay, Cromwell was a black man who was registered to vote in Portsmouth, had voted the previous fall, and was a "pronounced Readjuster and took part in Petersburg Convention of colored men in favor of Readjusters." Lewis Lindsay to Mahone, March 1882, box 187, MP.

60. Clipping, *Culpeper Times*, November 18, 1881, Mahone Scrapbooks, box 215, MP.

61. Box 187, MP.

62. Judge Bell to Mahone regarding P. E. Bragg as post office employee, and Slade to Mahone, both June 1882, box 187, MP. Williams was replaced by William J. Powers. Mahone was trying to ferret out Straight-Out Republican railway workers appointed by the Hayes and Garfield administrations.

63. Edwin James Harvie to Lewis E. Harvie, December 24, 1882, Harvie Family Papers, VHS.

64. Petition, Republicans of the Fourth Congressional District to President Arthur, n.d. [December 1881], box 179, MP.

65. Flyer, Mahone to County Chairmen, March 24, 1883: "I wish you would send me a list, on the back of this circular, of the colored churches in your county and the full name of all the colored Preachers, and the Post Office address of each." Mahone received a list from sixty counties. Box 189, MP.

66. Lists, county precincts, n.d. [September 1883?], ibid.; "Organization of the Readjuster Coalition Party of Isle of Wight Co. Va. and the Names of the Ex. Comm. and Leut. and Capts.," 1883; List of voters and squad captains for King & Queen Co. with salary costs, in Mahone's handwriting, box 189. See also "A List of the Col'd Voters at Buena Vista Prec't," box 188. The correspondence index for 1883 lists many letters from county chairmen begging for horses.

67. See Virginia Code of 1873, chap. 37, sec. 15. Apparently some Democratic county clerks resisted sending the lists of delinquent voters to the Readjusters. See the letter of Attorney General Frank S. Blair to Mahone (October 25, 1882, box 60, MP) affirming the Readjusters' right to this information and the obligation of the county clerks to transmit it.

68. The 1876 poll tax could be amended only by two consecutive votes in the General Assembly and then by popular ratification. The Readjuster legislature passed such amendments in 1879–80 and 1881–82, and the voters endorsed them in 1882.

69. Flyer, J. A. Noon of Staunton to Precinct Workers, October 7, 1882, box 58, MP. Sir George Campbell (*White and Black*, 283) recalled that Democratic tax collectors often failed to collect poll taxes from African Americans until after an election was over.

70. H. J. of Rappahannock to Mahone, October 3, 1883, box 79, MP.

See Flyer, Mahone to Local Readjuster Organizations, September 19, 1883: "Please send me as quickly as you can a list of the names of such Funders [Democrats] as you think are reasonably open to conviction, giving the Post Office of each." Box 78, MP.

71. Herring to Mahone, October 2, 1883, box 78, MP.

72. Hyman (*Anti-Redeemers*, 192) notes the weakness of hill country political organizational structures and their inability to withstand Democratic challenges.

73. On the 1884 presidential election and the Republican Party's "southern strategy" of aiding independent movements, see De Santis, *Republicans Face the Southern Question*, 182–227; Hirshson, *Farewell to the Bloody Shirt*, 118–22; and Kousser, *Shaping of Southern Politics*, 23–24.

74. Blake, *William Mahone*, 233.

75. Pincus, *Virginia Supreme Court*, 11. Mahone's correspondence index for 1879 shows dozens of petitions for positions as county judges. Box 168, MP. See also John B. Lady to Mahone, November 14, 1879, box 16, MP.

76. Pincus counts seventy-nine between 1870 and 1902, adding eight to Luther P. Jackson's old estimate. See Pincus, *Virginia Supreme Court*, 47 n. 118, and Jackson, *Negro Office-Holders*, 12–13, 30, 59, 61–67.

77. W. S. Fernald to General G. Raum (copy), April 9, 1881, box 28, MP. See also C. H. Causey to Mahone, November 6, 1880 (box 23, MP), in which Causey asserts that "wherever we have a good county judge there we have a powerful influence to start with." Conversely, William Blake, of the far eastern county of Matthews, insisted in a letter to D. H. Foster, January 2, 1880 (box 18, MP), that "if the legislature will give us a readjuster judg [*sic*] at the next election for the legislature you will see almost a unanimous vote for readjustment[;] if a funder judg[e,] readjustment will be dead in the county of Mathews forever." For more on the participation of black Virginians in the courtroom, see Pincus, *Virginia Supreme Court*, 17–50. In 1879 federal circuit court judge Alexander Rives charged his grand jury to examine the jury lists of state judges to determine if citizens were being excluded on account of race. Two grand juries indicted a total of fourteen county judges. The U.S. Supreme Court upheld the indictments in *Ex parte Virginia*, 100 U.S. 339 (1880). None of the judges was convicted, however, and Judge Rives's campaign to increase the numbers of black jurors came to little. All of the cases cited by Pincus in which multiple black jurors served came from the period of Readjuster dominance of the courts. See Pincus, *Virginia Supreme Court*, 20–22, 25 n. 26.

78. Clipping, *Richmond State*, September 13, 1889, Frank Gildart Ruffin Papers, 1874–92, AL (first quotation); *Marion Conservative Democrat*, September 1, 1882; *Staunton Spectator*, February 28, April 11 (second quotation), 1882. The Commissioner of Sales Bill passed the house (House Bill No. 2, extra sess., 1882) but was killed in the senate by the opposition of four former Readjusters.

79. Though less implicated in this relationship than whites, black Republican leaders were not exempt from charges of corruption. In the black-majority

county of Northampton, e.g., Afro-Americans received a token number of minor posts (constables, overseers of the poor) while the white minority divided the more prestigious and lucrative jobs with Conservatives on a five-to-four basis. In return, Northampton was represented in the legislature by an African American Republican, Peter J. Carter. On GOP-Conservative fusion, see Brooks Miles Barnes, "Triumph of the New South," 101–4. On black Virginia Republicans' dissatisfaction with their party, see George F. Bragg Jr. to *Journal of Negro History* 11 (October 1926). Republican/Conservative fusion in Virginia was representative of the conciliatory patronage policies of the southern GOP in the 1870s. See Eric Foner, *Reconstruction,* 347–51, and Powell, "The Politics of Livelihood."

80. Dungee to Mahone, April 8, 1881, box 28, MP.

81. Recognizing that Mahone needed the votes of Republicans as much as the Virginia GOP needed his leadership and popularity, President James Garfield refused to abandon the party organization in Virginia by turning over complete control of federal patronage to Mahone. Instead, the president divided the offices between the Straight-Outs and the Readjusters. DeSantis, *Republicans Face the Southern Question,* 150.

82. Corprew to Mahone, April 18, 1881, box 28, MP.

83. Quoted in *Petersburg Lancet,* September 2, 1882.

84. Lewis to Mahone, July 8, 1881, box 32, MP. See also William E. Cameron to H. H. Riddleberger, March 22, 1881 (box 1, folder 8, RP), in which he warns against meanness in "dealing with [black Readjusters'] little claims for places," as that would "furnish the Grip-Sackers a strong whip by which to lash them back before the Election comes."

85. Preston to Mahone, July 22, 1881, box 32, MP. This was Preston's second attempt to communicate on this topic with Mahone. In May he had written that "the people is a thinking hard of you and i have dune got shame myself teling the people miself that you are again to give the people something too due and dont due it and the callared People said last night [at a mass meeting] that Sampson P Baily was neither a member of congress and neather a senator and yet he could get people samthing to due in the government servise and they says it shows on your face that you are not a good friend as you have bin recomended to be." Preston to Mahone, May 13, 1881, box 30, MP.

86. Cameron to Riddleberger, March 22, 1881, box 1, folder 8, RP.

87. Fusion movements between Republicans and either disaffected Democrats or Independent/Greenbacker organizations emulating the Readjusters' efforts were supported by the Arthur administration in Texas, Mississippi, North Carolina, South Carolina, Georgia, Alabama, Tennessee, and Arkansas. The administration passed over similar constellations in Louisiana and Florida in favor of Straight-Out Republican organizations. In the congressional elections of 1882 the South elected only eight Republicans—one less than in 1880—but sent eight Independents—four more than in 1880—for a net gain of four anti-Democrats in the House, nearly doubling the size of ad-

ministration strength in the House from the South. This was important because of Republican losses in the North. Without the aid of southern anti-Democrats, the Republican Party stood little chance of retaining the executive in 1884. On Arthur's policy of aid to southern third-party movements, see De-Santis, *Republicans Face the Southern Question*, 182–227. See also Kousser, *Shaping of Southern Politics*, 23–24, and Hirshson, *Farewell to the Bloody Shirt*, 118–22, 138.

88. Flyer, Mahone to Readjuster County Chairmen, July 9, 1882, box 179, MP. "Please give me the names and postoffice address of (#) colored men, who would be glad to have employment in the Norfolk Navy Yard, or here in Washington, as laborers. . . . Let those persons you name be selected by the colored people themselves in your county. . . . Name only Readjusters, and such as stand by the caucus action of our party at Richmond and by President Arthur's administration." This final admonition was directed against supporters of James G. Blaine. In August this flyer was sent again to delinquent counties with a sharply worded request for action, indicating the high priority Mahone and his lieutenants placed on furthering black patronage and spreading it evenly throughout the state.

89. The economic importance of waterfront jobs in Norfolk would only increase: by the 1890s Norfolk was the world's leading port for coal (mined from the mountains of western Virginia and West Virginia), and by 1910 it was America's fourth largest port for cotton and the South Atlantic's source of exported lumber. Earl Lewis, *In Their Own Interests*, 12–13; Ransom and Sutch, *One Kind of Freedom*, chaps. 4–7; Moger, "Industrial and Urban Progress," 327. On relations between white and black dockworkers, see Arnesen, *Waterfront Workers of New Orleans*, esp. chaps. 3–5.

90. Statistics compiled from lists of Virginians employed by the federal government, n.d. [1882], boxes 179–87, MP.

91. *Nation*, March 1880, 204.

92. Rabinowitz, *Race Relations*, 282.

93. Richardson to Mahone, November 23, 1879, box 17, MP. See also D. J. Godwin to Mahone, November 12, 1879 (box 16, MP), J. M. Gills to Lewis E. Harvie, December 6, 1879 (Harvie Family Papers, VHS), and Lewis E. Harvie to Mahone, November 5, 1879 (box 16, MP), in which each writer urges immediate extension of patronage to the Readjusters' black Republican allies. The doorkeeper of the senate in the 1881–82 legislative session, Peter J. Carter of Northampton, was in fact African American, as was the second doorkeeper of the house, Charles Harris of Norfolk. In addition, there were two black clerks in the capitol, Richard Baptist of Mecklenburg and Bob Norton (son of Assemblyman Robert Norton) of York. See Bragg to *Journal of Negro History*, 673. For a list of black legislators, see Johnston, "Participation of Negroes," 262.

94. Moore, "Black Militancy," 181; Bragg to *Journal of Negro History*, 679.

95. Henderson, *Gilded Age City*, 74. Petersburg's African American citizens had enjoyed significant political power between 1869 and 1874, when white

conservatives managed to take control of the municipal government. Between 1872 and 1874, forty-one black men held city offices, including policemen and city councilmen. See Maddex, *Virginia Conservatives*, 200–202.

96. In 1885 John Mercer Langston became president of the institute. Two years later Democrats removed the black members of the Board of Visitors, failed to renew Langston's contract, and cut the budget, which in turn required a reduction in faculty. See Cheek and Cheek, "A Negro Runs for Congress," 14–15, and Henderson, *Gilded Age City*, 88, 139–40, 142–46.

97. The other three local black Readjusters were Captain James E. Hill, clerk of the Centre Market; George Dabney, keeper of the Powder Magazine; and Glemmory Henson, keeper of the Hay Scales. See *Petersburg Index-Appeal*, July 3, 1882; cf. *Petersburg Lancet*, July 15, 1882.

98. Henderson, *Gilded Age City*, 122–24.

99. Ibid., 134–36. Graded schools were a northern innovation and rare in the South before the 1890s.

100. Paige quoted in *Richmond Dispatch*, March 23, 1882.

101. Jackson, *Negro Office-Holders*, 92. See also Knight, "Reconstruction and Education," 28–34.

102. Quoted in Rabinowitz, "Half a Loaf," 579–80. Jacqueline Jones (*Soldiers of Light*, 65) notes the apparent desire of black parents to send their children to schools taught by native black teachers. For an overview of segregation and African American education in the New South, see Rabinowitz, *Race Relations*, 152–81.

103. *Staunton Spectator*, August 23, 1881.

104. *Virginia Star*, November 18, 1882, quoted in Rabinowitz, "Half a Loaf," 578.

105. Elsa Barkley Brown, "Uncle Ned's Children," 95, 97; Taylor, *Negro in the Reconstruction*, 160–63. In 1883 Richmond's new Readjuster-dominated school board hired black teachers and principals for all of the black schools except Richmond Normal. Williams, *Capt. R. A. Paul*, 27–28; Brown, "Uncle Ned's Children," 98–99.

106. Rabinowitz, "Half a Loaf," 579. White teachers in schools operated by the American Missionary Association and other religious organizations, on the other hand, were mainly from the North and better educated than their southern black colleagues. Black communities served by mission schools were frequently divided over the issue of black teachers, with many parents of the opinion that white instructors were superior to black instructors. In 1906 W. E. B. Du Bois argued in favor of integrated faculties, noting that "the only remaining point of intimate sympathetic broad-minded contact between the white and black world in the South is through the white teachers of Negro schools." McPherson, *Abolitionist Legacy*, 269–74, 292 (Du Bois).

107. *Virginia Star*, November 18, 1882.

108. *Petersburg Lancet*, July 15, 1882.

109. Shaw, *What a Woman Ought to Be*, 176, 185. The unsuitability of white teachers for black students was made in the petition presented to the Peters-

burg School Board: "It must appear to you that a white person, who by birth, education and breeding has always felt that the negro was intellectually, morally and socially inferior, is not the person to be put in charge of the intellectual and moral training of the children of that race. It must also appear to you that the persons who move in and out among the families of the children in a social way are best prepared to create and furnish means to supply in the school room that which the child lacks at home as an incentive to study; this your white teachers cannot do, and serious as the charge may be, in ninety-nine cases in a hundred the interest of the white teacher in charge of a colored school goes to the extent of drawing his or her monthly stipend—no further." *Petersburg Lancet,* July 15, 1882.

110. The resolutions of the Colored Virginia Baptist State Convention, which met in Staunton in May 1882, reveal the overlapping professional, moral, educational, and race concerns of Virginia's black citizens regarding the control of black schools: "Whereas, We believe that the educational interests of our children can be better promoted by being taught by colored teachers; and, Whereas, We believe that the colored youth that are graduating from the high schools of our country have a better right morally [than white graduates to teach in black schools], therefore, Resolved, That We will do all in our power to secure competent colored principals and teachers for all our public schools, with due respect to all." Minutes, Virginia Baptist State Convention, Colored, May 1882.

111. Henderson, *Gilded Age City,* 135–36.

112. Black Readjusters had approached Mahone before addressing the school board, hoping that he would back their drive for black teachers. But Mahone refused to support the black leaders, fearing a white backlash for this concession to African American political pressure. Henderson, *Gilded Age City,* 136.

113. *Petersburg Index-Appeal,* July 13, 1882. Cf. *Petersburg Lancet,* July 15, 1882.

114. *Petersburg Index-Appeal,* July 13, 1882.

115. Ibid.

116. The State Board of Education (which consisted of the governor, the state superintendent of education, and the attorney general) appointed, and could remove, city and county boards of education. Historians have noted the Readjusters' active control of the school system and portrayed it as distressingly partisan. Henderson (*Gilded Age City,* 134) repeats the mantra that "the politicization of teachers and principals" increased under the Readjusters, quoting Heatwole, *History of Education in Virginia,* 265.

117. *Petersburg Index-Appeal,* July 26, 1882.

118. *Petersburg Lancet,* August 5, 1882.

119. *Petersburg Index-Appeal,* July 26, 1882.

120. *Marion Conservative Democrat,* October 7, 1881, quoting *Petersburg Evening Star,* May 24, 1868.

121. Calhoun and Moore, "William Evelyn Cameron," 99. Cameron remains difficult to decipher owing to a lack of sources. The Library of Virginia

has only two small collections of his manuscripts; the executive correspondence is missing for the Readjuster era. The papers of Cameron's daughter, Susie Cameron Whitfield, are held at Florida State University. The Mahone Papers (at Duke University) and the Riddleberger Papers (at the College of William and Mary) contain many letters from Cameron, but these cannot replace the missing official gubernatorial correspondence.

122. Other prominent Readjusters who allied against Mahone, first in 1885 and then in 1888, were John F. Lewis, James D. Brady, H. H. Riddleberger, John S. Wise, and R. A. Paul. In 1890 Cameron returned to the Democratic Party over the tariff issue and the Lodge Federal Elections Bill. Moger, *Bourbonism to Byrd*, 59, 63, 66–67 n. 63.

123. *Petersburg Index-Appeal*, August 10, 1882.

124. *Acts of the General Assembly*, chap. 69.

125. *Petersburg Index-Appeal*, August 11, 16, 1882; *Petersburg Lancet*, August 19, 1882. Of the twelve new school board members, nine were Readjusters and three of these were black. See *Lancet*, September 2, 1882, quoting *Chicago Conservator*.

126. *Petersburg Lancet*, August 12, 1882.

127. *Petersburg Index-Appeal*, August, 23, 30, 1882; Henderson, *Gilded Age City*, 138. Henderson says that the faculties were integrated, but I find no evidence of this, and the *Index-Appeal* (August 30, 1882) states the contrary.

128. *Virginia Star*, December 9, 1882. A number of other urban black schools already had African American teachers in place. The black citizens of Liberty, who had employed black teachers for several years and attributed their success in this regard to the Readjusters, wrote to the *Lancet* to congratulate Petersburg blacks on their achievement. See *Lancet*, September 6, 1882, quoting from letters to the editor from Farmville and Liberty.

129. For increased educational appropriations and statistics about white and black schools under the Readjusters, see *Acts of the General Assembly*, 262–64, 473–74, and Farr, *Fifteenth Annual Report*, 1885, 243–47.

130. General Assembly, *Acts and Joint Resolutions*, 1881–82, 37.

131. In *Alston v. School Board* (1940), the U.S. Court of Appeals ruled that paying black teachers less than white teachers violated the due process and equal protection clauses of the Fourteenth Amendment. Sullivan, *Days of Hope*, 142. See also Tushnet, *NAACP's Legal Strategy*, 44–48, 70–81.

132. Historians of Jim Crow and disfranchisement have noted a correspondence between political power and school funding in the South. Per pupil expenditures in black schools dropped precipitously between 1890 and 1910. This decline parallels the chronology of African American disfranchisement, which began in Mississippi in 1890 and concluded with Georgia in 1908. Before then, black southerners used their political clout, as in Petersburg, to fight for parity in educational funding and facilities. Literacy rates are one measure of this progress. Between 1870 and 1890 the percentage of literate adults in Petersburg nearly doubled. Black education was a potent enemy of white supremacy, a fact recognized by southern whites and blacks alike. On the decline

in school spending for black southerners, see Kousser, *Shaping of Southern Politics*, 228–29. The literacy rate is cited in Hartzell, "Exploration of Freedom in Black Petersburg," 151.

133. *Petersburg Lancet,* September 2, 1882.

134. *Staunton Spectator,* July 11, 1882.

CHAPTER 3

1. On the efforts of Petersburg blacks to have an African American nominated in the 1882 congressional elections, see *Lancet,* July 1, August 1, 19, 1882. Mahone appears to have supported the drive for a black congressman from the Fourth District. See Mahone to Lewis E. Harvie, July 3, 1882, quoted in Moore, "Black Militancy," 183.

2. John S. Wise, *The Lion's Skin,* 195–96. See also Maddex, "Persistence of Centrist Hegemony."

3. *Staunton Spectator,* June 13, 1882.

4. In this I follow Armstead L. Robinson, "Beyond . . . Social Consensus," 277, commenting on Hays, *Political History as Social Analysis,* 49 (quotation).

5. For concentrated evidence of the Readjusters' move toward liberalism, see the scrapbook entitled "The Liberal Movement," box 215, MP.

6. The relationship of the antebellum South to liberal ideals remains hotly contested. Defining liberalism primarily in terms of capitalist labor relations, Eugene D. Genovese and Elizabeth Fox-Genovese (*Fruits of Merchant Capital*) have memorably described the slave South as "a bastard child of merchant capital" (p. 5), "in but not of the bourgeois world" (p. 55). Against this interpretation stands most forcefully James Oakes's *Slavery and Freedom* (pp. 60, 72) and *The Ruling Race* which stress the antebellum South's position within a market economy and focus on the region's legal and political system. Following Locke and Charles Taylor, Oakes defines liberalism in terms of individual rights and demonstrates, among other things, how liberalism's sanctification of private property could be utilized to defend the traffic in human beings.

As far as the postbellum period goes, most scholars continue to focus their discussion of southern liberalism exclusively on a small group of white intellectuals who considered black civic liberty compatible with white social, economic, and political dominance. Examples of such an approach include Sosna, *In Search of the Silent South;* Joel Williamson, *Crucible of Race,* 85–108; and Frederickson, *Black Image in the White Mind,* 198–227. For a new work that centers on liberal race policies but includes a broad spectrum of black twentieth-century liberals, see Gaines, *Uplifting the Race.*

7. Eric Foner, *Reconstruction,* 29; Thomas Holt, "'Empire over the Mind,'" 288 (quotation). Leslie Schwalm discusses the rejection of free labor tenets by South Carolina freedpeople and the confusion of both former slaves and former masters over the responsibilities and meaning of contracts. See Schwalm, *Hard Fight for We,* chap. 6 and 200 n. 49. For more on the reluctance

of freedpeople and former masters alike to embrace free labor relations, see Holt, " 'Empire over the Mind,' " esp. 288–89, 297–300; Hunter, *To Joy My Freedom,* 21–43; Stanley, "Beggars Can't Be Choosers" and *From Bondage to Contract;* Fields, "Advent of Capitalist Agriculture"; and Laura F. Edwards, *Gendered Strife,* chaps. 1–2. On differing conceptions—both race and class-based—of model family life after emancipation, see Schwalm, *Hard Fight for We,* chap. 7, and Edwards, chaps. 3–4.

8. Eric Foner, *Reconstruction,* 29. See also his *Nothing but Freedom* and *Politics and Ideology,* chap. 6.

9. In *The Virtues of Liberalism* (pp. 6, 8), James T. Kloppenberg stresses the conflictual nature of American liberalism and denies that there is a singular form of liberalism in America.

10. Myrdal, *American Dilemma,* 466.

11. The relationship of the Readjusters to liberalism conforms to Ronald Dworkin's ("Liberalism," 115–16) "skeptical thesis," which sees liberalism not as an authentic and coherent political morality but rather as a "cluster of political positions" tied to a set of political and economic propositions (such as a free market economy and one man, one vote). This interpretation of Readjuster liberalism accords with Peter Berkowitz's definition, quoting Judith Shklar, that liberalism is "a political doctrine" whose primary goal is "to secure the political conditions that are necessary for the exercise of personal freedom." Berkowitz adds to this characterization the idea that "liberalism rests on the fundamental premise of the natural freedom and equality of all human beings." Not all Readjusters shared this premise in its entirety. Berkowitz, *Virtue and the Making of Modern Liberalism,* 4–5; Shklar, "The Liberalism of Fear," *Political Thought and Political Thinkers,* 3.

12. This is Joel Williamson's assertion in *Crucible of Race,* 107.

13. Mahone quoted in *New York Herald,* reprinted in *Staunton Spectator,* April 26, 1881.

14. See, e.g., unidentified clipping, n.d. [*Star* or *Whig,* 1880], Wise Family Scrapbook, 1879–1901, SLV, and Moore, *Two Paths,* 64.

15. *New York Times,* June 20, 1881.

16. Former president Grant, who opposed repudiation, endorsed the coalition in 1881 because of its stand on the suffrage issue. See Ulysses S. Grant to James D. Brady, October 4, 1881, Williams Papers, AL. On the relationship of the national Republicans with the Readjusters, see DeSantis, *Republicans Face the Southern Question,* 141–60.

17. Broadside, "The Re-Adjuster Programme! An Address of the State Committee to the Readjuster Party of Virginia" (written by Mahone), January 4, 1881, Broadside Collection, VHS.

18. *Richmond Whig,* February 19, 1881, quoted in *Shenandoah Herald,* February 23, 1881.

19. *Richmond Whig,* June 24, 1881, quoted in Moore, *Two Paths,* 79.

20. *Richmond Whig,* June 18, 1881, quoting *New York Evening Post,* Mahone Scrapbooks, box 215, MP.

21. John R. Hathaway, editor of *Norfolk Day Book*, to *New York Times*, June 17, 1881, and *Times* editorial on the same day.

22. In 1878 local workingmen's parties organized nationally as the Independent or Greenbacker Party and elected fifteen Greenbacker congressmen and many local and state officials. Greenbackers attended the Readjusters' founding convention in 1879 and influenced the coalition's agenda as well as its organization. In Richmond, the Greenbackers served as a bridge to the Readjusters for the African American community. On black Greenbackers, see Rachleff, *Black Labor*, 84. On the Greenbackers generally and independent politics in the period following the Great Railroad Strike of 1876, see Painter, *Standing at Armageddon*, 27–30; Fink, *Workingmen's Democracy*, esp. chap. 6; and McLaurin, *Knights of Labor*.

23. *Petersburg Index-Appeal*, March 15, 1881. The Petersburg delegates passed resolutions calling for freedom of the ballot, equality of all before the law, improved public education, tax reductions for workingmen, the appointment of blacks as jurors, and a more equitable system of state taxation.

24. The evolution of the Readjuster program can be most easily traced in the party platform. See also Pearson, *Readjuster Movement*, 97–102, and Moore, *Two Paths*, 82. For legislation to renovate and expand the state penitentiary, see *Acts of the General Assembly*, 1881–82, 246–47. For food and vaccines for the poor, see *Acts*, 1881–82, 169, 230, 463.

25. *Staunton Spectator*, April 26, May 10, 17, 1881.

26. "An Appeal to the Voters of Lynchburg," n.d. [1881], box 200, MP. With regard to Democratic race rhetoric, John Wise argued that if black Virginians would only listen to what the funders were saying, "there will be no necessity for them to hear our speakers at all." Extract from Wise speech reported in *Richmond Dispatch*, November 2, 1880.

27. *Staunton Spectator*, April 5, October 4, 1881, quoting Daniel.

28. *Marion Conservative Democrat*, October 7, 1881 (first quotation); *Staunton Spectator*, November 1, 1881 (second quotation).

29. Clipping, editorial (George S. Rouse), *Culpeper Times*, December 2, 1881, Mahone Scrapbooks, box 215, MP.

30. Clipping, *Florida Weekly Telegraph*, December 3, 1881, box 215, MP.

31. Clipping, *Norfolk Review*, May 25, 1882, box 215, MP.

32. Clipping, [no title], n.p., Gouverneur, N.Y., January 12, 1882, box 215, MP.

33. Farr to Mahone, November 5, 1880, box 23, MP.

34. For an introduction to the vast literature on the definition and analytic usefulness of the public and private spheres, see the collections of essays edited by Benn and Gaus, *Public and Private in Social Life;* Craig Calhoun, *Habermas;* and Nancy Fraser, *Unruly Practices*. The Ur text of discussions about the public and the private is Habermas, *Structural Transformation of the Public Sphere*. On the gendered aspects of separate spheres, see Cott, *Bonds of Womanhood*.

35. McCurry, *Masters of Small Worlds*, 61, 213–15, 225, 236. For a condensed version of these arguments, see McCurry, "Politics of Yeoman Households."

For another formulation of the same idea, see Laura F. Edwards, *Gendered Strife,* 7: "in the decades before the Civil War, the gender, racial, and class dimensions of private and public power converged." Other historians applying the conceptual model of the household to southern history include Fox-Genovese, "Antebellum Southern" and *Within the Plantation Household,* 37–99, and Bardaglio, *Reconstructing the Household.*

36. Laura F. Edwards, "'The Marriage Covenant,'" 84.

37. For recent works that criticize the utility of concepts of public and private in understanding the lives of African Americans, see Bercaw, "Politics of Household"; Elsa Barkley Brown, "Uncle Ned's Children"; Frankel, *Freedom's Women;* Evelyn Brooks Higginbotham, *Righteous Discontent;* and Schwalm, *Hard Fight for We.*

38. Leonidas Bough to Mahone, May 31, 1881, box 30, MP.

39. Wise testimony, U.S. Senate *Report,* 449.

40. Rachleff, *Black Labor,* 93.

41. Pateman, *Sexual Contract,* 2.

42. Hodes, "Sexualization of Reconstruction Politics," and *White Women, Black Men,* chap. 7. See also Bardaglio, *Reconstructing the Household,* chap. 6.

43. *Congressional Journal,* 39th Cong., 1st sess., pt. 1, January 10, 1866, 179–80.

44. This connection had deep roots. On the eve of secession in 1860, for instance, a South Carolina minister warned white men that emancipation would not only liberate the slave, enabling him to be "his own master," but also make him the equal of every white man. The logical next step, he argued, would be the arrival of "Abolition preachers" to "consummate the marriage of your daughters to black husbands." Quoted in Channing, *Crisis of Fear,* 287. This discourse was not limited to the South. In the postwar North, where black suffrage was combated fiercely, similar rhetorical and symbolic linking of black political and sexual rights was commonplace. In Ohio in 1867, to take one example, Democrats staged processions with floats on which young white women carried banners inscribed, "Fathers, save us from negro suffrage." Fowler, *Northern Attitudes,* 231.

45. Avins, "Anti-Miscegenation Laws and the Fourteenth Amendment," 1227.

46. Although the Fifteenth Amendment (1870) deemed that the right to vote belonged to all citizens, section two of the Fourteenth Amendment (1868) effectively limited the franchise to male citizens twenty-one years of age or older. Some woman suffragists read the negative language of the Fifteenth Amendment ("the vote shall not be denied") as open to the possibility of female enfranchisement, but the Supreme Court ultimately upheld the interpretation of Elizabeth Cady Stanton and Susan B. Anthony at the time: that the amendments positively defined the franchise in masculine terms. On the passage of the suffrage amendments and the feminist response, see Gillette, *The Right to Vote,* and Ellen Carol Du Bois, *Feminism and Suffrage,* chap. 6.

47. Tourgée, *A Fool's Errand,* 378.

48. *Richmond Whig,* September 21, 1883.

49. Porter, "A Card to the Voters," October 29, 1883, box 192, MP. Cf. the definition of Readjuster liberalism offered by the *Shenandoah Herald,* February 23, 1881, as "[t]he harmonious union of both colors, to forward mutual interests and to protect mutual rights, without sacrificing either race to the other."

50. Virginia Revised Code, chap. 158, sec. 4, vol. 1, pp. 585–86 (1819); Virginia Code, chap. 109, sec. 1, vol. 1, p. 471 (1849), chap. 196, secs. 8–9, vol. 1, p. 740 (1849), chap. 109, sec. 1, p. 529, chap. 196, secs. 8–9, p. 804 (1860), and chap. 105, sec. 1, p. 850 (1873).

51. Virginia Acts of Assembly, chap. 371, sec. 5, p. 534 (1924).

52. Grossberg, "Guarding the Altar," 204. See also Grossberg, *Governing the Hearth,* chap. 4; Keller, *Affairs of State,* 149–50, 451–52; and Bardaglio, *Reconstructing the Household,* chaps. 5–6. Nancy F. Cott ("Giving Character to Our Whole Civil Polity," 115) notes that late-nineteenth-century American courts upheld a "double characterization of marriage (as private *and* public, contract *and* status)."

53. Peter Bardaglio (*Reconstructing the Household,* 176–89) provides a particularly clear analysis of the transformation of white southern legal concepts regarding marriage.

54. *New York Times,* May 20, 1879 (first half of quotation), May 21, 1879 (second half of quotation). On the Kinney case, see *Ex parte Kinney,* 14 F. Cas. 602 (C.C.E.D. Va. 1879) (No. 7825). In the decision Edmund Kinney is identified as black and Mary Hall as white. See Peter Wallenstein, "Race, Marriage, and the Supreme Court."

55. Clipping, n.d. (probably *Virginia Star* or *Richmond Whig,* 1880), Wise Family Scrapbook, 1879–1901.

56. *Virginia Star,* August 27, 1881.

57. For a similar argument for Reconstruction North Carolina, see Laura F. Edwards, " 'The Marriage Covenant.' "

58. Langston, *Freedom and Citizenship,* 158.

59. *Petersburg Lancet,* July 15, 1882. The *Philadelphia Evening Bulletin* of November 9, 1883, used precisely this language to explain the hatred of white Democrats for black Readjusters. Black Virginians had earned the wrath of the Bourbons there, it said, because "he who was a slave and a chattel is now a man and a voter."

60. Quoted in Rachleff, *Black Labor,* 99.

61. W. E. B. Du Bois, "The Niagara Movement," 374–75.

62. Laura F. Edwards, *Gendered Strife,* 196.

63. Quoted in Eric Foner, *Reconstruction,* 288.

64. Isabel V. Hull maps this relationship clearly in *Sexuality, State and Civil Society in Germany,* 288–89, 245–51. In America this relationship was articulated through the idiom of republicanism, with the manly republican citizen-subject defined as independent, courageous, self-reliant, commanding, productive, controlled, fiscally responsible: in a word, virtuous. See Smith-

Rosenberg, "Dis-Covering the Subject of the 'Great Constitutional Discussion,'" 850, 855–56.

65. This was true for African American women as well as men, although the meaning was not identical. See Laura F. Edwards, *Gendered Strife*, chap. 1.

66. As one black Union corporal from Virginia explained to his troops in 1866, "The Marriage Covenant is the foundation of all our rights. In slavery we could not have *legalised* marriage: *now* we have it." Quoted in Bardaglio, *Reconstructing the Household*, 132. On the contrasting expectations of marriage among black and white southerners, see Laura F. Edwards, *Gendered Strife*, 24–65. Edwards's analysis is based heavily on Noralee Frankel's dissertation. See also Schwalm, *Hard Fight for We*.

67. Leach, "Caste and Class Systems," 19. On marriage as a marker of equality, see also Seed, *To Love, Honor, and Obey in Colonial Mexico;* Gutiérrez, *When Jesus Came, the Corn Mothers Went Away;* and Marinez-Alier, *Marriage, Class and Colour in Nineteenth-Century Cuba.*

68. There is scattered but decisive evidence to suggest that antebellum Virginia communities frequently turned a blind eye to sexual liaisons that crossed the color line. Nansemond County's 1830 census taker, for instance, reported matter-of-factly nine cases where a free black man lived with "his white wife." Johnston, *Race Relations in Virginia*, 265–66 n. 105. In 1816 Robert Wright, the mixed-race son of planter Thomas Wright, petitioned the Virginia legislature for divorce from his white wife. See Buckley, "Unfixing Race." For examples of marriages that crossed the color line in seventeenth-century America, see Morgan, *American Slavery*, 334–35, and Kathleen Brown, *Good Wives*, 126–28, 135, 188. For a more comprehensive discussion of interracial sex in the nineteenth-century South, see Hodes, *White Women and Black Men* and "Wartime Dialogues on Illicit Sex." On the postwar South, see Berry, "Judging Morality," esp. 838–48. For more on miscegenation law, see Saks, "Miscegenation Law" and Applebaum, "Miscegenation Statutes."

69. Virginia Acts of Assembly, chap. 7, para. 3, p. 302 (1877–78).

70. *Kinney v. Commonwealth*, 71 Va. (30 Gratt.) 858 (1878); *Greenhow v. James' Executor*, 80 Va. 636 (1885).

71. Beginning in the 1850s, Martha Logan and James Miliam enjoyed a monogamous relationship in Pittsylvania County that lasted over fifty years. See Delany and Delany, *Having Our Say*, 41–51.

72. Wallenstein, "Race, Marriage, and the Law of Freedom," 403.

73. In *McPherson v. Commonwealth*, 69 Va. (28 Gratt.) 939 (1877), the trial court determined that George Stewart was white but his wife, the former Rowena McPherson, was not, and therefore their marriage was invalid. This decision was overturned by the state supreme court, which ruled on testimony about McPherson's mixed-race grandmother that McPherson was legally white. See also *Jones v. Commonwealth*, 70 Va. 213, 216–17 (1884), and its 1885 appeal *Jones v. Commonwealth*, 80 Va. 538, 541 (1885), in which the wife in a marriage alleged to be miscegenous denied that she was white.

74. *Loving v. Virginia*, 388 U.S. (1967).

75. *Richmond Star,* December 16, 1882.

76. *Richmond State,* March 8, 1880; Virginia Legislature, *House Journal,* 1881–82, 337. See also *Richmond Whig,* May 13, September 16, 1881, December 8, 1882, October 19, 1883.

77. Quoted in *Staunton Spectator,* April 25, 1882.

78. Quoted from Mahone's remarks on the Pendleton Bill (regulating federal patronage). Clipping, Scrapbooks, 1882–83, box 206, MP.

79. Franklin and Eaton, "The Role of Honor in Southern Society"; Kenneth S. Greenberg, *Honor and Slavery;* Wyatt-Brown, *Southern Honor;* Ayers, *Vengeance and Justice;* Stowe, *Intimacy and Power.*

80. Breen (*Tobacco Culture*) considers honor a mentality or worldview (in chap. 2, he refers to a "tobacco culture" that is virtually synonymous with honor), Kenneth S. Greenberg (*Honor and Slavery,* xi) refers to it as a language, and Wyatt-Brown (*Southern Honor,* xv) sees it as a system of ethics.

81. Edward L. Ayers is an exception, as is Gaines M. Foster, who explores the persistence of notions of honor in the creation of the Lost Cause. See, e.g., Ayers, *Vengeance and Justice,* and Foster, *Ghosts of the Confederacy,* 25–26. Bertram Wyatt-Brown (*Southern Honor*) notes the persistence of the culture of honor in the South after the war but leaves discussion to another day.

82. "Southern Curse: Why America's Murder Rate Is So High," *New York Times,* July 26, 1998.

83. Walker Percy, *Lancelot,* 60.

84. Historians tracing the evolution of Jim Crow segregation laws have pinpointed their genesis in centers of commensality and transportation, places where white women ventured forth into the world and were liable to come into close contact with men. As Ayers (*Promise of the New South,* 140) has observed, "the more closely linked to sexuality, the more likely was a place to be segregated." Barbara Y. Welke makes a similar, detailed observation in "When All the Women Were White, and All the Blacks Were Men." The postwar southern expansion of women's sphere parallels that of the antebellum North, where the definition of the private sphere "became an expansive doctrine: home was anywhere women and children were." Paula Baker, "Domestication of Politics," 620. On the expansion and articulation of domesticity and the private sphere in the North, see also Cott, *Bonds of Womanhood,* and Ryan, *Women in Public.*

85. Forrester, a dairy farmer and contractor, was wealthy enough to open bank accounts for each of his grandchildren as they were born. He had been a Republican since emancipation and served as city councillor in Richmond from Jackson Ward. See Rachleff, *Black Labor,* 19, and Jackson, *Negro Office-Holders,* 57. Paul was born a slave in Nelson County in 1846 and after the war accompanied his mother to Richmond, where he was employed as a waiter. Taught to read by his mother, Paul continued his education on his own and eventually served on the board of stewards of the Third Street African Methodist Episcopal Church. He was also a member of numerous African American societies. He was elected captain of a local militia unit and first became

active politically in 1874, when he opposed ring rule in the Republican Party. In 1878 he switched to Greenbackerism and later converted to the Readjusters on the strength of their legislative record. Under the Readjusters Paul served as a bailiff, a U.S. deputy marshal, and a mailing clerk in the Richmond Post Office. In 1882 he was appointed personal doorkeeper to Governor Cameron. See Williams, *Capt. R. A. Paul,* esp. 25–49.

86. Quoted in Rachleff, *Black Labor,* 104. This was not the first time that Cameron had replaced a school board. In 1882, propelled by Petersburg's large and active African American Readjuster community, he had removed a Democratic school board that refused to appoint black teachers in the city's black schools and replaced it with one dominated by Readjusters; see Chapter 2. Cameron's change in the Richmond board was upheld in a May court of appeals decision. His action at once dealt a blow to Democratic power in Richmond and appropriated coveted patronage positions for Readjusters. There was considerable overlap between the Richmond School Board and the common council. On membership of the school board and common council, cf. Records of the Richmond Common Council, vol. 21 (July 1, 1878–December 18, 1883, Richmond Public Library), with the school board members listed in *Richmond Dispatch,* February 1, 1883. On the judicial decision, see *Richmond Dispatch,* May 12, 1883.

87. *Richmond Dispatch,* February 23, 1883. Compare the *Dispatch*'s position to that of the *Norfolk Landmark* two years earlier. On May 3, 1881, after reporting the election of several African American Readjusters as Norfolk delegates to the forthcoming Readjuster state convention, where they would presumably influence party policy, the *Landmark* pronounced itself unequivocably opposed to black authority in public life: "We declare that we are not willing to see Negroes, because they are black, and have certain vested political rights, made overseers of the roads, County Commissioners, members of juries, Magistrates, Councilmen, Mayors, or lawmakers, and so on, and so on."

88. This is not an inherently liberal position: totalitarian regimes such as the USSR relied on the same logic to transform their own social realities.

89. *New York Globe,* October 20, 1883. The cartoon was published in newspapers and as a flyer, and there are multiple copies of it in the Mahone Papers.

90. Douglas, *Purity and Danger,* 144.

91. Boxes 71–73 of the Mahone Papers contain many letters from local Readjusters to Mahone seeking to replace a Democratic teacher or school principal with a Readjuster. See, e.g., Lee to Mahone, June 7, 1883 (box 73), in which Robert A. Lee, an African American from Nansemond County, claimed that he lost his school because Democratic school trustees objected to his Readjuster politics. Leading white Republican Readjuster James D. Brady put the matter squarely in the spring of 1883 regarding the reluctance of Richmond school superintendent Griffin Edwards to fire Democratic teachers in favor of Readjusters: "Cannot Mr. Griff Edwards, the Supt. be instructed that White Readjusters *must* teach the white schools, and colored Readjusters the colored schools? It is reported that he says 'Politics ought not to enter into these school

matters.' How did he become Supt. if not *entirely* through a *mistaken* idea of *his* politics." Brady to Mahone, May 7, 1883, box 71. Black Readjusters concurred. Richmond's black schoolteachers met in May 1883 to demand that the city "put none but colored men to be princaple [*sic*] in colored schools wether the whites be good Readjusters or not." Lewis Lindsay to Mahone, May 23, 1883, box 72.

92. According to the 1880 occupational census, roughly two-thirds of the teachers in Virginia were women. U.S. Census Office, *Tenth Census*, 742, table 31.

93. *Richmond Dispatch*, May 12, 1883.

94. Ibid.

95. Cross to Mahone, May 26, 1883, box 72, MP.

96. Deyer to Mahone, May 30, 1883, ibid. The May election was also complicated by Democratic charges that the Readjusters had ordered John L. Newsome, a black Republican leader, to be shot. See letters of Deyer and Cross and a Democratic flyer dated June 2, 1883 (box 73, MP) that read "READ, READ, READ! A Colored Republican SHOT DOWN IN COLD BLOOD by one of Mahone's white Democratic Readjusters—JOHN L. NEWSOME, OF FRANKLIN, is dead, in compliance with the order of Mahone, at the Custom House, Norfolk. REMEMBER NEWSOME AND VOTE AGAINST THE READJUSTERS."

97. Henley to Mahone, May 28, 1883, box 72, MP.

98. Rev. W. E. Talley to Mahone, June 6, 1883, box 73, MP.

99. *Lynchburg Virginian*, October 20, 1883.

100. *Lynchburg News,* September 5, 1883.

101. Heermans to Mahone, October 17, 1883, box 80, MP.

102. Kenny to Brady, October 23, 1883, ibid.

103. See the many letters of May–November 1883 in the Mahone Papers— e.g., Lewis P. Nelson to Mahone, October 31, 1883 (box 80), in which Nelson informs Mahone that a Colonel Gibson, who "is opposed to mixed schools, Negro Trustees or Negro managers where white children are going," will sweep the white vote in Culpeper County. One prominent Readjuster advised Mahone that the party's only chance to beat the Democrats in future was to "draw a *color line* under the name of *the white man's liberal Party of Virginia*." R[ichard] A. Wise to Mahone, November 8, 1883, box 81.

104. Gills to Mahone, November 23, 1883, box 82, MP. The reference to black men examining the daughters of white women could have referred either to the possibility of black school superintendents or to the fact that in at least one city (Petersburg), the physician to the poor was African American.

105. "I fear many of our best white men have left us permanently as they object to the appointment of negroes on School Board in Richmond," one county leader warned Mahone. Thomas H. Cross to Mahone, May 26, 1883, box 72, MP. Mahone reportedly denounced Cameron for injuring both party and school interests by his actions in Richmond. See S. Bassett French to Mahone, May 27, 1883, box 72, MP.

106. *Staunton Spectator,* September 4, 1883.

107. Arendt, "Reflections on Little Rock," 56, 48–49, 45, and "A Reply to Critics," 181. For a thoughtful reading of Arendt's purpose in the Little Rock essay, see Bohman, "Moral Costs of Political Pluralism."

108. The Supreme Court saw the relationship clearly enough. Given the opportunity to rule on the constitutionality of antimiscegenation legislation in 1954, with the *Brown* decision still awaiting implementation, the Court declined to openly address the issue of marriage across the color line "while strident opposition is being voiced to less controversial desegregation because it allegedly leads to intermarriage." Jack Greenberg, *Race Relations and American Law,* 345. As Peter Wallenstein points out, the educated guesses of astute Court watchers such as Greenberg regarding the relationship between the school desegregation cases and the antimiscegenation decisions were documented years later in the papers of the justices. Harvey M. Grossman, one of Justice William O. Douglas's law clerks, agonized about how to advise him when an opportunity arose for the Supreme Court to rule on antimiscegenation statutes in 1954. "It seems clear to me that the statute involved is unconstitutional," wrote Grossman. Yet "review at the present time would probably increase the tensions growing out of the school segregation cases and perhaps impede solution to that problem." Quoted in Wallenstein, "Race, Marriage, and the Supreme Court," 75. See also Wallenstein, "Race, Marriage, and the Law of Freedom," 415–16 and "Law and the Boundaries of Race and Place."

109. Douglas, *Purity and Danger,* 114.

CHAPTER 4

1. William Alexander Percy, *Lanterns on the Levee,* 307. In *The Negro: The Southerner's Problem* (1904), Thomas Nelson Page made similar veiled threats regarding (the lack of) black deference and the potential for white violence. See esp. pp. 203–4.

2. Hobsbawm, *Primitive Rebels;* Thompson, *Making of the English Working Class* and "Moral Economy of the English Crowd"; Field, *Rebels in the Name of the Tsar;* James Scott, *Weapons of the Weak* and *Domination;* Benda, "The Power of the Powerless," *Open Letters,* 193–96, 204, 213.

3. Aptheker, *American Negro Slave Revolts;* Genovese, *Roll, Jordan, Roll;* Levine, *Black Culture;* Raboteau, *Slave Religion;* Osofsky, *Puttin' on Ole Massa.* See also Bauer and Bauer, "Day to Day Resistance to Slavery," and Stuckey, "Through the Prism of Folklore."

4. Kelley, " 'We Are Not What We Seem,' " 78. Eugene Genovese makes a similar point in *Roll, Jordan, Roll:* "Such apparently innocuous and apolitical measures as a preacher's sermon on love and dignity or the mutual support offered by husbands and wives played . . . an indispensable part in providing the groundwork for the most obviously political action [insurrection and running away], for they contributed to the cohesion and strength of a social class threatened by disintegration and demoralization" (p. 598).

5. Kelley, "'We Are Not What We Seem,'" 109–10.

6. Rabinowitz, *Race Relations* and "From Exclusion to Segregation." On segregation, see Woodward, *Strange Career;* Wade, *Slavery in the Cities;* Cell, *Highest Stage of White Supremacy;* and Cox, "From Emancipation to Segregation." On the Woodward thesis and its critics, see Woodward, "The Strange Career of a Historical Controversy," *American Counterpoint,* 234–60, and "*Strange Career* Critics"; and Rabinowitz, "More Than the Woodward Thesis." On patterns of urban residential segregation in the South, see Blassingame, "Before the Ghetto" and *Black New Orleans;* Kellogg, "Negro Urban Clusters" and "Formation of Black Residential Areas in Lexington, Kentucky"; Groves and Muller, "Evolution of Black Residential Areas"; and Chesson, *Richmond after the War,* chap. 5. As a rule, the newer the city, the greater the residential segregation.

7. Kelley, "'We Are Not What We Seem,'" 101–2. As Kelley points out, many of these day-to-day struggles for black dignity under Jim Crow were fought out in public spaces, especially on public transportation. In the nineteenth century, African Americans protested civic attempts to segregate streetcars. See Fischer, "A Pioneer Protest"; Meier and Rudwick, "Boycott Movement"; McMillen, *Dark Journey,* 291–95; and Dittmer, *Black Georgia,* 16–19. A number of scholars stress the black quest for dignity in their attempts to undermine the Jim Crow system—e.g., Chafe, *Civilities and Civil Rights;* Earl Lewis, *In Their Own Interests;* Lipsitz, *Life in the Struggle;* Kelley, *Hammer and Hoe;* Honey, *Southern Labor and Black Civil Rights;* and Fairclough, *Race and Democracy.*

8. McMillen, *Dark Journey,* 11. In 1930 Robert Russa Moton, president of the Tuskegee Institute, recalled that "in the early days of the automobile . . . Negroes driving their own cars were dragged out and whipped, and their cars wrecked, for their imputed arrogance and impertinence in presuming to enjoy privileges to which whites alone were entitled." Moton, *What the Negro Thinks,* 213. On race-based rules of the road in Mississippi in the 1930s, see also Powdermaker, *After Freedom,* 49–50.

9. Bertram Wilbur Doyle, *Etiquette of Race Relations,* 168. On racial etiquette in the South, see Ray Stannard Baker, *Following the Color Line;* Dollard, *Caste and Class,* chaps. 5, 7–8, 12; and J. William Harris, "Etiquette, Lynching."

10. *Southern Workman,* January 1884, 2. Orra Langhorne, the sister of William Ruffner, Virginia's first superintendent of public education, was a white southern liberal who could, in the same breath, denounce the Bourbons, defend black civil rights, and promote educational qualifications for the suffrage, as she did in her column published in the *Southern Workman* in October 1883. For a cross section of Langhorne's writings, see Wynes, *Southern Sketches.*

11. Ravenel (1865) quoted in Litwack, *Been in the Storm So Long,* 259. Myrta Lockett Avary (*Dixie after the War,* 194) concurred with Ravenel: "The new manners of the blacks were painful, revolting, absurd. . . . Southerners had taken great pains and pride in teaching their negroes good manners. . . . It was with keen regret that their old preceptors saw them throw all their fine schooling in etiquette to the winds." On the adoption of "disrespectful" (to whites) forms of dress by freedwomen, see Jones, *Labor of Love,* 69–70.

12. Conrad, "Reminiscences of a Southern Woman," 410; Meriwether, *Recollections of 92 Years*, 167.

13. Margaret Mitchell, *Gone with the Wind*, 510; Cash, *Mind of the South*, 227.

14. Douglass, *Narrative*, 60; Wade, *Slavery in the Cities*, 108 (Richmond ordinance). According to Wade (p. 109), every southern city had such a code as this by the 1850s, when, as the issue of slavery reached a boiling point, the politics of street space became more insistent. In an August 10, 1852, letter to the *American Beacon*, "Discipline" complained about the behavior of Norfolk blacks who wore "Silks or Satins, broadcloth or bonnets" and who walked three or four abreast on the sidewalk, forcing whites into the street. The writer proposed that African Americans be forced to walk single file. Quoted in Foner and Pacheco, *Three Who Dared*, 85. Petersburg whites passed a similar law requiring free blacks to yield the sidewalk to whites. See Lebsock, *Free Women of Petersburg*, 94.

15. Ryan, *Women in Public*, 62. For the transformation of etiquette in the nineteenth-century urban North, see Kasson, *Rudeness and Civility*.

16. Erving Goffman ("The Nature of Deference and Demeanor," esp. 476) distinguishes between symmetrical and asymmetrical rules of conduct.

17. "Memorial of the Citizens of Charleston to the Senate and House of Representatives of the State of South Carolina [Charleston, 1822]," quoted in Fox-Genovese, *Within the Plantation Household*, 307.

18. Bourdieu, "Sentiment of Honor in Kabyle Society," 228. On honor in the nineteenth-century South, see Franklin, *Militant South;* Franklin and Eaton, "Role of Honor"; Wyatt-Brown, *Southern Honor;* Ayers, *Vengeance and Justice;* Gorn, " 'Gouge and Bite' "; Stowe, *Intimacy and Power;* and Kenneth S. Greenberg, *Honor and Slavery*.

19. Stanley ("Conjugal Bonds and Wage Labor") argues that in post–Civil War America the right to contract was increasingly viewed as the key to individual freedom and was incorporated via the Civil Rights Act of 1866 into a sovereign right of citizenship. For the history of contract and the equation between freedom and the right of contract, see MacPherson, *Political Theory of Possessive Individualism;* Hurst, *Law and the Conditions of Freedom;* David Brion Davis, *The Problem of Slavery;* Atiyah, *Rise and Fall of Freedom of Contract;* Fox-Genovese, "Property and Patriarchy." On the definition of the individual through contract and the importance of contract for civil society, see Seligman, *Idea of Civil Society*, 16, 28, 33.

20. Michel de Certeau (*Practice of Everyday Life*, 97–98) defines walking in a city as a "pedestrian speech act" that has a "triple 'enunciative' function: it is a process of *appropriation* of the topographical system on the part of the pedestrian (just as the speaker appropriates and takes on the language); it is a spatial acting-out of the place (just as the speech act is an acoustic acting-out of language); and it implies *relations* among differentiated positions, that is, among pragmatic 'contracts' in the form of movements (just as verbal enunciation is an 'allocution,' 'posits another opposite' the speaker and puts con-

tracts between interlocutors into action)." Breaking accepted social rules can also be a way of asserting self-identity. As Goffman ("Nature of Deference and Demeanor," 475) explains, "An act that is subject to a rule of conduct is, then, a communication, for it represents a way in which selves are confirmed. . . . An act that is subject to rules of conduct but does not conform to them is also a communication—often even more so—for infractions make news and often in such a way as to disconfirm the selves of the participants."

21. Walzer, "Civil Society Argument," esp. 154.

22. As Lefebvre (*Production of Space,* 416) puts it, "groups, classes or fractions of classes cannot constitute themselves, or recognize one another, as 'subjects' unless they generate (or produce) a space." The transformation of everyday life (especially the transformation of the political) can proceed only with the radical transformation of space because they are interconnected. As he wrote (*Survival of Capitalism,* 72), "To 'change society,' to 'change life' means nothing if there is not production of an appropriated space . . . for new social relations there must be new space and vice versa." Gottdiener, *Social Production of Urban Space,* 150–56.

23. Elias, *Power and Civility,* 325; Bruce, *Plantation Negro as a Freeman,* 46. Elias himself, of course, lived through a nightmare "period of transition": although he managed to escape Nazi Germany for England, his parents died within two years at Breslau and Auschwitz (p. vii).

24. *Southern Workman,* January 1884, 2.

25. Don H. Doyle, *New Men, New Cities,* 1, 11. On southern urbanization, see also Goldfield, *Cotton Fields and Skyscrapers;* Rabinowitz, "Continuity and Change"; Larsen, *Rise of the Urban South;* and Miller, "Urban Blacks in the South."

26. Brownell and Goldfield, *The City in Southern History,* 16 (quotation); Rabinowitz, "Continuity and Change," 104. The rate of urban growth in the South between 1870 and 1880 was 8.68 percent, but Virginia bucked this trend—its urban population during this period increased by 27.3 percent. U.S. Census Office, *Tenth Census,* 456.

27. *Historical Statistics of the United States,* 29. For statistics on southern outmigration between 1870 and 1950, see Cohen, *At Freedom's Edge,* 106, table 5; 295, table 13; and 296, table 14.

28. Cohen, *At Freedom's Edge,* 296, table 14. See also Wallenstein, "Cartograms and the Mapping of Virginia History," 102–5.

29. Goldfield, *Region, Race, and Cities,* 71; U.S. Census Office, *Compendium of the Eleventh Census,* 1:442–52.

30. Virginia's population grew only marginally between 1880 and 1900— from 1.51 million to 1.85 million. *Statistical Abstract of the United States,* 4, table 3. From 1890 to 1900 the state grew by only 12 percent. As Kerr-Ritchie (*Freedpeople,* 233) points out, only six states in the nation had smaller percentage increases.

31. Those African Americans who managed to vote throughout the Jim Crow era were disproportionately clustered in cities: in the 1940s, e.g., a full

85 percent of registered black southern voters lived in cities. Goldfield, *Black, White, and Southern,* 47.

32. Kerr-Ritchie, *Freedpeople,* 236–39; U.S. Bureau of the Census, 1900, *Statistical Abstract,* 148. See also Kerr-Ritchie, *Freedpeople,* 237, table 8.10. Howard Rabinowitz ("Continuity and Change," 92) observed that "the main difference between antebellum and postbellum urbanization was the filling in of the urban network through the growth of important interior southern cities." Danville and Roanoke are particularly clear examples of this trend.

33. U.S. Senate *Report,* 213.

34. Textile entrepreneurs spoke openly of increasing the number of white workers in Danville. Manufacturer R. A. Schoolfield recalled that in 1882 "the parties interested in developing the water power were anxious to bring white labor here to break negro rule." Schoolfield manuscript, Schoolfield Papers, AL.

35. On Danville, see Pollock, *Illustrated Sketch Book;* Tilley, *Bright-Leaf Tobacco Industry;* Hairston, *Brief History of Danville;* and Siegel, *Roots of Southern Distinctiveness.* Other information has been obtained from the Manuscript Census Returns, Tenth Census . . . Pittsylvania County; 1881–82 Danville City Directory, DPL; OB-E; Danville Proceedings; and U.S. Senate *Report.* The offices of the city's newspaper, the *Danville Register,* burned at the turn of the century, destroying back copies. The only local news reports for late-nineteenth-century Danville are clippings saved in private collections and a few back copies of the *Register* at the State Library of Virginia, Richmond, and Alderman Library, UVA.

36. Virginia Legislature, *House Journal,* 1881–82, 331. See also Danville Proceedings, April 7, 1882. The Readjusters did not expand the city's borders to achieve this: Danville was already a black-majority city. According to U.S. census data, in the three decades from 1870 to 1890 the total population of Danville was, in 1870, 3,463 (1,398 whites and 2,065 blacks, or 59.6 percent black), in 1880, 7,526 (3,129 whites and 4,397 blacks, or 58.4 percent black), and in 1890, 10,305 (4,764 whites, 5,538 blacks, and 3 Chinese, or 53.7 percent black). U.S. Census Office, *Tenth Census,* 425, table 6 (1870, 1880), and *Compendium of the Eleventh Census,* 577, table 17 (1890). The Danville Common Council reported in April 1884 a total population of 8,471, of which 4,890 citizens were black and 3,581 were white; this is the closest estimate for November 1883. For 1884 statistics, see Danville Proceedings, April 1, 1884.

37. Danville Proceedings, July 1, 1882. Withers was one of eight regularly elected policemen. See also testimony of J. D. Raulston (p. 465), John D. Blackwell (p. 359), and W. P. Robinson (pp. 390–411), U.S. Senate *Report.*

38. On the African American cemetery, see Danville Proceedings, October 11, December 8, 1882; on streets, see Danville Proceedings, October 11, 1882, January 3, 1883; on schools, see clipping, *Danville Daily Register,* August 5, 1882, Public School Report, in Danvile Proceedings; see also Danville Proceedings, September 1, October 3, 1882, May 14, August 7, October 2, 1883. On taxes, see Danville Proceedings, March 24, 1882, February 23, 1883.

39. State law imposed a fine of $15 to $50 for carrying a concealed weapon. During the summer of 1883 nearly a hundred indictments were filed in Danville against people who did so. Although the majority of these were white men, prominent black Readjusters, such as Squire Taliaferro, were arrested repeatedly for this offense. Majority Report (p. xxvi), testimony of R. J. Adams (p. 242) and W. H. Barksdale (p. 278), U.S. Senate *Report.* See also Report of the Mayor, Danville Proceedings, November 21, 1883, and OB-E, April 12, 1883–January 1, 1885. On illegal gaming, see OB-E, June 5, 1883. For a contemporary argument in favor of strengthening the laws against carrying a concealed weapon, see Redfield, *Homicide, North and South,* 193–207.

40. Despite the growth of the city, arrests under the Readjusters fell from a high of 163 in September 1882 to 126 in May 1883 to 78 in September 1883. The vast majority of these arrests involved misdemeanors. For crime statistics, see Danville Proceedings, January 1882–December 1884.

41. OB-E, October 2, 1883. The list of those indicted in October for violating the concealed weapons law reads like a Who's Who of Danville politics. This is because men who were politically opposed reported each other carrying concealed weapons; e.g., W. H. McCormick, a white Democrat, reported Squire Taliaferro; Readjuster W. H. Luck, who was himself indicted for this offense in May, informed on Democrat J. W. Hall in October; the same week, Hall turned in eight Readjusters, including three police officers (who were presumably off duty at the time). See also OB-E, October 5, 1883.

42. *Coalition Rule in Danville,* vii, ix; emphasis in the original.

43. See Rabinowitz, *Race Relations,* 41–43, 47, 266, 278, 296, 329, 350.

44. Police officers were selected by the common council to serve six-month terms. In 1882 the council chose one black officer, Walter S. Withers, and in 1883 it added a second, Robert J. Adams. Danville Proceedings, July 6, 1882, August 7, 1883. C.f. J. D. Raulston (president, Danville Common Council) testimony, U.S. Senate *Report,* 457; J. D. Blair (Democrat) testimony, *Danville Riot . . . Committee of Forty,* 39–40, VHS; (Readjuster) J. H. Johnston, "Address to the People," [November 1883], box 216, MP.

45. J. H. Johnston, "Address to the People." Cf. J. D. Raulston testimony, U.S. Senate *Report,* 457; J. D. Blair testimony, *Danville Riot . . . Committee of Forty,* 39–40, VHS; Raulston deposition, December 1883, box 192, MP.

46. Danville Proceedings, July 6, 1882; J. H. Johnston, "Address to the People"; J. D. Raulston testimony, U.S. Senate *Report,* 455, 458. Cf. Danville Proceedings, July 6, 1882, with J. D. Blair testimony, *Danville Riot . . . Committee of Forty,* 39–40, VHS, and John D. Blackwell testimony, U.S. Senate *Report,* 359. The sanitary policeman was a high-ranking city official who not only performed the duties of a scavenger but also enforced city regulations regarding sewerage, such as keeping ditches clear and gutters clean, and removing obstructions to the streams. In the latter capacity he came in contact with many businesses whose refuse accumulated. Although there is no evidence that Taliaferro harassed particular businessmen, one of the white city council members made repeated attempts to block his reappointment as sanitary

policeman and opposed Readjusters' attempts to extend his term. See Danville Proceedings, July 6, October 10, 1882, April 4, 1883.

47. J. D. Ruffin testimony, U.S. Senate *Report*, 462.

48. Testimony of John D. Blackwell (p. 367) and J. D. Ruffin (p. 462), ibid. W. P. Robinson, who was himself a magistrate, concurred with Blackwell, noting that Jones "understood the law very well, and seemed to be a very well educated negro. . . . I have seen him try white cases, and white men preferred to have him try them." W. P. Robinson testimony, ibid., 396.

49. W. P. Robinson deposition, December 1883, box 192, MP; Testimony of W. P. Robinson (pp. 392–93), J. D. Raulston (p. 459), and John D. Blackwell (pp. 360–61), U.S. Senate *Report;* Mahone handwritten speech #2, MP. Even Democrats admitted that the picture of the market under Democratic rule was overdrawn, noting that "[W]e never did have a good market in Danville . . . we didn't have any of the 'enticing meats' that these gentlemen speak of—at least I never got any of them." W. N. Ruffin testimony, U.S. Senate *Report,* 1006.

50. The council established a special committee to investigate the charges but found no evidence to support the complaint. Danville Proceedings, January 2, 1883.

51. *Coalition Rule in Danville.* Although conflict over sidewalk space was a universal condition in cities, Danville's old-fashioned walkways may have contributed to the problem. Most of the sidewalks consisted of two parallel rows of stone about twelve inches wide and raised a foot or more above street level. In Spring 1883 the common council ordered that the "stringers," as these sidewalks were called, be replaced with paving brick or stone. On April 13 the *Richmond Dispatch* noted: "That order necessitates the removal of much of those two parallel rows of stone stringers, the surrender of one or the other of which to persons meeting thereon taxes so heavily the politeness of some people." See also Danville Proceedings, February 9, 1883. For more white accounts of black appropriation of the language of gentility, see Litwack, *Been in the Storm So Long,* 256–57, and Ayers, *Promise of the New South,* 133–34.

52. Civil rights activist Virginia Durr recalled that in the 1920s, "I was taught by my environment and by my mother that you can't call a black woman a lady. You can't say 'A lady's here'; you have to say, 'A woman's here.'" Quoted in Bernard, *Outside the Magic Circle,* 19. Katharine Du Pre Lumpkin (*Making of a Southerner,* 189–93) recounted a pre–World War I crisis in her local YWCA over whether or not the white members would receive and address a black speaker as "Miss" Arthur. On the other hand, African Americans had ingenious methods of circumventing white prejudices. Hortense Powdermaker (*After Freedom,* 343) relates how one Mississippi family in the 1930s had their baby christened "Misjulia," thereby ensuring white use of her title.

53. See Reid Mitchell, *Civil War Soldiers,* 66. In his dramatization of the life of Sigmund Freud, Jean-Paul Sartre (*Freud Scenario,* 284–88, 321) links Freud's drive and self-identity to an incident in which the young Freud and his father were forced from the sidewalk by an anti-Semite ("Not on the sidewalk, Jew!") and suggests that memories of the incident triggered Freud's articulation of

the oedipal complex. See also Freud, *Complete Psychological Works,* 4:196–97, 212, and Schorske, *Fin-de-Siècle Vienna,* 191.

54. Graves testimony, U.S. Senate *Report,* 213, 212.

55. See esp. Jones, *Labor of Love;* Clinton, "Reconstructing Freedwomen" and "Freedwomen, Sexuality, and Violence"; Gilmore, *Gender and Jim Crow;* Laura F. Edwards, "Sexual Violence" and *Gendered Strife;* and Schwalm, *Hard Fight for We.*

56. W. N. Ruffin testimony, U.S. Senate *Report,* 999–1000. Cf. testimony of J. R. Pleasants (p. 1041), Thomas Fricker (p. 1071), and B. F. Wheatley (p. 1109), ibid.

57. Walter Gay deposition, December 1883, box 192, MP.

58. *Lynchburg Democratic Campaign,* October 29, 1883, quoted in Walter T. Calhoun, "Danville Riot," 36–37.

59. Munford, *Random Recollections,* 154.

60. By street etiquette, I mean what Erving Goffman ("Nature of Deference and Demeanor," 476–77) calls "rules of conduct," or "ceremonial rules," through which an individual "expresses his character or conveys his appreciation of the other participants in the situation." Street etiquette falls under Goffman's category of "symmetrical rules," or common courtesies, that are considered mutually binding.

61. Noel was 26 years old in 1880, which would have made him 28 or 29 in 1883. He is identified in the 1880 manuscript census as an unmarried clerk in a grocery store and a boarder in the home of Richard and Catherine Walk.

62. Noell testimony, *Danville Riot . . . Committee of Forty,* 11–12, VHS. The Committee of Forty report spells Noel's name as Noell. He is listed as Noel both in the census and in the index of the U.S. Senate *Report.* Lawson's full name was Henderson Lawson. He was 21 years old in 1880, which would have made him 23 or 24 in 1883. Lawson was identified as a porter in the 1880 census and as a waiter in Nicholas and Hessberg's restaurant in the 1881–82 Danville City Directory, DPL; he was unmarried as of 1880.

63. In the 1880 manuscript census Lewellyn is identified as 21 years old, which would have made him 23 or 24 in 1883. He worked in a tobacco factory and shared a room with a store clerk. He was unmarried in 1880.

64. On "getting too close" as a violation of personal honor, see Simmel, "The Secret and the Secret Society," 321.

65. Edward Ayers (*Vengeance and Justice*) has written of the propensity of white men in the postwar South to overreact to perceived African American insolence. "When black gestures signaled flagrant contempt," Ayers writes, "many white Southern men literally knew no way to react other than with violence. If a black man insulted a white man and the white did not strike back immediately, he had, in his own eyes and in the eyes of his peers, no honor left to lose" (p. 235). Cf. Bertram Wilbur Doyle, *Etiquette of Race Relations,* 117, and Litwack, *Been in the Storm So Long,* 278.

66. Sims testimony, contested election case, *Sims v. Hurt,* quoted in Mahone handwritten speech #1 (December 1883), box 192, MP. Cf. Sims testimony,

U.S. Senate *Report*, 701–4, and *Danville Times*, November 20, 1883 (entered as testimony in *Danville Riot . . . Committee of Forty*, 13–14, VHS). Sims described the audience as polite and controlled, whereas white Democrats portrayed it as "a vast crowd of Africans, who were yelling and whooping at the top of their voices." See Peter Boudin editorial in *Danville Times*, November 20, 1883, entered as testimony in *Danville Riot . . . Committee of Forty*, 13–14, VHS.

67. Although Cabell's name did not appear on the circular, his reputation was attached to it, as he had made speeches personally affirming its truth. See N. T. Reid testimony, *Danville Riot . . . Committee of Forty*, 22, VHS; Mahone handwritten speech #2, citing report of S. M. Dickey, Grayson County, to Mahone, box 192, MP.

68. Charles Friend testimony, *Danville Riot . . . Committee of Forty*, 21; B. B. Temple testimony, U.S. Senate *Report*, 49. According to Temple, between six hundred and seven hundred men assembled in the Opera House. Even *after* the violence, Democrats were obsessed with upholding the truth of the circular. In a mass meeting at the Richmond Armory Hall on November 4, Colonel John B. Purcell chaired a meeting called to denounce Mahone for casting aspersions on the honor of the white men of Danville by questioning the claims of the circular. Purcell moved to uphold the circular. *Lynchburg Virginian*, November 6, 1883.

69. Testimony of Noel (pp. 109–11), Lawson (p. 144), Lewellyn (pp. 157–58), Taylor (p. 29), and Lea (pp. 85–87), U.S. Senate *Report*. Taylor and Lea both singled out Lawson as the man Noel was after. Noel identified the man he saw on the street as the same man who pushed him off the pavement, who was Lewellyn.

70. The phrase "to insure fair play" belongs to the vocabulary of dueling. It is striking that the white men should use such language in regard to a fight with a black man that began, after all, over white resentment at being treated as a black equal. It is more likely that Noel's intent was to beat Lewellyn with brass knuckles while Lea and Taylor stood by armed. Or perhaps this fight can be seen as lying in the cultural middle between the older southern defense of honor, the duel, and its New South replacement, the street fight. On street fights, see Ayers, *Vengeance and Justice*, 268–70.

71. The tobacco factories and warehouses, where the majority of the black population in Danville worked, had half days on Saturday. Most people stopped work at twelve. For tobacco factory hours, see R. W. Glass testimony, U.S. Senate *Report*, 84.

72. Lawson and Lewellyn claimed that Noel was wearing "knucks," or brass knuckles. Noel, Taylor, and Lea insisted that Noel fought with his bare hands.

73. Testimony of Lea (p. 87), Lewellyn (pp. 158–59), Lawson (pp. 144–45), and Adams (pp. 238–39), U.S. Senate *Report*.

74. Testimony of R. J. Adams (p. 238) and W. R. Taylor (p. 30), U.S. Senate *Report*. Lea refused to say whether he had shot or not, fearing to incriminate himself.

75. The Democrats denied that there were women and children in the

crowd. But there is ample testimony that women and children were in the street, although none were injured. John F. Carl, keeper of the U.S. Cemetery, which lay within the corporate limits of Danville, estimated that "fully one half of (the crowd) were youths and children from 6 years upwards with a sprinkling of girls and women." The women and children were milling around at the back of the crowd, which accounts for the fact that all of the people who died were adult men. John F. Carl deposition, November 1883, contained in Mahone handwritten speech #1, box 192, MP. Cf. depositions of Rev. W. H. Barksdale and George W. West, ibid., and Sophia Powell testimony, U.S. Senate *Report,* 178–79.

76. Testimony of R. J. Adams, U.S. Senate *Report,* 239.

77. There was confusion among the crowd over who had fired at Adams, Lea or Taylor, who was also openly armed. Some people mistakenly demanded the arrest of Taylor, while others identified Lea as the shooter.

78. Walter S. Withers deposition, Mahone handwritten speech #1, box 192, MP.

79. Testimony of R. J. Adams (pp. 239–40), Walter S. Withers (pp. 1–2), W. R. Taylor (p. 30, quotation), J. C. Reagan (p. 64), and R. W. Glass (p. 75), U.S. Senate *Report.* Similar language was used in Richmond during the struggle over integrated streetcars there. In the spring of 1867, when three blacks refused to leave a whites-only streetcar, a crowd gathered, shouting, "let's have our rights." Rachleff, *Black Labor,* 42–43.

80. The number of dead is difficult to document, although there is general if undocumented agreement that five men were killed. See Wynes, *Race Relations,* 31, and Moore, *Two Paths,* 117. The records of the Virginia Bureau of Vital Statistics are not much help on this issue. Only two black men can be located—Terry Smith and Edward Davis—who died of gunshot wounds in Danville on November 3, and there is no record of black men dying of gunshot wounds in the surrounding counties, either. In addition, Walter Holland cannot be located in these records, although all testimony agrees that he died on the street that day. See Virginia Bureau of Vital Statistics (microfilm), reel 32, SLV. The Danville Common Council Proceedings for November 1883 report three deaths by gunshot wounds that month, all African American. Cf. R. W. Glass testimony, U.S. Senate *Report,* 79–80, and R. W. Glass deposition, in Mahone handwritten speech #1, box 192, MP.

81. Depositions of Charles Adams and L. L. Ivy (black), Mahone handwritten speech #1, box 192, MP; Testimony of J. C. Reagan (pp. 63–65) and Jack Redd (p. 14), U.S. Senate *Report.* Cf. testimony of Charles Adams (p. 234) and R. J. Adams (p. 241), U.S. Senate *Report.* Graves admitted encountering Adams and agreed that Adams was shot but argued that it was impossible for him to have fired the shot. Graves testimony, U.S. Senate *Report,* 210–11.

82. Testimony of Charles Friend (p. 21), James P. Harrison (p. 23), and R. M. Hubbard (p. 24), *Danville Riot . . . Committee of Forty,* VHS.

83. Flyer, "To the People of Danville," November 5, 1883, printed in *Danville Riot . . . Committee of Forty,* 31–32, VHS. According to Mayor Johnston, these

men had no authority to be on the streets, but they defied all attempts to disband them. Johnston testimony, U.S. Senate *Report*, 659. On November 7 the common council, over the protests of black Readjusters, created a special all-white police force of fifteen to patrol the city. It was still active in mid-November, and rather than discouraging crime, the force was implicated in it. In calling for its dispersal Johnston complained, "it is to be noted that since this constabulary force has been on duty there have been more successful burglaries, attempts at burglary, and house breaking without discovery of the perpetrators, committed in this town than ever before in the same space of time." Report of the Mayor, November 15, 1883, Danville Proceedings.

84. Powell deposition, December 1883, box 192, MP. Cf. R. A. Schoolfield manuscript (edited by his daughter, Blanch Church), Robert Addison Schoolfield Papers, AL, in which he recalls patrolling Saturday night and parts of Sunday and Monday nights. Violet Keeling, a friend of Sophie Powell, said that "we did not know how many people had been killed, and how many would be killed. We did not know where to run to, & we just stayed at home." Keeling testimony, December 1883, box 192, MP.

85. For 1883 election statistics, see Mahone Scrapbooks, vol. 2, box 216, MP. See also McKinney, *Southern Mountain Republicans*, 106, 239 n. 245. For more on the election, see Chapter 5 and the Epilogue below.

86. Lewis E. Harvie of Danville (Democrat) to Lewis E. Harvie of Amelia (Readjuster), December 8, 1883, Harvie Family Papers, VHS.

87. Clipping, *Washington Star*, n.d., Mahone Scrapbooks, vol. 31, box 216, MP. Cf. *Marion Conservative Democrat*, December 6, 1883. In light of Democratic behavior in other southern states, Mahone's charges of premeditated violence were credible. But in this case, the evidence is against Democratic premeditation of the assault in Danville, although the Democrats' election campaign was rife with predictions of "race war" in the event of a Readjuster victory. Democratic efforts to keep the white men of Danville in the Opera House until they had all signed the affidavit denouncing William Sims is the strongest piece of circumstantial evidence that the violence had not been planned. Also, the frenzied efforts of Representative Cabell to keep the peace, testified to by witnesses on both sides of the political divide, argues against a Democratic plot. Mayor Johnston, hardly a fan of Cabell's, nevertheless volunteered that immediately after the shooting he "found Colonel Cabell taking a very active part, trying to quiet the people, and but for his influence I think they would have torn things up generally . . . they were perfectly crazy—desperate." Johnston testimony, U.S. Senate *Report*, 655.

88. *Danville Riot . . . Committee of Forty*, 3–6, VHS.

89. There is no reliable testimony that any of the African Americans were armed with guns, much less that they had fired. In fact, it is unlikely that the black men and women on the streets that afternoon doing their marketing and otherwise passing the time would have courted the fines imposed for possession of concealed weapons. More to the point, the blacks outnumbered the whites by an estimated margin of ten to one. Had the black men been armed,

they might have massacred the white men on the sidewalk. Black policeman Walter Withers was quoted (in the *Danville Riot . . . Committee of Forty,* VHS) as having said that "the firing seemed to be on both sides right at each other," but in a deposition cited by Mahone, Withers insisted that he "used no such language nor any language intended to convey any such idea. I swear positively that I saw no colored man fire a shot nor did I see any colored man with any weapons in his hands, at that time." Withers deposition, Mahone handwritten speech #1, box 192, MP.

90. Report of the Grand Jury (p. 484) and Watkins testimony (pp. 483–85), U.S. Senate *Report.*

91. On lynching, see Raper, *Tragedy of Lynching;* Hall, *Revolt against Chivalry;* Ayers, *Vengeance and Justice,* 238–65; Wright, *Racial Violence in Kentucky;* and Brundage, *Lynching in the New South* and *Under Sentence of Death.* On the predecessor to lynching, the more overtly political mob violence of Reconstruction, see Gillette, *Retreat from Reconstruction;* Eric Foner, *Reconstruction,* 425–44; Trelease, *White Terror;* and Rable, *But There Was No Peace.* On Reconstruction violence in Virginia, see Maddex, *Virginia Conservatives,* 184–203; Chesson, *Richmond after the War,* chap. 4; and Taylor, *Negro in the Reconstruction,* chaps. 3–4.

92. Although the urban South was not the most likely home for lynching, southern cities still had to contend with threatened lynchings and other forms of urban violence. On urban lynchings, see Ingalls, "Lynching and Establishment Violence in Tampa," and Rabinowitz, *Race Relations,* 52–54. On urban violence in the New South, see Ayers, *Vengeance and Justice,* 223–65; Joel Williamson, *Crucible of Race,* 57–59, 115–19, 180–223; Shapiro, *White Violence and Black Response;* Hair, *Carnival of Fury;* and Prather, *We Have Taken a City.*

93. On Richmond, see Chesson, *Richmond after the War,* 102, 160. On Norfolk, see Taylor, *Negro in the Reconstruction,* 23.

94. Joel Williamson, *After Slavery,* 257 (fistfight in Charleston); Rabinowitz, *Race Relations,* 337.

95. Danville Proceedings, November 15, 21, 1883.

96. Chesnutt, *Marrow of Tradition,* 33.

97. Lea testimony, U.S. Senate *Report,* 88–89.

98. Quoted in Benjamin, "On Some Motifs in Baudelaire," 167. See also Buck-Morss, "The Flaneur, the Sandwichman and the Whore."

99. Brundage makes this point in *Lynching in the New South,* 155–56, 200. There were, of course, many uses to segregation. For instance, there is a gendered aspect to segregation as well as a racist one. The most basic spatial division in turn-of-the-century urban society was between a gendered public and private sphere. Scholars have shown for a variety of societies how women were restricted to preserve social order and to differentiate between political subjects and their dependents. The racialized demarcation of public space in the segregated American South can be seen, in part, as an emasculation of African American men, which constituted both a threat to black male identity and

an attack on black manliness paralleled by white efforts to ensure black disfranchisement.

100. Brundage, *Lynching in the New South*, 200.

101. But not in buses and streetcars: hence the volatility of the shifting no-man's-land between white and black sections. Cf. Kelley, " 'We Are Not What We Seem,' " 104.

102. Fauchet, *Origine desdinitez et magistrats de France*, quoted in Ginzburg, "Fiction as Historical Evidence," 381. The occasion for Fauchet's comment was his defense of the use of fiction in the writing of history. On Dixon and history, see Davenport, "Thomas Dixon's Mythology of Southern History."

103. On the Wilmington Riot, see Prather, *We Have Taken a City;* Shapiro, *White Violence*, 65–75; Gilmore, *Gender and Jim Crow*, chap. 4; Edmonds, *Fusion Politics in North Carolina*, 158–77; and McDuffie, "Politics in Wilmington and New Hanover County, N.C."

104. In 1896 populism split North Carolina's white vote, and the Populists combined with Republicans to create a third-party fusion government. The fusionist legislature altered the city charter of Wilmington, expanding its borders and concentrating its black Republican majority. On biracial rule in North Carolina, see Edmonds, *Fusion Politics in North Carolina*.

105. Dixon's (*Leopard's Spots*, 415) fictional version of the Manly editorial is an afterthought, mentioned almost parenthetically: "The incendiary organ of the Negroes, a newspaper that had been noted for its virulent spirit of race hatred, had published an editorial defaming the virtue of the white women of the community."

106. Dixon, *Leopard's Spots*, 414–15.

107. Ginzburg, "Fiction as Historical Evidence," 380. Ginzburg constructs this phrase to describe Aristotle's argument in the *Poetics* (1451 a) that "a poet's object is not to tell what actually happened but what could and would happen either probably or inevitably." Dixon was not a witness to the Wilmington Riot; he was in New York at the time, and, according to historians of the riot, the sidewalk shoving incident Dixon uses as a catalyst to violence in *The Leopard's Spots* never occurred. See Gilmore, *Gender and Jim Crow*, chap. 4. See also Gilmore, " 'One of the Meanest Books.' "

108. *New Bern Journal*, quoted in *Wilmington Messenger*, September 18, 1898; *Wilmington Messenger*, September 18, October 27, 1898; Prather, *We Have Taken a City*, 53–54.

109. Lumpkin, *Making of a Southerner*, 134. On Lefevbre's idea of the revelatory "moment," see *La somme et le reste*. Childhood did not always protect African American children from white wrath. In 1912 J. A. DeLaine, who later caused Clarendon County, S.C, to be one of the five cases brought before the Supreme Court in *Brown v. Board of Education*, was sentenced as a youngster to twenty-five lashes for pushing a white boy who had shoved DeLaine's sister off the sidewalk. Rather than submit, DeLaine ran away to Atlanta. See Kluger, *Simple Justice*, 12.

CHAPTER 5

1. Chap. 4, 3 Laws of Virginia 250, 251 (Hening, 1823) (enacted 1705); Chap. 78, 12 Laws of Virginia 184, 185 (Hening, 1823) (enacted 1785); *Virginia Acts of Assembly,* chap. 357 (1910) and chap. 371 (1924). For a fascinating overview of colonial and antebellum Virginia's shifting definitions of race and their legal and social consequences, see Higginbotham and Kopytoff, "Racial Purity and Interracial Sex." On the ambiguities of racial identity, see Johnston, *Race Relations in Virginia,* 191–215. On the 1924 law, see Sherman, " 'The Last Stand.' " For an analysis of twentieth-century court cases and the definition of race, see Pascoe, "Miscegenation Law, Court Cases." See also Bynum, "Miscegenation, Racial Identity, and the Law."

2. *Debates and Proceedings in the Congress of the United States, 1789–1791,* 1:998, 1284; 2:1148–56, 1162, 2264.

3. The federal Naturalization Law of 1790 reserved naturalization for "whites" only, thus providing a basis for barring Asian immigrants from citizenship.

4. *In re Halladjian,* 174 F. 834 (1909) (first quotation); *United States v. Akhay Kumar Mozumdar,* 296 F. 173 (1923) (second quotation). See also *In re Balsara,* 171 F. 294 (1909), and *United States v. Bhagat Singh Thind,* 261 U.S. 204 (1923). On this topic, see Almaguer, *Racial Fault Lines,* 10, and Takaki, *Strangers from a Different Shore,* 15, 298–300. On the law of race in America, see Stephenson, *Race Distinctions;* Jack Greenberg, *Race Relations and American Law;* Finkelman, "The Color of Law"; Gotanda, "Critique of 'Our Constitution Is Color-Blind' "; and Haney Lopez, *White by Law.* On the law of miscegenation, see Martyn, "Racism in the United States"; Joel Williamson, *New People;* Wadlington, "The *Loving* Case"; and Sickles, *Race, Marriage, and the Law.*

5. For a thorough and accessible introduction to this subject, see Gould, *Mismeasure of Man.*

6. Thomas Holt, "Marking: Race, Race-making, and the Writing of History," 14. See also David Roediger's (*Towards the Abolition of Whiteness,* 2) argument that "race is given meaning through the agency of human beings in concrete historical and social contexts, and is not a biological or natural category." The literature on the definition of race in America is vast and still growing. On the social construction of race, see, among many others, Fields, "Ideology and Race"; Roediger, *Wages of Whiteness;* Saxton, *Rise and Fall of the White Republic;* Jacobson, *Whiteness of a Different Color;* Almaguer, *Racial Fault Lines;* Pascoe, "Miscegenation Law, Court Cases"; Amy Robinson, "It Takes One to Know One"; and Hale, *Making Whiteness.* On scientific racism, see Horsman, *Race and Manifest Destiny;* Fredrickson, *Black Image in the White Mind;* Gossett, *History of an Idea in America;* Gould, *Mismeasure of Man;* and Barkan, *Retreat of Scientific Racism.*

7. W. E. B. Du Bois, "The Superior Race," in David Levering Lewis, *W. E. B. Du Bois Reader,* 477.

8. Evelyn Brooks Higginbotham, "Metalanguage of Race," 252.

9. *Scott v. Raub,* 88 Va. 721 (1892), 14 S.E. 178; Virginia Code of 1860, chap. 103, sec. 1; General Assembly, *Acts, 1865–1866,* chap. 18, 85–86. Prior to the passage of this last law, unions between free people of color and slaves were held to be legal nullities.

10. Virginia Code of 1873, chap. 105, sec. 1, 850.

11. *Scott v. Raub,* 722, 729; *Jones v. Commonwealth,* 80 Va. 538 (1885), 544–45. In insisting on a high standard of proof of African descent, the Virginia court recognized the serious legal penalties of blackness as well as the possibilities within such a racial system for slander and malicious accusation.

12. *Scott v. Raub,* 728, 729.

13. Ibid., 729; Goffman, *Interaction Ritual,* 85.

14. Thomas J. Buckley's "Unfixing Race," a fascinating interpretation of the mixed-race Wright family, is a notable exception, as is Ariela Gross's work, "Litigating Whiteness." See also Gross, *Double Character.*

15. Faulkner scholars agree that neither Christmas nor the reader is ever given proof of Joe's racial makeup. The narrator refers variously to Christmas as "white" and as a "nigger." "White" characters are described in the novel as darker than Christmas. See Snead, *Figures of Division,* 88.

16. The Readjusters provide an excellent example of Mary Douglas's ("Rightness of Categories," 240) critique of theories of identity that operate from "an implicit though dubious assumption that individual knowledge comes first and that public knowledge is built up afterwards." On the dynamic relationship between categories and the impossibility of defining any in isolation from others, see Butler, *Bodies That Matter,* 168.

17. Roediger, *Wages of Whiteness,* 170–81.

18. Pierpont to Dr. Wing, December 12, 1881, box 1, folder 11, RP.

19. William G. Mustard to Mahone, April 28, 1881, box 30, MP. Sidney Mosby, a black Readjuster from Charlotte County, complained to Mahone in the spring of 1883 that local white Readjusters refused to split the county offices with them. See Mosby to Mahone, April 12, 1883, box 70, MP. Local party organizations were integrated in 1881. See Bragg, *Journal of Negro History,* 675.

20. W. J. S. Bowe to Mahone, May 16, 1881, box 30, MP.

21. *Petersburg Index-Appeal,* September 9 (Wise), November 2, 1882; Letter to the editor, *Staunton Spectator,* September 13, 1881.

22. Virginia was granted an additional congressional representative based on the 1880 U.S. census, but the boundaries of the new district remained undrawn in 1881: hence the temporary position of "congressman-at-large."

23. *Marion Conservative Democrat,* November 3, 1882 (Massey); *Staunton Spectator,* May 5, 1881.

24. In 1883 Mahone estimated that "the Readjuster party . . . is composed of about 110,000 colored and about 65,000 white voters." *Richmond Whig,* June 15, 1883.

25. See the many articles on the 1881 and 1882 statewide elections in the *Staunton Spectator* and *Lynchburg Virginian.*

26. *Marion Conservative Democrat,* May 5, 1882, quoting *Patriot and Herald.*

27. W. E. B. Du Bois, *Black Reconstruction,* 700–701.

28. The phrase is from Lipsitz, "The Possessive Investment in Whiteness."

29. *Richmond Whig,* April 6, 1881 (Jefferson); Bond, "Extent and Character of Separate Schools," 326.

30. In 1863 Huxley differentiated between "mongrels" and "hybrids," saying that mongrels were crosses between distinct races, and thus capable of reproducing, whereas hybrids were crosses between distinct species and therefore sterile. Huxley, "Six Lectures to Working Men," in *Collected Essays,* 423–24. On the place of degeneration in American racial thought, see Fredrickson, *Black Image in the White Mind,* 54, 228–55, 258–83, 290, 300, 307; Stepan, "Biology and Degeneration"; Stanton, *Leopard's Spots;* and Gould, *Mismeasure of Man,* 39–40.

31. Young, *Colonial Desire,* 4.

32. Address of the Conservative State Executive Committee, June 1881, printed in *Staunton Spectator,* June 14, 1881; *Richmond Dispatch,* April 17, 1881. See also *Spectator,* April 19, 1881.

33. *Staunton Spectator,* February 8, 1881, quoting *Lynchburg Advance,* September 20, 1881 (Tucker).

34. See Ryan, *Women in Public,* 135. In 1864 Democrats coined the word "miscegenation" to denounce alleged Republican tendencies toward race mixing. On the 1864 election and this Democratic strategy, see Kaplan, "The Miscegenation Issue."

35. "Hermaphrodite" is a term that cropped up from time to time in southern politics after the Civil War, meaning generally that a man was incompletely male. For an example from Georgia in 1869, see Eric Foner, *Reconstruction,* 348 (one Republican against another); for an example in 1892, also from Georgia, see Ayers, *Vengeance and Justice,* 239 (a Democrat referring to a Populist). In the 1870s and 1880s the *Oxford (N.C.) Torchlight* occasionally printed cartoons that depicted Republican electoral candidates as women. See Laura F. Edwards, *Gendered Strife,* 234. "Hermaphrodite" could also refer to women, of course, and even to a state of mind. To give a famous example, in 1838 Rev. Henry F. Harrington said of women's rights activists Mary Wollstonecraft, Frances Wright, and Harriet Martineau, "They are only semi-women, mental hermaphrodites." Quoted in Welter, "The Cult of True Womanhood," 173.

36. Quoted in *Richmond Dispatch,* October 26, 1883. Ideas about race and gender had been linked in Virginia since colonial times, when the English connected them through rhetoric that drew on the "natural" differences among people. Once racial and gender differences had been naturalized, it was that much easier to see differentials in power based on racial and gender differences as equally natural and unchanging. For a clear yet nuanced account of the process of differentiation by race and gender in seventeenth-century Virginia, see Kathleen Brown, *Good Wives,* esp. 107–244.

37. Laura F. Edwards, *Gendered Strife,* 188, 232 (first quotation); Fink, *Workingmen's Democracy,* 163 (second quotation). Even in the postwar North, as

David Montgomery (*Fall of the House of Labor*, 25) has shown, codes of "manly behavior" were "usually cast in ethnic and racial terms." Examples of this sort of language and discursive strategy may be found across the South. Kousser (*Shaping of Southern Politics*, 37) notes that during the Populist era, "partisanship and racism became indistinguishable" in Democratic rhetoric.

38. Kantrowitz, *Ben Tillman*, MSS 315.

39. *Lynchburg Virginian*, October 15, 1883.

40. Ibid. On the lack of these rights under slavery, even for free blacks, see Berlin, *Slaves without Masters*, 316–17. In *Honor and Slavery*, Kenneth Greenberg argues for the interrelatedness of the southern culture of honor and racial slavery. In an earlier book, *Masters and Statesmen*, Greenberg notes that "the very act of sending a note to someone, even in confrontation, meant that you regarded your opponent as a social equal" (p. 35).

41. On dueling in Virginia during the Readjuster era, see Moore, "Death of the Duel." Men who would play prominent roles in the political struggles of the Readjuster years were involved in duels fought before 1879. In 1866 William Cameron was injured in a duel with Democrat Robert W. Hughes; both were newspaper editors at the time. In 1873 funder William Royall served as second to Page McCarty in a duel in which McCarty mortally wounded his antagonist, John B. Mordecai. See Royall, *Some Reminiscences*, 65–99.

42. John Wise fought one duel in 1882 after being foiled in an earlier attempt in 1880, when he was rejected for membership by the exclusive Westmoreland Club. Learning that he had been blackballed by Dr. George Ben Johnston, Wise demanded an explanation, the instigatory step in the ritual of dueling. Before the duel could occur, Johnston was arrested. Wise remained at large, eluding the police by disguising himself as a Jewish peddler so effectively that even his own son did not recognize him. After a week he voluntarily unmasked himself to the Richmond police. Wise's successful disguise (and stories about it) reestablished his honor almost as effectively as a duel would have. On this event, see Moore, "The Death of the Duel," 265. On Wise, see Curtis Carroll Davis, "Very Well-Rounded Republican." On the cultural significance of masks and other disguises to southern men of honor, and the importance of unmasking oneself versus being unmasked, see Kenneth S. Greenberg, *Honor and Slavery*, 24–50.

43. *Richmond Whig*, October 17, 1881 (Mahone letter). The correspondence between the protagonists in a duel was typically published, thus allowing the public to witness and judge the events that precipitated the confrontation.

44. On the importance of dueling as ritual reaffirmation of equality among the principals, see Kenneth S. Greenberg, *Honor and Slavery*, 58.

45. *Richmond Commonwealth*, January 30, February 5–6, 1880, quoted in Moore, "Death of the Duel," 263 (Royall); C. W. Bryan to Mahone, December 10, 1883, box 192, MP.

46. These tactics of intimidation did not always work out as planned. When R. R. Nolan, a Democratic candidate for the state legislature from Halifax County, told his tenant Simon Barksdale to vote Democratic or lose his lease,

Barksdale voted Readjuster and found himself a new place to live, taking his kinsmen with him. Barksdale affidavit, box 192, MP.

47. John R. Woods to Mahone, December 9, 1883, box 63, MP; Petition of Mechanics and Workingmen's Association of Lynchburg, April 1, 1883, box 70, MP. On threatened loss of credit, see T. S. Curlett to Mahone, November 23, 1883, box 82, and Caesar Phillips affidavit, handwritten depositions, box 216, MP. On eviction, see Simon Barksdale affidavit, December 1883, box 216, and D. S. Hale to Mahone, December 18–19, 1883, box 82, MP.

48. W. F. Jones to Mahone, December 14, 1883, box 192, MP. For an example of a prospective bride coercing her husband-to-be to vote Democratic, see O'Ferrall, *Forty Years of Active Service*, 222–23.

49. T. W. Payne to Mahone, n.d. [December 1883], box 192, MP. For additional evidence, see George W. Young to Mahone, December 18, 1883, box 192, MP, in which Young reports that in Mecklenburg County "[t]hreats of social ostracism and every other means were used with powerful effect to make every white man that was possible vote the bourbon ticket." One white Readjuster in Danville complained of an organized Democratic campaign of social and economic ostracism against Readjusters. See W. P. Robinson affidavit, box 192, MP.

50. If this failed to move the governor, a postscript supplied a coup de grâce: "P.S. I am an orphan." Wm. P. Barksdale to William E. Cameron, April 21, 1882, box 1, Cameron Executive Papers, SLV.

51. William P. Barksdale to William E. Cameron, April 21, 1882, box 1, Cameron Executive Papers, SLV.

52. John C. Duane to Mahone, n.d. (December 1883), box 192, MP.

53. Keiley, letter to the editor, *Marion Conservative Democrat*, March 8, 1883.

54. Waynesboro Democratic Club flyer, October 29, 1883, included in text of Mahone handwritten speech #1 (December 1883), p. 188, box 192, MP.

55. W. F. Jones to Mahone, December 14, 1883, box 192, MP. See also W. B. Blanton to Mahone, December 14, 1883, box 192, and C. A. Heermans to Mahone, October 17, 1883, box 80, MP, in which Heermans complains that "[Democratic] Men are employed by the day to ride and visit the people and the only song is nigger, nigger. It has the effect to scare some of our people."

56. Samuel J. Quinn to Mahone, n.d. [December 1883], box 192, MP; Wise County chairman to Mahone, n.d. (composed on the back of a March 24, 1883, circular from Mahone), box 189, MP; C. A. Heermans to Mahone, November 9, 1883, box 81, MP.

57. *Warrenton Index*, quoted in *Staunton Spectator*, July 10, 1883.

58. Lewis P. Nelson to Mahone, October 31, 1883, box 80; Rev. W. E. Talley to Mahone, June 6, 1883, box 73; and Cross to Mahone, May 26, 1883, box 72—all in MP.

59. Flyer, n.d. [1883], on J. E. Mason's candidacy for commonwealth attorney for Prince George County, Mahone Scrapbooks, box 216, MP; *Lynchburg News*, quoted in U.S. Senate *Report*, v; *Staunton Spectator*, May 22, 1883.

60. *Danville Times*, n.d. [March 1883], quoted in U.S. Senate *Report*, vi. Afri-

can American Readjusters tried without success to repeal the antimiscegenation laws. For more on this, see Chapter 4 above.

61. *Staunton Spectator,* headline editorial, "In Which Column Will You Stand?," October 30, 1883; *Lynchburg Virginian,* November 6, 1883 (Massey). Massey was still speaking in these terms in the late 1880s. As he explained on one occasion, "Two parties (I might say two races) are confronting each other in the Southern States." Hancock, *Autobiography of John E. Massey,* 271.

62. *Staunton Spectator,* quoting the *Virginian,* October 23, 1883.

63. *Staunton Spectator,* October 30, 1883.

64. *Lynchburg Advance,* September 5, 1883.

65. Mary Douglas makes this point in *Purity and Danger,* 115, where she argues that the body "is a model that can stand for any bounded system."

66. W. O. Austin to Mahone, December 26, 1883, box 192, MP. Three black men and one white man were killed outright during the shooting, and a fourth black man died later.

67. A. M. Willis Jr. to Mahone, October 19, 1883, box 80, MP. See also the many other letters in box 80 outlining the steps needed to counteract the circular.

68. *Staunton Spectator,* November 6, 1883. The story of this speech was reported repeatedly, beginning on October 30.

69. See the many letters asserting this in box 81, MP.

70. J. M. Gills to Mahone, November 23, 1883, box 82, MP (Tazewell County); Walker to Mahone, November 9, 1883, box 81, MP. For Readjuster rebuttals, see Meredith Watson to Mahone, December 15, 1883, box 82, MP, and *Staunton Spectator* October 30, November 6, 1883.

71. See R. J. Wollwine to Mahone, n.d. [December 1883], and Flyer, November 3, 1883, late afternoon, box 192, MP.

72. Perhaps nowhere in Virginia would stories about black insurrection cause such panic among whites as in Southampton County, home fifty years earlier to Nat Turner. Several New York and Virginia newspapers reported on November 10 "the startling intelligence that the whole white population of the county was much excited over rumors that the negroes were making arrangements for a general uprising and massacre." Small towns in Southampton "were making preparations to defend themselves, and . . . scouts had been sent out to watch the negroes." *New York Herald, New York World, New York Tribune,* and *Lynchburg Virginian,* all November 10, 1883. On rumor as political expression and white use of insurrectionary scares to tip the balance of power in the rural South, see Hahn, " 'Extravagant Expectations' of Freedom," esp. 146–58.

73. W. O. Harvie to Mahone, December 12, 1883 (first quotation), box 82, MP; Washington, D.C., *National Republican,* November 15, 1883, quoting a letter from Abingdon, November 14, 1883, box 81, MP. If it seems unlikely that an election could cause a war, recall that the secession of the southern states was sparked by the Republican victory in the presidential election of 1860.

74. Depositions of Walter Gay (first quotation) and William Powell, Decem-

ber 1883, box 192, MP. This loss of the black vote did not affect the Readjuster outcome in Pittsylvania County, as it and several nearby Piedmont counties were strongly Democratic. See Moore, *Two Paths*, 128–29, and S. F. Early deposition, box 192, MP.

75. H. Southworth, Essex County Chairman, to Mahone, December 14, 1883, box 82, MP (Essex County remained in the Readjuster camp); Ballard to Mahone, November 8, 1883, box 81, MP; Degler, *The Other South*, 298 (Hughes). Not all Virginia blacks supported the Readjusters, however: Robert F. Mays estimated that in 1883 approximately 25,000 black men voted the Democratic ticket, probably either because they were coerced or because the Democrats had allied with Straight-Out Republicans in some sections of the state. See Mays to Mahone, November 7, 1883, box 81, MP.

76. Although it is tempting to posit a causal relationship between the violence in Danville and the Readjuster defeat, evidence suggests that the coalition lost in the mountain regions not because of white defections but because of Democratic gains among first-time voters. For 1883 election statistics, see Mahone Scrapbooks, vol. 2, box 216, MP, and McKinney, *Southern Mountain Republicans*, 106, 239 n. 245. On Democratic premeditation of the violence, see Chapter 4, n. 89.

77. Joseph Porter to Mahone, November 23, 1883, box 192, MP. J. H. Ballard reported from Abingdon that "The Danville Riot completely demoralized the democratic [white] element of our party, and they deserted, like rats from a sinking ship. The Republicans, I am proud to say, stood to their guns like men—never saw them more determined, or united." Ballard to Mahone, November 8, 1883, box 81, MP.

78. On the 1884 presidential election and the Republican Party's "southern strategy" of aiding independent movements, see De Santis, *Republicans Face the Southern Question*, chap. 4; Kousser, *Shaping of Southern Politics*, 23–24; and Hirshson, *Farewell to the Bloody Shirt*, 118–22, 138.

79. Steven Elliott Tripp (*Yankee Town, Southern City*) provides a classic example of this static approach to white racism in his explanation of why Lynchburg whites failed to ally effectively with local blacks in the late 1880s. "Most whites," Tripp writes, "simply could not divorce themselves from their ancient [race] prejudices and were thus reluctant to share power with blacks" (p. 254).

80. J. L. Powell to Mahone, December 12, 1883, box 192, MP. See also C. L. Pritchard to Mahone and Jonathan T. Silman to Mahone, November 19, 1883 (ibid.), in which both men attribute the loss in Warren County to news of the violence in Danville. Another correspondent complained that "[o]n Tuesday hundreds of our party men who had never failed with their support turned a deaf ear to all persuasion and would hear nothing, fully bent on voting the only ticket they believed would save the state from negro domination." W. A. Wesson to Mahone, November 9, 1883, box 81, MP.

81. *Richmond Star*, December 16, 1882.

82. My framing of this question draws on Ruth Frankenberg's (*White Women, Race Matters*, 12) definition of whiteness as "an economic and political [and, we

should add, social] category maintained over time by a changing set of exclusionary practices, both legislative and customary." See also Dominquez, *White by Definition,* and Pascoe, "Race, Gender and Intercultural Relations."

83. *Marion Conservative Democrat,* February 5, 1881. According to the paper, the girl (or her family) brought suit under the Civil Rights Act in the U.S. District Court in Lynchburg.

84. Quoted in Berman, *Richmond's Jewry,* 231–33.

EPILOGUE

1. J. L. Powell to Mahone, December 12, 1883, box 82, MP.

2. Cobb, *The Most Southern Place.*

3. *Staunton Spectator,* November 13, 1883; *Richmond Dispatch,* November 4, 1883. The Democrats had a majority of only about 18,000 out of 267,000 votes.

4. Williams, *Capt. R. A. Paul,* 61.

5. In *Antoni v. Greenhow,* 17 Otto (U.S.) 770–82 (1883), the U.S. Supreme Court upheld the provisions of the Readjuster debt settlement that prohibited the payment of state taxes in bond coupons. This seeming resolution to the debt question allowed the Democrats to retreat from their opposition to the Readjuster debt legislation without losing face. Although the Democrats accepted the debt settlement, the bondholders did not. Various groups of bondholders continued to bring suit. In 1885 the Supreme Court reversed itself and struck down the principal Readjuster debt legislation. *Poindexter v. Greenhow,* 29 L. ed. 193 (1885). In 1892 Virginia's Democratic state government renegotiated the debt settlement, accepted a greater proportion of the antebellum debt than the Readjusters had, and agreed to pay interest for a century instead of the fifty years provided for in Readjuster debt legislation. See General Assembly, *Acts and Joint Resolutions,* 1891–92, 522–42. See also Moore, *Two Paths,* 114, 120.

6. Democratic slogan quoted in Sheldon, *Populism,* 150. There is a certain air of hopelessness to Mahone's ridicule in 1887 of Virginia Democrats, who, he said, "denouncing Republicanism and professing Democracy, acquiesced in the State Republican platform in 1883 and have adopted the National Republican platform in 1887!" Blake, *William Mahone,* 237.

7. Resolutions of the State Democratic Committee reported in *Richmond Dispatch,* November 23, 1883, and *Staunton Spectator,* November 27, 1883; Hope quoted in *Staunton Spectator,* November 27, 1883.

8. Moger, "Origin of the Democratic Machine."

9. Buni, *Negro in Virginia Politics,* 7; Wynes, *Race Relations,* 40 (quotation).

10. Pearson, *Readjuster Movement,* 169.

11. Ibid.

12. Blake, *William Mahone,* 235–38. Barbour died in 1892 and was succeeded in the senate by General Eppa Hunton.

13. Not all black Republicans favored Langston's candidacy—see Johnston, "Participation of Negroes," 269–70. Wise, Cameron, and John F. Lewis were more critical of Mahone's leadership style than his conduct vis-à-vis Langston. See Blake, *William Mahone*, 238–39.

14. Wynes, *Race Relations*, 42. Despite the victory in Virginia, Cleveland lost nationally and was replaced by Republican Benjamin Harrison. Cleveland returned to the White House in 1892. Langston ran against both the regular Republican nominee and Democrat Edward C. Venable, who was declared the victor.

15. Langston was not seated until the last week of the Fifty-first Congress, in September 1890. Denied reelection, he sat as a lame-duck representative until March 1891. For more on the 1888 congressional race, see Langston, *From the Virginia Plantation to the National Capitol*, and Cheek and Cheek, "A Negro Runs for Congress" (quotation, p. 30). On Langston more generally, see Cheek and Cheek, *John Mercer Langston*.

16. See Schewel, "Local Politics in Lynchburg," and Tripp, *Yankee Town, Southern City*, 252.

17. On the 1886 coalition, see Fink, *Workingmen's Democracy*, 156–59, and Rachleff, *Black Labor*, 157–78.

18. Blake, *William Mahone*, 252.

19. Kerr-Ritchie, *Freedpeople*, 196, 204.

20. Wynes, *Race Relations*, 47–49 (quotation, p. 47). A dispirited and diminished Republican vote was cast for several Populist congressional candidates in 1892. In 1893 the GOP had no nominees for governor or the General Assembly, which indirectly aided the third party. In 1895 a number of Virginia Republicans ran as "honest election" men in tandem with the Populist Party. Blake, *William Mahone*, 252–53.

21. Woodward, *Origins*, 261. Elections in Richmond were particularly brutal, as the Democrats fought to eliminate black men's votes. See Rabinowitz, *Race Relations*, 319–20. On fraud after the Anderson-McCormick law, see Moger, *Bourbonism to Byrd*, 98.

22. *Roanoke Times*, October 30, 1882, quoted in Ann F. Alexander, "'Like an Evil Wind,'" 179.

23. On this tactic, see Brewer, "The Ghosts of Jackson Ward," 27.

24. Between 1869 and 1900 twenty-four Virginia elections were contested in the House of Representatives. Of the twenty decided after 1874, sixteen were based on alleged fraud. Eleven of the sixteen were decided by Republican-controlled houses, and six Republicans were seated instead of the Democratic "victors." *Digest of Contested Election Cases*, 22; McDanel, *Virginia Constitutional Convention*, 11.

25. McKinney quoted in Elsa Barkley Brown, "Uncle Ned's Children," 379. On the Walton Act, see Kousser, *Shaping of Southern Politics*, 173 and table 6.9. The Walton Act inspired Mahone's final political intervention. Shortly before his death in 1895 Mahone convened a meeting in Petersburg to organize a campaign for honest elections. The meeting was attended by a number of lead-

ing Populists who, if they did not care for the black vote, did desire a fair count of the white vote. See Blake, *William Mahone*, 253, and Wynes, *Race Relations*, 52–53.

26. For North Carolina, see Gilmore, *Gender and Jim Crow*, 119–20, 129–30. As Gilmore puts it so well, "Since expulsion from electoral politics and expulsion from party politics occurred simultaneously, African Americans not only lost the vote but also lost the best way to regain it" (pp. 119–20).

27. *Richmond Planet*, February 21, 1885, quoted in Rachleff, *Black Labor*, 112.

28. Elsa Barkley Brown, "Uncle Ned's Children," 374–75. The Virginia GOP was in step with the national party. For a number of reasons, including a generational shift that paralleled an ideological change of focus, by 1896 the national Republican Party had dropped its support for a free ballot and a fair count in the South from its platform. On the Republican sea change, see Kousser, *Shaping of Southern Politics*, 31.

29. Elsa Barkley Brown, "Uncle Ned's Children," 386.

30. Ibid., 162.

31. Of Virginia's 100 counties, 52 opposed the call for convention, but the Democrats won the popular vote. Opponents of the convention carried 18 of the 35 counties with a black majority and 25 of the 32 counties west of the Blue Ridge Mountains. The use of "trick" tickets, in which the words "For Constitutional Convention" had to be marked out by the voter opposed to the convention while unmarked ballots were considered for it, also influenced the outcome. Kousser, *Shaping of Southern Politics*, 177–78. Moger (*Bourbonism to Byrd*, 186) notes that all eighteen cities voted in favor of the convention.

32. J. Morgan Kousser (*Shaping of Southern Politics*, 177) observes that of the 60 percent of voters who rejected the convention in 1897 and failed to vote in 1900, most must have been white, since the percentage of Republicans (who by 1897 were overwhelmingly African American) opposed to the convention was exactly the same in the May 1900 special election (44 percent) as in the November 1900 presidential election.

33. The suffrage restrictions of the 1902 constitution immediately cut the electorate in half. The 1900 presidential election vote in Virginia was 264,240; in 1904 it had been 130,544—a drop of 51 percent. In 1940, well after passage of the Nineteenth Amendment had significantly broadened the electorate through the inclusion of women, fewer than 10 out of every 1,000 Virginians voted, compared with 147 of every 1,000 in 1900. Woodward, *Origins*, 344–45.

34. *Proceedings and Debates*, 3014.

35. Quoted in Ayers, *Promise of the New South*, 308.

36. McDanel, *Virginia Constitutional Convention*, 42.

37. *Proceedings and Debates*, 3076–77.

38. Ibid., 3254–55. In Alabama—the only southern state that presented its revised constitution to the voters for ratification—the white counties rejected it and the black counties carried it by fraud. Woodward, *Origins*, 342.

39. Ayers, *Promise of the New South*, 307. On the connections between south-

ern disfranchisement and national imperialist projects, see Hunt, *Ideology and U.S. Foreign Policy,* 80–91, and Painter, *Standing at Armageddon,* 228–29.

40. Buni, *Negro in Virginia Politics,* 24–25, app. A, "November 1902 Voter Registration," 265; Pendleton, *Appalachian Virginia,* 457–59, 458 (*Lynchburg News*); Kousser, *Shaping of Southern Politics,* 181.

41. Buni, *Negro in Virginia Politics,* 34–47. The leadership of the Virginia GOP publicly criticized Wise for undertaking a legal challenge to the suffrage provisions (pp. 42–43).

42. *Jones v. Montague,* 194 U.S. 24 S. Ct. 611 (1904); *Richmond News Leader,* December 16, 1904, quoted in Buni, *Negro in Virginia Politics,* 47.

43. *Richmond Planet,* April 30, May 14 (quotation), 1904; Elsa Barkley Brown, "Uncle Ned's Children," 480–83; cf. Meier and Rudwick, "Boycott Movement." Trains in Virginia were first segregated by law in 1900. In 1904 the Jim Crow law was tightened to refuse admittance of any black person to Pullman, dining, parlor, chair, or compartment cars. In 1906 streetcars were segregated by law statewide. See Wynes, "Evolution of Jim Crow Laws," 417–18.

44. Quoted in Pearson, *Readjuster Movement,* 164.

45. Cohen, *At Freedom's Edge,* 295, table 13. Many thanks to Peter Wallenstein, who pointed out the significance of the Virginia chronology to my story.

46. In a letter to Walter White, national head of the NAACP, Jackson explained that a primary goal of *Negro Officeholders* was to "stimulate the Negroes of this state to a sense of their political duties." Jackson to White, March 19, 1946, Luther Porter Jackson Papers, Johnston Memorial Library, Virginia State University, box 42. My thanks to Larissa Smith for bringing this to my attention. Biographical information on Jackson is from Logan and Winston, *Dictionary of American Negro Biography,* 342–43. According to the *Dictionary,* there is evidence that Jackson's great-grandfather was the brother of Mary Todd Lincoln.

47. In 1920 the regular Republicans failed to challenge Democrat Carter Glass for the U.S. Senate. Black Republicans nominated attorney Joseph R. Pollard, who polled 17,576 votes. This represented 20 percent of the 87,458 votes cast in Virginia for GOP presidential nominee Warren G. Harding. In 1921 black Republicans in Richmond formally broke with the state organization and nominated a "lily-black" state ticket headed by John Mitchell. Also included was the first woman nominated for state office in Virginia—prominent businesswoman Maggie Lena Walker, for superintendent of public instruction. Buni, *Negro in Virginia Politics,* 80–81, 84.

48. Ibid., 106, 117–20. The actions of Virginia blacks paralleled the strategy of the national NAACP. In 1930 NAACP head James Weldon Johnson called for a declaration of African American political independence and counseled southern blacks to vote in Democratic primaries. On the migration of southern blacks into the Democratic Party before 1936, see Gilmore, "False Friends and Avowed Enemies." On the partisan switch after 1936, see Weiss, *Farewell to the Party of Lincoln.*

49. Buni, *Negro in Virginia Politics,* 127–28.

50. Sullivan, *Days of Hope,* 204–5. William Lawrence won a seat on the Nansemond County Board of Supervisors. See Larissa M. Smith, "Challenging the Byrd Machine," 2.

51. Lawson, *Black Ballots,* 134, table 1. In 1950, 65,286 black Virginians were registered to vote.

52. See, e.g., John Douglas Smith, "Managing White Supremacy," and Larissa M. Smith "Where the South Begins."

53. Glasgow, *Voice of the People,* 441.

54. Ibid., 316.

BIBLIOGRAPHY

PRIMARY SOURCES

Archival and Manuscript Collections

Charlottesville, Virginia
Alderman Library, University of Virginia
  Barringer Family Papers
  Thomas S. Bocock Papers
  Broadside Collection, 1877
  Burwell Family Papers
  John Warwick Daniel Papers
  R. T. W. Duke Papers
  Hamlet Family Papers
  Harrison Family Papers
  Hunter-Garnett Papers
  Leonard Family Papers
  William Hodges Mann Papers
  McCabe Family Papers
  John E. Massey Papers
  Frank Gildart Ruffin Papers
  Robert Addison Schoolfield Papers
  James Harrison Williams Papers

Danville, Virginia
Danville Circuit Court
  Common Law Order Book E
Danville Public Library
  Danville City Directory

Durham, North Carolina
Perkins Library, Duke University
  William Mahone Papers

Hampton, Virginia
Hampton University Newspaper Clipping Files (microfilm)

Moultie, North Carolina
William Henry Ruffner Papers

Petersburg, Virginia
Johnston Memorial Library, Virginia State University
    Luther Porter Jackson Papers

Richmond, Virginia
Richmond Public Library
    Records of the Richmond Common Council (July 1878–December 1883)
State Library of Virginia
    William Evelyn Cameron Executive Papers, 1882, 1884–86
    Frederick W. Holliday Executive Papers, 1879
    Proceedings of the Danville Common Council, 1881–84
    Virginia Bureau of Vital Statistics (microfilm), reel 32
Virginia Baptist Historical Society, University of Richmond
    Minutes, Baptist General Association of Virginia, 1871–85
    Minutes, Shiloh Baptist Association of Virginia, 1868–75, 1883
        (a.k.a. Colored Shiloh Baptist Association)
    Minutes, Virginia Baptist State Convention, 1869–83, 1891
Virginia Historical Society
    Allen Family Papers
    Anderson Family Papers
    Bagby Family Papers
    Baskerville Family Papers
    Bouldin Family Papers
    Broadside Collection
    Danville Riot, November 3, 1883: Report of the Committee of Forty with Sworn
        Testimony of Thirty-seven Witnesses (Richmond, 1883)
    Armistead Churchill Gordon Papers
    Harvie Family Papers
    Hunter Family Papers
    Lewis Family Papers
    Wickham Family Papers
    Wise Family Papers

Williamsburg, Virginia
Swem Library, College of William and Mary
    Harrison Holt Riddleberger Papers

Newspapers and Periodicals

Alexandria Picayune
Boston Globe
Culpeper Times
Florida Weekly Telegraph
Lynchburg Advance

Lynchburg Virginian
Marion Conservative Democrat
Nation
New National Era
New York Age
New York Evening Post
New York Globe
New York Herald
New York Times
Norfolk Day Book
Norfolk Landmark
Norfolk Review
Petersburg Index-Appeal
Petersburg Lancet
Philadelphia Evening Bulletin
Richmond Dispatch
Richmond Planet
Richmond Star
Richmond State
Richmond Whig
Scribner's Monthly
Shenandoah Herald
Southern Workman
Staunton Spectator
Washington, D.C., National Republican

Government Documents

Alvord, John W. *Inspector's Report of Schools and Finances.* U.S. Bureau of
    Refugees, Freedmen, and Abandoned Lands. Washington, D.C.: GPO,
    1866.
———. U.S. Bureau of Refugees, Freedmen, and Abandoned Lands. *Semi-
    Annual Report on Schools for Freedmen.* Vol. 1. Washington, D.C.: GPO,
    1866.
Annual Message from the Governor to the General Assembly of Virginia. December
    4, 1878. Richmond: R. G. Fraser, 1878.
*Communication from the Governor of Virginia in Response to the Resolution of the
    Senate.* March 7, 1878. Virginia Historical Society, Richmond.
Congressional Directories. 1877–97.
Congressional Globe. 41st Congress. 1870.
Congressional Journal. 39th Congress. 1866.
Congressional Record. 43d Congress. 1874.
———. 47th Congress. 1881.
Debates and Proceedings in the Congress of the United States, 1789–1791.
    Washington, D.C.: Gales and Seaton, 1834–56.

Debates and Proceedings of the Constitutional Convention of the State of Virginia. 1868.

Digest of All the Contested Election Cases in the House of Representatives of the United States from the First to the Fifty-sixth Congress, 1789–1901. Washington, D.C.: GPO, 1901.

General Assembly of Virginia. *Acts and Joint Resolutions.* 1869–70, 1870–71, 1881–82, 1891–92.

Historical Statistics of the United States, 1789–1945: A Supplement to the Statistical Abstract of the United States. Washington, D.C.: U.S. Bureau of the Census, 1949.

Journal of the Virginia Constitutional Convention, 1868.

Manuscript Census Returns, Tenth Census of the United States, 1880, Pittsylvania County, Virginia.

Proceedings and Debates of the Constitutional Convention . . . of Virginia. Vol. 2. 1901–2.

U.S. Bureau of the Census. *Statistical Abstract of the United States.* No. 24. Washington, D.C.: GPO, 1901.

U.S. Census Office. *Compendium of the Eleventh Census, 1890.* 3 vols. Washington, D.C.: GPO, 1892–97.

———. *The Statistics of the Population of the United States: Tenth Census.* 3 vols. Washington, D.C.: GPO, 1883.

U.S. Senate Committee on Privileges and Elections. *Report on the Danville Riot.* 48th Cong., 1st sess., 1884. No. 579. Serial 2178.

Virginia Acts of Assembly. 1865–66, 1866–67, 1869–70, 1877–78, 1910, 1924. Alderman Library, University of Virginia, Charlottesville.

Virginia Department of Public Instruction. *Virginia School Report: Annual Report of the Superintendent of Public Instruction.* Richmond: Superintendent of Public Printing, 1871–84

Virginia Legislature. *House Journal.* 1874, 1877–78, 1881–82.

———. *Senate Journal.* 1869–70, 1873–74, 1876–77.

Printed Primary Sources

Avary, Myrta Lockett. *Dixie after the War: An Exposition of Social Conditions Existing in the South during the Twelve Years Succeeding the Fall of Richmond.* New York: Doubleday, Page and Co., 1906.

Baker, Ray Stannard. *Following the Color Line: An Account of Negro Citizenship in the American Democracy.* New York: Doubleday, Page and Co., 1908.

Bruce, Philip Alexander. *The Plantation Negro as a Freeman.* New York: G. P. Putnam's Sons, 1889.

Campbell, George. *White and Black: The Outcome of a Visit to the United States.* New York: R. Worthington, 1879.

Chesnutt, Charles Waddell. *The Marrow of Tradition.* 1901. Reprint, Ann Arbor: University of Michigan Press, 1969.

Coalition Rule in Danville: To the Citizens of the Southwest and Valley of Virginia

(Danville Circular). N.p., n.d. [1883]. Reprinted in U.S. Senate *Report,* vii–ix, from which quotations are cited in the text. Numerous original copies exist.

Conrad, Georgia Bryan. "Reminiscences of a Southern Woman." *Southern Workman* 30 (July 1901).

Dixon, Thomas. *The Leopard's Spots: A Romance of the White Man's Burden, 1865–1900.* New York: Doubleday, Page and Co., 1902.

Douglass, Frederick. *Narrative of the Life of Frederick Douglass.* 1845. Reprint, Cambridge: Harvard University Press, 1960.

Du Bois, W. E. B. "The Superior Race." *Smart Set* 79 (April 1923): 55–60.

Farr, Richard R. *Fifteenth Annual Report of the Superintendent of Public Instruction.* Richmond: Superintendent of Public Printing, 1885.

Fortune, T. Thomas. *Black and White: Land, Labor and Politics in the South.* 1884. Reprint, New York: Arno Press, 1968.

Hancock, Elizabeth H., ed. *Autobiography of John E. Massey.* New York: Neale Publishing Co., 1909.

Hill, Benjamin H. "Fidelity to Trusts the Highest Duty." Washington, D.C., 1881.

Huxley, T. H. *Collected Essays.* Vol. 2. London: Macmillan, 1893–95.

Kennaway, John H. *On Sherman's Track: The South after the War.* London: Seeley, Jackson, and Halliday, 1867.

King, Edward. *The Great South.* 1873. Reprint, Baton Rouge: Louisiana State University Press, 1972.

Langston, John Mercer. *Freedom and Citizenship: Selected Lectures and Addresses.* 1883. Reprint, Miami: Mnemosyne Publishing Inc., 1969.

———. *From the Virginia Plantation to the National Capitol: An Autobiography.* 1894. Reprint, New York: Bergman Publishers, 1969.

McConnell, John Preston. *Negroes and Their Treatment in Virginia from 1865 to 1867.* Pulaski, Va.: B. D. Smith and Brothers, 1910.

Meriwether, Elizabeth Avery. *Recollections of 92 Years, 1824–1916.* Nashville: Tennessee Historical Commission, 1958.

Munford, Beverley. *Random Recollections.* N.p., 1905.

O'Ferrall, Charles T. *Forty Years of Active Service.* New York: Neale Publishing Co., 1904.

Page, Thomas Nelson. *The Negro: The Southerner's Problem.* New York: Scribner's, 1904.

Pollock, Edward. *Illustrated Sketch Book of Danville, Virginia: Its Manufactures and Commerce.* Petersburg: N.p., 1885.

Pryor, Mrs. Roger A. *Reminiscences of Peace and War.* New York: Macmillan, 1905.

Redfield, H. V. *Homicide, North and South.* Philadelphia: Lippincott, 1880.

Reid, Whitelaw. *After the War: A Southern Tour.* Cincinnati: Moore, Wilstach and Baldwin, 1866.

Royall, William L. *History of the Virginia Debt Controversy: The Negro's Vicious Influence in Politics.* Richmond: 1897.

———. *Some Reminiscences.* New York: Neale Publishing Co., 1909.

Ruffner, William Henry. "The Co-Education of the White and Colored Races." *Scribner's Monthly,* May 1874, 86–90.

———. *Second Annual Report of the Superintendent of Public Instruction.* Richmond: Superintendent of Public Printing, 1872.

———. *Seventh Annual Report of the Superintendent of Public Instruction.* Richmond: Superintendent of Public Printing, 1877.

———. *Ninth Annual Report of the Superintendent of Public Instruction.* Richmond: Superintendent of Public Printing, 1879.

Stuart, Alexander A. A. *A Narrative of the Leading Incidents of the Organization of the First Popular Movement in Virginia . . . and of the Subsequent Efforts of the "Committee of Nine."* Richmond: W. E. Jones, 1888.

Tourgée, Albion W. *A Fool's Errand, by One of the Fools.* 1879. Reprint, Cambridge: Harvard University Press, 1961.

Williams, D. B. *A Sketch of the Life and Times of Captain R. A. Paul.* Richmond: Johns and Goolsby, Printers, 1885.

Wise, Barton H. *The Life and Times of Henry A. Wise of Virginia, 1806–1876.* London: Macmillan, 1899.

Wise, John S. *The Lion's Skin: A Historical Novel and a Novel History.* New York: Doubleday, Page and Co., 1905.

SECONDARY SOURCES

Abramowitz, Jack. "The South: Arena for Greenback Reformers." *Social Education* 17 (March 1953): 108–10.

Alexander, Ann Field. " 'Like an Evil Wind': The Roanoke Riot of 1893 and the Lynching of Thomas Smith." *Virginia Magazine of History and Biography* 100 (April 1992): 173–206.

Alexander, Thomas. "Persistent Whiggery in the Confederate South, 1860–1877." *Journal of Southern History* 27 (August 1961): 305–29.

———. "Political Reconstruction in Tennessee, 1865–1870." In *Radicalism, Racism, and Party Realignment: The Border States during Reconstruction,* edited by Richard O. Curry, 37–79. Baltimore: Johns Hopkins University Press, 1969.

Allen, James S. *Reconstruction: The Battle for Democracy, 1865–1876.* New York: International Publishers, 1937.

Almaguer, Tomas. *Racial Fault Lines: The Historical Origins of White Supremacy in California.* Berkeley: University of California Press, 1994.

Ambler, Charles Henry. *Francis H. Pierpont: Union War Governor of Virginia and Father of West Virginia.* Chapel Hill: University of North Carolina Press, 1937.

———. *Sectionalism in Virginia from 1776 to 1861.* Chicago: University of Chicago Press, 1910.

Anderson, Eric. *Race and Politics in North Carolina, 1872–1901: The Black Second*. Baton Rouge: Louisiana State University Press, 1981.

Anderson, James D. *The Education of Blacks in the South, 1860–1935*. Chapel Hill: University of North Carolina Press, 1988.

―――. "Ex-Slaves and the Rise of Universal Education in the New South, 1860–1880." In *Education and the Rise of the New South*, edited by Ronald K. Goodenow and Arthur O. White, 1–25. Boston: G. K. Hall, 1981.

Applebaum, Harvey M. "Miscegenation Statutes: A Constitutional and Social Problem." *Georgetown Law Journal* 53 (1964): 49–91.

Aptheker, Herbert. *American Negro Slave Revolts*. New York: Columbia University Press, 1945.

Arendt, Hannah. "Reflections on Little Rock." *Dissent* 6 (Winter 1959): 45–56.

―――. "A Reply to Critics." *Dissent* 6 (Winter 1959): 179–81.

Argersinger, Peter H. "'A Place on the Ballot': Fusion Politics and Antifusion Laws." *American Historical Review* 85 (April 1980): 287–306.

Arnesen, Eric J. *Waterfront Workers of New Orleans: Race, Class, and Politics, 1863–1923*. New York: Oxford University Press, 1991.

Aron, Cindy Sondik. *Ladies and Gentlemen of the Civil Service: Middle-Class Workers in Victorian America*. New York: Oxford University Press, 1987.

Atiyah, Patrick S. *The Rise and Fall of Freedom of Contract*. New York: Oxford University Press, 1979.

Avins, Alfred. "Anti-Miscegenation Laws and the Fourteenth Amendment: The Original Intent." *Virginia Law Review* 52 (1966): 1224–55.

Ayers, Edward L. *Promise of the New South: Life After Reconstruction*. New York: Oxford University Press, 1992.

―――. *Vengeance and Justice: Crime and Punishment in the 19th Century American South*. New York: Oxford University Press, 1984.

―――. "The World the Liberal Capitalists Made." *Reviews in American History* 19 (June 1991): 194–99.

Baker, Paula. "The Domestication of Politics: Women and American Political Society, 1780–1920." *American Historical Review* 89 (June 1984): 620–47.

Baldwin, James. *Notes of a Native Son*. Boston: Little, Brown, 1955.

Balk, Jacqueline, and Ari Hoogenboom. "The Origins of Border State Liberal Radicalism. In *Radicalism, Racism, and Party Realignment: The Border States during Reconstruction*, edited by Richard O. Curry, 220–44. Baltimore: Johns Hopkins University Press, 1969.

Bardaglio, Peter. *Reconstructing the Household: Families, Sex, and the Law in the Nineteenth-Century South*. Chapel Hill: University of North Carolina Press, 1995.

Barjenbruck, Judith. "The Greenback Political Movement: An Arkansas View." *Arkansas Historical Quarterly* 36 (Summer 1977): 107–22.

Barkan, Elazar. *Retreat of Scientific Racism: Changing Concepts of Race in Britain*

and the United States between the World Wars. New York: Cambridge
University Press, 1992.

Barnard, Hollinger F., ed. *Outside the Magic Circle: The Autobiography of
Virginia Foster Durr.* University, Ala.: University of Alabama Press, 1985.

Barnes, Brooks Miles. "Triumph of the New South: Independent
Movements in Post-Reconstruction Politics." Ph.D. diss., University of
Virginia, 1991.

Barnes, Kenneth C. *Who Killed John Clayton? Political Violence and the Emergence
of the New South, 1861–1893.* Durham: Duke University Press, 1998.

Bauer, Raymond A., and Alice H. Bauer, "Day to Day Resistance to Slavery."
Journal of Negro History 27 (October 1942): 388–419.

Benda, Václav. *Open Letters: Selected Prose, 1965–1990.* Edited and translated
by Paul Wilson. Boston: Vintage, 1992.

Benjamin, Walter. "On Some Motifs in Baudelaire." In *Illuminations,* edited
by Hannah Arendt, 155–200. New York: Schocken Books, 1969.

Benn, S. I., and G. F. Gaus. *Public and Private in Social Life.* New York: St.
Martin's Press, 1983.

Bercaw, Nancy. "The Politics of Household: Domestic Battlegrounds in the
Transition from Slavery to Freedom in the Yazoo-Mississippi Delta, 1850–
1860." Ph.D. diss., University of Pennsylvania, 1996.

Berkowitz, Peter. *Virtue and the Making of Modern Liberalism.* Princeton:
Princeton University Press, 1999.

Berlin, Ira. *Slaves without Masters: The Free Negro in the Antebellum South.* New
York: Pantheon, 1974.

Berman, Myron. *Richmond's Jewry, 1769–1976: Shabbat in Shockoe.*
Charlottesville: University Press of Virginia, 1979.

Berry, Mary Frances. "Judging Morality: Sexual Behavior and Legal
Consequences in the Late-Nineteenth-Century South." *Journal of
American History* 78 (December 1991): 835–56.

Blake, Nelson Morehouse. *William Mahone of Virginia: Soldier and Political
Insurgent.* Richmond: Garrett and Massie, 1935.

Blassingame, John W. "Before the Ghetto: The Making of the Black
Community in Savannah, Georgia, 1865–1880." *Journal of Social History*
6 (Summer 1973): 463–88.

———. *Black New Orleans, 1860–1880.* Chicago: University of Chicago Press,
1973.

Bohman, James. "The Moral Costs of Political Pluralism: The Dilemmas of
Difference and Equality in Arendt's 'Reflections on Little Rock'." In
Hannah Arendt: Twenty Years Later, edited by Larry May and Jerome Kohn,
53–80. Cambridge: Harvard University Press, 1996.

Bond, Horace Mann. "The Extent and Character of Separate Schools in the
United States." *Journal of Negro Education* 4 (July 1935): 321–27.

Bourdieu, Pierre. "The Sentiment of Honor in Kabyle Society." In *Honour
and Shame: The Values of Mediterranean Society,* edited by J. G. Peristiany,
191–241. Chicago: University of Chicago Press, 1966.

Bragg, George F., Jr., "Letter to the Editor." *Journal of Negro History* 11 (October 1926): 669–82.

Breen, T. H. *Tobacco Culture: The Mentality of the Great Tidewater Planters on the Eve of Revolution.* Princeton: Princeton University Press, 1985.

Brewer, James H. "The Ghosts of Jackson Ward." *Negro History Bulletin* 22 (November 1958): 27–30.

Brown, Elsa Barkley. "Negotiating and Transforming the Public Sphere: African American Political Life in the Transition from Slavery to Freedom." *Public Culture* 7 (Fall 1994): 107–46.

———. "Uncle Ned's Children: Negotiating Community and Freedom in Postemancipation Richmond, Virginia." Ph.D. diss., Kent State University, 1994.

Brown, Kathleen. *Good Wives, Nasty Wenches, and Anxious Patriarchs: Gender, Race, and Power in Colonial Virginia.* Chapel Hill: University of North Carolina Press, 1996.

Brown, Robert Euell. "The Rise and Fall of the Lynchburg Readjusters." Special Scholar Thesis in History, University of Virginia, 1966.

Brownell, Blaine A., and David R. Goldfield. *The City in Southern History: The Growth of Urban Civilization in the South.* Port Washington, N.Y.: Kennikat Press, 1977.

Brundage, W. Fitzhugh. *Lynching in the New South: Georgia and Virginia, 1880–1930.* Urbana: University of Illinois Press, 1993.

———, ed. *Under Sentence of Death: Lynching in the South.* Chapel Hill: University of North Carolina Press, 1997.

Buck, Solon. *The Granger Movement: A Study of Agricultural Organization and Its Political, Economic, and Social Manifestations, 1870–1880.* Cambridge: Harvard University Press, 1933.

Buckley, Thomas E., S.J. "Unfixing Race: Class, Power, and Identity in an Interracial Family." *Virginia Magazine of History and Biography* 102 (July 1994): 349–80.

Buck-Morss, Susan. "The Flaneur, the Sandwichman and the Whore: The Politics of Loitering." *New German Critique* 39 (Fall 1986): 99–139.

Buni, Andrew. *The Negro in Virginia Politics, 1902–1965.* Charlottesville: University Press of Virginia, 1967.

Burton, Vernon. "Race and Reconstruction: Edgefield County, South Carolina." *Journal of Social History* 12 (Fall 1978): 31–56.

Butler, Judith. *Bodies That Matter: On the Discursive Limits of "Sex."* New York: Routledge, 1993.

Bynum, Victoria E. " 'White Negroes' in Segregated Mississippi: Miscegenation, Racial Identity, and the Law." *Journal of Southern History* 64 (May 1998): 247–76.

Calhoun, Craig, ed. *Habermas and the Public Sphere.* Cambridge: MIT Press, 1992.

Calhoun, Walter T. "The Danville Riot and Its Repercussions on the Virginia Election of 1883." In *Studies in the History of the South, 1875–1922,* edited by Walter T. Calhoun, 25–51. Greenville, N.C.: East Carolina Publications in History, 1966.

Calhoun, Walter T., and James Tice Moore. "William Evelyn Cameron: Restless Readjuster." In *The Governors of Virginia, 1860–1978,* edited by Edward Younger and James Tice Moore, 95–109. Charlottesville: University Press of Virginia, 1982.

Cartwright, Joseph H. *The Triumph of Jim Crow: Tennessee Race Relations in the 1880s.* Knoxville: University of Tennessee Press, 1976.

Cash, W. J. *The Mind of the South.* New York: Knopf, 1941.

Cell, John W. *The Highest Stage of White Supremacy: The Origins of Segregation in South Africa and the American South.* Cambridge: Cambridge University Press, 1982.

Certeau, Michel de. *The Practice of Everyday Life.* Translated by Steven F. Rendall. Berkeley: University of California Press, 1984.

Chafe, William H. *Civilities and Civil Rights: Greensboro, North Carolina, and the Black Struggle for Freedom.* New York: Oxford University Press, 1980.

Channing, Steven A. *Crisis of Fear: Secession in South Carolina.* New York: Simon and Schuster, 1974.

Cheek, William, and Aimee Lee Cheek. *John Mercer Langston and the Fight for Black Freedom, 1829–65.* Urbana: University of Illinois Press: 1989.

———. "A Negro Runs for Congress: John Mercer Langston and the Virginia Campaign of 1888." *Journal of Negro History* 52 (January 1967): 14–34.

Chesson, Michael B. *Richmond after the War, 1865–1890.* Richmond: Virginia State Library, 1981.

Clinton, Catherine. "Freedwomen, Sexuality, and Violence during Reconstruction." In *Half-Sisters of History: Southern Women and the American Past,* edited by Catherine Clinton, 136–53. Durham, N.C.: Duke University Press, 1994.

———. "Reconstructing Freedwomen." In *Divided Houses: Gender and the Civil War,* edited by Catherine Clinton and Nina Silber, 306–19. New York: Oxford University Press, 1992.

Cobb, James. *The Most Southern Place on Earth: The Mississippi Delta and the Roots of Regional Identity.* New York: Oxford University Press, 1992.

Cohen, William. *At Freedom's Edge: Black Mobility and the Southern White Quest for Racial Control, 1861–1915.* Baton Rouge: Louisiana State University Press, 1991.

Cott, Nancy F. *The Bonds of Womanhood: "Woman's Sphere" in New England, 1780–1835.* New Haven: Yale University Press, 1977.

———. "Giving Character to Our Whole Civil Polity: Marriage and the Public Order in the Late Nineteenth Century." In *U.S. History as Women's History: New Feminist Essays,* edited by Linda K. Kerber, Alice Kessler-Harris, and Kathryn Kish Sklar, 107–21. Chapel Hill: University of North Carolina Press, 1995.

Cox, LaWanda. "From Emancipation to Segregation." In *Interpreting Southern*

History: Essays in Honor of Sanford W. Higginbotham, edited by John B. Boles and Evelyn Thomas Nolen, 199–253. Baton Rouge: Louisiana State University Press, 1987.

Cullen, Jim. " 'I's a Man Now': Gender and African American Men." In *Divided Houses: Gender and the Civil War,* edited by Catherine Clinton and Nina Silber, 76–96. New York: Oxford University Press, 1992.

Dabney, Virginius. *Virginia: The New Dominion.* 1929. Reprint, Garden City, N.Y.: Doubleday, 1971.

Davenport, F. Garvin, Jr. "Thomas Dixon's Mythology of Southern History." *Journal of Southern History* 36 (August 1970): 350–67.

Davis, Curtis Carroll. "Very Well-Rounded Republican: The Several Lives of John S. Wise." *Virginia Magazine of History and Biography* 71 (October 1963): 461–87.

Davis, David Brion. *The Problem of Slavery in the Age of Revolution, 1700–1823.* Ithaca: Cornell University Press, 1975.

Degler, Carl N. *The Other South: Southern Dissenters in the Nineteenth Century.* New York: Harper and Row, 1974.

———. *Place over Time: The Continuity of Southern Distinctiveness.* Baton Rouge: Louisiana State University Press, 1977.

Delany, Sarah, and A. Elizabeth Delany, with Amy Hill Hearth. *Having Our Say: The Delany Sisters' First 100 Years.* New York: Kodansha International, 1993.

DeSantis, Vincent. "Negro Dissatisfaction with Republican Policy in the South, 1882–1884." *Journal of Negro History* 36 (April 1951): 148–59.

———. "President Arthur and the Independent Movements in the South in 1882." *Journal of Southern History* 19 (August 1953): 346–63.

———. "President Hayes's Southern Policy." *Journal of Southern History* 21 (November 1955): 476–94.

———. *Republicans Face the Southern Question: The New Departure Years, 1877–1897.* Baltimore: Johns Hopkins University Press, 1959.

Dittmer, John. *Black Georgia in the Progressive Era, 1900–1920.* Urbana: University of Illinois Press, 1977.

Dollard, John. *Caste and Class in a Southern Town.* New York: Oxford University Press, 1937.

Dominquez, Virginia R. *White by Definition: Social Classification in Creole Louisiana.* New Brunswick, N.J.: Rutgers University Press, 1986.

Douglas, Mary. *Purity and Danger: An Analysis of Concepts of Pollution and Taboo.* Boston: Routledge and Kegan Paul, 1980.

———. "Rightness of Categories." In *How Classification Works: Nelson Goodman among the Social Sciences,* edited by Mary Douglas and David Hull, 239–71. Edinburgh: Edinburgh University Press, 1992.

Doyle, Bertram Wilbur. *The Etiquette of Race Relations in the South: A Study in Social Control.* Chicago: University of Chicago Press, 1937.

Doyle, Don H. *New Men, New Cities, New South: Atlanta, Nashville, Charleston, Mobile, 1860–1910.* Chapel Hill: University of North Carolina Press, 1990.

Du Bois, Ellen Carol. *Feminism and Suffrage: The Emergence of an Independent Women's Movement in America, 1848–1869.* Ithaca: Cornell University Press, 1978.

Du Bois, W. E. B. *Black Reconstruction in the United States, 1860–1880.* New York: Harcourt, Brace, 1935.

Dworkin, Ronald. "Liberalism." In *Public and Private Morality,* edited by Stuart Hampshire, 113–43. New York: Cambridge University Press, 1978.

Eaton, Clement. "Henry A. Wise: A Liberal of the Old South." *Journal of Southern History* 7 (November 1941): 482–94.

Edmonds, Helen G. *The Negro and Fusion Politics in North Carolina, 1894–1901.* Chapel Hill: University of North Carolina Press, 1951.

Edwards, Laura F. *Gendered Strife and Confusion: The Political Culture of Reconstruction.* Urbana: University of Illinois Press, 1997.

———. " 'The Marriage Covenant Is at the Foundation of All Our Rights': The Politics of Slave Marriages in North Carolina after Emancipation." *Law and History Review* 14 (Spring 1996): 81–124.

———. "Sexual Violence, Gender, Reconstruction, and the Extension of Patriarchy in Granville County, North Carolina." *North Carolina Historical Review* 68 (July 1991): 237–60.

Edwards, Rebecca. *Angels in the Machinery: Gender in American Party Politics from the Civil War to the Progressive Era.* New York: Oxford University Press, 1997.

Elias, Norbert. *Power and Civility.* Vol. 2 of *The Civilizing Process.* Translated by Edmund Jephcott. New York: Urizen Books, 1978–82.

Escott, Paul D. *Many Excellent People: Power and Privilege in North Carolina, 1850–1900.* Chapel Hill: University of North Carolina Press, 1985.

Fairclough, Adam. *Race and Democracy: The Civil Rights Struggle in Louisiana, 1915–1972.* Athens: University of Georgia Press, 1995.

Faulkner, William. *Light in August.* New York: H. Smith and R. Haas, 1932; Vintage, 1990.

Field, Daniel. *Rebels in the Name of the Tsar.* Boston: Houghton Mifflin, 1976.

Fields, Barbara Jeanne. "The Advent of Capitalist Agriculture: The New South in a Bourgeois World." In *Essays on the Postbellum Southern Economy,* edited by Thavolia Glymph and John J. Kushna, 73–94. College Station: Texas A&M Press, 1985.

———. "Ideology and Race in American History." In *Region, Race, and Reconstruction: Essays in Honor of C. Vann Woodward,* edited by J. Morgan Kousser and James M. McPherson, 143–77. New York: Oxford University Press, 1982.

———. "Slavery, Race, and Ideology in the United States of America." *New Left Review* 181 (May–June 1990): 95–118.

Fink, Leon. *Workingmen's Democracy: The Knights of Labor and American Politics.* Urbana: University of Illinois Press, 1983.

Finkelman, Paul. "The Color of Law." *Northwestern University Law Review* 87 (1993): 937.

Fischer, Roger A. "A Pioneer Protest: The New Orleans Street-Car Controversy of 1867." *Journal of Negro History* 53 (July 1968): 219–33.

Fitzgerald, Michael W. *The Union League Movement in the Deep South: Politics and Agricultural Change during Reconstruction.* Baton Rouge: Louisiana State University Press, 1989.

Foner, Eric. *Freedom's Lawmakers: A Directory of Black Officeholders during Reconstruction.* New York: Oxford University Press, 1993.

———. *Nothing but Freedom: Emancipation and Its Legacy.* Baton Rouge: Louisiana University Press, 1983.

———. *Politics and Ideology in the Age of the Civil War.* New York: Oxford University Press, 1980.

———. *Reconstruction: America's Unfinished Revolution, 1863–1877.* New York: Harper and Row, 1988.

Foner, Philip S., and Josephine F. Pacheco. *Three Who Dared: Prudence Crandall, Margaret Douglass, Myrtilla Miner: Champions of Antebellum Black Education.* Westport, Conn.: Greenwood, 1984.

Foner, Philip S., and George E. Walker, eds. *Proceedings of the Black National and State Conventions, 1865–1900.* Vol. 1. Philadelphia: Temple University Press, 1986.

Foster, Gaines M. *Ghosts of the Confederacy: Defeat, the Lost Cause, and the Emergence of the New South, 1865–1913.* New York: Oxford University Press, 1987.

Fowler, David H. *Northern Attitudes toward Interracial Marriage: Legislation and Public Opinion in the Middle Atlantic and the States of the Old Northwest, 1780–1930.* New York: Garland Press, 1987.

Fox-Genovese, Elizabeth. "Antebellum Southern Households: A New Perspective on a Familiar Question." *Review* 7 (Fall 1983): 215–53.

———. "Property and Patriarchy in Classical Bourgeois Political Theory." *Radical History Review* 4 (Spring–Summer 1977): 36–59.

———. *Within the Plantation Household: Black and White Women of the Old South.* Chapel Hill: University of North Carolina Press, 1988.

Frankel, Noralee. *Freedom's Women: Black Women and Families in Civil War Era Mississippi.* Bloomington: Indiana University Press, 1999.

Frankenberg, Ruth. *White Women, Race Matters: The Social Construction of Race.* Minneapolis: University of Minnesota Press, 1993.

Franklin, John Hope. *The Militant South, 1800–1861.* Cambridge: Harvard University Press, 1956.

———. *Reconstruction: After the Civil War.* Chicago: University of Chicago Press, 1961.

Franklin, John Hope, and Clement Eaton. "The Role of Honor in Southern Society." *Southern Humanities Review* 10 (Special Bicentennial Issue, 1976): 47–58.

Fraser, Nancy. *Unruly Practices: Power, Discourse, and Gender in Contemporary Social Theory.* Minneapolis: University of Minnesota Press, 1993.

Fraser, Walter J., Jr. "William Henry Ruffner and the Establishment of

Virginia's Public School System, 1870–1874." *Virginia Magazine of History and Biography* 79 (July 1971): 259–79.

Fredrickson, George M. *The Arrogance of Race: Historical Perspectives on Slavery, Racism, and Social Inequality.* Middletown, Conn.: Wesleyan University Press, 1988.

———. *The Black Image in the White Mind: The Debate on Afro-American Character and Destiny, 1817–1914.* Middletown, Conn.: Wesleyan University Press, 1971.

Freehling, Alison Goodyear. *Drift toward Dissolution: The Virginia Slavery Debate of 1831–1832.* Baton Rouge: Louisiana State University Press, 1982.

Freeman, Douglas Southall. *Lee's Lieutenants: Gettysburg to Appomattox.* Vol. 3 of *Lee's Lieutenants.* New York: Scribner's, 1944.

Freud, Sigmund. *Standard Edition of the Complete Psychological Works of Sigmund Freud.* 24 vols. Edited and translated by J. Strachey, A. Freud, A. Strachey, and A. Tyson. London: Hogarth Press, 1953–74.

Gaines, Kevin K. *Uplifting the Race: Black Leadership, Politics, and Culture in the Twentieth Century.* Chapel Hill: University of North Carolina Press, 1996.

Gatewood, Willard B. *Aristocrats of Color: The Black Elite, 1880–1920.* Bloomington: Indiana University Press, 1990.

Genovese, Eugene D. *Roll, Jordan, Roll: The World the Slaves Made.* New York: Vintage Books, 1972.

———. *The World the Slaveholders Made.* New York: Pantheon Books, 1969.

Genovese, Eugene, and Elizabeth Fox-Genovese. *Fruits of Merchant Capital: Slavery and Bourgeois Property in the Rise and Expansion of Capitalism.* New York: Oxford University Press, 1983.

Giddings, Paula. *When and Where I Enter: The Impact of Black Women on Race and Sex in America.* New York: Bantam, 1984.

Gillette, William. *Retreat from Reconstruction, 1869–1879.* Baton Rouge: Louisiana State University Press, 1979.

———. *The Right to Vote: Politics and the Passage of the Fifteenth Amendment.* Baltimore: Johns Hopkins University Press, 1965.

Gilmore, Glenda Elizabeth. "False Friends and Avowed Enemies: Southern African Americans and Party Allegiances in the 1920s." In *Jumpin' Jim Crow: Southern Politics from Civil War to Civil Rights,* edited by Jane Dailey, Glenda Gilmore, and Bryant Simon. Princeton: Princeton University Press, 2000.

———. *Gender and Jim Crow: Women and the Politics of White Supremacy in North Carolina, 1896–1920.* Chapel Hill: University of North Carolina Press, 1996.

———. "'One of the Meanest Books': Thomas Dixon, Jr., and *The Leopard's Spots.*" *North Carolina Literary Review* 2 (Spring 1994): 87–101.

Ginzburg, Carlo. "Fiction as Historical Evidence: A Dialogue in Paris, 1646." In *Rediscovering History: Culture, Politics, and the Psyche,* edited by Michael S. Roth, 378–88. Stanford: Stanford University Press, 1994.

Glasgow, Ellen. *The Voice of the People*. New York: Doubleday, 1900.

Goffman, Erving. *Interaction Ritual: Essays on Face-to-Face Behavior*. Garden City, N.J.: Anchor Books, 1967.

———. "The Nature of Deference and Demeanor." *American Anthropologist* 58 (June 1956): 473–502.

Goldfield, David R. *Black, White, and Southern: Race Relations and Southern Culture, 1940 to the Present*. Baton Rouge: Louisiana State University Press, 1990.

———. *Cotton Fields and Skyscrapers: Southern City and Region, 1607–1980*. Baton Rouge: Louisiana State University Press, 1982.

———. *Region, Race, and Cities: Interpreting the Urban South*. Baton Rouge: Louisiana State University Press, 1997.

Goodrich, Carter. "Public Aid to Railroads in the Reconstruction South." *Political Science Quarterly* 71 (September 1956): 407–42.

Goodwyn, Lawrence. "Populist Dreams and Negro Rights: East Texas as a Case Study." *American Historical Review* 76 (December 1971): 1435–56.

Gorn, Elliott J. " 'Gouge and Bite, Pull Hair and Scratch': The Social Significance of Fighting in the Southern Backcountry." *American Historical Review* 90 (February 1985): 18–43.

Gossett, Thomas F. *Race: The History of an Idea in America*. Dallas: Southern Methodist University Press, 1963.

Gotanda, Neil. "A Critique of 'Our Constitution Is Color-Blind'." *Stanford Law Review* 44 (November 1991): 1–68.

Gottdiener, M. *The Social Production of Urban Space*. Austin: University of Texas Press, 1985.

Gould, Stephen J. *The Mismeasure of Man*. New York: Norton, 1981.

Green, Fletcher M. "Ben E. Green and Greenbackerism in Georgia." *Georgia Historical Quarterly* 30 (March 1946): 1–13.

Greenberg, Jack. *Race Relations and American Law*. New York: Columbia University Press, 1959.

Greenberg, Kenneth S. *Honor and Slavery: Lies, Duels, Noses, Masks, Dressing as a Woman, Gifts, Strangers, Humanitarianism, Death, Slave Rebellions, the Proslavery Argument, Baseball, Hunting, and Gambling in the Old South*. Princeton: Princeton University Press, 1996.

———. *Masters and Statesmen: The Political Culture of American Slavery*. Baltimore: Johns Hopkins University Press, 1985.

Greenwood, Janette Thomas. *Bittersweet Legacy: The Black and White "Better Classes" in Charlotte, 1850–1910*. Chapel Hill: University of North Carolina Press, 1994.

Gross, Ariela. *Double Character: Slavery and Masters in the Antebellum Southern Courtroom*. Princeton: Princeton University Press, 2000.

———. "Litigating Whiteness: Trials of Racial Determination in the Nineteenth-Century South." *Yale Law Journal* 108 (October 1998): 109–88.

Grossberg, Michael. *Governing the Hearth: Law and the Family in Nineteenth-Century America.* Chapel Hill: University of North Carolina Press, 1985.

———. "Guarding the Altar: Physiological Restrictions and the Rise of State Intervention in Matrimony." *American Journal of Legal History* 26 (July 1982): 197–226.

Grossman, James R. *Land of Hope: Chicago, Black Southerners, and the Great Migration.* Chicago: University of Chicago Press, 1988.

Groves, Paul A., and Edward K. Muller. "The Evolution of Black Residential Areas in Late-Nineteenth-Century Cities." *Journal of Historical Geography* 1 (April 1975): 169–91.

Gutiérrez, Ramón. *When Jesus Came, the Corn Mothers Went Away.* Stanford: Stanford University Press, 1991.

Gutman, Herbert G. "Black Coal Miners and the Greenback Labor Party in Redeemer Alabama, 1878–79: The Letters of Warren D. Kelley, Willis Johnson Thomas, 'Dawson,' and Others." *Labor History* 10 (Summer 1969): 506–35.

———. "Schools for Freedom: The Post-Emancipation Origins of Afro-American Education." In *Power and Culture: Essays on the American Working Class,* edited by Ira Berlin, 260–97. New York: Pantheon, 1987.

Habermas, Jürgen. *The Structural Transformation of the Public Sphere: An Inquiry into a Category of Bourgeois Society.* Cambridge: MIT Press, 1965, 1989.

Hahn, Steven. " 'Extravagant Expectations' of Freedom: Rumour, Political Struggle, and the Christmas Insurrection Scare of 1865 in the American South." *Past and Present* 157 (November 1997): 122–58.

———. "Hunting, Fishing, and Foraging: Common Rights and Class Relations in the Postbellum South." *Radical History Review* 26 (October 1982): 37–64.

———. "The Politics of Black Rural Laborers in the Postemancipation South." Paper delivered at the Commonwealth Fund Conference on Two Souths: Toward an Agenda for Comparative Study of the American South and the Italian Mezzogiorno, University College London, January 1999. In author's possession.

———. "A Response: Common Cents or Historical Sense?" *Journal of Southern History* 59 (May 1993): 243–58.

———. *The Roots of Southern Populism: Yeomen Farmers and the Transformation of the Georgia Upcountry, 1850–1890.* New York: Oxford University Press, 1983.

———. *To Build a New Jerusalem: The African-American Political Experience in the Rural South, 1860–1900.* Cambridge: Harvard University Press. Forthcoming.

Hair, William Ivy. *Carnival of Fury: Robert Charles and the New Orleans Race Riot of 1900.* Baton Rouge: Louisiana State University Press, 1976.

Hairston, L. Beatrice W. *A Brief History of Danville, Virginia, 1728–1954.* Richmond: Dietz Press, 1955.

Hale, Grace Elizabeth. *Making Whiteness: The Culture of Segregation in the South, 1890–1940*. New York: Pantheon, 1998.

Hall, Jacquelyn Dowd. "'The Mind That Burns in Each Body': Women, Rape, and Racial Violence." In *Powers of Desire: The Politics of Sexuality*, edited by Ann Snitow, Christine Stansell, and Sharon Thompson, 328–49. New York: Monthly Review Press, 1983.

———. *Revolt against Chivalry: Jessie Daniel Ames and the Southern Women's Campaign against Lynching*. New York: Columbia University Press, 1979.

Halsell, Willie D. "James R. Chalmers and 'Mahoneism' in Mississippi." *Journal of Southern History* 10 (February 1944): 37–58.

———. "Republican Factionalism in Mississippi, 1882–1884." *Journal of Southern History* 7 (February 1941): 84–101.

Haney Lopez, Ian F. *White by Law: The Legal Construction of Race*. New York: New York University Press, 1996.

Harris, Carl V. "Stability and Change in Discrimination against Black Public Schools: Birmingham, Alabama, 1877–1931." *Journal of Southern History* 51 (August 1985): 375–416.

Harris, J. William. "Etiquette, Lynching, and Racial Boundaries in Southern History: A Mississippi Example." *American Historical Review* 100 (April 1995): 387–410.

Hartz, Louis. *The Liberal Tradition in America: An Interpretation of American Political Thought since the Revolution*. New York: Harcourt, Brace, 1955.

Hartzell, Lawrence L. "The Exploration of Freedom in Black Petersburg, Virginia, 1865–1902." In *The Edge of the South: Life in Nineteenth-Century Virginia*, edited by Edward L. Ayers and John C. Willis, 134–56. Charlottesville: University Press of Virginia, 1991.

Hays, Samuel P. *Political History as Social Analysis*. Knoxville: University of Tennessee Press, 1980.

Heatwole, Cornelius. *A History of Education in Virginia*. New York: Macmillan, 1916.

Henderson, William D. *Gilded Age City: Politics, Life, and Labor in Petersburg, Virginia, 1874–1889*. Washington, D.C.: University Press of America.

Henri, Florette. *Black Migration: Movement North, 1900–1920*. Garden City, N.Y.: Anchor Press, 1975.

Higginbotham, A. Leon, Jr., and Barbara K. Kopytoff. "Racial Purity and Interracial Sex in the Law of Colonial and Antebellum Virginia." *Georgetown Law Journal* 77 (1989): 1967–2029.

Higginbotham, Evelyn Brooks. "African-American Women's History and the Metalanguage of Race." *Signs* 17 (Winter 1992): 251–74.

———. *Righteous Discontent: The Women's Movement in the Black Baptist Church, 1880–1920*. Cambridge: Harvard University Press, 1993.

Hirshson, Stanley. *Farewell to the Bloody Shirt: Northern Republicans and the Southern Negro, 1877–1893*. Bloomington: Indiana University Press, 1962.

Hobsbawm, Eric J. *Primitive Rebels: Studies in Archaic Forms of Social Movement in the 19th and 20th Centuries*. New York: Praeger, 1963.

Hodes, Martha. "The Sexualization of Reconstruction Politics: White Women and Black Men in the South after the Civil War." *Journal of the History of Sexuality* 3 (January 1993): 402–17.

———. "Wartime Dialogues on Illicit Sex: White Women and Black Men." In *Divided Houses: Gender and the Civil War,* edited by Catherine Clinton and Nina Silber, 230–42. New York: Oxford University Press, 1992.

———. *White Women, Black Men: Illicit Sex in the Nineteenth-Century South.* New Haven: Yale University Press, 1997.

Holt, Sharon Ann. "Making Freedom Pay: Freedpeople Working for Themselves, North Carolina, 1865–1900." *Journal of Southern History* 60 (May 1994): 229–62.

Holt, Thomas. *Black over White: Negro Political Leadership in South Carolina during Reconstruction.* Urbana: University of Illinois Press, 1977.

———. " 'An Empire over the Mind': Emancipation, Race, and Ideology in the British West Indies and the American South." In *Region, Race, and Reconstruction: Essays in Honor of C. Vann Woodward,* edited by J. Morgan Kousser and James M. McPherson, 283–313. New York: Oxford University Press, 1982.

———. "Marking: Race, Race-making, and the Writing of History." *American Historical Review* 100 (February 1995): 1–20.

Honey, Michael. *Southern Labor and Black Civil Rights: Organizing Memphis Workers.* Urbana: University of Illinois Press, 1993.

Hoogenboom, Ari. *Outlawing the Spoils: A History of the Civil Service Reform Movement, 1865–1883.* Urbana: University of Illinois Press, 1968.

———. "The Pendleton Act and the Civil Service." *American Historical Review* 64 (January 1959): 301–18.

Horsman, Reginald. *Race and Manifest Destiny: The Origins of American Racial Anglo-Saxonism.* Cambridge: Harvard University Press, 1981.

Horst, Samuel L. *Education for Manhood: The Education of Blacks in Virginia during the Civil War.* Lanham, Md.: University Press of America, 1987.

Hull, Isabel V. *Sexuality, State and Civil Society in Germany, 1700–1815.* Ithaca: Cornell University Press, 1996.

Hunt, Michael H. *Ideology and U.S. Foreign Policy.* New Haven: Yale University Press, 1987.

Hunter, Tera W. *To 'Joy My Freedom: Southern Black Women's Lives and Labors after the Civil War.* Cambridge: Harvard University Press, 1997.

Huntzinger, Victoria MacDonald. "The Birth of Southern Public Education: Columbus, Georgia, 1864–1904." Ph.D. diss., Harvard University, 1992.

Hurst, James Willard. *Law and the Conditions of Freedom in the Nineteenth-Century United States.* Madison: University of Wisconsin Press, 1956.

Hyman, Michael R. *The Anti-Redeemers: Hill-Country Political Dissenters in the Lower South from Redemption to Populism.* Baton Rouge: Louisiana State University Press, 1990.

Ingalls, Robert P. "Lynching and Establishment Violence in Tampa, 1858–1935." *Journal of Southern History* 53 (November 1987): 613–44.

Jackson, Luther Porter. *Negro Office-Holders in Virginia, 1865–1895.* Norfolk: Guide Quality Press, 1945.

Jacobson, Matthew Frye. *Whiteness of a Different Color: European Immigrants and the Alchemy of Race.* Cambridge: Harvard University Press, 1998.

Johnston, James Hugo. "The Participation of Negroes in the Government of Virginia from 1877 to 1888." *Journal of Negro History* 14 (July 1929): 251–71.

———. *Race Relations in Virginia and Miscegenation in the South, 1776–1860.* Amherst: University of Massachusetts Press, 1970.

Jones, Jacqueline. *Labor of Love, Labor of Sorrow: Black Women, Work, and the Family from Slavery to the Present.* New York: Basic Books, 1985.

———. *Soldiers of Light and Love: Northern Teachers and Georgia Blacks, 1865–1873.* Chapel Hill: University of North Carolina Press, 1980.

Jordan, Winthrop. *White over Black: American Attitudes toward the Negro, 1580–1812.* Chapel Hill: University of North Carolina Press, 1968.

Kahn, Kenneth. "The Knights of Labor and the Southern Black Worker." *Labor History* 18 (Winter 1977): 49–70.

Kantor, Shawn Everett. *Politics and Property Rights: The Closing of the Open Range in the Postbellum South.* Chicago: University of Chicago Press, 1998.

Kantor, Shawn Everett, and J. Morgan Kousser. "Common Sense or Commonwealth?: The Fence Law and Institutional Change in the Postbellum South." *Journal of Southern History* 59 (May 1993): 201–42.

———. "Rejoinder: Two Visions of History." *Journal of Southern History* 59 (May 1993): 250–66.

Kantrowitz, Stephen. *Ben Tillman and the Reconstruction of White Supremacy.* Chapel Hill: University of North Carolina Press, 2000.

Kaplan, Sidney. "The Miscegenation Issue in the Election of 1864." *Journal of Negro History* 34 (July 1949): 274–343.

Kasson, John F. *Rudeness and Civility: Manners in Nineteenth-Century Urban America.* New York: Hill and Wang, 1990.

Keller, Morton. *Affairs of State: Public Life in Late Nineteenth Century America.* Cambridge: Harvard University Press, 1977.

Kelley, Robin D. G. *Hammer and Hoe: Alabama Communists during the Great Depression.* Chapel Hill: University of North Carolina Press, 1990.

———. " 'We Are Not What We Seem': Rethinking Black Working-Class Opposition in the Jim Crow South." *Journal of American History* 80 (June 1993): 75–112.

Kellogg, John. "The Formation of Black Residential Areas in Lexington, Kentucky, 1865–1887." *Journal of Southern History* 48 (February 1982): 21–52.

———. "Negro Urban Clusters in the Postbellum South." *Geographical Review* 67 (July 1977): 310–21.

Kelly, Alfred H. "The Congressional Controversy over School Segregation, 1867–1875." *American Historical Review* 64 (April 1959): 537–63.

Kerber, Linda K. "Separate Spheres, Female Worlds, Woman's Place: The Rhetoric of Women's History." *Journal of American History* 75 (June 1988): 9–39.

Kerr-Ritchie, Jeffrey. *Freedpeople in the Tobacco South: Virginia, 1860–1900.* Chapel Hill: University of North Carolina Press, 1999.

Keve, Paul W. *The History of Corrections in Virginia.* Charlottesville: University Press of Virginia, 1986.

Key, V. O. *Southern Politics in State and Nation.* New York: Knopf, 1950.

Kloppenberg, James T. *The Virtues of Liberalism.* New York: Oxford University Press, 1998.

———. "The Virtues of Liberalism: Christianity, Republicanism, and Ethics in Early American Political Discourse." *Journal of American History* 74 (June 1987): 9–33.

Kluger, Richard. *Simple Justice.* New York: Knopf, 1975.

Knight, Edgar W. "Reconstruction and Education in Virginia." *South Atlantic Quarterly* 15 (January 1916): 25–40.

———. ed. *A Documentary History of Education in the South before the Civil War.* 5 vols. Chapel Hill: University of North Carolina Press, 1949–53.

Kousser, J. Morgan. *Dead End: The Development of Nineteenth-Century Litigation on Racial Discrimination in Schools.* New York: Oxford University Press, 1986.

———. "Post-Reconstruction Suffrage Restrictions in Tennessee: A New Look at the V. O. Key Thesis." *Political Science Quarterly* 87 (December 1973): 655–83.

———. *The Shaping of Southern Politics: Suffrage Restriction and the Establishment of the One-Party South, 1880–1910.* New Haven: Yale University Press, 1974.

Larsen, Lawrence. *The Rise of the Urban South.* Lexington: University of Kentucky Press, 1985.

Lawson, Steven F. *Black Ballots: Voting Rights in the South, 1944–1969.* New York: Columbia University Press, 1976.

Leach, Edmund. "Characterization of Caste and Class Systems." In *Caste and Race: Comparative Approaches,* edited by Anthony de Rueck and Julie Knight, 17–27. Boston: Little, Brown, 1967.

Lebsock, Suzanne. *The Free Women of Petersburg: Status and Culture in a Southern Town, 1784–1860.* New York: Norton, 1984.

Lefebvre, Henri. *La somme et le reste.* Paris: La Nef de Paris, 1959.

———. *The Production of Space.* Translated by Donald Nicholson-Smith. Cambridge, Mass.: Blackwell, 1991.

———. *The Survival of Capitalism.* Translated by Frank Bryant. London: St. Martin's Press, 1976.

Lemann, Nicholas. *The Promised Land: The Great Black Migration and How It Changed America.* New York: Knopf, 1991.

Letwin, Daniel L. *The Challenge of Interracial Unionism: Alabama Coalminers, 1878–1921.* Chapel Hill: University of North Carolina Press, 1998.

———. "Interracial Unionism, Gender, and 'Social Equality' in the Alabama Coalfields, 1878–1908." *Journal of Southern History* 61 (August 1995): 519–54.

Levine, Lawrence W. *Black Culture and Black Consciousness: Afro-American Folk Thought from Slavery to Freedom.* New York: Oxford University Press, 1977.

Lewis, David Levering, ed. *W. E. B. Du Bois Reader.* New York: Henry Holt, 1995.

Lewis, Earl. *In Their Own Interests: Race, Class, and Power in Twentieth-Century Norfolk, Virginia.* Berkeley: University of California Press, 1991.

Lichtenstein, Alex. *Twice the Work of Free Labor: The Political Economy of Convict Labor in the New South.* New York: Verso, 1996.

Link, William A. *A Hard Country and a Lonely Place: Schooling, Society, and Reform in Rural Virginia, 1870–1920.* Chapel Hill: University of North Carolina Press, 1986.

Lipsitz, George. *A Life in the Struggle: Ivory Perry and the Culture of Opposition.* Philadelphia: Temple University Press, 1995.

———. "The Possessive Investment in Whiteness: Racialized Social Democracy and the 'White' Problem in American Studies." *American Quarterly* 47 (September 1995): 369–87.

Litwack, Leon F. *Been in the Storm So Long: The Aftermath of Slavery.* New York: Vintage Books, 1979.

———. *Trouble in Mind: Black Southerners in the Age of Jim Crow.* New York: Knopf, 1998.

Logan, Rayford W., and Michael R. Winston. *Dictionary of American Negro Biography.* New York: Norton, 1982.

Lowe, Richard G. *Republicans and Reconstruction in Virginia, 1856–70.* Charlottesville: University Press of Virginia, 1991.

Lumpkin, Katharine Du Pre. *The Making of a Southerner.* New York: Knopf, 1947.

MacPherson, C. B. *The Political Theory of Possessive Individualism: Hobbes to Locke.* Oxford: Oxford University Press, 1962.

Maddex, Jack P., Jr. *The Virginia Conservatives, 1867–1879: A Study in Reconstruction Politics.* Chapel Hill: University of North Carolina Press, 1970.

———. "Virginia: The Persistence of Centrist Hegemony." In *Reconstruction and Redemption in the South,* edited by Otto H. Olsen, 113–50. Baton Rouge: Louisiana State University Press, 1980.

Maddox, William Arthur. *The Free School Idea in Virginia before the Civil War.* New York: Arno Press, 1969.

Mancini, Matthew J. *One Dies, Get Another: Convict Leasing in the American South, 1866–1928.* Columbia: University of South Carolina Press, 1996.

Manent, Pierre. *Tocqueville and the Nature of Democracy.* Lanham, Md.: Rowman and Littlefield, 1996.

Marinez-Alier, Verena. *Marriage, Class and Colour in Nineteenth-Century Cuba: A Study of Racial Attitudes and Sexual Values in a Slave Society.* Cambridge: Cambridge University Press, 1974.

Martin, Albro. "The Troubled Subject of Railroad Regulation in the Gilded Age: A Reappraisal." *Journal of American History* 61 (September 1974): 339–71.

Martyn, Byron C. "Racism in the United States: A History of Anti-Miscegenation Legislation and Litigation." Ph.D. diss., University of Southern California, 1979.

Marx, Karl. *Capital: A Critique of Political Economy.* 10 vols. New York: 1967.

McCurry, Stephanie. *Masters of Small Worlds: Yeoman Households, Gender Relations, and the Political Culture of the Antebellum South Carolina Low Country.* New York: Oxford University Press, 1995.

———. "The Politics of Yeoman Households in South Carolina." In *Divided Houses: Gender and the Civil War,* edited by Catherine Clinton and Nina Silber, 22–38. New York: Oxford University Press, 1992.

———. "The Two Faces of Republicanism: Gender and Proslavery Politics in Antebellum South Carolina." *Journal of American History* 78 (March 1992): 1245–64.

McDaniel, Ralph Clipman. *The Virginia Constitutional Convention of 1901–1902.* Baltimore: Johns Hopkins University Press, 1928.

McDuffie, Jerome A. "Politics in Wilmington and New Hanover County, N.C., 1865–1900: The Genesis of a Race Riot." Ph.D. diss., Kent State University, 1979.

McFarland, George M. "The Extension of Democracy in Virginia, 1850–1895." Ph.D., Princeton University, 1925.

McGrane, Reginald C. *Foreign Bondholders and American State Debts.* New York: Macmillan, 1935.

McKinney, Gordon B. *Southern Mountain Republicans, 1865–1900: Politics and the Appalachian Community.* Chapel Hill: University of North Carolina Press, 1978.

McLaurin, Melton Alonza. *The Knights of Labor in the South.* Westport, Conn.: Greenwood Press, 1978.

McMillen, Neil R. *Dark Journey: Black Mississippians in the Age of Jim Crow.* Urbana: University of Illinois Press, 1989.

McPherson, James M. *The Abolitionist Legacy: From Reconstruction to the NAACP.* Princeton: Princeton University Press, 1975.

———. *Battle Cry of Freedom: The Civil War Era.* New York: Oxford University Press, 1988.

———. *Ordeal by Fire: The Civil War and Reconstruction.* New York: Knopf, 1982.

———. "White Liberals and Black Power in Negro Education, 1865–1915." *American Historical Review* 75 (June 1970): 1357–86.

Meier, August, and Elliott Rudwick. "The Boycott Movement against Jim Crow Streetcars in the South, 1900–1906." In *Along the Color Line:*

Explorations in the Black Experience, edited by Meier and Rudwick, 267–89.
Urbana: University of Illinois Press, 1976.

Miller, Zane L. "Urban Blacks in the South, 1865–1920: The Richmond,
Savannah, New Orleans, Louisville, and Birmingham Experience." In *The
New Urban History: Quantitative Explorations by American Historians,* edited
by Leo F. Schnore, 184–204. Princeton: Princeton University Press, 1975.

Mitchell, Margaret. *Gone with the Wind.* New York: Macmillan, 1936.

Mitchell, Reid. *Civil War Soldiers: Their Expectations and Their Experiences.* New
York: Viking, 1988.

Moger, Allen W. "Industrial and Urban Progress in Virginia from 1880 to
1900." *Virginia Magazine of History and Biography* 66 (July 1958): 307–36.

————. "The Origin of the Democratic Machine in Virginia." *Journal of
Southern History* 8 (May 1942): 183–209.

————. "Railroad Practices and Policies in Virginia after the Civil War."
Virginia Magazine of History and Biography 59 (July 1951): 423–57.

————. *Virginia: Bourbonism to Byrd, 1870–1925.* Charlottesville: University
Press of Virginia, 1968.

Montgomery, David. *The Fall of the House of Labor: The Workplace, the State, and
American Labor Activism, 1865–1925.* Cambridge: Harvard University
Press, 1987.

Moore, James Tice. "Black Militancy in Readjuster Virginia, 1879–1883."
Journal of Southern History 41 (May 1975): 167–86.

————. "The Death of the Duel: The *Code Duello* in Readjuster Virginia,
1879–1883." *Virginia Magazine of History and Biography* 83 (July 1975):
259–76.

————. "Origins of the Solid South: Redeemer Democrats and the Popular
Will, 1870–1900." *Southern Studies* 22 (Fall 1983): 285–301.

————. "Redeemers Reconsidered: Change and Continuity in the
Democratic South, 1870–1900." *Journal of Southern History* 44 (August
1978): 357–78.

————. *Two Paths to the New South: The Virginia Debt Controversy, 1870–1883.*
Lexington: University of Kentucky Press, 1974.

Morgan, Edmund. *American Slavery, American Freedom: The Ordeal of Colonial
Virginia.* New York: Norton, 1975.

Morris, Robert C. *Reading, 'Riting, and Reconstruction: The Education of
Freedmen in the South, 1861–1870.* Chicago: University of Chicago Press,
1981.

Morrison, Toni. *Jazz.* New York: Knopf, 1992.

Morton, Richard L. *The Negro in Virginia Politics, 1865–1902.* Charlottesville:
University Press of Virginia, 1919.

Moton, Robert Russa. *What the Negro Thinks.* Garden City, N.Y.: Doubleday,
1930.

Myrdal, Gunnar. *An American Dilemma: The Negro Problem and Modern
Democracy.* New York: Harper and Brothers, 1944.

Newby, Cassandra Lynn. "'The World Was All before Them': A Study of the

Black Community in Norfolk, Virginia, 1861–1884." Ph.D. diss., College of William and Mary, 1992.

Oakes, James. *The Ruling Race: A History of American Slaveholders.* New York: Knopf, 1982.

———. *Slavery and Freedom: An Interpretation of the Old South.* New York: Knopf, 1990.

O'Brien, John Thomas, Jr. "From Bondage to Citizenship: The Richmond Black Community, 1865–1867." Ph.D. diss., University of Rochester, 1974.

Olsen, Otto H. *A Carpetbagger's Crusade: The Life of Albion Winegar Tourgée.* Baltimore: Johns Hopkins University Press, 1965.

Osofsky, Gilbert, ed. *Puttin' on Ole Massa: The Slave Narratives of Henry Bibb, William Wells, and Solomon Northrup.* New York: Harper and Row, 1969.

Painter, Nell Irvin. *Exodusters: Black Migration to Kansas after Reconstruction.* New York: Knopf, 1977.

———. "'Social Equality,' Miscegenation, Labor, and Power." In *The Evolution of Southern Culture,* edited by Numan V. Bartley, 47–67. Athens: University of Georgia Press, 1988.

———. *Standing at Armageddon: The United States, 1877–1919.* New York: Norton, 1987.

Pascoe, Peggy. "Miscegenation Law, Court Cases, and Ideologies of 'Race' in Twentieth-Century America." *Journal of American History* 83 (June 1996): 44–69.

———. "Race, Gender and Intercultural Relations: The Case of Interracial Marriage." *Frontiers* 12 (Summer 1991): 5–18.

———. "Race, Gender, and the Privileges of Property: On the Significance of Miscegenation Law in the U.S. West." In *Over the Edge: Remapping the American West,* edited by Valerie J. Matsumoto and Blake Allmendinger, 215–30. Berkeley: University of California Press, 1998.

Pateman, Carole. *The Sexual Contract.* Stanford: Stanford University Press, 1988.

Pearson, Charles Chilton. *The Readjuster Movement in Virginia.* New Haven: Yale University Press, 1917.

Pendleton, William C. *Political History of Appalachian Virginia, 1776–1927.* Dayton, Va.: Shenandoah Press, 1927.

Percy, Walker. *Lancelot.* New York: Farrar, Straus and Giroux, 1977.

Percy, William Alexander. *Lanterns on the Levee: Recollections of a Planter's Son.* Baton Rouge: Louisiana University Press, 1990.

Pincus, Samuel N. *The Virginia Supreme Court, Blacks, and the Law, 1870–1902.* New York: Garland Publishing Co., 1990.

Poland, Charles Preston, Jr. *From Frontier to Suburbia.* Marceline, Mo.: Walsworth Publishing Co., 1976.

Powdermaker, Hortense. *After Freedom: A Cultural Study in the Deep South.* New York: Viking, 1939.

Powell, Lawrence N. "The Politics of Livelihood: Carpetbaggers in the Deep

South." In *Region, Race, and Reconstruction: Essays in Honor of C. Vann Woodward,* edited by J. Morgan Kousser and James M. McPherson, 315–48. New York: Oxford University Press, 1982.

Prather, H. Leon, Sr. *We Have Taken a City: Wilmington Racial Massacre and Coup of 1898.* Rutherford, N.J.: Fairleigh Dickenson University Press, 1984.

Rabinowitz, Howard N. "Continuity and Change: Southern Urban Development, 1860–1900." In *The City in Southern History: The Growth of Urban Civilization in the South,* edited by Blaine A. Brownell and David R. Goldfield, 92–122. Port Washington, N.Y.: Kennikat Press, 1977.

———. "From Exclusion to Segregation: Southern Race Relations, 1865–1890." *Journal of American History* 63 (September 1976): 325–50.

———. "Half a Loaf: The Shift from White to Black Teachers in the Negro Schools of the Urban South, 1865–1890." *Journal of Southern History* 40 (November 1974): 565–94.

———. "More Than the Woodward Thesis: Assessing *The Strange Career of Jim Crow.*" *Journal of American History* 75 (December 1988): 842–56.

———. *Race Relations in the Urban South, 1865–1890.* Urbana: University of Illinois Press, 1979.

Rable, George C. *But There Was No Peace: The Role of Violence in the Politics of Reconstruction.* Athens: University of Georgia Press, 1984.

Raboteau, Albert J. *Slave Religion: The "Invisible Institution" of the Antebellum South.* New York: Oxford University Press, 1978.

Rachleff, Peter J. *Black Labor in Richmond, 1865–1890.* Urbana: University of Illinois Press, 1989.

Randall, James G. "The Virginia Debt Controversy." *Political Science Quarterly* 30 (1915): 553–77.

Randolph, B. C. "Foreign Bondholders and the Repudiated Debts of the Southern States." *American Journal of International Law* 25 (1931).

Ransom, Roger, and Richard Sutch. *One Kind of Freedom: The Economic Consequences of Emancipation.* New York: Cambridge University Press, 1977.

Raper, Arthur. *The Tragedy of Lynching.* Chapel Hill: University of North Carolina Press, 1933.

Ratchford, B. U. *American State Debts.* Durham, N.C.: Duke University Press, 1941.

Roberts, Frances. "William Manning Lowe and the Greenback Party in Alabama." *Alabama Review* 5 (April 1952): 100–121.

Robinson, Amy. "It Takes One to Know One: Passing and Communities of Common Interest." *Critical Inquiry* 20 (Summer 1994): 715–36.

Robinson, Armstead L. "Beyond the Realm of Social Consensus: New Meanings of Reconstruction for American History." *Journal of American History* 68 (September 1981): 276–97.

Roediger, David R. *Towards the Abolition of Whiteness: Essays on Race, Politics, and Working Class History.* New York: Verso, 1994.

————. *The Wages of Whiteness: Race and the Making of the American Working Class.* London: Verso, 1991.

Rogers, William W. *The One-Gallused Rebellion: Agrarianism in Alabama, 1865–1896.* Baton Rouge: Louisiana State University Press, 1970.

Rothman, David J. *Politics and Power: The United States Senate, 1869–1901.* Cambridge: Harvard University Press, 1966.

Ryan, Mary P. *Women in Public: Between Banners and Ballots, 1825–1880.* Baltimore: Johns Hopkins University Press, 1990.

Sabean, David. *Power in the Blood: Popular Culture and Village Discourse in Early Modern Germany.* Cambridge: Cambridge University Press, 1984.

Saks, Eva. "Representing Miscegenation Law." *Raritan* 8 (Fall 1988): 39–69.

Saloutos, Theodore. *Farmer Movements in the South, 1865–1933.* Berkeley: University of California Press, 1960.

————. "The Grange in the South, 1870–1877." *Journal of Southern History* 19 (November 1953): 473–87.

Sartre, Jean-Paul. *The Freud Scenario.* Translated by Quintin Hoare. Chicago: University of Chicago Press, 1988.

Saville, Julie. *The Work of Reconstruction: From Slave to Free Laborer in South Carolina, 1860–1870.* New York: Cambridge University Press, 1994.

Saxton, Alexander. *The Rise and Fall of the White Republic: Class Politics and Mass Culture in Nineteenth Century America.* London: Verso, 1990.

Schewel, Michael J. "Local Politics in Lynchburg, Virginia, in the 1880s." *Virginia Magazine of History and Biography* 89 (April 1981): 170–80.

Schorske, Carl E. *Fin-de-Siècle Vienna: Politics and Culture.* New York: Vintage, 1981.

Schwalm, Leslie. *A Hard Fight for We: Women's Transition from Slavery to Freedom in South Carolina.* Urbana: University of Illinois Press, 1997.

Scott, Emmett J. *Negro Migration during the War.* 1920. Reprint, New York: Arno and New York Times, 1969.

Scott, James. *Domination and the Arts of Resistance: Hidden Transcripts.* New Haven: Yale University Press, 1990.

————. *Weapons of the Weak: Everyday Forms of Peasant Resistance.* New Haven: Yale University Press, 1985.

Seed, Patricia. *To Love, Honor, and Obey in Colonial Mexico: Conflicts over Marriage Choice, 1574–1821.* Stanford: Stanford University Press, 1988.

Seligman, Adam B. *The Idea of Civil Society.* New York: Maxwell Macmillan International, 1992.

Sellers, Charles Grier, Jr. "Who Were the Southern Whigs?" *American Historical Review* 59 (January 1954): 335–46.

Shade, William G. *Democratizing the Old Dominion: Virginia and the Second Party System, 1824–1861.* Charlottesville: University Press of Virginia, 1996.

Shapiro, Herbert. *White Violence and Black Response: From Reconstruction to Montgomery.* Amherst: University of Massachusetts Press, 1988.

Shaw, Stephanie J. *What a Woman Ought to Be and to Do: Black Professional*

Women Workers during the Jim Crow Era. Chicago: University of Chicago
    Press, 1996.
Sheldon, William DuBose. *Populism in the Old Dominion: Virginia Farm Politics,
    1885–1900.* Glouster, Mass.: Peter Smith, 1967.
Sherman, Richard B. " 'The Last Stand': The Fight for Racial Integrity in
    Virginia in the 1920s." *Journal of Southern History* 54 (February 1988):
    69–92.
Shifflett, Crandall A. "Gilbert Carlton Walker: Carpetbag Conservative." In
    The Governors of Virginia, 1860–1978, edited by Edward Younger and
    James Tice Moore, 57–67. Charlottesville: University Press of Virginia,
    1982.
————. *Patronage and Poverty in the Tobacco South: Louisa County, Virginia,
    1860–1900.* Knoxville: University of Tennessee Press, 1982.
Shklar, Judith. *Political Thought and Political Thinkers.* Chicago: University of
    Chicago Press, 1998.
Sickles, Robert J. *Race, Marriage, and the Law.* Albuquerque: University of
    New Mexico Press, 1972.
Siegel, Frederick F. *The Roots of Southern Distinctiveness: Tobacco and Society in
    Danville, Virginia, 1780–1856.* Chapel Hill: University of North Carolina
    Press, 1987.
Simmel, Georg. "The Secret and the Secret Society." In *The Sociology of Georg
    Simmel,* edited and translated by Kurt H. Wolff, 307–76. New York: Free
    Press, 1950.
Simon, Bryant. "The Appeal of Cole Blease of South Carolina: Race, Class,
    and Sex in the New South." *Journal of Southern History* 62 (February 1996):
    57–86.
Skowronek, Steven. *Building a New American State: The Expansion of National
    Administrative Capacities, 1877–1920.* New York: Cambridge University
    Press, 1982.
Smith, John Douglas. "Managing White Supremacy: Politics and Culture in
    Virginia, 1919–1939." Ph.D. diss., University of Virginia, 1998.
Smith, Larissa M. "Challenging the Byrd Machine: Civil Rights Activism in
    Virginia during the 1940s." Paper presented at Sydney Sussex College,
    University of Cambridge, March 1999. In author's possession.
————. "Where the South Begins: Black Politics and Civil Rights Activism in
    Virginia, 1930–1954." Ph.D. diss., Emory University, in progress.
Smith-Rosenberg, Carroll. "Dis-Covering the Subject of the 'Great
    Constitutional Discussion,' 1786–1789." *Journal of American History* 79
    (December 1992): 841–73.
Snead, James A. *Figures of Division: William Faulkner's Major Novels.* New York:
    Methuen, 1986.
Sosna, Morton. *In Search of the Silent South: Southern Liberals and the Race Issue.*
    New York: Columbia University Press, 1977.
Stanley, Amy Dru. "Beggars Can't Be Choosers: Compulsion and Contract

in Postbellum America." *Journal of American History* 78 (March 1992): 1265–93.

———. "Conjugal Bonds and Wage Labor: Rights of Contract in the Age of Emancipation." *Journal of American History* 75 (September 1988): 471–500.

———. *From Bondage to Contract: Wage Labor, Marriage, and the Market in the Age of Slave Emancipation.* New York: Cambridge University Press, 1998.

Stanton, William. *The Leopard's Spots: Scientific Attitudes Towards Race in America, 1815–1859.* Chicago: University of Chicago Press, 1960.

Stein, Judith. "'Of Mr. Booker T. Washington and Others': The Political Economy of Racism in the United States." *Science and Society* 38 (Winter 1974–1975): 422–63.

Stepan, Nancy. "Biology and Degeneration: Races and Proper Places." In *Degeneration: The Dark Side of Progress,* edited by J. Edward Chamberlain and Sander L. Gilman, 97–120. New York: Columbia University Press, 1985.

Stephenson, Gilbert Thomas. *Race Distinctions in American Law.* 1910. Reprint, New York: AMS Press, 1969.

Sterling, Dorothy. *The Trouble They Seen: Black People Tell the Story of Reconstruction.* New York: Doubleday, 1976.

Stevenson, Brenda E. *Life in Black and White: Family and Community in the Slave South.* New York: Oxford University Press, 1996.

Stover, John F. *The Railroads of the South, 1865–1900.* Chapel Hill: University of North Carolina Press, 1955.

Stowe, Steven M. *Intimacy and Power in the Old South: Ritual in the Lives of the Planters.* Baltimore: Johns Hopkins University Press, 1987.

Stuckey, Sterling. "Through the Prism of Folklore: The Black Ethos in Slavery." *Massachusetts Review* 9 (Summer 1968): 417–37.

Sullivan, Patricia. *Days of Hope: Race and Democracy in the New Deal Era.* Chapel Hill: University of North Carolina Press, 1996.

Summers, Mark W. *Railroads, Reconstruction, and the Gospel of Prosperity: Aid under the Radical Republicans, 1865–1877.* Princeton: Princeton University Press, 1984.

Sundquist, Eric, ed. *The Oxford W. E. B. Du Bois Reader.* New York: Oxford University Press, 1996.

Takaki, Ronald. *Strangers from a Different Shore: A History of Asian Americans.* Boston: Little, Brown, 1989.

Taylor, Alrutheus Ambush. "The Negro in the Reconstruction of Virginia." *Journal of Negro History* 11 (April and July 1926): 243–415 and 425–537.

———. *The Negro in the Reconstruction of Virginia.* New York: Russell and Russell, 1969.

Thompson, Edward P. *The Making of the English Working Class.* New York: Vintage Books, 1966.

———. "The Moral Economy of the English Crowd in the Eighteenth Century." *Past and Present* 50 (February 1971): 76–136.

Thornton, J. Mills, III. "Fiscal Policy and the Failure of Reconstruction in the Lower South." In *Region, Race, and Reconstruction: Essays in Honor of C. Vann Woodward,* edited by J. Morgan Kousser and James M. McPherson, 349–94. New York: Oxford University Press, 1982.

Tilley, Nannie May. *The Bright-Leaf Tobacco Industry, 1860–1929.* Chapel Hill: University of North Carolina Press, 1948.

Trelease, Allen W. *White Terror: The Ku Klux Klan Conspiracy and Southern Reconstruction.* New York: Harper and Row, 1971.

Tripp, Steven Elliott. *Yankee Town, Southern City: Race and Class Relations in Civil War Lynchburg.* New York: New York University Press, 1997.

Trotter, Joe William, Jr., ed. *The Great Migration in Historical Perspective: New Dimensions of Race, Class, and Gender.* Bloomington: Indiana University Press, 1991.

Tushnet, Mark. *The NAACP's Legal Strategy against Segregated Education, 1925–1950.* Chapel Hill: University of North Carolina Press, 1987.

Varon, Elizabeth R. "Tippecanoe and the Ladies, Too: White Women and Party Politics in Antebellum Virginia." *Journal of American History* 82 (September 1995): 494–520.

————. *We Mean to Be Counted: White Women and Politics in Antebellum Virginia.* Chapel Hill: University of North Carolina Press, 1998.

Vaughn, William Preston. *Schools for All: The Blacks and Public Education in the South, 1865–1877.* Lexington: University Press of Kentucky, 1974.

Voss, Kim. *The Making of American Exceptionalism: The Knights of Labor and Class Formation in the Nineteenth Century.* Ithaca: Cornell University Press, 1993.

Wade, Richard C. *Slavery in the Cities: The South, 1820–1860.* New York: Oxford University Press, 1964.

Wadlington, Walter. "The *Loving* Case: Virginia's Anti-Miscegenation Statute in Historical Perspective." *Virginia Law Review* 52 (1966): 1189–1223.

Wallenstein, Peter. "Cartograms and the Mapping of Virginia History, 1790–1990." *Virginia Social Science Journal* 23 (1993): 90–110.

————. *From Slave South to New South: Public Policy in Nineteenth-Century Georgia.* Chapel Hill: University of North Carolina Press, 1987.

————. "Law and the Boundaries of Place and Race in Interracial Marriage: Interstate Comity, Racial Identity, and Miscegenation Laws in North Carolina, South Carolina, and Virginia, 1860s–1960s." *Akron Law Review* 32 (1999): 557–76.

————. "Race, Marriage, and the Law of Freedom: Alabama and Virginia, 1860s–1960s." *Chicago-Kent Law Review* 70 (1994): 371–437.

————. "Race, Marriage, and the Supreme Court from *Pace v. Alabama* (1883) to *Loving v. Virginia* (1967)." *Journal of Supreme Court History* 2 (1998): 65–86.

Walzer, Michael. "The Civil Society Argument." In *Theorizing Citizenship,* edited by Ronald Beiner, 153–74. Albany: State University of New York Press, 1995.

Watson, Harry L. *Liberty and Power: The Politics of Jacksonian America.* New York: Noonday Press, 1990.

Weir, Robert E. *Beyond Labor's Veil: The Culture of the Knights of Labor.* University Park: Pennsylvania State University Press, 1996.

Weiss, Nancy J. *Farewell to the Party of Lincoln: Black Politics in the Age of FDR.* Princeton: Princeton University Press, 1983.

Welke, Barbara Y. "When All the Women Were White, and All the Blacks Were Men: Gender, Class, Race, and the Road to *Plessy,* 1855–1914." *Law and History Review* 13 (Fall 1995): 261–316.

Welter, Barbara. "The Cult of True Womanhood: 1820–1860." *American Quarterly* 18 (Summer 1966): 151–74.

Williamson, Chilton. *American Suffrage: From Property to Democracy, 1760–1860.* Princeton: Princeton University Press, 1960.

Williamson, Joel. *After Slavery: The Negro in South Carolina during Reconstruction, 1861–1877.* Chapel Hill: University of North Carolina Press, 1965.

———. *The Crucible of Race: Black-White Relations in the American South since Emancipation.* New York: Oxford University Press, 1984.

———. *New People: Miscegenation and Mulattoes in the United States.* New York: Free Press, 1980.

Wilson, Theodore Brantner. *The Black Codes of the South.* University, Ala.: University of Alabama Press, 1965.

Woodman, Harold D. "Economic Reconstruction and the Rise of the New South, 1865–1900." In *Interpreting Southern History: Essays in Honor of Sanford W. Higginbotham,* edited by John B. Boles and Evelyn Thomas Nolen, 254–307. Baton Rouge: Louisiana State University Press, 1987.

Woodward, C. Vann. *American Counterpoint: Slavery and Racism in the North-South Dialogue.* Boston: Little, Brown, 1971.

———. *Origins of the New South, 1877–1913.* Baton Rouge: Louisiana State University Press, 1951.

———. "*Strange Career* Critics: Long May They Persevere." *Journal of American History* 75 (December 1988): 857–68.

———. *The Strange Career of Jim Crow.* New York: Oxford University Press, 1955.

———. *Thinking Back: The Perils of Writing History.* Baton Rouge: Louisiana State University Press, 1986.

Wright, George C. *Life behind a Veil: Blacks in Louisville, Kentucky, 1865–1930.* Baton Rouge: Louisiana State University Press, 1985.

———. *Racial Violence in Kentucky, 1865–1940: Lynchings, Mob Rule, and "Legal Lynchings."* Baton Rouge: Louisiana State University Press, 1990.

Wyatt-Brown, Bertram. *Southern Honor: Ethics and Behavior in the Old South.* New York: Oxford University Press, 1982.

Wynes, Charles E. "The Evolution of Jim Crow Laws in Twentieth Century Virginia." *Phylon* 28 (Winter 1967): 416–25.

―――. *Race Relations in Virginia, 1870–1902.* Charlottesville: University
   Press of Virginia, 1961.
―――, ed., *Southern Sketches from Virginia, 1881–1901.* Charlottesville:
   University Press of Virginia, 1964.
Young, Robert J. C. *Colonial Desire: Hybridity in Theory, Culture and Race.*
   London: Routledge, 1995.
Younger, Edward, and James Tice Moore, Jr. *The Governors of Virginia, 1860–
   1978.* Charlottesville: University Press of Virginia, 1982.

INDEX

Abingdon, 151

Abingdon Virginian, 148

"Act for the Preservation of Racial Integrity," 88

Adams, George, 122–23

Adams, Robert J., 122, 123, 127

African Americans: and suffrage, 1, 2, 5, 9, 16, 18–19, 20, 21, 59, 86, 91, 106, 109, 111, 146, 175 (n. 21); and Readjuster Party, 1, 36–37, 45–47, 48, 50–51, 52–53, 55, 62, 63, 64, 65–70, 74, 77, 89, 110, 137–38, 153, 230 (n. 75); and political power, 1, 37, 49–50, 53–54, 65–66, 67, 68–69, 73–76, 77, 79, 81, 93, 112, 113, 115, 129, 139–40, 147, 171–72 (n. 4), 173 (n. 17); and jury service, 1, 53–54, 64, 86, 153; and migration, 2, 10, 111, 167; and voting, 4, 16, 160–61, 167–68, 214–15 (n. 31); disfranchisement of, 5, 14, 160–66, 171–72 (n. 4); and patronage, 11, 36, 47, 59, 64, 65–76, 77–78, 115, 116, 138, 139–40, 196–97 (n. 79); and public assertions of equality, 12, 94, 103–8, 109, 116, 118, 130, 142–43; and political activism, 16, 20, 70, 72–74, 96–97, 110, 161, 166, 167–68, 234 (n. 48); and civil rights, 16, 86, 91, 92, 104–5, 106, 107, 109, 153, 213

(n. 19); and education, 22–25, 46, 69, 70–76, 111, 146, 177 (n. 41), 178–79 (n. 52), 201–2 (n. 132); and Republican Party, 35, 36, 46–47, 48, 50, 53–54, 66, 67, 161, 167, 233 (n. 28), 234 (n. 47); in General Assembly, 36, 46–47, 68, 81, 92, 94, 114, 156, 183 (n. 95); and debt policy, 43–44, 46–47; churches of, 49, 62, 161; militias of, 49, 188 (n. 6); fraternal organizations of, 49, 188–89 (n. 6); labor unions of, 53–54; and corporal punishment, 55, 108; and Democratic Party, 65, 167–68, 188 (n. 5), 230 (n. 75); as post office workers, 67, 94, 114; male, 68, 76, 86–87, 95–96, 97, 98–99, 118, 139, 208 (n. 84); and gender, 85–86, 117–18; female, 95, 116, 118, 130; and "place," 106, 119, 166–67; as police, 114–15, 116, 122, 123; and economic competition, 115–16; and Populist Party, 160

Alexandria, 16

Alexandria Gazette, 145

"Amalgamation," 141. *See also* Sex, interracial

Amelia County, 101, 151

Anderson-McCormick election law, 157–58

269

56–57, 61, 62, 192 (n. 40); and
U.S. senators, 57, 192–93 (n. 42);
and jobs, 57–58, 63–64, 66–68,
69, 98, 196 (n. 77); and women,
60; and General Assembly, 63–64;
and racial hierarchy, 68, 90, 96;
and interracial sex, 99
Paul, John, 138
Paul, Robert A., 50, 96, 98, 101, 156,
189 (n. 11), 208–9 (n. 85)
Peabody, George, 25
Pearson, Charles Chilton, 9
Pendleton, William, 164–65
Pendleton Act, 56, 192 (n. 40)
Percy, William Alexander: *Lanterns
on the Levee,* 103
Petersburg, 32, 64, 68–76, 38, 164,
167
Petersburg Lancet, 73, 75, 76, 90
Pierpont, Francis H., 16, 17, 19, 137,
177 (n. 40)
Pittsylvania County, 121, 151
Poland, Charles Preston, Jr., 9
Police, African American, 114–15,
116, 122, 123
Poll tax, 5, 32, 45, 55, 62, 63, 81,
139, 163, 168
Populist Party, 3, 14, 157, 159–60
Populist-Republican coalition, 4,
129, 223 (n. 104)
Private sphere. *See* Public versus
private spheres
Pryor, Alfred S., 75
Public space, 12, 106, 214 (n. 22).
See also Etiquette, racial: in urban
spaces
Public versus private spheres, 85–
88, 89, 93, 96, 97, 102, 105, 127
Punishment, corporal, 37, 47, 55,
69, 89, 108

Quakers, 23, 177 (n. 41)

Rabinowitz, Howard N., 105, 215
(n. 32)

Race: as political issue, 5, 83–84,
132–54, 155; hierarchies of, 68,
90, 96, 97; and liberalism, 84;
definitions of, 132, 133–35, 142,
153; as social construct, 133–
34, 135, 145, 224 (n. 6). *See also*
Coalitions, interracial; Etiquette,
racial; Marriage, interracial; Sex,
interracial; Whiteness
—as identity: and politics, 10, 132–
54; and social performance, 93,
149; and legislation, 132; fluidity
of, 132–33, 135, 149, 152–53, 166;
and court cases, 133–34, 152, 207
(n. 73); fictional portrayals of,
135. *See also* Race; Whiteness
Racism, 9, 10, 155; and race baiting,
12, 78, 82–83, 96, 98, 100–101,
105, 114–16, 138, 139, 140–42,
145, 146–52
Railroads: 17–18, 29, 39–40, 53, 82,
184 (n. 111); 184–85 (n. 112)
Raub, Sarah, 133–34
Readjuster Party: in *Jazz,* 1, 2; as
interracial coalition, 1, 3, 5, 43,
59, 76, 78, 79, 84, 89, 96; and
African American suffrage, 1, 9,
11, 81, 86; and patronage, 1, 11,
47, 55–61, 63–64, 66–76, 137–
38, 144, 146, 158; and African
Americans, 1–2, 36–37, 45–47,
48, 50–51, 52–53, 55, 59, 63,
64, 65–70, 74, 77, 89, 110, 137,
138, 153, 230 (n. 75); legacy of, 2,
14, 156–57, 168, 169; failure of,
9, 12, 13, 139–40, 152, 156, 230
(n. 76); and racial divisions, 9, 52,
92, 137–38, 158; historiography
of, 9, 152, 169; and liberalism,
11, 78–79, 81–85, 86, 97, 105,
137, 138; and whiteness, 13, 58–
59, 112, 136–37, 139–40, 141,
147, 153; origins of, 15–47; social and economic composition
of, 32, 33, 82, 137; geographic

Walker, Gilbert C., 24–25, 27, 28, 40, 180–81 (n. 67), 182 (n. 87)
Walker, Richard F., 150
Wallenstein, Peter, 178 (n. 42)
Walton, M. L., 160
Walton Act, 160, 161, 165, 232–33 (n. 25)
Washington, Booker T., 22
Welke, Barbara Y., 208 (n. 84)
West Virginia, 16, 18, 175 (n. 13)
Whig. See *Richmond Whig*
Whigs, former, 19, 20, 36
Whiteness: threatened, 13, 93, 112, 140, 141–42, 147, 148; and Democratic Party, 14, 139, 145; and honor, 94, 136; privileges of, 136, 139, 152; fear of loss of, 140, 142, 153. *See also* Race; Race—as identity; White supremacy
Whites: reaction to African American political power by, 2, 76, 78, 94, 95–96, 125, 139; and liberalism, 84–85; female, 86, 95,

98–99, 101; threatened by black patronage, 98–101, 139–40, 146; disapprove of white-on-black violence, 110; fear African American violence, 150–51, 229 (n. 72). *See also* Whiteness
White supremacy, 79; establishment of, 5, 6, 153; and Democratic Party, 14, 153, 156; challenged, 48, 96, 141, 146
Williamsburg, 32, 93
Wilmington, N.C., 105, 129–30, 223 (nn. 105, 107)
Wise, Henry A., 22, 23, 33, 174 (n. 1)
Wise, John S., 77, 86, 138, 143, 158, 165–66, 227 (n. 42)
Wise County, 146
Withers, Walter S., 113, 122
Woodman, Harold D., 8
Woodward, C. Vann, 6–7
Workingmen's Reform Party, 159

GENDER AND AMERICAN CULTURE

How Am I to Be Heard?: Letters of Lillian Smith, *edited by Margaret Rose Gladney (1993)*

Entitled to Power: Farm Women and Technology, 1913–1963, *by Katherine Jellison (1993)*

Revising Life: Sylvia Plath's Ariel Poems, *by Susan R. Van Dyne (1993)*

Made From This Earth: American Women and Nature, *by Vera Norwood (1993)*

Unruly Women: The Politics of Social and Sexual Control in the Old South, *by Victoria E. Bynum (1992)*

The Work of Self-Representation: Lyric Poetry in Colonial New England, *by Ivy Schweitzer (1991)*

Labor and Desire: Women's Revolutionary Fiction in Depression America, *by Paula Rabinowitz (1991)*

Community of Suffering and Struggle: Women, Men, and the Labor Movement in Minneapolis, 1915–1945, *by Elizabeth Faue (1991)*

All That Hollywood Allows: Re-reading Gender in 1950s Melodrama, *by Jackie Byars (1991)*

Doing Literary Business: American Women Writers in the Nineteenth Century, *by Susan Coultrap-McQuin (1990)*

Ladies, Women, and Wenches: Choice and Constraint in Antebellum Charleston and Boston, *by Jane H. Pease and William H. Pease (1990)*

The Secret Eye: The Journal of Ella Gertrude Clanton Thomas, 1848–1889, *edited by Virginia Ingraham Burr, with an introduction by Nell Irvin Painter (1990)*

Second Stories: The Politics of Language, Form, and Gender in Early American Fictions, *by Cynthia S. Jordan (1989)*

Within the Plantation Household: Black and White Women of the Old South, *by Elizabeth Fox-Genovese (1988)*

The Limits of Sisterhood: The Beecher Sisters on Women's Rights and Woman's Sphere, *by Jeanne Boydston, Mary Kelley, and Anne Margolis (1988)*